S0-CLP-402

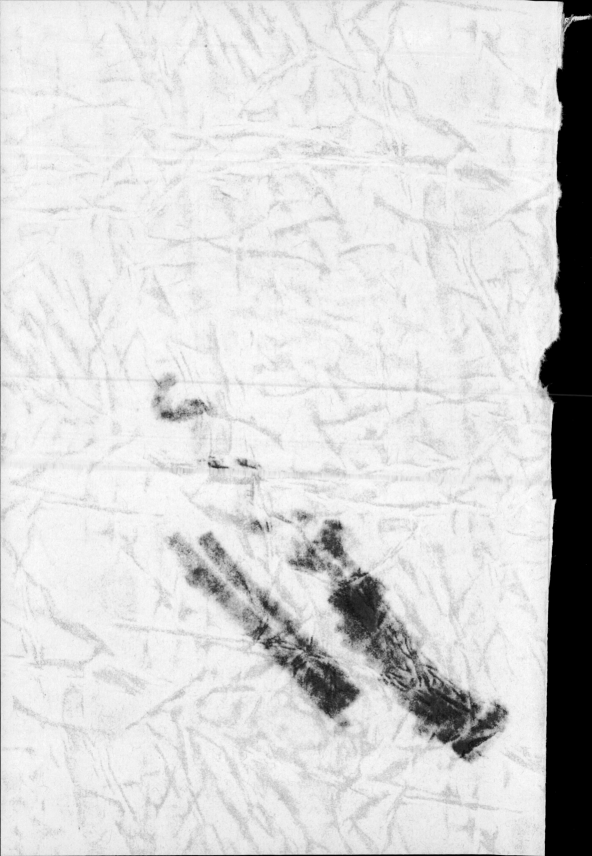

U.S.-KOREAN RELATIONS
1882-1982

IFES RESEARCH SERIES NO. 17

U.S.-KOREAN RELATIONS 1882-1982

Edited by

TAE-HWAN KWAK
Eastern Kentucky University

in collaboration with

JOHN CHAY
Pembroke State University

SOON SUNG CHO
University of Missouri-Columbia

SHANNON McCUNE
University of Florida

THE INSTITUTE FOR FAR EASTERN STUDIES
KYUNGNAM UNIVERSITY

Library of Congress Cataloging in Publication Data
  Kwak, Tae-Hwan, 1938-

Main entry under title: U.S.-Korean Relations, 1882-1982.
  Includes index.
  Contents: U.S.-Korea Security Relations/Tae-Hwan Kwak—The First
  Three Decades of American-Korean Relations, 1882-1910/John Chay—
  American Policy Toward Korean Unification, 1945-1980/Soon Sung
  Cho—American Image of Korea in 1882/Shannon McCune—[etc.]

  Westview's ISBN 0-86531-608-2   (hb)

Published in 1982 by Kyungnam University Press
  28-42 Samchung-dong, Chongro-ku, Seoul 110, Korea

Copyright © 1982 by Tae-Hwan Kwak and IFES, Kyungnam University.
First Printing, 1982.
Second Printing, 1983.
  All rights reserved. No part of this book may be reproduced or trans-
  mitted in any form or by any means, electronic or mechanical, including
  photo copying, recording, or by any information on storage and retrieval
  system, without permission in writing from the copyright owner and/or
  the publisher except in the case of brief quotations embodied in critical
  article, and reviews.

Printed in the Republic of Korea
  by Seoul Computer Press

CONTENTS

PREFACE

Korea and the United States observed the centennial anniversary of their mutual relations in May 1982. In 1882 when the Treaty of Amity and Commerce between the two countries was signed, the United States took interest in Korea as no more than a port in which her merchant ships could harbor on their way to and from China. It seems that American businessmen did not perceive much economic interest in this "Land of the Morning Calm" at that time. Nor does it seem that American political leaders found strategic value in the Korean peninsula at that juncture of our history. Judging from the lack of interest in Korea on the part of the United States, it is quite natural that she remained mostly non-committal to the national fate of Korea during the initial period of Korean-American relations.

In contrast, after the end of the Second World War the United States came to adopt a policy of almost total commitment to Korea. As is well-known, she occupied and ruled Korea for the first three years in the post-war period, and the story of her military and economic commitment to Korea for the last 37 years is too familiar to be repeated here. Needless to say, such a radical change of American policy toward Korea was based upon the awareness that the Korean peninsula possessed strategic importance in the new international framework of the postwar era. In other words, the United States has found a bastion in Korea for the security of the whole Pacific area including Japan.

Korean policy toward the United States has not changed as much as U.S. policy toward Korea over the last one hundred years. At the time of the Treaty of Amity and Commerce, King *Kojong* wished to play American power off against other big powers coveting Korea in order to keep the independence of the country. During the period of the Japanese rule over Korea, both the leaders and people of Korea sought American intervention in Japanese colonialism on behalf of

Korean independence. In the postwar era, Korean policy toward the United States has consistently been to secure American commitment to Korea not only for the defense of the country but for the industrialization of its economy.

From this comparison of U.S. policy toward Korea and Korean policy toward the U.S., it may be concluded that Korean people have kept a sort of one-sided "love affair" with the United States for a very long time. Such a state of mind on the part of Koreans has become much stronger in the postwar period as it was grounded on the material dependency of Korea upon the United States.

However, it must be pointed out that mutually beneficial relations between the two countries can be made more enduring and lasting only upon the basis of more equal Korean-American relations than the existing ones. Then, the goal of Korean-American relations in the decades ahead is to establish a symmetric relationship between them, and the prospect of accomplishing it is very bright since the leaders of both countries share a desire to build such a partnership. This book is a collection of articles reviewing the one hundred years of Korean-American relations written by outstanding scholars teaching in the universities of both countries. I am sure that this book will lay an academic foundation upon which to build a mature partnership between Korea and the United States in the near future.

I wish to express my deep appreciation to Dr. Tae-Hwan Kwak (Eastern Kentucky University) for his leadership and contributions to the publication of this centennial volume.

July 1982
Seoul, Korea

Jae Kyu Park, Ph.D.
Director, The Institute for
Far Eastern Studies,
Kyungnam University

ACKNOWLEDGMENTS

This book would not have been possible without the assistance and contributions of numerous individuals and institutions. Financial support came primarily from the Korea-U.S.A. Centennial Program Committee in Seoul. We wish to acknowledge with special appreciation the Committee's financial support. We wish to express our special thanks to Dr. Tae-Yung Rhee, President of Daegu University and Dr. Jae Kyu Park, Dean of Graduate School and Director of the Institute for Far Eastern Studies at Kyungnam University, for their financial support for the publication of this centennial volume. Without their understanding, support and faith in this volume, this book would not have been published in commemoration of the centennial of the establishment of diplomatic relations between Korea and the U.S. in 1982.

We wish to express our sincere appreciation to all of those who actively participated in the five panels organized and presented by the Centennial Program Committee on U.S.-Korean Relations at the 23rd Annual Convention of the International Studies Association in Cincinnati, Ohio, on March 24-27, 1982, in commemoration of the centennial anniversary of diplomatic relations between the U.S. and Korea. Those paper presenters and discussants were: Ardath W. Burks, John Chay, Soon Sung Cho, Chong-Ki Choi, Gerard H. Clarfield, Thomas A. D'Elia, Han-Kyo Kim, Ki-Hoon Kim, Hong N. Kim, Se-Jin Kim, Yu-Nam Kim, Tae-Hwan Kwak, Chung Hoon Lee, J. K. Lee, Manwoo Lee, Sang Ho Lee, John R. Merrill, Shannon McCune, Andrew C. Nahm, Fred W. Neal, Edward A. Olsen, John Outland, Wayne Patterson, Jai Poong Ryu, Young Il Shin, Sheldon Simon, Clarence N. Weems, Gregory F. T. Winn, and Yong Soon Yim.

This centennial volume is an outgrowth of the centennial program organized by the Centennial Program Committee on U.S.-Korean

Relations whose members were John Chay, Soon Sung Cho, Chang-Yoon Choi, Youngnok Koo, Tae-Hwan Kwak (Chairman), Edward A. Olsen, Wayne Patterson, and Yong Soon Yim. We wish to express our special thanks to them for their dedication and contributions.

Kwak wishes to thank Dr. Charles Whitaker (Eastern Kentucky University) for his constructive comments and Mr. Dong Moon Suh (Eastern Kentucky University) for his research assistance, proofreading and other contributions to this volume. Kwak also wishes to express his sincere thanks to staff members of the Institute for Far Eastern Studies, Kyungnam University. We also wish to thank Mr. Jin Wang Kim, President of Seoul Computer Press, for his support and faith in this centennial volume. This book is dedicated to those who have worked hard for better understanding of U.S.-Korean relations and the promotion of Korean-American friendship.

T. H. Kwak
J. Chay
S. S. Cho
S. McCune

August 1982
Seoul, Korea

THE CONTRIBUTORS

ARDATH W. BURKS is Professor Emeritus of Asian Studies at Rutgers University, and the author of *The Government of Japan* (Thomas Y. Crowell, 1964) and *Japan: Profile of a Postindustrial Power* (Westview Press, 1981).

JOHN CHAY is Professor and Chairman of History at Pembroke State University. Dr. Chay is the editor of *The Problems and Prospects of American-East Asian Relations* (Westview Press, 1977).

SOON SUNG CHO is Professor of Political Science at the University of Missouri-Columbia. Dr. Cho is the author of *Korea in World Politics* (University of California Press, 1968). He has also published numerous articles in Korean, Japanese and English.

CHONG-KI CHOI is Professor of Public Administration at Seoul National University and President of the Korean Institute of International Studies, Seoul, Korea. Dr. Choi is the editor of *Korean Journal of International Studies*.

GERARD H. CLARFIELD is Professor of History at the University of Missouri-Columbia. Dr. Clarfield is the author of *Timothy Pickering and the American Republic* (University of Pittsburgh Press, 1980).

THOMAS A. D'ELIA is a U.S. government economist. Dr. D'Elia has published his articles in professional journals.

KI-HOON KIM is Professor of Economics at Central Connecticut State College. Dr. Kim has contributed numerous articles to journals in the U.S. and Korea.

YU-NAM KIM is Associate Professor of International Relations and Director of Research Department II at the Institute of Foreign Affairs and National Security, Ministry of Foreign Affairs, Republic of Korea. Dr. Kim has published numerous articles in scholarly journals.

TAE-HWAN KWAK is Professor of Political Science at Eastern Kentucky University and Chairman of the Centennial Program

Committee on U.S.-Korean Relations. Dr. Kwak is the co-editor of *The Two Koreas in World Politics* (forthcoming), and has published numerous articles in scholarly journals in Korea, the U.S., Hong Kong, and West Germany.

CHUNG HOON LEE is Professor of Economics at University of Hawaii at Manoa. Dr. Lee has authored numerous articles.

SANG HO LEE received Doctor of Theology from Boston University in 1972 and is presently affiliated with First United Methodist Church, Williamstown, Massachusetts.

SHANNON McCUNE is Professor Emeritus of Geography at University of Florida. He has authored numerous articles and is the author of *Korea, Land of Broken Calm* (D. Van Nostrand Co., 1966).

ANDREW C. NAHM is Professor of Asian History and Director of Center for Korean Studies, Western Michigan University. Dr. Nahm is the author and editor of several books on Korea. He has authored numerous articles on Korean affairs.

EDWARD A. OLSEN is Professor of National Security Affairs and Coordinator of Asian-Pacific Studies at U.S. Naval Postgraduate School. Dr. Olsen authored numerous articles and is the author of *Japan: Economic Growth, Resource Scarcity, and Environmental Constraints* (Westview Press, 1978).

JAE KYU PARK is Professor of International Relations at Kyungnam University, and Director of the Institute for Far Eastern Studies, Seoul, Korea. Dr. Park is the publisher of *Asian Perspective*.

JAI POONG RYU is a member of Sociology Department at Loyola College in Maryland. Dr. Ryu has published numerous articles in professional journals.

YOUNG IL SHIN is a member of Department of History and Social Science at Northfield Mount Hermon School.

GREGORY F. T. WINN is a member of Office of Research at the U.S. International Communication Agency, where he evaluates West European foreign and defense policy issues and serves as a consultant on East Asian affairs. Dr. Winn has published articles on Korean and Japanese decision-making, and North Korean political/strategic issues in professional journals.

YONG SOON YIM is Associate Professor of Political Science at Virginia Commonwealth University. Dr. Yim is the author and co-editor of several books on Korean affairs. He has published numerous articles in journals in the U.S., Hong Kong, and Korea.

U.S.-KOREAN RELATIONS
1882-1982

INTRODUCTION

The Editors

The advent of the United States to a position of unqualified importance was the most striking event in the history of East Asian international relations since the late nineteenth century. The United States
was the first Western country to open the door of Japan in 1854 and
also the Hermit Kingdom of Korea in 1882. The U.S. became the first
nation which introduced Western civilization to Korea. The year 1982
marks the centennial anniversary of American-Korean relations. In
retrospect, a century of American-Korean relations was a turbulent
era of the deep sense of frustration and hope, trust and distrust, and
a feeling of apathy and friendship.

In order to commemorate the centennial anniversary of U.S.-Korean
relations, the idea for a conference or a symposium that would make
a comprehensive examination of American-Korean relations, including not only the usual political, military, and economic, but also
social and cultural dimensions, was conceived about a half dozen
years ago by a group of specialists in U.S.-Korean relations. An idea,
like all other living entities, needs time to grow. After several years of
incubation, more definite and detailed plans were made by the editors
of this volume during the annual convention of the International
Studies Association in Philadelphia in the spring of 1981. An important factor for this definite step was the coming of the centennial year
of the Shufeldt Treaty of May 22, 1882, which opened the formal
diplomatic relations between the two nations. Without this significant
impetus, the realization of the idea would have been delayed even
longer, or would have died during the incubation period.

As originally formulated by a number of Korean political scientists and historians in the United States, the plan for a conference had four parts: diplomatic relations, security relations, economic relations, and socio-cultural relations. This plan was later executed without any significant alteration, but with the addition of one more dimension to the annual program of the International Studies Association held in Cincinnati in the spring of 1982. A consideration of the future of U.S.-Korean relations was added to make the centennial program even more comprehensive by adding one more temporal dimension. The future panel also included a spatial extension by bringing in North Korea and Japan. Thus five panels dealing with all aspects of U.S.-Korean relations were presented at the 1982 annual convention of the International Studies Association.

Unlike the two other major areas of specialization for Asian scholars—American-Chinese and American-Japanese relations—the area of American-Korean relations claims only a small number of specialists. While most of these scholars are political scientists and historians, a few concentrate in the fields of economics, sociology, and the humanities. The organizers of the Centennial Program Committee on U.S.-Korean Relations of the International Studies Association made an effort to include representatives from all these fields. Even though the ideal was not always realized, the centennial program committee also made a special effort to distribute the participants in the program equally among three groups: Korean scholars in the United States, scholars in Korea, and American scholars specializing in U.S.-Korean relations.

As was already pointed out, the centennial occasion served as an important catalyst for execution of the centennial program. Of course, the role of the centennial was much more than catalytic; it had a very part in determining the content of the project. Therefore, before introducing the reader to the chapters of this volume, a few general observations will be made on the meaning of the centennial project and its organization.

A great hope in the minds of the planners of this centennial project is that it will bring some sense of history to the people of both Korea and the United States. Both nations are now fully in the realm of modern society; and one of the main characteristics of modern society is its ahistorical nature. Because great and continuous change is one of the most important aspects of modern society, things of the past tend to be considered as a hindrance to change in this society. Hence, almost by necessity, modern society is ahistorical. However, stability is also an important factor for health of every society, especially for modern society, because of the speed and amount of change. This stability comes largely from tradition, which in turn comes from a sense of history. For modern-day Koreans and Americans, looking back to the beginnings of their diplomatic relations in the early 1880s is to turn to the origin and roots of the relationship. They can see the development of a time-tested tradition when they examine the process of American-Korean relations in the following century. Thus, for both nations—especially for the Americans—gaining a sense of the history of the relations between the two nations is to gain a temporal comprehension of the relationship which is very much needed at this point.

It is also hoped that this centennial project will give the two nations an opportunity for reflection. Another important characteristic of modern society is its action-orientedness. Since development and progress come from actions, this orientation is a necessary part of the modern society. But, like other good elements of a living organization, when it becomes excessive or when it is not harmonized with an adequate amount of a moderating element, it begins to be destructive to the society. And this element that harmonizes and moderates actions is reflection. Unless a people, like an individual human being, stops and thinks once in a while, its action becomes meaningless and society loses its direction. Reflection will help both nations discover the meaning of the development and progress, and will also help put the present status of the nations in a proper historical perspective. Thus, the opportunity for reflection will assist the two nations to see clearly the fundamental nature and principles of the relationship between the two countries.

Along with its urge for looking back toward the past, the project will help also the people to look forward to the future relations between the U.S. and Korea. Understandably, modern society is a present-oriented society. Along with the sense of history and an opportunity for reflection, the two states need a sense of direction and a vision not only for their prosperity but also for their very survival in the coming decades. And this sense of direction and vision comes from the futuristic perspective. Although the coverage is probably not completely adequate, the future section includes special papers paying attention to North and South Korea, the U.S. and Japan. And since the unification issue will be the most important issue involving the Korean peninsula in the coming decades, the inclusion of North Korea in a consideration of the future of U.S.-Korean relations is quite logical.

The organizers of the centennial program also hoped to give the two nation-states an opportunity of seeing the bilateral relationship in a wholistic way. One of the most important characteristics of modern society is its emphasis on science. And, an emphasis on science naturally makes the people more analytic; without a highly developed analytical spirit and methods, modern science would be impossible. But, it is also axiomatic that, like all other dynamic systems, modern society needs a synthesis or a wholistic attention for its satisfactory functioning. Along with the usual diplomatic, military, and economic aspects, the project devotes at least one part to the socio-cultural dimension. The space allocated to these two areas may not be quite adequate, but the project has taken a step for further advancement in this direction. The project recognizes at least that the social and cultural dimension, which seem to be less important and urgent than the political, security and economic dimensions for international relations, is in the long run the most fundamental and important factor in international relations.

Lastly, the project is a fruit of a meaningful cooperation between the scholars of the two countries and that cooperation is very significant. As it is evident in the following chapters, one of the most important—probably the single most important—points of U.S.-Korean relations is its asymmetrical nature. The needs, the interests, the importance, and the amount of attention between the two nations is far from equal, or asymmetrical. Like all other dynamic relationship, to be satisfactory, the American-Korean relationship should be pushed toward a point of symmetry. Fortunately, the post-World War II trend in relations between large-small nations, in which the gap in the role and importance of the two sides has narrowed gradually, is very helpful for the American-Korean case. Even more and sustained cooperation between American and Korean specialists in U.S.-Korean relations is hoped in the future for a step in the realization of more symmetrical relations between the U.S. and Korea.

The editors of this volume have collected nineteen papers presented at the annual meetings of the International Studies Association and the Association for Asian Studies and other conferences in Korea and abroad in commemoration of one hundred years of U.S.-Korean relations, 1882-1982. The nineteen chapters are arranged in five parts: Part I deals with the political-diplomatic dimensions of U.S.-Korean relations; Part II deals with U.S.-Korean cultural and social relations; Part III discusses the military-security dimensions of the two nations; Part IV analyzes U.S.-Korean economic relations; and Part V deals with the future of U.S.-Korean relations in the 1980s.

Let us take a brief look at major points of the contributors presented in this volume. Part I, "U.S.-Korean Relations: The Political-Diplomatic Dimensions," reassesses and reflects political-diplomatic relations between the U.S. and Korea:

— Chapter 1, "The First Three Decades of American-Korean Relations, 1882-1910: Reassessments and Reflections," by John Chay analyzes the major issues of American-Korean diplomatic relations during the first three decades of official contact. In addition to examining American gunboat diplomacy in Korea, the treaty-making process in 1882, and American policy toward Korea, this article explores the options open to the Koreans in those thirty years. Major themes treated in the chapter suggest that American gunboat diplomacy existed in Korea through the late 1890s; that there was a single, consistent American policy of strict neutrality and non-intervention with regard to Korea; and that the Koreans wasted three valuable decades trying to rely upon a disinterested and distant nation when they should have been working to strengthen themselves.

—Chapter 2, "U.S. Policy and the Japanese Annexation of Korea," by Andrew C. Nahm offers a new interpretation of U.S. policy toward the Japanese annexation of Korea. His analysis reveals that president Theodore Roosevelt "abandoned" Korea to the Japanese, not because of his concern for the security of the Philippines, but because of his desire to establish the open door in Manchuria. Economically, Manchuria seemed much more important than Korea to the United States which had only a marginal economic interest in the peninsula. For this reason, Roosevelt advanced his own version of "Korea for Manchuria (*Man-Kan kokan* in Japanese)." He had no sympathy or respect for Korea, and he elected to "give" Korea to Japan in order to secure Japanese consent to the open door in Manchuria. Roosevelt had already encouraged the Japanese to "take" Korea as early as March 1904, and he made similar remarks to the Japanese before July 1905. When did Roosevelt make his final concession on Korea to the Japanese? The secret memoir of Kaneko Kentaro strongly suggests that Roosevelt did so in late August 1905. Therefore, Nahm argues that the Taft-Katsura Memorandum has little historical significance as far as the fall of Korea was concerned. Whatever the reasons for

Roosevelt's unwillingness to help Korea in 1905 may have been, all his hopes in the Far East were frustrated and he failed to establish the open door in Manchuria and his plan to maintain the balance of power in East Asia were frustrated by the Japanese.

— Chapter 3, "The Last Domino: America, Japan, and the Blair House Decisions," by Gerard H. Clarfield reassesses American involvement in the Korean War. Several key decisions regarding America's overall Asian policy which were made immediately following the North Korean attack were all intended to serve the same end — the establishment of a strong and viable relationship between Japan and the U.S. The defense of Korea and Formosa were primarily political moves intended to assure the Japanese that the U.S. could be depended upon as a determined and reliable ally. The decisions to aid the French in Indochina and to help the Philippines Government put down the Hukbalahap rebellion were likewise influenced by concerns for the future of Japan. Intent upon reviving Japan economically and at the same time keeping her from re-establishing close ties with Peking, the Truman Administration viewed the markets and raw materials of Southeast Asia as crucial to Japan's future. These considerations led to the decisions to intervene in Viet Nam and Philippines. In one of the more remarkable ironies of modern history Truman and Secretary of State Dean Acheson set out to create for Japan an economic sphere similiar to the one Japan's leaders sought to acquire by force in the late 1930s.

— Chapter 4, "American Policy Toward Korean Unification, 1945-1980," by Soon Sung Cho describes and analyzes those forces and effects (both internal and external) that were brought to bear on U.S. policy makers in formulating Korean unification policy. Defining policy as a specific, deliberate course of action for achieving some objectives, the central hypothesis of this study is that the United States had no viable foreign policy towards the reunification of Korea. The U.S. followed a policy reaction (rather than initiating action) aimed towards holding the Korean situation at a status quo. It was a policy of temporary expediency aimed towards protecting the national interest of the U.S. and the security of Japan.

— Chapter 5, "American-Korean Diplomatic Relations, 1961-1982," by Chong-Ki Choi describes, analyzes and evaluates Korea-U.S. relations from a South Korean perspective from the military revolution in 1961 to the present. He emphasizes the strategic importance of Korea to the security of Japan and the U.S.

Part II, "U.S.-Korean Cultural and Social Relations," examines the social, educational, and cultural dimensions of U.S.-Korean relations:

— Chapter 6, "Native Contributions to the Success of America's Missionary Educational Work in Korea," by Sang Ho Lee examines whether the indigenous enthusiasm for learning among Koreans had any significant role in contributing in the success of America's missionary-initiated educational enterprise in Korea from the 1880s to the present. This study reveals much of the facts known to Korean scholars. The significant one is that there had always been an overwhelming desire among many far sighted Koreans for a shift from the traditional toward Western system of education. The desire is grown out of their national consciousness, and this has served as a hidden, driving force behind the success of American missionary's educational work in Korea.

— Chapter 7, "American Image of Korea in 1882: A Bibliographical Sketch," by Shannon McCune looks at American interest in Korea. In 1882 the American knowledge of Korea was limited. It was a period of rapid industrialization and urbanization; railroads were being built to tie the diverse areas of the U.S. together. Thus, a distant, strange peninsula, located for across the Pacific was not a matter of concern for most Americans. However, there were three books on Korea, one by John Ross, written from the viewpoint of Manchuria: *History of Korea,* Paisley, Scotland, 1880, another by Ernest Oppert, written from the viewpoint of Shanghai: *A Forbidden Land: Voyages to the Corea,* New York, 1880 and the third by William Elliot Griffis, written from the perspective of Japan: *Corea, the Hermit Nation,* New York, 1882. Unfortunately these books used little Korean source material and gave somewhat distorted views of Korea.

— Chapter 8, "Koreans in America: Past and Present," by Jai Poong Ryu looks at Korean immigrants to the United States. The Korean American community will become more diversified according to his opinion. As the volume of Korean immigration has increased in recent years, so has the probability that the immigrants are bringing with them increasingly diverse background in culture, socio-economic experiences, and so on. Further, as Korean Americans are more dispersed in settlement than other groups, they may also be subjected to more diverse set of circumstances in the United States.

— Chapter 9, "American Protestant Missions to Korea and the

Awakening of Political and Social Consciousness in the Koreans between 1884 and 1941,'' by Young Il Shin analyzes, first, the vital roles played by American missionaries in awakening the Koreans to their politico-social consciousness and responsibilities, and secondly, the works and activities of those Koreans who were awakened and Christians between 1884 and 1941. The missionaries were prohibited from taking part in domestic politics of Korea, but they disseminated quite freely the Western democratic principles and ideas of social obligation and service, which were Christian in their belief, into the minds of the Korean people. It was they who fostered common Korean men and women to be active participants in the nation's politics and social service works.

Part III, "U.S.-Korean Relations: The Military-Security Dimensions," reviews and evaluates U.S.-South Korean military-security relations from the birth of the two Koreas to the present:

— Chapter 10, "U.S.-Korea Security Relations," by Tae-Hwan Kwak reviews U.S.-Korea security relations and makes policy recommendations regarding Korean security, U.S. troop withdrawal, and unification. The U.S. and the Republic of Korea have been alliance partners, and the U.S. has become the ultimate military guarantor of Korean security against a North Korean attack. Carter's troop withdrawal policy was based on strategic miscalculations and indefensible premises, and could disrupt the military balance between the two Koreas, thereby weakening an effective, credible deterrent force against another North Korean attack. A continued U.S.-Korea security cooperation would best serve the security interests of the two allies. Kwak maintains that the U.S. 2nd Army Division in Korea and U.S. air force units as a symbol of U.S. firm commitment to the security of South Korea should continue to stay in Korea until South and North Korea will conclude a non-aggression agreement and as long as the U.S.-ROK Mutual Defense Treaty is in force. The U.S. firm commitment and ROK self-reliant defense forces only can deter a renewed war on the Korean peninsula, and can also insure stability and peace in Northeast Asia in the coming decade.

— Chapter 11, "U.S.-Korean Security Interdependence," by Yu-Nam Kim discusses a new U.S.-South Korean security interdependence vis-a-vis the Soviet challenge to peace and security in Northeast Asia, emphasizing (1) the Soviet challenge in the Pacific, (2) the Japanese reaction, and (3) the role of South Korea. His main topics are Korea's security perspective and its future role with non-Communist nations, specifically the U.S., Japan and the ASEAN countries. South Korea may play a significant role in counterbalance Soviet expansionism in East Asia with other Asian countries.

— Chapter 12, "Riding the Tiger: Military Confrontation on the Korean Peninsula," by Gregory F. T. Winn looks at the military confrontation between South and North Korea. The general pattern of the two Koreas' military growth indicates that both nations in the late 1970s and early 1980s were locked into an exponential arms race. Both were also busy building up a munitions industry and modernizing their weapons systems. Economic and psychic constraints may eventually lead Korean leaders to explore alternatives to the present conflict situation. A preferred stratagem for the Korean situation might be to first alter the "nature" of armed forces (limiting their relative "offensive" capabilities) prior to actually reducing their numbers. Other arms control and disarmament proposals may also prove useful. There are few instances in history where an escalating arms race did not lead to war. The present confrontational situation is like riding a tiger, and it is difficult to get off once mounted.

— Chapter 13, "U.S. Strategic Doctrine, Arms Transfer Policy, and South Korea," by Yong Soon Yim takes a close look at U.S. arms transfer policy toward South Korea. U.S. strategic doctrine has constantly been in motion, and American arms transfer policy toward Korea followed its strategic doctrine. This change of the doctrine also changed the flow of the arms transaction between the two nations. Postwar arms supply took various forms, from the government grants under the military assistance program to the government-to-government sales program. This change of arms transaction to South Korea was due to the overall strategic, political, economic, and other requirements of the United States. Projecting 1980s trend, U.S. arms supply to South Korea will continue for several reasons; (1) U.S. strategic requirements in the Far East; (2) an increase in North Korea's military capability; (3) the continued expansion of the Soviet Union in the Pacific areas; (4) South Korea's increased economic capability; and (5) U.S. economic needs.

Part IV, "U.S.-Korean Economic Relations," examines U.S.-ROK economic relations and U.S. direct investment in Korea:

— Chapter 14, "The Development of Contemporary U.S.-ROK Economic Relations," by Ki-Hoon Kim analyzes and evaluates the development of contemporary economic relations between the two nations during the post-World War II period. It focuses on the role of

U.S. foreign aid and its impact on the Korean economy, which was followed by remarkable economic growth, especially in Korea's foreign trade since 1962. Korea has been transforming her economy from an aid-sustained to a trade-sustained growth process. U.S. and Korea have established an indispensable and steadfast economic relationship, from a unilateral aid to a bilateral trade partnership.

— Chapter 15, "U.S.-ROK Economic Interdependence," by Thomas A. D'Elia examines U.S.-South Korean economic relations in terms of trade, investment, technology, and capital flows and the importance of these flows to each economy. Economic ties between the U.S. and South Korea have grown rapidly over the past 30 years and the relationship has shifted from the one-way relationship of the 1950s and 1960s to a more mutual beneficial, two-way association. The two economies are, to a considerable extent, complementary. The U.S. is South Korea's most important economic partner. The U.S., for its part, benefits from close ties to one of the world's most dynamic economies.

— Chapter 16, "United States Direct Investment and Its International Production in Korean Manufacturing Industries," by Chung Hoon Lee investigates some of the salient characteristics of U.S. direct investment in Korean manufacturing industries and the effects of its interational production on the Korean economy. Where appropriate, the characteristics of U.S. direct investment are compared with those of Japanese direct investment in Korea. Its main conclusions are that U.S. direct investment was, at least up through 1978, largely in the capital-intensive, high-technology industries, carried out at a relatively large scale of $5 million or more and that its affiliates' output was primarily for the local market. It is also concluded that direct foreign investment has not been a dominant link connecting the U.S. and the Republic of Korea.

Part V, "The Future of U.S.-Korean Relations in the 1980s," examines the future relations between the U.S. and North Korea, the triangular relationship among Korea, the U.S. and Japan, and Northeast Asian security options:

— Chapter 17, "The Triangle: Korea, the United States and Japan," by Ardath Burks discusses Korea-the U.S.-Japan relations. In the author's opinion, most likely is a steady increase in American military presence, not only in Northeast and in East Asia, but also through Southeast Asia and into the Indian Ocean. More slowly but steadily, Japan will increase the quality (if not quantity) of strategic capacity, not only for the defense of Japan but also for wider coordinated functions. These functions will include protection of vital sea lanes approaching Northeast Asia, and, even more likely, joint planning with the U.S. and ROK to maintain stability and peace on the Korean peninsula.

— Chapter 18, "North Korean Policy toward the United States," by Jae Kyu Park discusses the history of the North Korean policy toward the U.S. from the time of Korean War to the present, and examines the organizations, contents and methods of North Korean propaganda toward the U.S. since propaganda has been a major means of the North Korean government not only to express its policy toward the U.S. but also to implement it. Park attempts to assess the impact of the North Korean policy toward the U.S. on the security of the Republic of Korea. Park argues that the North Korean policies toward the U.S., whether belligerent or reconciliatory, are totally geared to a forceful unification of the Korean peninsula by North Korea.

— Chapter 19, "Northeast Asian Security: Sharing Responsibilities," by Edward A. Olsen examines Northeast Asian security options in the changing international environment of East Asia. Olsen argues that if the U.S. commitments are to remain viable, Washington's allies in the area—Japan and South Korea—will have to cooperate more extensively with each other and trilaterally with the U.S. Washington must try to compel closer cooperation via various incentives. Without visible Japanese armed support for regional security, a second Korean war might well produce popular American refusal to back the United States' existing commitments to its Northeast Asian allies.

PART I

U.S.-KOREAN RELATIONS:
THE POLITICAL-DIPLOMATIC DIMENSIONS

CHAPTER 1

THE FIRST THREE DECADES OF AMERICAN-KOREAN RELATIONS, 1882-1910: REASSESSMENTS AND REFLECTIONS

John Chay

The first three decades, more exactly the 28 years, between 1882—the year in which the first treaty between the United States and Korea was signed—and 1910—the year in which this first period American-Korean relationship came to end with the end of the Korean kingdom itself—was an important formative period in the relations of the two-nations for at least three reasons. During this period, the forces and factors for the relationship between the two countries were first brought into full operation. Moreover, the two-nation relationship turned out to have at least some impact on the Korean history during the following 35 year period. And, finally, these 28 years were filled with dramatic events, and questions still remain to be answered and issues to be dealt with before a full understanding of the relationship between the two countries is achieved.

For official American-Korean relations, the first important event was the opening of the hermit kingdom by the United States in 1882, an event that occurred exactly a hundred years ago. However, it should hastily be pointed out that this first formal event was preceded by at least two major events which cannot be neglected: the 1866 General Sherman case and the follow-up actions which include the 1871 American expedition to the Korean peninsula. During the 28 year period following the opening of the nation to the Western world, a series of crises occurred in which the United States was involved to a various degrees: the 1882 military rebellion, the 1884 coup, the Sino-Japanese War of 1894-1895, the Russo-Japanese War of 1904-

1905, and the annexation of Korea by Japan in 1910. Since 1922, when the publications of Tyler Dennett, one of the leading scholars on the subject of American-Korean relations, began to appear,[1] a number of scholars have written books and articles that deal with American policies and actions in Korea during these crises. Although a number of important issues were treated in these publications, many of them still remain open for further consideration; these include the issue of U.S. gunboat diplomacy in Korea; the motives, issues, and consequences involved in the treaty of 1882; the exact nature of American policy toward Korea during the period; and the nature of the Korean policy toward the United States. The main objective of this essay is to reexamine these issues and to reflect on the meaning of these events and issues in a broad context.

I. U.S. Gunboat Diplomacy in Korea

Characterizing clearly and accurately American policy and actions toward Korea before 1882 is an important task for a student for American-Korean relations. This is a part of the much broader issue of American policy toward the Far East in the latter half of the 19th century. It is certainly not unfair to argue that the Open Door Policy, the major and almost the only policy the United States had for the region, had existed in the latter half of the 19th century due to the placement of the most-favored nation principle in the treaties with all three powers in the region. Until John Hay verbalized this policy at the turn of the century through a series of notes and circulars, it was more action-oriented, and the action component of the Policy may be called "gunboat diplomacy." The question to be raised here is whether the American action in Korea before 1882 was an example of gunboat diplomacy. One author goes at far as to say that even Commodore Shufeldt's act of opening Korea in 1882 was one of the "most vivid examples of episodes in a well-defined pattern of global gunboat

---

[1] Tyler Dennett, *Americans in Eastern Asia: a Critical Study of United States Policy in the Far East in the Nineteenth Century* (New York: Barnes & Noble, 1922); "American Good Offices in Asia," *American Journal of International Law*, 16 (1922): 1-5; "Seward's Far Eastern Policy," *American Historical Review*, 28 (1922): 145-62.

diplomacy.''[2] Others do not go that far, but many of them do not hesitate to admit that the American naval expedition of 1871 was an act of the gunboat diplomacy.[3]

Before examining further a series of actions on the Korean coast, it seems to be in order to define the concept of gunboat diplomacy. In simple and straightforward terms, gunboat diplomacy is diplomacy supported by use of a gunboat or a naval force. The use of a gunboat may be explicit in an action or only implicit in a sheer display of force. Whether explicit or implicit, when the use of a naval force is involved gunboat diplomacy exists. Here, the question to be explored is whether use of naval force was involved in the formation and execution of American policy toward Korea during the period under consideration.

A series of American actions of the Korean coast in the 1860s emerged from the unfortunate General Sherman incident of 1866. While on the Taedong River near Pyongyang, the entire crew of the American Schooner General Sherman was killed by Koreans mainly because of the behavior, or misbehavior of the crew, and the ship was burnt. Two judicious fact-finding American naval expeditions followed in the next two years. Apparently frustrated by these futile efforts and ready to seize an opportunity for carrying out a cooperative policy with France, Secretary of State William H. Seward approached in the summer of 1868 the French representative in Washington, whose country also had difficulties in Korea because of the Koreans' ruthless suppression of Catholics, about a joint punitive expedition. Fortunately, the French government turned down the American proposal for a forceful action.[4] However, a forceful American policy was eventually carried out in the 1871 expedition. Equipped with the authorization of Secretary of State Fish, Minister Low and Admiral

---

[2] Kenneth J. Hogan, *American Gunboat Diplomacy and the Old Navy, 1877-1889* (Westport, Connecticut: Greenwood, 1973), p. 10.

[3] Dennett, *Americans in Eastern Asia*, p. 453; Charles O. Paulin, *Diplomatic Negotiations of American Naval Officers 1778-1883* (Baltimore: Johns Hopkins University Press, 1912, 1967), p. 287; Takehiko Okutaira, *Chosen Kaikoku Koshyo Shimatsu* (Diplomacy for Opening of Korea) (Tokyo: Kanae Shoin, 1969), p. 14; Wonmo Kim, *Kundae Hanmi Oegyosa* (The Modern History of United States-Korean Relations, 1852-1871: the Gunboat Diplomacy toward Korea) (Seoul: Hongsungsa, 1979), pp. 303-308; Ilkeun Park, *Mikukwi Oegyochungchaekkwa Hanmi Oegyokwanke* (United States Open Nation Policy and Korean-American Relations) (Seoul: Ilchokak, 1981), p. 115.

[4] Dennett, *Americans in Eastern Asia,* p. 419; "Seward's Far Eastern Policy," p. 59.

Rogers launched an expedition with five gunboats carrying 85 guns and 1,230 men with the dual objectives of finding more about the General Sherman case and making a treaty with the Koreans for opening of the country to the West.[5] The original intention of the mission, which was modeled upon the Perry Mission to Japan of 1853-1854 was a peaceful one. However, while carrying out a survey in a sensitive zone of the waterway near Inchon, the gateway to the Korean capital, the American boats were fired upon. In the following punitive operation, the American force won a decisive military victory, destroying five Korean forts, killing 350 Korean soldiers, and capturing some war prisoners and arms. After failing to achieve its political objectives, the expeditionary force withdrew to the Chinese waters.[6] Wonmo Kim and F.C. Jones point out that the cause of the failure was the employment of force.[7] Thus, both in the abortive joint expedition of 1868 and the Low-Rogers naval expedition of 1871, the use of naval force was involved. The role of gunboat diplomacy in Korean-American relations is quite clear.

Furthermore, American gunboat diplomacy in Korea did not end with the opening of the country in 1882, and the presence of American gunboats in Korean harbors for diplomatic purposes continued through the 1880s and the 1890s with a short period of relaxation in the early 1890s.[8] The dual objectives of the presence of American gunboats in Korea harbors was to protect American lives and material interests in the country and to strengthen the American position in dealing with other powers. Beyond these particular reasons, there was a general political reason. The continuing presence of the American gunboats in Inchon strengthened the American position in Korea. Oddly enough, the host country did not dislike the presence of the foreign gunboats; they, in fact, welcomed the Americans. Because the Koreans did not have a modern navy, the presence of the American gunboats in their harbors gave them a sense of

---

[5] Low to Fish, 18 February 1871, #32, Instructions, China, National Archives (NA).

[6] Dennett, "American Good Offices in Eastern Asia," p. 2; Kim, *Kundae Hanmi Oegyosa,* p. 352; F. C. Jones, "Foreign Diplomacy in Korea, 1866-1894," 1935 Harvard University Ph.D. dissertation, p. 64.

[7] Kim, *Kundae Hanmi Oegyosa,* p. 363; Jones, "Foreign Diplomacy in Korea," p. 64.

[8] Frelinghuysen to Chandler, 14 March 1883, Domestic File, Department of State, NA, microcopies (m) 40 roll (r) 98; Chandler to Frelinghuysen, 16 March 1883, Misc., State, NA, m178 r627; Whitney to Bayard, 3 August 1887, Misc., State, NA, m179 r731; Belknap to Teacy, 6 January 1890, Area File, Navy, NA, m625 r351; Harmony to Herbert, 19 May 1893, in Herbert to Gresham, 23 June 1893, NA, m179 r867.

security against both internal and external threats. The king repeatedly asked the Americans to keep a gunboat in Inchon.[9]

If is necessary now to put the subject in a broader context. Like imperialism, "gunboat diplomacy" has a bad flavor. But, when looked at in a much broader context and in a more realistic framework, the concept becomes less ugly. The main American interests in Korea in those years concerned a small number of missionaries and other American citizens and small amount of commercial and other economic interests. Throughout most of the 19th century, the United States had an almost ridiculously small army, often not more than 30,000 men in peacetime, and a correspondingly small navy equipped with rapidly deteriorating old wooden vessels after the Civil War, which was almost a "laughing stock" to other nations until the emergence of the new navy toward the end of the century.[10] In sum, even though the terminology sounds awesome and ugly, American gunboat diplomacy, with the exception of the 1871 expedition, did not amount to much more than the presence of one old warship in Inchon harbor charged to protect its small interest there and comfort the Korean monarch against his mostly internal foes.

II. Opening of the Korean Door by the United States: the Issues

Two prominent authors, one a leading historian in American-Far Eastern relations and the other a specialist in American naval history, have declared that the American act of opening of Korea in 1882 was "by far the most important action undertaken by the United States in Asia until the occupation of the Philippines" and it was "the most notable success of the American navy in the peaceful field of diplomacy."[11] Without much risk of exaggeration, one can state at least

[9] David to Chandler, 28 May 1883, NA, m40 r98; Foote to Frelinghuysen, 19 July 1883, Despatches, Korea, NA, m134 rl; Foulk to Bayard, 7 September 1888, Despatches, Korea, NA, m134 r3; Miller to Chandler, 26 May 1887, in Chandler to Whitney, 11 June 1887, NA, rg45.

[10] Heard to Blaine, 17 May 1890, Despatches, Korea, NA, m134 r6; Harold and Margaret Sprout, *The Rise of American Naval Power 1776-1918* (Princeton: University Press, 1939, 1967), pp. 165, 166, 170, 175; *New York Times,* 4 June 1891, 8:1-2.

[11] Dennett, *Americans in East Asia,* p. 450; Charles O. Paulin, *Diplomatic Negotiations of American Naval Officers 1778-1883* (Baltimore: Johns Hopkins University Press, 1912, 1967), p. 328.

that the year 1882 was definitely the most important year in the hundred year history of American-Korean relations. In view of the great impact of treaty-making upon the history of East Asian international relations in the following century, this year should also be considered as one of the most important in East Asian history. The major issues involved in the treaty-making to be considered in this essay are: the motives of the three countries for the decision to make the treaty—the United States, China, and Korea; the issues in the negotiation; and the impact of the treaty.

Major American motives for opening the Korean door in 1882 were pragmatic: In addition to improving the treatment of shipwrecked citizens on the Korean coast, the Americans wanted to open Korea for trade. These were very similar to the motives that underlay the opening of Japan in 1854. These motives were clearly spelled out in the two instructions the Secretaries of State sent to Commodore Shufeldt in the winter of 1881 and 1882.[12] It should be pointed out that of the two motives, that of caring for shipwrecked sailors was far more important for the Americans, because they knew well that Korea was a poor country and there was not much prospect for trade. In addition to these two national motives, there was a third. Probably the most powerful one, it falls into a different category. Behind Commodore Shufeldt's acts lay personal ambition and strong sense of glory. Without doubt, Shufeldt sought to emulate Perry and he was very conscious about the historical significance of his act.[13] The author of a special study on Secretary Blaine's foreign policy criticizes Shufeldt when she argues that the opening of Korea was carried out mainly because of Shufeldt's personal "desire" not because of the "concern" of the Secretary of State who gave the original instruction for the mission.[14] When the first American Minister, Lucius H. Foote, had his first audience with the Korean king, he told the Oriental monarch that, in negotiating the treaty, the American government was motivated "only by the highest motives"; he defined this high motive as "the comfort and happiness" of the Korean

---

[12] Blaine to Shufeldt, 14 November 1881, #1112, Instructions, China, NA; Frelinghuysen to Shufeldt, 6 January 1882, Instructions, China, NA. See also Shufeldt to Korean King, 4 May 1880, Enclosure #2, in Bingham to Evarts, 31 May 1880, #1126, Despatches, Japan, NA.

[13] Robert W. Shufeldt to Mary A. Shufeldt, 28 April 1882, Shufeldt MSS.

[14] Alice F. Tyler, *The Foreign Policy of James G. Blaine* (Hamden, Connecticut: Archon, 1965), p. 262.

people.[15] Foote was an honorable man and was not telling a lie in expressing his feeling to the king, but it is doubtful whether this altruistic motive was in the heart of the people in Washington. At least three interests—shipwrecked sailors, trade, and Shufeldt's personal ambition—are evident as the bases for American acts.

The motives of Li Hung-chang and his government in helping Shufeldt and the Korean government for the 1882 treaty are equally clear. They were twofold: the Chinese wanted to enlist American asssistance in checking Japanese influence in Korea, which had been increasing rapidly since 1876, and to safeguard the peninsula, which they considered important for their own security against the more-than-imaginary Russian threat. Finally, they wanted to make clear the control China had over the Korean kingdom. American policy makers in Washington and their representatives in the Far East knew fully well the nature of Chinese motives.[16]

No one seemed to pay any attention to Korea and to her concerns in opening the country to the United States in 1882. Judging from the king's enthusiasm and from his determination dating from 1880 to open his country to a Western nation, it is clear that the Koreans also desired this historical act. At least two reasons can be detected without much difficulty: The King of course desired to bring in American influence to combat the weight of three powerful neighbors—Japan, Russia, and China. From domestic concerns, which originated in the Queen's power struggle with her father-in-law Taewongun who had held the Korean door tightly closed for many years, came the second.[17] Shufeldt himself sensed the "absolute necessity" of the Koreans to make the treaty as a security measure against the "aggressive surrounding powers."[18]

For almost a year, from the middle of June 1881 to late May of the following year, Shufeldt had a trying time in China. The hardest part was waiting idly to hear words from the Korean government.

[15] Foote to Korean King, 20 May 1883, note, American Legation, NA r84.

[16] Shufeldt to Frelinghuysen, 23 January 1882, Instructions, China, NA; Holcome to Blaine, 19 December 1881, #30, Despatches, China, NA; Bingam to Blaine 20 June 1881, #1318, Despatches, Japan, NA. See also for a somewhat different view Frederick Foo Chen, *The Opening of Korea: a Study of Chinese Diplomacy 1876-1885* (Hamden, Connecticut: Archon, 1967), p. 92.

[17] Ilkeun Park, *Gundae Hanmi Oegyosa* (Modern History of Korean-American Relations) (Seoul: Pakwoosa, 1968), p. 237.

[18] Shufeldt to Thompson 13 October 1880, in Thompson to Evarts, 14 December 1880, misc., State, NA, m179 r576.

However, once the negotiations with Li and his aides began, they moved quickly, and the treaty was practically completed except one unresolved issue within a month, by May 19th of 1882. The only difficult issue he had to deal with, on which the negotiations were almost wrecked, was the dependency issue. The first article of the Chinese draft, which was the revised version of the draft brought from Korea, began with a sentence: "Choseun, being a dependent state of the Chinese Empire, has nevertheless hitherto exercised her own sovereignty in all matters of internal administration and foreign relations."[19] Very understanding and flexible, Shufeldt did not deny that a dependent state could also make a treaty with another power, but he thought its political implications were not satisfactory. Li apparently did not want to see a termination of the negotiation on this issue and conceded a step by proposing a substitute measure which consisted of two letters by Schufeldt and the King to the Chinese government referring to the dependent relationship between Korea and China. Disregarding the legal effect of the letters, Shufeldt proceeded to conclude the negotiation.[20]

Two minor issues remained outstanding: one was resolved in China and the other in Korea. In the early 1880s, Christianity was still a very emotional issue in Korea and the original Korean draft had a clause prohibiting missionary activities. Shufeldt objected to the inclusion of the clause in the treaty, and Li managed to convince the Koreans and the issue was dropped.[21] Shufeldt's activities in Korea between May 12th and 24th, 1882 were largely ceremonial, and the only issue handled there was that of prohibiting exportation of rice from the open port.[22] The good offices clause which became a source of difficulty in the later years, did not even come up as an issue in the negotiations. Chiefly because of Shufeldt's magnanimity and tact-fulness, the negotiations proceeded smoothly.

The treaty was ratified, receiving Senatorial approval early in the following year of 1883, and became effective in May through an

[19] Enclosure, Shufeldt to Frelinghuysen, 10 April 1882, Despatches, China, NA.

[20] Shufeldt to Frelinghuysen, 11 March 1882, Shufeldt to Li, 4 April 1882, in Shufeldt to Frelinghuysen, 10 April 1882, 28 April 1882, Despatches, China, NA.

[21] Holcome to Frelinghuysen, 29 May 1882, #117 Despatches, China, NA; Ilpyŏng Mun, *Hanmi Osipnyunsa* (Fifty Year History of Korean-American Relations) (Seoul: Chokwangsa, 1945), pp.40-42.

[22] Shufeldt to Frelinghuysen, 23 August 1882, Despatches, China, NA, Mun, *Hanmi Osipnyunsa*, p. 45.

exchange of the ratifications which took place in Seoul exactly a year after the treaty was signed.[23] The first treaty between the United States and Korea consisted of 14 articles. It was much like the treaties the United States had concluded with two other Asian countries, but it had some new and favorable features. The Americans achieved their main objectives through the clause on shipwrecks (Article III), trade (Article V), and diplomatic and consular privileges (Article II). Extraterritoriality and the most-favored nation privileges, with a favorable feature for the Koreans, were also included. Beneficial to the Koreans were arrangements prohibiting the opium trade (Article VII), prohibiting the exportation of rice and ginseng (Article VIII), specifying a liberal tariff rate of 10% for ordinary goods and 30% for the luxury goods, which was much higher than the 5% rate in the Chinese and the Japanese treaties, and the good office clause (Article I).[24] Most of these advantages came from Li's past experience in China, and he well deserved Korean gratitude. The inclusion of the good offices clause, which also was in the Tientsin Treaty of 1858, came from his political acuity.

The immediate reaction of the world to the treaty was mostly favorable. Most people who paid attention to the treaty thought it was generous to the Koreans and good. John Bingham, the American minister in Tokyo, enthusiastically hailed it as "more liberal and just" than any other treaties concluded between the Oriental nations and the Western powers.[25] The treaty became a model for the treaties concluded soon between Korea and the European powers. Some of the spectators were unhappy with the treaty for selfish reasons. The British thought the generosity exhibited in the tariff rate and extraterritoriality clause would cause a problem in China and tried to prevent ratification in the United States.[26] Some were critical later about the long-range impact of the treaty. Dennett called the American act of opening Korea "an act of absentmindedness," which "set Korea adrift in an ocean of intrigue" finally leading to its absorption by the Japanese in 1910.[27] But viewed from a longer-range view, it should be

---

[23] Foote to Frelinghuysen, 24 May 1883, Despatches, Korea, NA, m134 rl.

[24] *The Statutes at Large of the United States of America,* 23 (Washington: Government Printing Office, 1885): 720-725.

[25] Bingham to Frelinghuysen, 19 August 1883, #1547, Despatches, Japan, NA.

[26] Bingham to Frelinghuysen, 19 August 1882, #1547, 13 January 1883, #1630; 13 February 1883, #1632; 19 May 1883, #1687, Despatches, Japan, NA.

[27] Tyler Dennett, *Roosevelt and Russo-Japanese War* (New York: Doubleday, 1925),

pointed out that the Korean door was bound to be opened sooner or later by someone, that the demise of the Korean kingdom came from much more deep-seated reasons, and that the sooner the door was opened the better it was for the Koreans. It is regrettable that the last Oriental hermit kingdom was not opened 28 years earlier in 1854 by Robert McLane, or at least 12 years earlier in 1868 by George F. Seward.[28]

III. Closing of the Korean Door and the United States: A Policy or Policies?

There is much temptation to raise a question at the outset as to whether there was one American policy or many policies toward Korea during the first 28-year period of her relationship with Korea. The answer is that there was only one policy. Even though the existing fragmentary studies on the subject give to the reader an impression that there were many American policies toward Korea in these years, there was really only one constituent policy line. This one policy was described best, in plain language, by Lawrence H. Battistini: "The United States had no clearly defined policy or program with which to confront the rivalries of powers in Korea other than the somewhat nebulous tradition of favoring the development of strong and independent states everywhere in the Orient."[29] When verbalized in clearer language, this "nebulous tradition" becomes the Open Door Policy. The only American policy in Korea throughout these three decades was, in short, one of a strict neutrality and absolute non-intervention. Of course some deviations or aberrations from this policy did occur in that long period, and because of these deviations, an impression of many policies was created. These deviations came partly from the personality factor of those involved in policy-making and execution and partly from the conditions and circumstances of the particular time. It should also be noted that this straight line of policy, with some zigzags to be revealed by a close

---

pp. 103-104. See also Philip Low Bridgham, "American Policy Toward Korean Independence," 1951 Fletcher School of Law and Diplomacy Ph.D. dissertation, p. 19.

[28] Marcy to McLane, 9 November 1853, #2 Despatches, China, NA, m77 r38.

[29] Lawrence H. Battistini, *Rise of Influence in Asia and the Pacific* (West-port, Connecticut: Greenwood, 1960), p. 181.

examination, moved from the high or favorable beginning point to the low or unfavorable ending point. This gradually regressing single policy line may be subdivided for analytical purposes into five segments or sub-periods: the first from 1882 to 1894, the second from 1894 to 1895, the third from 1895 to 1904, the fourth from 1904 to 1905, and fifth and final from 1905 to 1910.

The single most important condition on the Korean peninsula during the first period was the rising influence of China; consequently, the main issue the American government had to deal with was the Chinese claim of suzerainty over the Korean kingdom. Because of the character of the individuals who handled diplomacy in Seoul during this 12-year period, there is an impression that American policy towards Korea during the first six years of this period was very favorable. It was very unfavorable during the latter half of the 12 years. However, American policy was very consistent throughout the whole period and adhered to a posture of strict neutrality and absolute nonintervention and, at the same time, a posture of recognizing Korea as an independent sovereign state. As soon as Lucius H. Foote, the first American representative, arrived in Seoul, Secretary of State Frelinghuysen wrote an instruction, which began: "The relations of the United States toward Korea are clear." He continued, "As far as we are concerned Korea is an independent sovereign power, with all the attendant rights, privileges, and duties and responsibilities. In her relations to China we have no desire to interfere unless action should be taken prejudicial to the rights of the United States."[30] His successors, Bayard and Blaine, adhered strictly to this policy line and did not show even a slight deviation.[31]

Diplomacy or the action policy in Seoul, however, showed some zigzags in those 12 years. During the first five years before 1887, when Minister Foote and Charge Foulk were representing the United States in Seoul, American diplomacy there was very active and pro-Korean almost to the extent of deviating too far from the main policy line. In the following seven years, from 1887 to 1894, when Ministers Dinsmore and Heard occupied the Seoul position, American diplo-

---

[30] Frelinghuysen to Foote, 17 March 1883, #3, Instructions, Korea, NA, m77 r109. See also Frelinghuysen to Young, 11 April 1883, #107, Instructions, China, NA.

[31] Bayard to Denby, 16 November 1885, #15, Instructions, China, NA; Bayard to Foulk, 19 August 1885, Instructions, Korea, NA, m77 r109; Blaine to Dinsmore, 7 May 1889, Instructions, Korea, NA, m77 r109; Blaine to Denby, #453, 27 June 1890, Instructions, China.

macy in Seoul was very inactive and it gave an impression of a policy change in Washington.[32] Both Foote and Foulk had great capabilities, magnanimity, and a great sense of humanity, and they tried to meet the challenges which came from the political coup of 1884 and from the dynamic character of Yuan Shih-Kai who happened to be representing China during this period. During the following seven years, this personal quality was lacking and Korea was quietly in the firm grip of Chinese hands.

Then, the Sino-Japanese War of 1894-1895 came, and American-Korean relations met the first severe test. With Cleveland and Gresham in Washington and John M. B. Sill in Seoul—all very traditional and humanely oriented persons—the stage was set for a brief period of aberration. In the summer of 1894, war was imminent in Korea and, reading accurately the consequence of war on the peninsula kingdom, the Korean government made an appeal to the American government. Responding to this appeal, Secretary Gresham instructed Sill in Seoul "to use every possible effort for the preservation of peaceful conditions" in Korea.[33] In Seoul, Sill presented a joint note, drafted with the cooperation of the representatives of the European powers to the representatives of two contending powers in Seoul.[34] Ignoring the verbal gesture of the Western powers, the Japanese took a further step on the next day in Seoul, and the helpless Korean monarch sent more appeals to the American government stating his wish to avert the conflict. When the fifth Korean appeal arrived, Gresham decided to send the "spirited message" directly to Tokyo. After pointing out that the Japanese had failed to withdraw their troops from Korea even after the rebellion was crushed and peace was restored, Gresham instructed the minister to convey the President's message to the Japanese government that he would be "painfully disappointed should Japan visit upon her feeble and helpless neighbor the horror of an unjust war."[35] The Japanese answer was easy and simple: They would not fight the Koreans, which was technically correct, and would insure "peace, good government, and sovereignty of Korea."[36] This act of aberration, however, was

---

[32] Robert E. Reordan, "The Role of George Clayton Foulk in the United States-Korean Relations, 1884-1887," 1955 Fordham University Ph.D. dissertation, p. 258.

[33] Uhl to Sill, 23 June 1894, Instructions, Korea, NA, m77 r109.

[34] Sill and others to Yuan and Otori, 25 June 1894, Enclosure, Sill to Gresham, Despatches, Korea, NA, m134 r11.

[35] Tel., Gresham to Dun, 7 July 1894, Instructions, Japan, NA, m133 r67.

momentary, and a few hours after his message left Washington, Gresham returned to the traditional line of policy when he confided to the Japanese minister in Washington that his government "could not and would not intervene in behalf of Korea otherwise than with its good offices."[37] The message was certainly in line with the American policy but the act was an unnecessary one for an apparent tactical reason. Anyway, this was the last act of verbal diplomacy; the American government did not participate in any joint effort of the powers to the end of the war.[38]

The America policy of neutrality and no intervention was carried out even more strictly in Korea during the eight and a half year period between 1895 and 1904. Gresham's successors in the State Department—Richard Olney, John Sherman, William R. Day, and John Hay—all did not have any interest in Korea and much of the time they could spare for that country was spent keeping their representatives in line with Washington's policy. Korea was going through another period of turbulence right after the Sino-Japanese War. Because of the urgency coming from a series of unusual events, including the assassination of the Queen, in which the Japanese minister was heavily involved, and the King's seeking refuge in the Russian Legation, and because of the sense of justice, it was difficult for the American representatives in Seoul not to be involved in the local politics. Olney was firm in his telegram to Sill in the late fall of 1895: "Confine yourself strictly protection of American citizens and interest. You have no concern internal affairs."[39] In the fall of 1897, Sherman reminded the newly appointed minister Horace N. Allen: "This government is no sense the counselor of Korea as to its internal destinies, neither is it bound to Korea by protective alliance." Further, the instruction indicated that not only the governmental representative but also the American citizens in Korea should hold "the attitude of absolute neutrality."[40] Because of Allen's caution and quietness in Korea—the calm before the storm—the early 1900s were eventless years for American-Korea relations. But in these quiet years, the Japanese were stepping up their economic penetration in

---

[36] Dun to Gresham, 10 July 1894, Despatches, Japan, NA.

[37] Memorandum, 7 July 1894, Notes, Japanese Legation, NA, m63 r5.

[38] Gresham to Bayard, 20 July 1894, *Papers Relating to the Foreign Relations of the United States, 1894* (Washington: Government Printing Office, 1895), Appendix I: 30.

[39] Tel., Olney to Sill, 20 November 1895, Instructions, Korea, NA, m77 r109.

[40] Sherman to Allen, 19 November 1897, Instructions, Korea, NA, m77 r109.

Korea, and Theodore Roosevelt and John Hay, who were sitting in Washington with an attitude and mood quite different from those of their predecessors, were preparing the ground for the coming period.

If the Sino-Japanese War was the first test for American-Korean relations, the Russo-Japanese War brought a second severe test. The Japanese domination of Korea was so much advanced by 1903 that Korea was not even an issue during the Russo-Japanese pre-war negotiations of 1903-1904, and the Japanese victory in the War sealed the fate of Korea. During the War, the United States judically carried out the traditional policy of neutrality. Secretary Hay instructed Allen soon after the war broke out: "Presume you will do all possible for the protection of American interests consistent with absolute neutrality."[41] The desperate Korean government turned to Allen for help, but he clearly knew what was at stake in the war and carried out cautiously throughout the entire period of the war the policy of neutrality and non-involvement.[42] Roosevelt and Hay were faithful to the Open Door Policy as far as China was involved and, as soon as the war broke out, they wrote notes to the belligerent powers expressing their desire that the neutrality and administrative integrity of China should be respected.[43] However, they would not do the same for the Koreans. Roosevelt later offered a good office for the conclusion of the war and even went as far as making an intervention for the successful conclusion of the peace at Portsmouth. But, he would not raise a finger for the Koreans.

The main controversy regarding Roosevelt's Korean policy centers around the issue of offering good offices for the Koreans as specified in the first article of the 1882 Treaty and the Taft-Katsura Memorandum of 1905. The entire good office clause reads: "If other powers deal unjustly or oppressively with either government, the other will exert their good offices, and being informed of the case, to bring about an amicable arrangement, thus showing their friendly feeling." Philip L. Bridgham among others, was very clear about the United States policy toward Korea under the leadership of Roosevelt. "The United States was guilty of violating both in spirit and substance a treaty."[44] It was by no means difficult for the Koreans to

---

[41] Tel., Hay to Allen, 2 March 1904, Instructions, Korea, NA, m77 r109.

[42] Allen to Townsend, 15 May 1904, Allen MSS; Allen to Horace E. and Maurice Allen, 9 March 1905, Allen MSS.

[43] Hay to American Representatives, 20 February 1904, *Foreign Relations of the United States, 1905*, p. 3.

show the Americans that they were being treated both unjustly and oppressively by the Japanese. The main difficulty the Koreans had was "informing" the Americans. The Koreans made at least four serious efforts to reach the President in the winter of 1905, but all of them failed because Roosevelt took a formalistic view and told them to come through an official diplomatic channel which was already under the Japanese control.[45]

On his way to the Philippines in the summer of 1905, Taft visited Tokyo and held a conversation with the Japanese Prime Minister Katsura on the subjects of Korea and the Philippines. The memorandum of the conversation became later a source of scholarly controversy.[46] Whether it was an "honest exchange of view," a "deal," or an understanding, the Japanese thought the American government gave them a sanction for taking over Korea, even before the conclusion of the Portsmouth Peace Conference. The Americans were equally hasty when they withdrew their legation in Seoul as soon as they saw the signal from Japan, becoming the first nation to terminate formal diplomatic relationship with Korea. Former Minister Allen commented resentfully: "We might have given them an expression of sympathy and waited till the funeral was over before nailing up the coffin."[47]

In view of Roosevelt's realistic outlook, his emphasis on the balance of power in the Far East, and his pro-Japanese and anti-Korean sentiment, and above all, the conditions in the region after the war, Roosevelt could not possibly have acted otherwise for the Koreans in 1905. However, he should and could have listened to Korean complaints about the Japanese and he could have made a formal offer of good offices for the Koreans. A forceful intervention on behalf of the Koreans in 1905 was unthinkable. Even a threat was not possible.[48]

---

[44] Bridgham, "American Policy toward Korean Independence," p. 151.

[45] Jongsuk Chay, "The United States and the Closing Door in Korea: American-Korean Relations, 1894-1905," 1965 University of Michigan Ph.D. dissertation, pp. 153-158.

[46] Raymond A. Esthus, *Theodore Roosevelt and Japan* (Seattle: University of Washington Press, 1966), pp. 102-107; Jongsuk Chay, "The Taft-Katsura Memorandum Reconsidered," *Pacific Historical Review*, 37 (1968): 321-326; Hong Yol Yoo, "The Unwritten Part of Korean-American Diplomatic Relations," *Koreana Quarterly*, 5 (1963), 78.

[47] Allen to Stevens, 29 November 1905, Allen MSS.

[48] Philip Jessup, *Elihu Root* (Hamden, Connecticut: Archon, 1964), II:62.

Whatever was left of American-Korean relations after the Russo-Japanese War belonged to an anti-climax. Even though it retained some vestiges of an embassy, the main function of the Seoul post was that of a Consul General—protection of the American citizens and their interests. All special treaty rights remained, and American businessmen and missionaries were left alone to carry out their activities as before. However, American business enterprizes were sold one after another to the Japanese and, by the time of annexation, the only American investment left in Korea was the mines.[49] Toward the end of August 1910, the Treaty of Annexation was signed in Seoul, and the first 28 years of American-Korean relations came to an end, to be opened again officially only after the end of the Second World War.

Like any other piece of foreign policy, the American policy toward Korea should be evaluated in terms of ends and means. The major American interest in Korea was economic, and it was certainly small. Even though American capital investment was not negligible, especially from the Korean perspective, the trade interest was close to none. The annual average Korean share of American trade between 1894 and 1904 was a little over $200,000, a level ranging between $100 and a little over $1,000,000 marks. This was less than one-hundredth of one percent of the American total foreign trade—indeed a small figure.[50] The only other American interest in Korea was the missionary work. This area was a little better than the trade, but not markedly better. It is true that American missionaries had an unusual success in Korea, but the number of converts was still very small during our period. There were only about 40,000 Christians in Korea in 1905, a little over one percent of the total number of converts the American mission work counted in that year.[51] The Americans never had any other interest in Korea in these early years. If any political concerns came into the picture, it was usually as a negative factor. Especially for Roosevelt, who considered the position of Japan very important to counter the Russian threat in Asia, the Korean "embarrassment" was rather burdensome. For these small ends, the available means were also very meager. The United States had an efficient modern but still small navy in the 1900s and had a surprisingly small army. No

---

[49] Carr to Thomas, 2 February 1909, Seoul Consular Document, NA, gp84; Thomas to O'Brien, 8 June 1909, Seoul Consular Document, NA, gp84.

[50] Chay, "The United States and the Closing Door in Korea," Appendix A.

[51] Chay, "The United States and the Closing Door in Korea," p. 17.

matter what force it had, however, it was not even thinkable for the United States to send it to the Far East in the 1900s to fight the Japanese for the Koreans. The only available means to implement American foreign policy in the Far East in the 1900s was a verbal one—the Open Door Policy. But, as noted earlier, Roosevelt would not use even this doubtful weapon for the Koreans. Even if the Policy was also applied in Korea, this paper bullet was inadequate to fight the march of Japanese imperialism. One may be reminded that Pearl Harbor was the price the Americans later paid for their lack of vision and determination in the early years and eventually the Americans had to intervene for the Koreans in 1950. But who could have persuaded Roosevelt to send the American army to Asia to fight for the Koreans in 1905?

IV. Closing Door in Korea and the Koreans

Korea was treated more as an object than a subject and was almost completely neglected as an actor in the Far Eastern international system in our period. Did Korea also have a foreign policy, especially towards the United States in the late 19th and the early 20th centuries? The choices she had in those years deserve some attention. First of all, it must be recognized that, because of her location and the size of her territory and population, she was in a very difficult situation. Because of this geopolitical factor, she was often a victim among the "millstones" or a "bone of contention among the neighboring dogs." Still, this difficult situation cannot deny them completely chances and choices; the implication seems to be that the people face a very difficult task and they have to double or triple their effort to meet the challenge. What were, then, the choices the Koreans had at the turn of the century? It seems to be that they had at least five choices: one, independence with Chinese protection; two, independence following the Japanese model and assistance; three, independence with American assistance; four, neutralization with an international guarantee; five, independence through self-reliance.

China herself had a problem in the late 19th century and was in no position to be helpful for the Koreans during this period. If, however, she had not changed her policy after 1882 to economic and political, and even military, domination in Korea, Korea would probably have been able to maintain the pre-1882 relationship with China. With the end of the Sino-Japanese War, this chance was lost forever. Many Koreans admired the progress Japan had made since the restoration and tried to learn from her for their own modernization process. It is regretful that the 1884 coup failed. But it is doubtful whether Korea's efforts to modernize would have succeeded with Japanese help. Japan showed much shortsightedness in her policy in Korea in 1894-1895 and especially during the five year period after the end of the Russo-Japanese War. It seems to be that there was not much chance for the first two choices.

The third choice of trying to maintain independence with American assistance was the most attractive one for the Koreans and was the route they took. To them, the Americans gave an image of being fair, unselfish, and "disinterested." They perceived correctly that the United States was different from their three greedy neighbors, or even from the European powers, in not having any territorial or political ambitions. Furthermore, some of the American representatives—especially Allen and Foote and even Foulk—gave an impression to the King that Korea would be able to rely on their country in time of need. "In this progressive age, there is a moral power more potent than standing armies, and the weakness of a nation is sometimes its strength."[52] This was what Foote told the King in his first audience. Probably these were the words the Oriental monarch wanted to hear from the American representative. The crux of the problem here was the disinterestedness. Logically, where there was no interest the Americans did not have any business. The Koreans seem to have realized this logical pitfall and the King tried to create as much American interest as possible in Korea by giving everything possible— the best gold mine, the rights for electricity, railway, the waterway, and street cars, and other privileges. But these were not enough. Thus, there was a logical defect in the third choice, and in this sense American-Korean relations in this period had a tragic element.

The notion of neutralization of Korea through an international guarantee is an interesting and peculiar one. Not only the Koreans themselves, but also all three neighbors were attracted by it at one time or another. But, an interesting fact was that the powers grabbed the idea as a mechanism to check the influence of their rivals, and as soon as the power configuration changed in their favor, they forgot

---

[52] Foote to Korean King, 20 May 1883, #3, Note, American Legation, NA, rg84.

quickly the idea. The powers never came up with the idea at the same time; hence, this was an interesting idea but it was never tried seriously during our period. It will remain as an interesting idea but will be also a hard one to realize.

The fifth and the last choice, that of self-reliance, was probably the best and the hardest one for the Koreans to choose. It was the best because it was the most reliable method, or probably the only reliable one. It was the hardest for the Koreans because the Koreans lacked strength, while at the same time, they were not allowed the luxury of time to nourish it, as is usual under such circumstances. The pressures coming from strong and greedy neighbors at the turn of the century were too strong and urgent. Being helpless, the Koreans turned to outside help and it never worked. The method of self-reliance was the longest and the hardest road but it also was the best and surest one, and it is regrettable that the Koreans at the turn of the century wasted valuable time while searching for a reliable friend.

Horace Allen, who arrived in Korea in 1884 and spent the critical 20 years in that country, first as a medical missionary and later as an American representative from 1897, was not a noble person by any means but was a perceptive one. Back in Ohio, he made later the following observation:

> The Koreans are reaping the harvest of their sawing through the twenty years during which they enjoyed more or less independence. Instead of heeding good advice and clearing up their premise so no powerful neighbor would have excuse for doing this for them, they played at all manner of silly pastime.[53]

Looking back, we now realize how crucial was this 20 year time at the turn of the century. Turning to the today's condition in Korea, one is surprised to find how similar the situation is to what it was a century ago. My wish is that a century from now another Allen will not make a similar observation.

---

[53] Horace N. Allen, *Things Korean: a Collection of Sketches Missionary and Diplomatic* (New York: Revell, 1908), p. 249.

CHAPTER 2

U.S. POLICY AND THE JAPANESE ANNEXATION OF KOREA

Andrew C. Nahm

The United States might not have anticipated the Japanese annexation of Korea when the Taft-Katsura Memorandum of July 1905 was exchanged between the United States and Japan. However, the policy adopted and actions taken during the Roosevelt administration contributed to the demise of the Korean nation in 1910. Abandoned by Great Britain and the United States, which rendered their moral support to the Japanese, Korea was powerless to avoid the tragic event.

The writings of Tyler Dennett, A. Whitney Griswold and others, who dealt with American involvement in Far Eastern affairs of the late nineteenth and early twentieth centuries, led many to believe that in the Taft-Katsura Memorandum the United States gave her consent to Japanese seizure of Korea in exchange for the disavowal of the Japanese of any hostile intentions against the Philippines, and with it the United States refused to help Korea to preserve her independence.

That the Taft-Katsura Memorandum constituted a milestone in the Korea policy of the United States cannot be disputed. It encouraged the Japanese to be more aggressive in Korea, but it was neither the first time "a green light" was given to the Japanese by the United States to establish their control in Korea, nor was it the final step taken by the United States to abandon Korea entirely to the Japanese. Be that as it may, the Roosevelt administration directly or indirectly contributed to the Japanese seizure of Korea.

The purpose of this paper is to examine the policy of the United States in dealing with the Korean question in general, and make some contribution to the promotion of more accurate knowledge about

U.S. policy toward Korea in the 1904-05 period which affected the destiny of Korea.

I. Traditional U.S. Policy Toward Korea

The Chemulp'o (Shufeldt) Treaty of May 22, 1882 established diplomatic and commerical relations between the United States and Korea. When Lucius H. Foote arrived in Seoul a year later in May 1883 as the first American minister to the Kingdom of Korea, the Korean king "danced with joy,"[1] because he and his ministers viewed the American treaty as "a wedge to free Korea from Chinese domination,"[2] and the United States would help Korea in time of difficulties.

What led the Koreans to anticipate American assistance and protection? Both the "good offices" clause in the treaty and what Foote said to the Korean king may have encouraged the Koreans to expect American assistance and even protection. The "good offices" clause in the treaty stated that "If other powers deal unjustly or oppressively with either Government, the other will exert good offices, and ... bring about amicable arrangement, thus showing their friendly feeling." When Foote had his first audience with the Korean king in May 1883, he said to the Korean king that "the highest motive" of the United States in Korea was to enhance "the welfare and happiness of the Korean people."[3] Moreover, the American said to the Korean king that "In this progressive age, there is a moral power more potent than standing armies, and the weakness of a nation is sometimes its strength."[4] Such expressions and gestures made by the American minister only encouraged the Korean king and his officials to rely on American assistance to, and even "protection" for Korea.

The United States had no such intentions. U.S. policy toward

---

[1] Foulk to Secretary of Navy, enclosure in No. 128, Foote to Frelinghuysen, December 17, 1884 in George M. McCune and John A. Harrison ed. with an Introduction, *Korean-American Relations: Documents Pertaining to the Far Eastern Diplomacy of the United States.* Vol. I. The Initial Period, 1883-1886 (Berkeley and Los Angeles: University of California Press, 1951), p. 105.

[2] *Ibid.*

[3] Foote to Korean King. May 20, 1882. Note. American Legation. National Archieves, r84.

[4] *Ibid.*

Korea was that of strict neutrality in political affairs. In his instruction to Minister Foote in March 1883, Secretary of State Frederick T. Frelinghuysen clearly stated that in Korea's relations with China and other nations, "we have no desire to interfere unless action should be taken prejudicial to the rights of the United States."[5] As a result, despite efforts made by Minister Foote and his Naval Aide George C. Foulk to promote political influence and commercial interests of the United States in Korea, the United States was little more than a detached onlooker.

Considering Korea unimportant and American interests being so minimal at best, the American government, in July 1884, even reduced the rank of American minister to Korea from Envoy Extraordinary and Minister Plenipotentiary to that of Minister Resident and Consul General. Disappointed, Minister Foote resigned, and in his letter of September 1884 to Frelinghuysen, he stated that his "sole purpose" was to extend the influence of the United States and open new fields for American commerce.[6]

The policy of neutrality and absolute non-intervention in Korea was streadfastly maintained by the successor of Frelinghuysen. Only when the Sino-Japanese War was about to begin and the Korean government made appeals to the American government, Secretary of State Walter Q. Gresham instructed American minister to Korea John M.B. Sill to use "every possible effort for the preservation of peaceful conditions in Korea."[7] Secretary Gresham, however, told the Korean envoy in Washington on July 9, 1894, that the American government would not intervene, either forcibly or jointly, with the European power in favor of Korea, and it would maintain "impartial neutrality." But, after receiving repeated appeals for help from the Korean government, Gresham said that he would advise the Japanese only in a "friendly way." Subsequently, Gresham asked the Japanese minister in Washington that Japan should treat her "feeble neighbor" "kindly and fairly."[8] Meanwhile, Gresham sent a "spirited message" to the

---

[5] Frelinghuysen to Foote, March 17, 1884. Instruction, No. 3. McCune and Harrison, *op. cit.,* p. 25.

[6] *Ibid.*

[7] [Edwin J. Uhl] to Sill, June 23, 1894. Instruction. Korea. National Archieves, n77. r109.

[8] Tyler Dennett, *Americans in Eastern Asia: A Critical Study of United States Policy in the Far East in the Nineteenth Century* (New York: Barnes and Nobles, 1922), p. 498.

Tokyo government via American minister to Japan Edwin Dun. In his message, Gresham instructed Dun to convey the President's message to the Japanese government that he would be "painfully disappointed should Japan visit upon her feeble and helpless neighbor the horror of an unjust war."[9] Gresham, however, confided to the Japanese minister in Washington that his government "could not and would not intervene in behalf of Korea otherwise with its good offices."[10]

Korea was not an important country as far as the United States was concerned. The economic interests of the United States in Korea was only marginal at best. The annual average value of trade between Korea and the United States during the period between 1894 and 1904 was a little over $200,000, which was one-hundredth of one per cent of the total foreign trade of the United States.[11] The most important economic activity of the Americans in Korea was gold mining at Unsan. "Flag follows dollar," and in the age of mercantile imperialism and dollar diplomacy, Korea had no commercial value for the United States. Political and military concerns of the United States in the Far East were yet to develop.

Despite the failure of the United States to intervene in behalf of Korea when the Japanese were encroaching upon Korea during the Sino-Japanese War, as late as January 1904, a short time before the outbreak of the Russo-Japanese War which determined the fate of Korea, Yi Wan-yong, Prime Minister of Korea, told a British correspondent[12] that Korea's "independence was guaranteed by America and Europe," and "we had the promise of America. She will be our friend no matter what happens."[13] Horace N. Allen, American minister to Korea, wrote in April 1904 that the Korean Emperor "falls back in his extremity upon his friendship with America..." and the United States would "do something for him ... to retain as much of his independence... as possible."[14]

---

[9] Gresham to Dun. July 7, 1894. Instructions. Japan. National Archieves, m133 r67.

[10] Memorandum, July 7, 1894. Notes. Japanese Legation. National Archives, m63 r5.

[11] Jongsuk Chay, "The United States and the Closing Door in Korea: American-Korean Relations, 1894-1905." Ph.D. dissertation (Michigan, 1965), Appendix A.

[12] Frederick A. McKenzie.

[13] Frederick A. McKenzie, *Korea's Fight for Freedom* (New York: 1920), pp. 77-78.

[14] *Ibid.;* Allen to Rockhill, January 4, 1904, quoted in Esthus, *op. cit.,* p. 49; Fred Harvey Harrington, *God, Mammon and the Japanese: Dr. Horace N. Allen and Korean-American Relations, 1884-1905* (Madison, Wisconsin: The University of Wisconsin Press, 1944), p. 326. The Korean King adopted imperial title for the first

Being unacquainted with modern diplomatic tactics and international law, and being inexperienced in the diplomacy of power politics, the Korean monarch and his officials were under an illusion that the good offices clause in the American-Korean treaty of May 1882 was an American guarantee for the security of Korea. Although they were counting on American assistance and intervention in behalf of Korea against the Japanese, the United States would do no such thing, and her assistance was not forthcoming.

II. U.S. Policy Toward Korea During the Period between 1904 and 1910

On November 17, 1905, four months after the exchange of the memorandum of conversation between U.S. Secretary of War, William Howard Taft, and Japanese Prime Minister, Katsura Tarō in July, the Japanese forced the Korean Emperor to sign the Treaty of Protection, putting his empire under Japanese protection. Following this, the Japanese established the Residency-General (*Tōkanfu*), and in August 1910 the Japanese annexed Korea against her will.

The Taft-Katsura Memorandum of conversation of July 27, 1905, has been widely interpreted as a secret pact between the United States and Japan whereby the United States approved Japanese seizure of Korea and establishment of their suzereinty over Korea in return for a Japanese disavowal of any aggressive intentions toward the Philippines. Therefore, it was regarded as a bargain with *quid pro quo*.[15] However, careful studies of the background and contents of the memorandum do not support this contention. It was a secret document, for it was kept secret, but it was neither as secret bargain with a *quid pro quo,* nor was it an agreement in which the United States gave complete freedom of action to the Japanese in Korea.

---

time in Korea history in 1898, and the Kingdom of Korea became the Empire of Korea (*Tae-Han cheguk*).

[15] A. Whitney Griswold, *The Far Eastern Policy of the United States* (New Haven and London: The Yale University Press, 1938), pp. 125-126; Tyler Dennett, "President Roosevelt's Secret Pact With Japan," *Current History*, XXI (1924), 15-21; Tyler Dennett, *Roosevelt and the Russo-Japanese War* (New York, 1925), pp. 112-114; C. I. Eugene Kim and Han-kyo Kim, *Korea and the Politics of Imperialism, 1876-1910* (Berkeley and Los Angeles: University of California Press, 1967), p. 126.

Available documentary evidence shows that in the 1904-05 period the United States was not concerned with the security of the Philippines. There were no threats of Japan towards the American colony in the Far East, and the Japanese did not make any preparations to take over the Philippines by force in 1905. The Japanese did not show any signs that they were contemplating to commit such an aggression in the future. Moreover, Takahira Kogorō, Japanese minister to the United States, and Kaneko Kentarō, who was Roosevelt's Harvard classmate, had told the American president at a luncheon on June 6, 1904 that "all talks of Japan's even thinking of seizing the Philippines were nonsense."[16] Therefore, the reasons for the exchange of the Taft-Katsura Memorandum must be sought elsewhere.

The foreign policy objectives of the Roosevelt administration in the Far East and American concessions made to Japan regarding Korea, particularly in the Taft-Katsura Memorandum, should be examined in a broader context.

The maintenance of the balance of power in East Asia and the establishment of the open door in Manchuria were two cornerstones of U.S. Far Eastern policy of the Roosevelt administration. It was Roosevelt's scheme to reduce Russian influence in the Far East, particularly in Manchuria, but not to destory Russian influence altogether in that region. Roosevelt expressed his hope that Japan would take her place among the great powers in the Fat East and establish "a paramount interest" in the area surrounding the Yellow Sea.[17] He did not wish to confront or challenge the Anglo-Japanese Alliance of 1902, which was formed with Russia in mind. However, since Japan might destory Russian influence in East Asia entirely, upset the balance of power in that area, and destory any chance for the United States to establish the open door in Manchuria, it was expedient for him to establish an understanding with Japan regarding the open door in Manchuria when the Russo-Japanese War commenced.

Since the United States had no sphere of influence in China, it looked toward Manchuria.[18] The Russian occupation of Manchuria

---

[16] Henry P. Pringle, *Theodore Roosevelt: A Biography* (New York: Harcourt, Brace and Co., 1931). p. 41.

[17] Esthus, *op. cit.,* p. 41. Roosevelt said this to the Japanese in 1904 and again in July 1905.

[18] John K. Fairbank, *The United States and China* (Cambridge: Harvard University Press, 1959), p. 256.

following the Boxer affairs was regarded as a rebuff to the United States and it was a direct challenge to the U.S. open door policy. Since the United States was unable to check Russian expansionism in the Far East, Roosevelt had hoped that Japan play a key role in checking Russian expansionism in East Asia.

When the Russo-Japanese War broke out in February 1904, the United States had written off Korea. A.W. Rockhill, adviser to Roosevelt, wrote a letter to Minister Allen in late February that the fall of Korea was inevitable. He said:

> I fancy that the Japanese will settle [the Korean] question when the present war is finished. The annexation of Korea to Japan seems to be absolutely indicated as the one great and final step westward of the extension of the Japanese ...[19]

Roosevelt concluded that "since America could not prevent Japanese absorption of Korea, the next best thing was to recognize the inevitable and secure something in return."[20] As a result, Roosevelt advanced his own version of the "Korea for Manchuria (*Man-Kan kōkan* in Japanese)" idea in order to establish the open door in Manchuria. In March 1904, Roosevelt told Baron Suematsu Kenchō, who visited Washington that Japan should have a position in Korea, "*just like we have with Cuba.*"[21] By inference, Roosevelt conceded to certain rights of Japan in Korea. Meanwhile, he informed Speck von Sternberg, German minister to Washington, that Korea should belong to Japan and Manchuria should be made a neutral zone under Chinese control.[22] Moreover, Roosevelt told the German minister Sternberg that Russia should retain a "leading position" in Manchuria but surrender Port Arthur and observe the open door for commerce in that region.[23]

In addition to the lack of economic interests in Korea on the part of the United States, the latter's policy toward Korea was heavily influenced by the personality of Roosevelt. A believer in Social Darwinism

---

[19] Rockhill to Allen, February 20, 1904, *Rockhill Papers*. Houghton Library, Harvard University.

[20] Thomas A. Bailey, *Diplomatic History of the American People* (New York: Appleton-Century-Croft, 1956), p. 399.

[21] Hayashi Gonsuke to Komura Jutarō, March 15, 1904, quoted in Esthus, *op. cit.*, p. 101. (Italics mine).

[22] Sternberg to the Foreign minister, May 9, 1904, quoted in *Ibid.*, p. 39.

[23] Sternberg to the Foreign minister, May 9, 1904, quoted in *Ibid.*

and the "Big Stick diplomacy" in international affairs, Roosevelt had a contemptuous attitude toward Korea, to say nothing of lack of sympathy for the Koreans.[24] He admired and respected the fighters and winners. He said that he was a "pro-Japanese,"[25] and he had no respect for Korea which had shown "its utter inability to stand by itself," and "could not strike a blow in her own behalf."[26]

On June 6, 1904 at a luncheon, Roosevelt told Japanese Minister to Washington, Takahira, and his former classmate at Harvard, Kaneko, who was in the United States to solicit American support for Japan, that Japan should "take over Korea," and he promised that the United States would excercise her influence to enable Japan to enjoy "the full fruits of her victory over Russia,"[27] without infringing upon American rights and interests in Korea and Manchuria. Secretary of State John Hay had already told the Japanese minister on May 12, 1903 that however marginal American interests may be in Korea "if American interests in Korea were threatened by any power, the United States might use force."[28]

In the spring and summer of 1905, Roosevelt's Manchurian scheme seemed to be in jeopardy. The Japanese won a major victory at the Battle of Mukden in March, followed by another great naval victory in the Korea Strait in May. Following these, Foreign Minister Komura Jutarō informed Roosevelt in June that Japan would not agree to make Manchuria a neutral area or put it under international guidance as Roosevelt had proposed earlier.[29] Moreover, the Japanese, insisted in collecting a large sum of war indemnity and taking some territories away from Russia.

Roosevelt was anxious that the Japanese didn't press too far to the north in Manchuria and, in order to arrive at some understanding with the Japanese regarding Manchuria, he would drop the idea about the neutralization of Manchuria itself if the Japanese would give their assurance to the open door there.

Roosevelt misread the signals from Tokyo. He thought that the Japanese militarists wanted to continue the war to win Russian territories. It was not the case. After the great victory at Mukden, the

---

[24] For his personality, see Pringle, *op. cit.*, pp. 35 ff.

[25] Quoted in Griswold, *op. cit.*, p. 120.

[26] Dennett, *Roosevelt and the Russo-Japanese War*, p. 110.

[27] Esthus, *op. cit.*, p. 43.

[28] *Ibid.*, p. 12.

[29] *Hay Diary*, June 26, 1905, quoted in *Ibid.*, p. 62.

opinion of many, including that of the militarists, was that the early conclusion of peace was desirable. The Japanese were waiting for an overture from St. Petersberg, and Motono Ichirō, Japanese Minister to France, informed French Foreign Minister Delcase to that effect. However, in public, the Japanese insisted upon collecting an indemnity and taking Vladivostok, the Liaoting region, and Sakhalin Island from Russia. However, in April 1905, the Japanese cabinet had decided that Russia's territorial concessions were not necessarily mandatory, and only if possible Japan should pursue efforts to secure Russian concession.

Roosevelt had no objections to Japanese occupation of Port Arthur and the Port Arthur-Harbin railroad, but he did not wish to weaken Russian influence in Manchuria too drastically. He said that he did not object Japan's expansion of her war aims if her aims were reasonable and would guarantee peace in the Far East.[30]

However, when the Japanese seemed to expand their war aims, Roosevelt reminded the Japanese that Secretary Hay had already told them on June 23, 1904 that they should not take that action.[31] Other neutral nations also expressed their hopes that no territorial appropriations in China should be made by the victor. Roosevelt maintained his hope to see Manchuria restored to China and the open door maintained there.[32] For this reason, he refused to act as a mediator between Japan and Russia without Japanese assurance for the open door in Manchuria. However, he knew that unless the United States was prepared to go to war against Japan, the maintenance of the open door in Manchuria was not possible.[33]

Being anxious to end the war, the Japanese Foreign minister informed Roosevelt in April 1905 that Japan would maintain the open door in Manchuria and restore it under Chinese control,[34] but after the victory at sea in May and their occupation of Sakhalin Island in July, the Japanese stood firm on their ground for Russian territorial concessions.

Roosevelt made futile efforts to persuade Japan to abandon her demands for indemnity and territorial concessions from Russia. Mean-

---

[30] *Ibid.,* p. 44.

[31] *Ibid.*

[32] Roosevlt to R. W. Meyer, U.S. Minister to St. Petersberg, February 6, 1905, quoted in *Ibid.,* p. 61.

[33] Roosevelt to Taft, December 22, 1919, quoted in Griswold, *op. cit.,* p. 132.

[34] Dennett, *Roosevelt and the Russo-Japanese War,* pp. 177-180.

while, George Kennan met Prime Minister Katsura in Tokyo and conveyed Roosevelt's thoughts on Port Arthur and Korea in March 1905, and in April Roosevelt dismissed Allen, U.S. minister to Korea, who expressed his anti-Japanese and pro-Russian sentiments, and appointed Edwin V. Morgan as new Minister to Korea in June 1905.

It was one of those "unexpected happenings,"[35] when Taft, Secretary of War and temporary Secretary of State, appeared in Tokyo while on his way to the Philippines. Although Taft had no mandate from Roosevelt to negotiate with the Japanese on Korea or on the Philippines, Katsura seized the opportunity to elicit a statement from Taft on the Korean question although he had already been informed by Kennan that Roosevelt had already resolved that Japan must hold Korea.[36]

During the conversation held on the morning of July 27, 1905 between Taft and Katsura, Taft remarked to Katsura that although "some pro-Russians in the United States would have the public believe that the victory of Japan would be a certain prelude to her aggression in the direction of the Philippines," in his opinion "Japan's only interest in the Philippines would be to have the islands governed by a strong and friendly nation like the United States and not to have them placed either under the misrule of the natives yet unfit to self government or in the hands of some unfriendly European power."[37] Katsura "confirmed in strongest terms the correctness of" Taft opinion about Japan's interest, and "positively stated" to Taft that "Japan does not harbour any aggressive design whatever on the Philippines." Katsura remarked that "all the insinuations of the 'Yellow Peril' type are nothing more or less than malicious and clumsy slanders calculated to do mischief to Japan" by pro-Russians in America.

Regarding Korea, Katsura stated that Korea "being the direct cause of our war with Russia it is a matter of absolute importance to Japan that a complete solution of the peninsula question should be made. . ." He further remarked that "If left to herself after the war, Corea

---

[35] Hilary Conroy, *The Japanese Seizure of Korea, 1868-1910: A Study of Realism and Idealism in International Relations* (Philadelphia: University of Pennsylvania Press, 1960), pp. 221 ff.

[36] In February 1905, Roosevelt told Richard Barry, a writer for *Coolier's,* that Japan must hold Port Arthur and Korea, and Barry relayed Roosevelt's message to Kennan who was in Tokyo.

[37] See Appendix A.

would certainly drift back to her former habit of improvidently entering into any agreements or treaties with other powers, thus resuscitating the same international complications as existed before the war." Therefore, Katsura expressed his view that Japan was "absolutely constrained to take some definite step with a view to precluding the possibility of Corea falling back into her former condition and of placing us again under the necessity of entering upon another foreign war."

Although Taft had no mandate from Roosevelt to confer with the Japanese with regard to Korea, or had any "authority to give assurance to" the Japanese, he was confident that Roosevelt "would concur" with his views on Korea, and seeing "the justness of the Count's observations" on Korea, Taft remarked to Katsura "to the effect that in his personal opinion the establishment of *a suzerainty over Corea enter into no foreign treaties without the consent of Japan* was the logical result of the present war and would directly contribute to permanent peace in the Far East."[38]

The discussion on the Philippines and Korea ended there, and the Taft-Katsura Memorandum could hardly be a secret agreement. It said nothing about the Japanese taking-over Korea and turning her into a colony. As the memorandum stated, the United States agreed with Japan that Japan should have her control over the foreign affairs of Korea, requiring that the Korean government conclude any agreements with other powers only after receiving the consent of the Japanese, and the Japanese control over Korea was to be no more than what the United States had over Cuba, as Roosevelt had said in March 1904 to Baron Suematsu. However, as one writer said, the United States went to the very threshold of a secret agreement with Japan for the absorption of Korea by Japan.[39]

On July 31, 1905, Roosevelt expressed his concurrence with Taft's opinions on Korea and the Philippines and statements made to Katsura. Evidently, Roosevelt believed what Katsura said to Taft about the American colony in the Far East, but he made it known to the Japanese that if any one threatened the security of the Philippines, "we would be quite competent to defend ourselves." Roosevelt had some misgivings that the Japanese victory over Russia "may possibly mean a struggle between them and us *in the future,*" but he said that

---

[38] *Ibid.* (Italics mine).
[39] Pringle, *op. cit.*, p. 269.

he did not believe that such would be the case.[40] At least, he did not hope that to be so. He was certain that the United States was competent to prevent any "meddling" by the Japanese with the Philippines and the United States needed no Japanese "guarantee of assistance to preserve our territorial integrity."[41]

The Japanese deliberately misinterpreted and misrepresented the understanding contained in the Taft-Katsura Memorandum in order to justify their aggressive designs and actions which had already been taken in Korea as well as future actions in Korea. Although Katsura denied that his government leaked the contents of the memorandum to the press, a Japanese newspaper, the *Kokumin Shimbun,* a government organ, printed a news item in October 1905, within a month after the Portsmouth Treaty was signed, and stated that the Taft-Katsura "agreement" was a secret political bargain between the United States and Japan regarding Korea and the Philippines.[42]

Roosevelt himself complained that the memorandum was "merely to clear up Japanese attitude" toward the Philippines, and regarding Korea he said that his Korean policy was not the result of a bargain in which Japan guaranteed the security of the Philippines. He added that "we neither ask nor give any favor to anyone as a reward for not meddling with any American territory. . ."[43] It was too late, however, for him to undo what he and Taft had done earlier, particularly what he had done in late August 1905 during the peace talks between Japan and Russia at Portsmouth.

Roosevelt was disturbed by excessive demands presented by the Japanese to Russia as he was anxious to see the war ended without delay. He feared that if the war went on, Russia might lose eastern Siberia to Japan, the Yellow Perilism and anti-Japanese feelings in Europe and America would grow, and the balance of power in the Far East would be completely upset. Although he said that he became "far more stronger pro-Japanese than before,"[44] he complained to his son that "The Japanese ask too much."[45]

During the negotiations for peace between Japan and Russia at

---

[40] Roosevelt to Spring Rice, June 13, 1904, quoted in Esthus, *op. cit.,* pp. 43, 102. (Italics mine).

[41] Roosevelt to Taft, October 5, 1905, quoted in *Ibid.,* p. 104.

[42] *Ibid.,* p. 105.

[43] Roosevelt to Taft, October 7, 1907, quoted in *Ibid.,* p. 104.

[44] Quoted in Griswold, *op. cit.,* p. 120.

[45] Roosevelt to Kermit, August 25, 1905, quoted in *Ibid.,* p. 89.

Portsmouth, the Japanese government instructed Foreign Minister Komura to secure, among other, a "free hand in Korea," as well as Russia's surrender of Sakhalin Island, demilitarization of Vladivostok, and payment of a large sum ($1,000 million) of indemnity to Japan. The Japanese were willing to agree to return the northern half of Sakhalin Island if Russia would agree to pay $600 million for it. At the end of August 1905, when Russia rejected all demands, except her willingness to take her hands off Korea, the peace conference was about to collapse.

Roosevelt refused to accept failure as a mediator for peace. He first attempted to make the Japanese drop their demand for an indemnity. Failing in that, he attempted to change the nature of monetary demand from indemnity to "redemption," but the Japanese refused to do so and stood firmly on their ground. Roosevelt grew desperate as things seemed hopeless. It was at this juncture that Roosevelt had a secret talk with Kaneko Kentarō, one of the members of the Japanese commission at Portsmouth, who had his own independent channel of communication with both his government and Roosevelt.

The full details of the Roosevelt-Kaneko talk on Korea in late August may never been known, but it is evident that Roosevelt urged the Japanese to go further than the limit in the Taft-Katsura understanding regarding Korea as a price for their abandoning excessive demands on Russia.

What made Roosevelt become more pro-Japanese? How did he induce the Japanese to reduce their demands on Russia? What further concession did he make to the Japanese regarding Korea?

The secret memoir of Kaneko Kentarō offered some clues to the mystery surrounding the "final" American-Japanese understanding on Korea. Kaneko wrote that during his talks with Roosevelt, the American president said to him:[46]

> [Japan] does not need money. You talk about collecting indemnity. Instead, take Sakhalin, Manchurian railway, Port Arthur, and coal mine at Lushun. *Sooner or later, it will be better for Japan to take Korea. I think Japan ought to take Korea.* It will be good for the Koreans and Asia. *I don't think Japan should take Korea right away, but sooner or later it will be better for [Japan] to take her.*

---

[46] Kaneko Kentarō, *Nichi-Ro kōwa ni kanshi Beigoku ni okeru yo no katsudō ni tsuite* (Concerning my activities in the United States during the Japanese-Russian peace negotiations)." Confidential. Japan. Ministry of Foreign Affairs. Research Division. First Section. Special Edition. No. 5. January 1939. p. 53. (Italics mine.)

Perhaps, it was a few days after Kaneko had his secret talks with Roosevelt, Japan agreed to keep only the southern half of Sakhalin and dropped the demand for indemnity entirely. The Portsmouth Treaty was signed on September 5, 1905, and Roosevelt won the Nobel Peace Prize in 1906. The way in which the Japanese responded to Roosevelt's last proposal made him "far more stronger pro-Japanese."

Indeed, it was in late August 1905 that Roosevelt gave a clear-cut green signal and "a free hand" to the Japanese in Korea. Kaneko further stated that when the American minister to Korea and other ministers of European powers sought further instructions from their government shortly after the signing of the Treaty of Protection, which was forced upon the Korean Emperor by the Japanese, on November 17, Roosevelt instructed the American minister that he should "pack and come home because the annexation of Korea by Japan will be good for Korea as well as Japan." Kaneko's secret memoir strongly suggests that he received an unmistakable signal from Roosevelt for Japan to annex Korea. Under the pressure, accompanied by military threats, on the Korean government to accept Japanese "protection," Roosevelt's daughter, Alice, Senator Francis G. Newlands and Congressman Frederick H. Gillette visited Korea. They were given a reception by the Korean Emperor and they were informed by him what the Japanese intentions in Korea were and what they were doing to him.

It is not clear what those American visitors said or wrote to Roosevelt regarding Korea. However, Llyod C. Griscom, American minister to Japan, wrote to Roosevelt on October 12 to the effect that the United States ought to throw its "whole moral weight" to prevent the Japanese from abusing the Koreans and "going too far."[47] Evidently, Griscom knew nothing about the attitude of Roosevelt toward Korea and the Taft-Katsura understanding. Be that as it may, soon after Griscom wrote to Roosevelt, Roosevelt talked with Japanese Minister Takahira about the Korean situation, and Takahira relayed Roosevelt's concerns to Tokyo. Katsura sent a telegram to Roosevelt saying that the Japanese government would carefully watch over the conduct of the Japanese in Korea. At the same time, Katsura confided to Roosevelt that Japan would shortly assume charge of Korea's external

---

[47] Griscom to Roosevelt, October 12, 1905. Roosevelt Papers. Quoted in Esthus, *op. cit.,* p. 109.

affairs. Roosevelt raised no objections as he took no further actions in behalf of Korea. Meanwhile, Minister Morgan in Seoul may have been notified by Roosevelt about the new Roosevelt-Kaneko understanding of late August 1905.

On November 17, 1905, the helpless Korean Emperor signed the Treaty of Protection, thereby putting his empire under Japanese protection and the foreign affairs of his government under Japanese supervision. Two days later, the United States closed down its legation in Seoul without giving "expression of sympathy" to the Korean or "waiting till the funeral was over." After that, other foreign missions left Seoul "like the stampede of rats from a sinking ship," as Willard Straight, U.S. Vice Consul in Seoul, had described.

When the Korean envoys sent to Washington appealed to the American government for help in late 1905, Secretary of State Elihu Root and Roosevelt turned deaf ears to the Korean envoys, for they knew that there was no way now for the United States to stop the Japanese in Korea. Secretary of State John Hay had already stated in 1903 to the Koreans that "our interests in Korea were more commercial than political,"[48] and that as long as the Japanese respected American interests and rights in Korea, the United States would not interfere with the Japanese. As an American scholar pointed out, by not doing anything for Korea, the United States became "guilty of violating both the spirit and substance of the 1882 treaty."[49]

Following the establishment of Japanese protectorate over Korea, the Japanese systematically took away sovereign rights of the Korean Emperor. In 1907, the Japanese forced Emperor Kojong to abdicate and put a puppet emperor on the throne. Finally, on August 22, 1910, the Japanese annexed Korea.

III. Conclusion

Korea fell primarily because of her own weaknesses and ineptitude. But Roosevelt's power politics and his vain hope to establish the open door in Manchuria and maintain the balance of power in East Asia by

---

[48] Dennett, *Roosevelt and the Russo-Japanese War*, pp. 110-113; Harrington, *op. cit.*, p. 324.

[49] Philip L. Bridgham, "American Policy Toward Korean Independence," Ph.D. dissertation (Fletcher, 1952), p. 151.

helping the Japanese contributed directly and indirectly to the growth of aggressiveness in Korea. The importance of the Taft-Katsura Memorandum with regard to the fall of Korea was exaggerated, for it was one of many signals given by Roosevelt to the Japanese regarding the establshment of their control in Korea. The more crucial decision with regard to Korea's fate was perhaps made during the Roosevelt-Kaneko talks in late August 1905.

Needless to say, Roosevelt failed to accomplish any of his objectives in the Far East. Russian influence in East Asia steadily diminished after the Russo-Japanese War, although she was able to hold her own territories and railway in northern Manchuria for a while. The open door collapsed in Manchuria completely as Japanese interests there grew. The balance of power in the Far East was upset with the rise of imperialist Japan. Roosevelt once believed that the "Japs have played our game,"[50] but it was his illusion.

The Taft-Katsura Memorandum served no useful purpose as far as the United States was concerned. However, it was effectively used by the Japanese in justifying their imperialistic activities in Korea. It neither safeguarded the security of the Philippines, nor promoted friendly relations between the United States and Japan as the history of U.S.-Japanese relations since September 1905 would attest. In 1906, war talk was such that Roosevelt sent urgent instructions to General Leonard Wood, Commander of U.S. troops in the Philippines, to prepare for a Japanese attack. Not only that, Roosevelt felt that it was necessary to send an American fleet to Japan to demonstrate U.S. Naval power to the Japanese.[51]

Three years later, in the Root-Takahira Agreement of November 20, 1908, Roosevelt received another Japanese disavowal of aggressive intentions toward the Philippines, but the United States gave Japan "a free hand in Manchuria"[52] as it had done so in Korea earlier.

Roosevelt's lack of sympathy and respect for Korea and remarks which he made in 1904 and 1905 regarding Japan's role in Korea

---

[50] Esthus, *op. cit.*, p. 43.

[51] For details of American-Japanese crisis of 1906-07, see Thomas A. Bailey, *Theodore Roosevelt and the Japanese-American Crisis* (New York: 1934), Chapters 9-11; Esthus, *op. cit.*, Chapters 8-11.

[52] Griswold, *op. cit.*, p. 129. On December 22, 1910, recognizing that the "vital interest of the Japanese" was in Manchuria and Korea, Roosevelt advised President Taft that it "is. . . peculiarly our interest not to take any steps as regards Manchuria which will give the Japanese cause to feel, with or without reasons, that we are hostile to them, or menace—in however slight a degree—to their interests." *Ibid.*, p. 131.

encouraged the Japanese to nurture their ambitions in Korea. The lack of positive economic interests on the part of the United States in Korea led to the absence of strong actions against the Japanese in Korea. Once Japanese control was established in Korea in 1905 with American assent, it was easy for the Japanese to bring about the demise of the Korean nation in August 1910.

APPENDIX A.

The full text of the Taft-Katsura Memorandum reads as follows:*

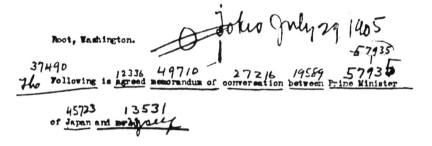

Count Katsura and Secretary Taft had a long and confidential conversation on the morning of July 27th. Among other topics of conversation, the following views were exchanged regarding the question of the Philippine Islands, of Corea, and of the maintenance of general peace in the East:

First. In speaking of some pro-Russians in America who would have the public believe that the victory of Japan would be a certain prelude to her aggression in the direction of the Philippine Island, Secretary Taft observed that Japan's only interests in the Philippine would be in his opinion to have these Islands governed by a strong and friendly nation like the United States, and not to have them placed either under the misrule of the natives yet unfit for self government or in the hands of some unfriendly European power. Count Katsura confirmed in strongest terms the correctness of his views on the point and positively stated that Japan does not harbour any aggressive design whatever on the Philippines, adding that all the insinuations of the "Yellow Peril" type are nothing more or less than malicious and clumsy slanders calculated to do mischief to Japan.

Second. Count Katsura observed that the maintenance of general

---

*The memorandum was sent to Secretary of State Root, dated July 29, 1905 in a telegraph in secret codes.

The remainder of Taft's telegraphic message dealt with Chinese diplomats who were on the way to Washington and conditions in China.

peace in the extreme East forms the fundamental principle of Japan's international policy. Such being the case, he was very anxious to exchange views with Secretary Taft as to the most effective means for insuring this principle. In his opinion, the best and, in fact, the only means for accomplishing the above objective would be to form good understanding between the three governments of Japan, the United States and Great Britain, which have common interest in upholding the principle of "Open Door." The Count well understands the traditional policy of the United States in this respect and perceives fully the impossibility of their entering into a formal alliance of such nature with any foreign nation. But in view of our common interests, he cannot see why some good understanding or an alliance, in practice, if not in name, should not be made between those three nations in so far as respects the affairs in the East. With such understanding firmly formed, general peace in these regions would be easily maintained to the great benefit of all powers concerned.

Secretary Taft said that it was difficult, indeed impossible, for the President of the United States to enter even into any understanding amounting in effect to a confidential informal agreement without the consent of the Senate, but that he felt sure that without any agreement at all the people of the United States were so fully in accord with a policy of Japan and Great Britain in the maintenance of peace in the Far East that whatever occasion arose appropriate action of the Government of the United States in conjunction with Japan and Great Britain for such a purpose could be counted on by them quite as confidently as if the United States were under treaty obligations to take it.

Third. In regard to the Corean question, Count Katsura observed that Corea being the direct cause of our war with Russia it is a matter of absolute importance to Japan that a complete solution of the peninsula question should be made as the logical consequence of the war. If left to herself after the war, Corea will certainly drift back to her former habit of improvidently entering into any agreements or treaties with other powers, thus resuscitating the same international complications as existed before the war. In view of the foregoing circumstances, Japan feels absolutely constrained to take some definite step with a view to precluding the possibility of Corea falling back into her former condition and of placing us again under the necessity of entering upon another foreign war.

Secretary Taft fully admitted the justness of the Count's observations and remarked to the effect that in his personal opinion the establishment of a suzerainty over Corea enter into no foreign treaties without the consent of Japan was the logical result of the present war and would directly contributed to permanent peace in the Far East. His judgement was that President Roosevelt would concur in his views in this regard, although he had no authority to give assurance of this. Indeed Secretary Taft added that he felt much delicacy in advancing the views he did, for he had no mandate for the purpose from the President, and since he left Washington Mr. Root had been appointed Secretary of State, and he might seem thus to be trespassing on another's Department. He could not, however, in view of Count Katsura's courteous desire to discuss the questions, decline to express his opinions which he had formed while he was temporarily discharging the duties of Secretary of State under the direction of the President; and he would forward to Mr. Root and the President a memorandum of the conversation. Count Katsura said that he would transmit the same confidentially to Baron Komura.

End of quotation.

Prime Minister quite anxious for interview. If I have spoken too freely or inaccurately or unwisely I know you can and will correct it. Do not want to butt in but under circumstances difficult to avoid statement and so told truth as I believe it. Count Katsura especially requested that our conversation be confined to you and the President so have not advised Griscom. If necessary under your direction Foreign Office can give him a copy.

CHAPTER 3

THE LAST DOMINO: AMERICA, JAPAN, AND THE BLAIR HOUSE DECISIONS

Gerard H. Clarfield

Two days after North Korean forces crashed across the thirty-eighth parallel beginning the Korean War, at a meeting held in Blair House the President made a series of important decisions. Acting on the recommendations of Secretary of State Dean G. Acheson he committed American naval and air forces to the defense of South Korea, reversed American policy toward the Chinese Civil War by ordering the Seventh Fleet to protect the Nationalist regime on Taiwan, approved an aid program for the Government of the Philippines which was then attempting to put down the communist led Hukbalahap rebellion, and approved stepped up aid for the French in their struggle for Indochina.

Inevitably, students of the period have focused their attentions on the decision to intervene in Korea. They have described President Truman as rushing to defend the recently created system of collective security, as waging war to check the advance of Asian Communism, and, most commonly, as having been influenced by lessons from the past. An act of aggression had taken place across what American policy makers viewed as a legitimate international boundary. For Truman's generation that immediately raised the specter of the 1930's, of Czechoslovakia, of Munich.

No matter what the explanation, however, the intellectual focus has remained on Korea and the war that was fought there. While that emphasis is certainly justified, it has nevertheless tended to obscure a relationship that existed between Washington's concern for the future of Japanese-American relations and the four decisions made by the President following the North Korean attack. Yet each of these, including the defense of South Korea, was in one degree or another taken with Japan in mind.

During the summer of 1949 Dean Acheson, Paul Nitze, and others high in policy making circles at the State Department developed serious concerns about future Soviet intentions. They were particularly disturbed because they believed defense spending, which had been limited to $13.5 billions by the President, seemed hopelessly inadequate to meet the needs created by America's expanding commitments. The discovery in August that the Soviets had exploded an Atomic Bomb well "ahead of schedule," and the largely unsuccessful efforts of Nitze, Acheson and others to awaken the federal bureaucracy, Congress, and the public to the need for a program of massive rearmament, made matters worse. The final collapse of the Chinese Nationalists and the treaty of friendship that soon followed between Moscow and Peking produced even further alarm. By early 1950 key State Department personnel were suffering from a serious case of the jitters. For the first time the Soviets seemed in a position to take the initiative in the Cold War. Few believed that Stalin was ready for a direct confrontation. The United States still enjoyed nuclear superiority and policy makers knew from experience that it would take years for the Soviets to build a significant nuclear arsenal of their own. But they were alert to the possibility of some sort of military action on the periphery of the Soviet empire. Remarked one high State Department official, "You couldn't tell where it was going to happen but [y]ou thought the time was ripe, it was sort of anticipated."[1]

Staff members of the National Security Council were by no means immune to this pervasive sense of pessimism and foreboding. Throughout the last half of 1949 they labored in concert with State and Defense Department officials, the Central Intelligence Agency, and the National Security Resources Board to develop an American policy for Asia. NSC 48/2, approved by President Truman on December 30, 1949, painted a dismal picture. The Soviets had not only attracted China into their orbit, they seemed on the verge of absorbing Southeast Asia as well. If that part of the world was "also swept by Communism," the authors of NSC 48 predicted apocalypse. "[W]e shall have suffered a major political rout the repercussions of which will be felt throughout the rest of the world, especially in the

---

[1] The Princeton Seminars, July 9, 23, 1953, Harry S. Truman Library. Hereafter the Truman Library will be referred to as *HSTL*.

Middle East and in a then critically exposed Australia."[2]

Haunted by their fears anxious policy makers agreed that "our immediate objective must be to contain and where feasible reduce the power and influence of the USSR in Asia." But how was that to be accomplished? According to NSC 48 there remained two major Asian power centers outside the Communist orbit. India and Pakistan together constituted one, but far more important was Japan. "If Japan, the principle component of a Far Eastern war making complex, were added to the Stalinist bloc," NSC 48/2 warned, "the Soviet Asian base could become a source of strength capable of shifting the balance of world power to the disadvantage of the United States. . . ."[3] At all costs Japan would have to be denied to the Soviet Union and brought into a close and lasting relationship with the United States.

Obviously America could no longer afford to treat Japan as a defeated enemy. In mid-1949 even before NSC 48/2 was approved, the political aspect of occupation policy began to change. The Japanese Government was granted increased authority while General MacArthur's powers were reduced. Because political reform inside Japan no longer played a role in American calculations and was also thought to have impeded economic recovery, the General was instructed "not to press upon the Japanese Government any further reform legislation." He was also instructed to reduce the pressure on Japanese officials for compliance with reforms already enacted.[4] Not only was the political purge virtually abandoned, some Japanese who had previously been stripped of their political rights now had them restored. While all of this was going on State and Defense Department officials laid plans for the implementation of a non-punitive peace treaty with Japan, so designed that the Chinese and Soviets could not undercut it later by making a more liberal offer.[5]

That in effect is where matters stood in June, 1950, when North Korean forces crossed the thirty-eighth parallel. Almost without exception those American policy makers who expressed an opinion viewed the attack as Soviet directed and intended for the benefit of

---

[2] NSC 48/2, Dec. 30, 1949, *Foreign Relations of the United States*, 1949, VII Pt. 2, 1215-1220. Hereafter the *Foreign Relations* series will be referred to as *FRUS*.

[3] *Ibid.*

[4] NSC 13/3, May 6, 1949, *FRUS*, VII, Pt. 2, 733.

[5] Frederick S. Dunn, *Peacemaking and the Settlement with Japan* (Princeton, 1963), 84-86.

the Japanese. George Kennan, Herbert Feis, John Allison, John Foster Dulles—they were unanimously of that opinion.[6] A State Department intelligence estimate produced on the very day of the attack emphasized the same point. The United States had little choice but to react to the North Korean aggression, the authors of the analysis contended. Otherwise Soviet control of the peninsula "would give Moscow an important weapon for the intimidation of the Japanese in connection with Japan's future alignment with the U.S." Our response would in effect "determine Japan's future course as an independent nation." If we did not stop the North Koreans, the "neutralist trend already gaining strength in Japan" would become more widespread. On the other hand, a swift and effective response "would increase Japanese confidence in us and strengthen the possible future Asian partnership."[7] There is little sense in belaboring the point. When Secretary Acheson recommended intervention in Korea the future of Japanese-American relations was very much on his mind.

The decision to intervene in China's civil war by stationing the Seventh Fleet in the Taiwan Straits was taken for similar reasons, at least in part. In December, 1949, after all economic and political efforts had seemingly failed to strengthen the Nationalist regime on Taiwan, the President, acting on Secretary Acheson's advice, officially washed his hands of the situation. In spite of this, however, State and Defense Department officials continued to fight a running battle over what to do about Taiwan. The Joint Chiefs, though unwilling to commit scarce ground and air forces to the island's defense, nevertheless insisted that it was strategically important to keep it from falling to a potential enemy. Unfriendly bases there, they insisted, would threaten the American position in the Philippines, Okinawa, and Japan. They wanted the State Department to continue to pursue diplomatic and economic approaches to the problem and even proposed stationing naval units in Taiwanese ports as a warning to potential invaders.[8]

---

[6] George Kennan, *Memoirs, 1935-1950,* (New York, 1967), 512-13; John M. Allison, *Ambassador From the Prairie* (Boston, 1973), 130; Princeton Seminars, Feb. 13 and March 15, 1954; Ernest Gross, Oral Interview, Columbia University Oral History Project.

[7] Intelligence Estimate, June 25, 1950, *FRUS,* 1950, VII, 151-52.

[8] NSC 37/3 and NSC 37/7, Feb. 10 and Aug. 22, 1949, *FRUS,* 1949, IX, 284-86; 376-78. Princeton Seminars, July 23, 1953.

Secretary of State Acheson was unimpressed by the strategic argument. He told the Chairman of the House Committee on Foreign Affairs that "there seems to be some magic that flows from the use of the term 'island' which seems to immediately give everyone the jitters, whereas, if Formosa had happened to be a peninsula we would probably have heard nothing more about it."[9] The prevailing sentiment both in the State Department and at the CIA was that the Peking Government would in all likelihood not have to bother invading the island. The Nationalist regime, which they viewed as a government in name only, would probably collapse of its own weight. Peking would then simply step in and take over.[10] To commit American prestige to the Nationalists a second time would be foolhardy. One might make the same mistake somewhere else, the urbane Acheson told the Washington press corps, "but not in the same place twice."[11]

The internal debate over Taiwan intensified down to the day of the North Korean attack. In fact, one of the more curious aspects of the US military's behavior at this time was that for the first thirty-six hours of the Korean War the Joint Chiefs showed far more concern for Taiwan than Korea. General Omar Bradley, Chairman of the Joint Chiefs, used the occasion of the Korean attack to prepare yet another memo for the President on the importance of Taiwan. This plea was never forwarded, because, a hand written note on Bradley's draft explains, "events which transpired during the evening and night of the 26th and the Presidential endorsement on the 27th made it unnecessary.[12] One of these developmets—critical to what followed— was that Secretary Acheson reversed himself, informing Bradley that he was now prepared to recommend the defense of the island.

Acheson had not suddenly been converted to the strategic argument. He explained to his staff just before the first of two high level conferences at Blair House that he feared a chain of disasters. If Korea should fall (on the afternoon of June 26 he viewed that as a

---

[9] Official Conversations and Meetings of Dean Acheson, January 4, 1950, The Presidential Documents Series, University Publications of America, Microfilm.

[10] Princeton Seminars, July 23, 1953; Dean G. Acheson, *Present At the Creation,* (New York, 1969), 350-53.

[11] Press Conferences of Secretary of State Dean Acheson, January 5, 1950, University Publications of America, Microfilm.

[12] Bradley to Vandenberg, Collins, Sherman, and Davis, June 25, 1950, Records of the Joint Chiefs of Staff, The Far East, University Publications of America, Microfilm.

distinct possibility) and Peking then took Taiwan, the entire Far Eastern policy of the United States would be in a shambles. George Kennan, who was at that staff meeting, later explained Acheson's thinking more explicitly to Dr. J. Robert Oppenheimer. If Formosa had been taken in the aftermath of the Korean attack "it would have set up the impression of a chain reaction in the Far East that might have affected the situation in the Philippines very disastrously and then, of course, the morale of Japan itself."[13]

The decision to intervene in the Philippines and to step up support for the French in Indochina was in like fashion influenced by Japanese considerations. But in these instances economic rather than political factors were preponderant. As the Cold War intensified the economic revival of Japan was given an increasingly high priority in Washington.[14] By early 1948 policies initiated in the immediate post war period were being sharply revised. In January, General Frank R. McCoy, the American representative on the Far Eastern Commission, told our former Pacific allies that since the war economic chaos in Japan had only been averted "at the expense of the American people who have financed the importation of vital food and other materials required to prevent widespread disease and unrest." But the annual cost had averaged $900 millions. McCoy made it clear to his listeners that the American taxpayer was not going to continue to foot the bill. Therefore, he announced that it would be the policy of the United States "to bring about the early revival of the Japanese economy on a peaceful, self-supporting basis."[15] In the years that followed, and much against the inclinations of our former allies, American policy makers abandoned attempts to dissolve the *zaibatsu,* authorized far higher levels of industry for Japan than had earlier been contemplated, and made it impossible for the victims of Japanese aggression to collect reparations.[16]

Japan had an industrial base, managerial talent, and a substantial force of skilled labor. But she lacked raw materials and could not feed her large population. Nor was her domestic market large enough

---

[13] Princeton Seminars, July 23, 1953; Feb. 13, 1954.

[14] Memo for the National Security Council, Feb. 26, 1951, Papers of Harry S. Truman, The President's Secretaries File, Papers of the National Security Council, *HSTL.*

[15] Jerome B. Cohen, *Japan's Economy in War and Reconstruction* (Minneapolis, 1949), 422.

[16] *Ibid.,* 417-47.

to absorb her potential industrial production. She would prosper or languish depending upon the state of her foreign trade. And that fact created concern in Washington. Prior to World War II China, including Manchuria and Taiwan, accounted for approximately twenty-five percent of Japan's total foreign trade.[17] The Communist victory in China, therefore, raised some serious questions. As late as 1949 some policy makers toyed with the idea of encouraging a renewal of Japan's China trade, hoping in this way to encourage Japanese economic revival and simultaneously entice Peking away from her close relationship with Moscow.[18] But that was never a majority view. Trade was a two-way street. Japan might be drawn in the other direction. General Albert Wedemeyer, remarking on this problem, predicted the failure of "present U.S. efforts to make the Japanese economy self-sufficient." Without China as a market and source of raw materials, he warned, the United States would have to accept Japan as a permanently weak dependancy. Otherwise she would be forced "to join the Soviet orbit as the only remaining means of survival."[19] A CIA estimate done two months later confirmed the General's judgment. "Over the long term, exclusion of Japan from Northeast Asia trade would so drastically distort Japan's natural trade pattern that economic stability could only be maintained if the United States were prepared to underwrite substantial trade deficits on a continuing basis." Short of that "economic distress might easily force Japan to align itself with the USSR as the only means of returning to economic normality."[20]

Nor did the CIA place any confidence in the natural affinity some thought Japanese leaders felt for a continuing American connection. The Japanese were for the moment totally dependent upon the United States. Moreover, they understood that if the United States was to maintain its position in the Far East their revival was essential. "Thus Japan continues to be" what the CIA described as "a purchasable asset." Under other circumstances, however, "if the U.S. position

[17] "Japan's International Economic Position," Oct. 14, 1950, Papers of Harry S. Truman, The President's Secretaries File, Defense Department File, *HSTL*.

[18] ORE Report 69-49, Sept. 12, 1949, *ibid.*, Records of the CIA. President's Secretaries File, *HSTL*.

[19] Wedemeyer to Forrestal, March 29, 1948, Records of the Joint Chiefs of Staff, Geographic File, China, 1948-50, Box 9, National Archives.

[20] ORE Report 43-48, May 24, 1948, Truman Papers, President's Secretaries Files, Records of the CIA, *HSTL*.

appeared untenable, Japan would realistically consider seeking the best possible bargain with the USSR and its communist supporters."[21]

If the prognosis was grim, that only made the need seem more acute in Washington. NSC 13/3, endorsed by the President in May, 1949, held that "second only to U.S. security interests, economic recovery should be made the primary objective of United States policy in Japan for the coming period."[22] But just how was that to be accomplished? State Department analysts assumed that Japan and America could never be partners in a significant direct trade. True, Japan could absorb large quantities of American food, raw materials, and manufactured goods. But having lost the silk market she had little to sell in return.[23] Since the war Japan had run huge deficits in this one-way trade. The chronic dollar shortage that resulted had bedeviled attempts by General MacArthur's staff to encourage economic recovery.[24]

American policy makers viewed South and Southeast Asia, including the Philippines and Indonesia, as the answer to Japan's needs.[25] The nations of this region could provide food and raw materials while serving as needed markets for Japan's industrial production. But policy makers struck on a potential solution to one thorny problem only to encounter another. The economy of the region, ravaged by war and revolution, was in no condition to play the role assigned to it by American planners. As a result, until well into 1950 Japanese industry languished, achieving only 95% of the levels of production set during the darkest days of the Great Depression. "The chief handicap to further achievement of economic recovery in Japan through exports," wrote Under Secretary of the Army Tracy Voorhees, "had been the inability of these areas to pay Japan for manufactured products which they desire from her, and require."[26] It would therefore be necessary for the United States to encourage the growth of these nations' economies through foreign

---

[21] Review of the World Situation, April 20, 1949, *ibid.*

[22] NSC 13/3, May 6, 1949, *FRUS,* VII, Pt. 2, 733-35.

[23] Japan's International Economic Position, Oct. 14, 1950, Papers of Harry S. Truman, President's Secretaries File, Defense Department File, *HSTL.*

[24] *Ibid.*

[25] *Ibid.*

[26] Voorhees to the National Security Council, Jan. 10, 1950, appended to Memo for the National Security Council, Feb. 26, 1951, Truman Papers, President's Secretaries File, Papers of the National Security Council, *HSTL.*

aid. This meant a degree of industrial development for the countries of South and Southeast Asia, but only a degree. They must never cease to provide Japan with food and raw materials or to serve as markets for Japan's industries. In summing things up Voorhees wrote: "Continuing or even maintaining Japan's economic recovery depends upon keeping Communism out of Southeast Asia, promoting economic recovery there and in further developing those countries, together with Indonesia, the Philippines, Southern Korea and India as the principle trading areas for Japan."[27] A CIA report dated September, 1949, made much the same point. The United States had no immediate economic interest in the Far East. But she did wish to deny Japan's industrial potential to Communism and retain access to Southeast Asia for her own convenience "and because of the great economic importance of that area to Western Europe and Japan." The "exclusion of Japan from trade with Southeast Asia," another CIA report concluded, "would seriously frustrate Japanese prospects for economic recovery."[28]

Washington was doing more than talking. The Economic Cooperation Administration was using its not inconsiderable resources to transform dream into reality. ECA Administrator William C. Foster explained to Thomas Blaisdell, Jr., Professor of Political Science at the University of California, that "we are laying more and more stress on Japan as a source for industrial materials in the Far East and Southeast Asia." Japan, Foster continued, had the plant capacity and could easily increase industrial production if it could acquire raw materials. "There is the off-set factor too, that Japan must import from the countries to which its industrial products might well go."[29]

Before Southeast Asia could fulfill its envisioned role in the regional economic plan evolving in Washington, peace and political stability would have to be restored to the area. State Department officials and the Joint Chiefs agreed that though the rebellion in the Philippines was a serious problem it could be quelled if the social and economic problems that underlay it were properly addressed.[30]

---

[27] *Ibid.*

[28] ORE Report 29-50, Oct. 13, 1950; ORE Report, 69-49, Sept. 12, 1949, *ibid.,* Papers of the CIA.

[29] William C. Foster to Thomas C. Blaisdell Jr., May 7, 1951, Blaisdell Papers, *HSTL.*

[30] JCS to Secretary of Defense, Sep. 6, 1950, Truman Papers, President's Secretaries File, Office of the Secretary of Defense, *ibid.*; Lacy to Rusk, March 30, 1950, *FRUS,*

The situation in Indochina was something else again. The French would never be able to restore colonial rule there, that much seemed certain.[31] Bao Dai, the puppet emperor who headed the make-believe Associated States of Viet Nam was unpopular with his people and in any event considered untrustworthy. (The CIA believed that if Bao Dai actually attained power he night negotiate a settlement with "the resistance.") And Ho Chi Minh, who according to one intelligence estimate controlled ninty percent of the territory of Viet Nam and enjoyed the support of eighty percent of the people was, unhappily, an agent of the Kremlin.

The political problems of Southeast Asia, of course, remained unresolved when, at the outset of the Korean War, Secretary Acheson recommended that the United States provide economic and military aid for the Philippines and increased support for the French in Indochina. If saving the situation in the Philippines would be difficult, the Indochinese gambit was an act of desperation. Acheson did not advise expanding the American involvement there because he believed the French could win. He did so because he was certain that if we failed to act they would lose. The recently formed alliance between Moscow and Peking, the recognition of the Government of Ho Chi Minh by the two Communist powers, and the fact that Chinese forces were stationed near the Indochinese border suggested that some sort of intervention was in the offing. The Korean attack confirmed that judgment. The Secretary was convinced that Soviet foreign policy had entered a new, more aggressive phase and that Communist pressure would soon be sharply increased at other points. "The invasion of Southern Korea cannot be regarded as an isolated incident," he told President Truman. "It alters the strategic realities of the area and is a clear indication of the pattern of aggression under a general internationalist Communist plan." He advised "quick affirmative action" in other "troublespots" while assuring Truman that such action would "contribute to the disposal of the Korean situation and also to forestalling a deterioration of the entire Far Eastern situation."[32]

Acheson believed that America's position in the Far East rested on

---

1950, VI, 1428-32; Acheson to Truman, April 20, 1950, *ibid.*, 1440-44; Memo, "The Situation in the Philippines," June 20, 1950, *ibid.*, 1461-63.

[31] Intelligence Memo #231, Oct. 7, 1949, Truman Papers, President's Secretaries File, Papers of the CIA.

[32] Points Requiring Presidential Decision, June 25, 1950, Papers of George Elsey, Box 71, *HSTL*.

her ability to keep an independent Japan in the Western camp. This in turn meant that Washington would have to prove itself a credible ally while simultaneously so structuring the Asian economic order that Japan could prosper without cultivating a close economic relationship with China. Each of the decisions recommended by Acheson and approved by the President in the days following the North Korean attack served one or the other of these purposes. South Korea and Formosa were not defended because of any inherent strategic or economic value placed upon them by the Secretary and the President, but at least in part because the Japanese required reassurance in the face of an overt military threat in their part of the world. The Containment Doctrine was quickly extended to Southeast Asia in order to insure that the region would remain non-communist and open to Japanese exploitation.[33] Secretary Acheson, a firm believer in what President Eisenhower would later dub the *domino theory,* felt that the Administration had to act in Southeast Asia or Japan, the last and most important domino in the Far East, would be denied the food, raw materials, and markets essential to her economic recovery. It was an article of faith in Washington that this would have left her little alternative, once sovereignty was restored, but to drift into neutralism or join the Soviet bloc. The key to America's anti-communist Asian policy seemed in jeopardy.

---

[33] It is important to note that the United States had already begun to move in this direction prior to the Korean War. The North Korean attack simply made the problem in Southeast Asia and the Philippines seem more dangerous. Programs that might have taken many months to develop were as a result decided upon in days.

CHAPTER 4

AMERICAN POLICY TOWARD KOREAN UNIFICATION, 1945-1980

Soon Sung Cho

One of the most tragic consequences of the Cold War following World War II has been the division of the nations of Viet Nam, Germany, and Korea. These divided areas stand as an ever present reminder of a divided world and the tremendous cost in natural resources, human energy, and human life produced by this division. Although having a life, will, and purpose of their own, these areas have been caught between greater forces and have suffered the tragic consequences. The most evident and lasting consequence has been the division of the people into two ideological camps and nations and into separate territorial and governmental entities. As the leader of the Western World, the United States has been one of these dividing forces, to a certain extent the division of these areas being a result of the foreign policy of the United States. The reunification of these areas will likewise depend greatly upon the foreign policy of the United States.

This paper will concentrate on U.S. policy towards the reunification of Korea during the post-war period. Although the birth of two Republics in Korea resulted from the failure of the Joint U.S.-Soviet Commission and the United Nations Temporary Commission on Korea to secure reunification in 1948, the separate identity of North and South Korea was made concrete by the Korea War of 1950. An investigation of American foreign policy towards the reunification of Korea and the environment in which it has operated since the end of the Second World War seems an advantageous focus in seeking to understand the current dilemma of two Koreas. This study will seek to describe and analyze those forces and effects (both internal and

external) that were brought to bear on U.S. policy makers in formulating Korean unification policy. Defining policy as a specific, deliberate course of action for achieving some objective, the central
hypothesis of this study is that the United States has had no viable
foreign policy regarding the reunification of Korea. The United States
has followed a policy reaction (rather than initiating action) aimed towards maintaining a status quo Korea situation. It has been a policy
of temporary expediency aimed towards protecting the national
interest of the United States and the security of Japan.

Korea, prior to the closing days of World War II, was virtually an
unknown land to Americans. At Cairo in December of 1943, China,
Great Britain, and the United States agreed that in "due course"
Korea would become a free and independent nation. The implication
of the wording of the Cairo Declaration was that America was
concerned about the Korean situation. Although President Roosevelt
had some reservations about Korea's immediate future and independence, nowhere in the documents of the war-time conferences was
there an indication that the American government favored the permanent division of Korea.[1] Similarly, there was almost no preparation
for military occupation of Korean independence prior to the end of
the war.[2] At the time President Roosevelt and his military advisors
were planning the post-war future, Korea was considered strategically
unimportant; and, as a result, little effort was made toward
cementing together a firm U.S. policy for Korea. At Cairo, President
Roosevelt proposed forty years of political tutelage and then, at
Yalta, shortened this time to twenty or thirty years.

The 38th parallel, as a dividing line in Korea, had never been the
subject of international discussion among the wartime leaders. The
parallel, which was destined to be so tragic in later years, was
neither debated nor bargained for by either side. As Dean Rusk, an
eye-witness to the birth of the situation at the 38th parallel, stated, it
was intended to be a purely military demarcation of a temporary
nature to facilitate the surrender to the Japanese forces in Korea. It
was proposed by the United States to limit Soviet occupation to
approximately half of Korea, since America could not, at that time,

---

[1] Soon Sung Cho, *Korea in World Politics* (Berkeley, 1967), pp. 13-34.

[2] Edward G. Meade, *American Military Government in Korea* (New York, 1951),
p. 46. For the more recent study of American occupational policy see, Bruce Cummings,
The Origin of the Korean War (Princeton, 1981), pp. 122-131. See also Gregory
Henderson, *Korea: The Politics of the Vortex* (Cambridge, 1968), pp. 113-147.

send forces to Korea in sufficient numbers to accept the Japanese surrender any further north than the 38th parallel.[3]

The first serious American attempt to reunify Korea was the implementation of Roosevelt's old trusteeship ideas. Early in May 1945, Harry Hopkins was sent to Moscow to clarify Truman's policy after Roosevelt's death. At this time Stalin definitely agreed that "there should be a trusteeship for Korea under the United States, China, Great Britain and the Soviet Union."[4] At the same time, Hopkins suggested that the period of trusteeship ought to be twenty-five years or less, but, "It would certainly be five or ten years." Since Stalin neither criticized this suggestion nor offered any alternatives, American policy planners felt that trusteeship was the most viable solution, despite vehement Korean opposition. On October 21, 1945, John Carter Vincent, the State Department's Chief of Far Eastern Affairs, publicly announced that:

> Korea, after years of subjugation to Japan, is not immediately prepared to exercise self-judgment. We, therefore, advocate a period of trusteeship during which Koreans will be prepared to take over the independent administration of their country. How long that will require neither you nor I can say. We will agree, however, that the briefer the period the better.[5]

Thus, even though it was apparent at the time of the Moscow Conference (December, 1945) that the Korean people would unanimously oppose a trusteeship, the United States advocated governing the Korean people through a High Commission and an Executive Council of representatives of the four powers. The United States' proposal included a five-year trusteeship with the possibility of an additional five year extension.[6] The fatal fallacy of this proposal lies in the fact that the reaction of the Korean people was ignored. U.S. policy makers lacked the vision to foresee the strong under-current which would later surge over the whole of Asia and Africa in the name of nationalism.

On the basis of the Moscow Agreement, a positive step toward Korean unification was initiated by the establishment of the Joint

---

[3] United States Department of State, *Foreign Relations of the United States,* Vol. VI (Washington D.C., 1969), p. 1039.

[4] Robert E. Sherwood, *Roosevelt and Hopkins: An Intimate History* (New York, 1948), p. 903. See also, Cho, *op. cit.,* pp. 95-97.

[5] *Department of State Bulletin,* October 21, 1945, p. 646.

[6] *The Soviet Union and the Korean Question* (London, 1950), pp. 14-16.

American-Soviet Commision, which was sponsored to assist in the formation of a provisional Korean government through consultations with democratic Korean political parties and social organizations. The first Joint Conference lasted from March 20, 1946 to May 6, 1946. After twenty-four fruitless sessions it was finally adjourned sine die on May 8, 1946, without having solved a single problem. A second conference was held from May 21, 1947 to October 18, 1947, in an effort to break the deadlock. In the course of debate there were numerous proposals and counter-proposals made by the two dele- gations, but no substantial progress was recorded. Officially, the failure was attributed to differences of interpretation over what were "democratic social groups or parties" and "what was the definition of 'freedom of speech.'" The fundamental reason for the failure, however, lay in the clash of opposing powers. This was clearly manifested in the opening speech of General Shtykov in the meeting of 1946. He unequivocally stated that the Soviet Union wanted to see Korea become a nation friendly to the Soviet Union so that in the future it would not become a base for an attack on the Soviet Union.[7] The Soviets thus endeavored to create a Soviet-oriented Korea by eliminating practically all pro-American rightist parties from the con- sultation. Therefore, further discussion with the Soviet Union in the Joint Commission was rendered useless.

Faced with vehement opposition from Koreans, the United States had been forced to abandon the idea of Korean trusteeship as an unworkable solution; with the failure of the Joint Commission, the idea of achieving unification through a bi-lateral negotiation with the Soviet Union was now abandoned as well. Further complications arose when United States foreign policy shifted toward containment with the enunciation of the Truman Doctrine on March 12, 1947. Consequently, the United Nations was almost the only remaining means through which the U.S. could negotiate with the Soviet Union concerning the issue of unification. In an attempt to break a total impasse over Korean unification the United States presented the Korean issue to the United Nations, calling for the establishment of a United Korean government in the name of the United Nations and transferal of most of U.S. responsibilities in Korea to the interna- tional organization. Thus, under sponsorship of the United States, the

---

[7] *Source Materials on Korean Politics and Ideology* (New York, 1950) compiled by Donlad G. Tewksbury, p. 78. See also *Voice of Korea,* April 6, 1946.

General Assembly of the U.N. adopted a resolution on November 14, 1947, calling for elections throughout Korea under the supervision of the United Nations Temporary Commission on Korea. The Soviet command, however, denied the U.N. Commission permission to enter its zone, thus depriving North Korea of the right to participate in any free election. As a result, the Republic of Korea was organized on August 15, 1948, under the supervision of the United Nations Commission. The Soviet Command, defying the United Nations, established the Democratic People's Republic of Korea in the North. Thus, two separate governments within one nation resulted from power politics rather than the will of the Korean people. It was a foregone conclusion that once the case was brought before the General Assembly of the United Nations, it would result in the establishment of two separate governments in Korea rather than one. The Soviet Union made it clear before the final voting that it would not accept the recommendation of the General Assembly. In a sense the United States made heavy and unrealistic demands on the United Nations, knowing that the organization was too weak to bear such a burden.[8] Because of this unhappy prospect many South Korean leaders also opposed U.S. proposals to bring the Korean case before the United Nations. Nevertheless, from 1947 on, United States policy toward the unification of Korea has been intertwined with the United Nations policy toward unification.

Although the United States had pursued since September 1947, two major objectives in Korea—the establishment of a unified, independent and democratic Korean government, and the containment of Communist expansion in Asia—its policy in Korea differed in both scope and method from the policy pursued in Europe. Its policies were oriented toward withdrawal in Asia, both from the mainland and from Korea. As early as 1947, American military authorities concluded that from the point of view of its own military security, the United States had little strategic interest in Korea. In fact, it was the judgment of the Joint Chiefs of Staff that in the event of hostilities in the Far East, American forces in Korea would be "a military liability."[9] In light of these developments, American world strategy was confronted with the problem of relieving itself of an

---

[8] Leland M. Goodrich, *Korea: A Study of United States Policy in the United Nations* (New York, 1956), p. 41.

[9] Harry S. Truman, *Years of Trial and Hope* (New York, 1956), pp. 325-326. See also Carl Berger, *The Korean Knot* (Philadelphia, 1957), pp. 74-83.

embarrassing situation in Korea without losing prestige with either the Korean people or the rest of the world. Thus, the reunification of Korea became a secondary issue in the face of more pressing problems. The primary objective of the United States was the earliest possible liquidation of American responsibilities in Korea, the U.S. seeking to transfer its burden unto the U.N. The leaders of the United States constantly viewed the Korean problem as an "unhappy burden" and "a needless liability to the free world." In a sense, political, military and geographical factors made it difficult for the United States to evolve a policy consistent with its moral commitment toward Korean unification and with American national interest.

Because of this presumed remoteness from American national interests, Secretary of State Acheson, in a speech before the National Press Club on January 12, 1950, inadvertently extended an invitation for North Korea to invade the South. Acheson unwisely implied that the defense perimeter of the United States in Asia no longer included either Formosa or Korea. He made it clear that "no person can guarantee these areas against military attack."[10] Subsequently, the first major attempt toward Korean unification by military means took place in the early morning of June 25, 1950. Because of the lack of a definite military aid policy to Korea; South Korean security forces were totally unprepared in terms of numbers, equipment and training. Although by June 1950, the ROK Army had reached a strength of nearly one hundred thousand men, the United States had supplied armaments sufficient for only sixty-five thousand men. Furthermore, at this time, fifteen percent of the army's weapons and thirty-five percent of its vehicles were unserviceable. The American Military Advisory Group estimated that the ill-equipped, ill-trained men that made up the ROK army could hold out for no more than fifteen days.[11] When the well trained North Korean Army with more than one hundred and fifty tanks and fighter planes attacked South Korea, it was certain that unless the U.S. intervened, Korea would be unified by force under the control of North Korea.

Why did the United States reverse a Korean policy which its military leaders had so long considered unrealistic? If the United States felt so strongly in January 1950, about the military indefensibility of Korea, it appears strange that the U.S. reversed this policy in order to

---

[10] For the full text of Acheson's statement, see *Department of State Bulletin*, January 23, 1950, pp. 111-116.

preserve U.S. prestige in June. Intervention in Korea represented a case in which the U.S. had a realistic foreign policy on paper, but it was one not commensurate with U.S. ideals. President Truman declared, "We were fighting in Korea. . . to carry out our commitment of honor to the South Koreans and to demonstrate to the world that the friendship of the United States is inestimable in time of adversity."[12] Besides this idealism, the North Korean aggression suddenly was seen as a "challenge to the whole system of collective security;" not only in the Far East, but everywhere in the world." Truman, at the initiation of the conflict, considered the impact of the war as crucial in maintaining the security of the Western world. Collective security included not only defense alignment in Europe, but also the future of the United Nations. Since the U.N., along with the United States, had played godfather at the birth of the Republic of Korea, the northern invasion was an attack on the authority of the world peacekeeping organization. Furthermore, the security of Japan, the most important area of the U.S. defense perimeter, was threatened.[13]

Whatever the reasons for American intervention, did the possibility of Korean reunification ever enter into the decision to intervene? This consideration apparently was never one of the factors which were weighed by those involved in the decision. America's immediate policy was only to reestablish the status quo ante bellum along the 38th parallel. It is interesting to note that in the President's directions to General MacArthur, as well as in the two resolutions of June 25 and June 27, 1950, in the United Nations, no mention was made of any desire to unify Korea. Evidence strongly suggests that policy makers from the beginning were intent upon confining the war to a limited scope.[14] Although the United States was revising its policy in

---

[11] Department of the Army, *Military Advisors in Korea: KMAG in Peace and War,* Prepared by Major Robert K. Sawyer and edited by Walter G. Hermes, (Washington D.C., 1962), p. 69 and pp. 73-75. See also, Roy E. Appleman, *U.S. Army in the Korean War: South to the Naktong, North to the Yalu* (Washington D.C., 1961), pp. 14-15.

[12] Richard Rovere and Arthur Schlessinger Jr., *The General and the President* (New York, 1951), p. 104. See also Glenn D. Paige, *The Korean Decision* (New York, 1968). For a new interpretation of the origin of the Korean war, see Robert R. Simmons, "The Communist Side: An Exploratory Sketch" in *the Korean War: 25 year Perspective* (Lawrence, 1977), pp. 197-208.

[13] George Kennan, "Japanese Security and American Policy," *Foreign Affairs,* October, 1964, p. 15.

Korea, it was not a total reversal. General MacArthur saw it as his duty to clear Asia of Communism, while President Truman saw the policy transformation as simply a means of pursuing containment.[15]

A major change in Korean policy appeared to be in order after the Inchon victory. It appeared North Korea's war machine was rapidly collapsing in the face of the offensive campaign being waged by U.N. forces. Consequently, the United States now pushed for the approval of its pre-war goal, political reunification of Korea in the United Nations. The U.S. hoped to obtain United Nations approval for military action beyond the 38th parallel, but it realized that such approval could hardly be obtained in the Security Council now that the Soviet delegation had returned. As early as September 20, 1950, U.S. officials pushed in the General Assembly for the acceptance of a United States resolution which indirectly called for offensive action above the 38th parallel. After considerable maneuvering, the United States obtained a favorable response in the form of a resolution which called for a "unified and independent" Korea. It was no secret that the United States desired to extend the war and settle the thorny problem of Korea permanently. Despite the fact that the initial U.N. resolution made it clear that the objectives of the UNC were to repel the invasion from the North and to reestablish the status quo at the 38th parallel, ROK troops crossed the parallel on October 1, 1950. It seemed obvious to the U.S. that the advantages outweighed the disadvantages in carrying the attack to the North. The boundary which had been so significant in June took on a less important meaning in October. Secretary of State Acheson noted that "troops could not be expected. . . to march up to a surveyors line and stop." As early as September 11, 1950, President Truman had approved a National Security Council policy which had stipulated that General MacArthur had the freedom, if there was no indication of Soviet or Chinese intervention, . . . "to extend his operation north of the parallel and to make plans for the occupation of North Korea." It seemed that the United States, regardless of the outcome of the U.N. resolution of October 7, 1950, was prepared to cross the parallel.[16] In essence, Washington now adopted a policy of reunifying Korea by military forces; yet, the United States was not prepared to conduct a general

[14] David Rees, *Korea: the Limited War* (New York, 1964), pp. 21-35.

[15] John W. Spanier, *The Truman-MacArthur Controversy and the Korean War* (New York, 1965), pp. 257-279.

[16] *Ibid.*, pp. 84-103.

war with China or the Soviet Union over the issue of Korean unification.

The gamble that the movement of U.N. forces across the 38th parallel would not engender Chinese intervention was misplaced. The vision of Korean unification by military forces rapidly diminished. By the end of October, reports of Chinese troops (volunteers) were confirmed and in December the U.N. forces were pushed once again below the 38th parallel. The United States had inaccurately estimated China's willingness to enter the war in spite of seemingly adequate warning given by the Chinese as to the necessity of their intervention in the Korean conflict if U.N.C. troops crossed the parallel. During the course of a conversation with Chinese Premier, Chou En-lai, K.M. Panikkar was informed that "if the Americans crossed the 38th parallel, China would be forced to intervene in Korea." The United States, however, had placed little credence in this warning passed on by the Indian ambassador.[17]

Was Korean reunification worth the risk of a general war? The only possible military solution to counter Chinese intervention called for the use of all-out war. Washington policy makers maintained that at no time had they intended to fight a general war in Korea. General MacArthur, unaccustomed to the limitations imposed by using only partial force, questioned the validity of the new policy, thus opening debate on limited warfare vs. general warfare. To MacArthur, escalation of the war had changed the conceptual framework for decision making established when the hostilities began, and consequently new policy guidelines should have been constructed in Washington. For the General, the U.N.C. objective of liberation and unification of Korea still existed, and the approval of a United States resolution in the U.N. General Assembly on February 1, 1951, branding "China as an aggressor," served to intensify the conflict between MacArthur and his government. MacArthur continued his criticism of Washington's policy throughout the winter, implying that rather than having a policy, the U.S. in reality had none. Finally, Truman was unable to tolerate the mounting pressure from MacArthur and dismissed him in April of 1951.[18]

With General MacArthur's dismissal the chances for Korean reuni-

---

[17] David Rees, *op. cit.,* pp. 106-107. K. M. Panikkar, *In Two Chinas* (London, 1956), p. 108. For Chinese policy at this time, see Allen S. Whitting, *China Crosses the Yalu* (Standford, 1960), pp. 68-115.

[18] Spanier, *op. cit.,* pp. 165-186.

fication as a result of military force were permanently eliminated. The General's demise signified not only the supremacy of the civilian authority over the military, but also indicated that the Korean unification policy would shift from military conquest to peaceful political settlement. Once again the United States found itself locked into its pre-war position, although now the rigid stalemate between Russia and the U.S. began to break down. This relaxing of tensions culminated, on June 23, 1951, almost one year after the fighting had originated, with Jacob Malik, the Soviet representative to the U.N. Security Council, hinting that neogtiations on the Korean armistice could be started. In response, General Ridgway issued an invitation to the Communists on June 30, suggesting that cease-fire talks be initiated. It is significant that this invitation was extended in spite of President Rhee's vehement opposition to any negotiation prior to unification of Korea by military means.

The inauguration of a new president in Washington in 1953 did not alter American policy orientations, which required an early end to the Korean War. As a presidential candidate, Eisenhower's immediate goal was to terminate the Korean War with honor; but in terms of foreign policy statements, it appears that the unification issue was not incorporated into the reality of ending the war. Eisenhower viewed war as perhaps the last and most remote of any alternative solutions to international disputes. Thus, on the 2nd of December, 1952, Eisenhower visited Korea and promised military and economic assistance to South Korea if President Rhee would agree to accept an Armistice to end the fighting. But President Rhee would not accept any end to the fighting which left Korea a divided nation, and threatened to remove all R.O.K. forces from the U.N. Command. Eventually, Rhee accepted the inevitability of a UNC armistice under strong pressure from General Clark and President-elect Eisenhower, but he nevertheless attempted to fight on alone. Eisenhower noted that Walter Robertson, the President's personnel representative, "day by day . . . argued with this fiercely patriotic but recalcitrant old man on the futility of going it alone."[19] To appease President Rhee the United States made five pledges: (1) The promise of a US-ROK security pact, (2) A loan of $200,000,000, (3) An agreement on the part of the United States to withdraw from the political conference after ninety days if nothing constructive resulted, (4) Aid in expand-

---

[19] Robert Murphy, *Diplomat Among Worriors* (New York, 1964), pp. 349-361.

ing the ROK Army, (5) An agreement to hold high level US-ROK talks on all aspects of the issue before the conference for the unification of Korea opened. Eisenhower assured Rhee that the U.S. would not renounce its efforts to unify Korea "by all peaceful means," and he threatened to carry an atomic war to the Chinese mainland if the Communists did not end the war soon.[20]

Despite last ditch efforts on the part of Rhee to wreck negotiations, the Korean Armistice was signed on July 27, 1953. A few days later a mutual defense treaty between the United States and Korea was signed. The treaty promised that "the parties will consult together whenever, in the opinion of either, their political independence or security is threatened." It also stated in Article 2 that the parties will "maintain and develop appropriate means to deter armed attack." But, the treaty made it clear that each party would act to meet the common danger in accordance with its constitutional processes (Article 3). Apparently, at this time the South Korean government did not notice the future implication of Article 3 and the differences between it and Article 5 of NATO to which both had earlier agreed. NATO Article 5 stated, ". . . each of the parties will assist one another if attacked by taking forthwith, individually and in concert with the other parties, such action as it deems necessary, including the use of armed forces, to restore and maintain the security of the North Atlantic Treaty." When the Senate passed the US-Korean mutual defense treaty in 1954. it did not forget to attach an understanding clause in which it required "the advice and consent of the Senate of the United States to implement Articles 2 and 3." This clause also made it clear that the obligation under Article 3 applied only in the event of an external armed attack.[21] In short, under the terms of the mutual defense treaty, the United States has no obligation to help South Korea when South Korea itself initiates hostilities. Obviously, the United States attempted to eliminate any implication that the unification of Korea through military action could be undertaken with the assistance of U.S. armed forces.

According to Article 60 of the Armistice Agreement, within three months after the signing of the armistice a political conference was to be held which would settle the problem of withdrawal of all foreign forces from Korea, as well as the problem of Korean unification.

---

[20] David Rees, *op. cit.*, pp. 404-406.
[21] Kyung Cho Chung, *Korea Tomorrow* (New York, 1961), pp. 270-273.

However, as October neared, the opening of the conference appeared no more imminent than it had prior to the armistice. It was not until April, 1954, than an agreement was reached to meet in Geneva with U.S. participation in this new conference to be dominated by the reality that as long as Korea remained divided, the possibility of another war existed. In other words, the United States saw the Geneva Conference as the best opportunity to unify Korea by peaceful means, which in turn would eliminate any possibility of forced American involvement in another war. Delegations from the United Nations command, including the ROK, met with delegations from the Soviet Union, Communist China, and North Korea. Problems immediately arose over whether or not elections should be conducted by secret ballot under the supervision of the U.N. North Korea, with the support of Communist China and the Soviet Union, refused to accept UN supervision on the grounds that the United Nations was a belligerent party in the Korean War and had lost the moral authority and competence to deal with Korean unification. Instead, its delegates proposed acceptance of the Communist Chinese position of elections supervision by a commission composed of neutral nations. What was at stake was not merely Korean unification but the authority and competence of the United Nations.[22] Acceptance of the North Korean proposal would, in effect, have resulted in the negation of all actions taken by the United Nations for unification of Korea since September 1947.

For two months conference members haggled over what constituted correct solutions to the Korean question. Agreement could not be reached on several issues: (1) Supervision of an all-Korean election, (2) Withdrawal of foreign troops, (3) Extent of U.N. authority, and (4) Allowance of a veto over the unification process. Unable to resolve these vital issues, the conference adjourned on June 15, 1954, without solving the question of unification, and thus the Korean War ended with the United States in basically the same position as in 1947. Reestablishment of the 38th parallel status quo found the UNC in control of 2,350 square miles of territory which at the beginning of hostilities had been in the hands of the North. Thus a more or less arbitrary demarcation, after causing three years of fighting and approximately 155,000 UNC casualties, solidified into a political

---

[22] Soon S. Cho, "The Politics of North Korea's Unification Policies," *World Politics*, Vol. XIX (January, 1967), pp. 218-224.

barrier which symbolized not only the division of communists and noncommunists, but also permanent division of Korea for the future.[23]

After the war, the United Nations became the last real hope for Korean unification. Yet, U.S. manipulation of the U.N. during the war for its own purposes had set a precedent which would continue to prevent realization of this hope. The United States first sought approval for its actions in Korea, and then solicited acceptance of a number of resolutions which, in reality, represented an abuse rather than proper utilization, of the United Nations. In all likelihood, the United States could have done as well militarily in Korea without reliance upon the United Nations because with the exception of small British, Australian, and Turkish contingents, actions in Korea were conducted by U.S. military forces. Thus, to the Soviets and Chinese, the U.N. was only a facade which provided the U.S. with an international shield for its own policy objectives.

In February 1953, the U.S.S.R. requested that member nations agree to invite representatives of the DPRK [Democratic People's Republic of Korea] to participate in discussions of the Korean question. The Soviet Union took the position that North Korea was not the aggressor, but rather that the Rhee regime was an aggressor and had provoked the war. The Soviet Union also called for the termination of the United Nations Korean Reconstruction Agency activities and stated that this agency was not capable of fulfilling its objectives. Finally, the U.S.S.R. also called for the termination of United Nations Committee for the Unification of the Republic of Korea. Meanwhile, in August of 1953, after the Armistice had been signed; the Soviets again called for admission of the Chinese People's Republic and the DPRK into discussions concerning the Korean question. The Soviet Union had no intention of seeing North Korea fall from the sphere of its influence, while the United States had equally no intention of losing South Korea as a buffer against Chinese and Soviet expansion. The unification of Korea had by now become overwhelmed by political and military realities of the cold war.

Hereafter, all efforts of the U.S. toward Korea concentrated on preventing the Armistice Agreement from forcing another war and on the restoration of the war-wrecked Korean economy. As a result, during the period of 1953-1958, the U.S. government provided South

---

[23] Kim Chum-Kon, *The Korean War* (Seoul, 1973), pp. 737-741.

Korea with more than 1.3 billion dollars in economic aid, and it was during this period of heavy financial outlay that the U.S. ignored an April, 1956 Communist Chinese note, sent via the British, which requested a conference to consider the withdrawal of all foreign troops from Korea. In October 1958, Communist China announced its intention to unilaterally withdraw its volunteer forces from Korea and requested a similar withdrawal move from the U.S. North Korea and Communist China demanded that after withdrawal of all foreign forces, all-Korea free elections would be held under supervision of a neutral nations organization.[24] Although the prospect of China withdrawing its troops sparked a renewed interest in the unification of Korea the issue never reached a serious level of debate. From these events we may draw two conclusions: (1) After the Geneva Conference of 1954 the U.S. followed a policy of insisting that Korean unification could be achieved only through the United Nations, and (2) The United States displayed a diminishing interest in Korean unification during the Eisenhower administration.

During the Kennedy administration there were no basic changes in U.S. policy toward the reunification of Korea via United Nations machinery. It is notable, however, that Adlai Stevenson, the American Ambassador to the U.N., suggested that the North Korean delegate be seated for discussion of the Korean question if the government of North Korea recognized the competence and authority of the United Nations.[25] This was apparently a move away from the previous, and somewhat harder American line, which had been a complete rejection of all North Korean delegates. This new attitude may have been occasioned by a genuine softening of U.S. policy toward North Korea, and may as well have been a response to the unsure voting situation in the U.N. created by the influx of Afro-Asian nations into the world organization. Stevenson's proposal did not change the basic American policy toward North Korea, in view of the fact that the DPRK still refused to accept the authority and competence of the U.N.

Even though the U.S. has regularly presented the issue of Korean

---

[24] Kim Il-sung's Report to the Central Committee of the Labor Party on April 24, 1956 in Kim Il-sung, *Minami Chōsen Kakumei to Sokokuno Tōitsu* (South Korean Revolution and the Unification of the fatherland) (Tokyo, 1970), pp. 148-157. See also Kim's speech on August 14, 1960 in *Kim Il-Sung Son-jip* (Pyongyang, 1965). For an analysis of North Korean unification policy, see Byung-Chul Koh, *The Foreign Policy of North Korea* (New York, 1969), pp. 125-157.

reunification in the United Nations, the American policy toward Korea in the 1960's was geared toward creating a South Korean government capable of withstanding Communist subversion. President Kennedy and his "new frontier" group were not, for the most part, satisfied with the Eisenhower-Dulles policies toward Korea, dubbed by Reischauer as "dike-building." Kennedy concluded that recognition of Communist China could not be negotiated at the onset of his administration, and devoted more attention to other problems. The short-run goal of his policy initially seems to have been to maintain strong, pro-American governments on the frontiers of Communism.[26] One of the ultimate objectives was to establish a viable and democratic government in South Korea, one which could bargain from a position of equal strength with North Korea should unification become a reality. However, American policy was not primarily directed toward the immediate reunification of Korea. President Kennedy gave strong, moral and economic support to the first real democratic government in the South organized by Chang-myon after a student revolution toppled the autocratic government of Syngman Rhee on April 19, 1960. In his twelve years in office, President Rhee had become increasingly reluctant to submit to the mandate of the polls, and had become insensitive to the demands of the people. The political scene during this time had been dominated by his Liberal Party with only minor harassment from the smaller and ineffectual Democratic Party. Even though the new democratic government proved to be quite ineffective in many areas, it guaranteed the rights of freedom of speech and assembly, and consequently the Kennedy administration wanted to provide strong support to Chang.[27]

Less than one month after the first anniversary of the student revolution, on May 16, the situation changed abruptly as the military junta under Park Chung-hee overthrew the democratic government. When Park set his military in motion, only 3,600 soldiers were needed to bring the government down and push Chang into hiding. Imme-

---

[25] Yil-Hyung Chyung, *The United Nations and the Korean Question* (Seoul, 1961), pp. 352-358.

[26] Roger Hilsman, *To Move a Nation* (New York, 1964), pp. 302-320. See also U.S. Congress, *The Future United States Role in Asia and in the Pacific* (Hearing before the House subcommittee on Asian and Pacific affairs, 90th Congress, 2nd session) (Washington D.C., 1968), pp. 22-23.

[27] For an analysis of Chang Myun regime, see Sungjoo Han, *The Failure of Democracy in Korea* (Berkeley, 1974).

diately after the coup officials at the American embassy and the United Nations Command voiced their strong opposition.[28] The U.S. promptly refused to endorse the new regime, and General Park was aware that South Korea's regime and its creaking economy would collapse overnight if U.S. support were totally withdrawn.

By mid-July American attitudes toward the military·junta began to change; the U.S. decided to accept the coup and to work with the new military government. This change may have been due to the realization on the part of the U.S. that continued negative reaction to the issue of viability of the military junta would inevitably translate into increased confusion, and possibly bloodshed, in South Korea. If the economic and political environment deteriorated to too great an extent, there was an imminent danger of another North Korean attack. Under these circumstances a joint statement was issued on July 7, 1961 by a representative of the military junta and Secretary of State Dean Rusk, wherein friendship and cooperation were reaffirmed. Subsequently, in a statement on July 28, Rusk stated that the U.S. welcomed "the vigorous and prompt step that the military government has taken in its efforts to root out corruption and to provide a firmer base for democracy." Following the assassination of President Kennedy and the initial period of adjustment of the Johnson administration, President Johnson sent Secretary of State Rusk to Seoul, as part of an Asian tour. The American commitment to Korea, as reaffirmed by Rusk, was one of continued cooperation in the economic and military sectors. The Johnson policy which appears to have held this view of Korean-American relations during the Kennedy administration, reached its fullest development of February 12, 1964, when Ambassador Berger outlined an "irrevocable" four-part commitment of the United States to South Korea: first, "to help safeguard the national integrity and independence of the Republic of Korea and share in its defense; second, to maintain its policy of economic assistance until Korea has achieved a large measure of independence from outside aid; third, to support efforts of the Korean people to establish an effective democratic government on a durable basis; fourth, to seek the ultimate reunification of Korea on a basis which will assure national independence and security against attack or subversion, freedom and peace."[29]

---

[28] Se-Jin Kim, *The Politics of Military Revolution in Korea* (Chapel Hill, 1971), pp. 93-121.

By late 1964, fulfillment of the second of these commitments appeared to have been progressing quite favorably, for in December of that year it was reported that South Korea had increased rice and fertilizer production, and had achieved a surplus in cement production. Exports had increased from 20 million dollars in 1959 to 175 million dollars in 1965, while import expenditures had decreased. Such progress was viewed quite favorably by the U.S. for the American economy was beginning to strain under the pressure of expenditures in Vietnam. The U.S. could not possibly afford a Vietnam-type situation to flare up in Korea during this critical time. Consequently, any signs of increased political and economic stability in South Korea were welcomed by American officials, who also began pushing South Korea to normalize relations with Japan in an attempt to introduce Japanese capital into Korea, thus further stabilizing the South Korean economy.

During President Johnson's administration the major concern of United States policy toward Korea was how to enlist Korean forces in the war effort of Vietnam. The United States needed Korean troops not only to assist in military operation, but also for public relations reasons. As the Vietnamese War was becoming increasingly unpopular both inside and outside of the United States, President Johnson had to "sell the war" as an important concern of the free world. While most of American allies were reluctant to commit their troops in Vietnam, Korea alone showed its interest in joining the United States in the war-effort. South Korean leaders wanted to demonstrate to the free world their determination to join in the resistance against Communist aggression at all costs and to repay American efforts for saving its independence during the Korean War. Furthermore, the benefit of additional payment from the United States for the Korean combat unit in Vietnam would greatly assist the economic development which they were pushing vigorously since 1963. From 1966 through 1973 South Korea maintained a force level of about 50,000 and earned about $1 billion as the compensation for its troop commitment in the Vietnam War, the South Korean government benefiting from the high pay rate the United States provided for its troops. Korean troops were paid at close to U.S. pay levels but, according to Ambassador William Porter, "the money was remitted

---

[29] United States Congress, *Investigation of Korean-American Relations* (Report of the Subcommittee on International Organization in 95th Congress 2nd Session) (Washington D.C., 1978), pp. 20-22.

to the government which then paid its troops at levels which were substantially less.''[30] Furthermore, Johnson committed the United States to deliver $150 million in development loans in 1965.

The South Korean's involvement in the Vietnam War dramatically increased the tensions between North and South. The border clashes increased and provocations as well as the infiltrations from the North were intensified. The tension reached a peak January 21, 1968 when a group of 31 North Korean commandos attempted to raid the Blue House to assassinate the President. Two days later, North Korea captured the intelligence ship U.S.S. Pueblo which was allegedly 15 miles from shore, 3 miles outside North Korean territorial water. One crewmember was killed and the other 82 were captured. Then, on April 14, 1969, a naval intelligence plane, an EC-121 operating out of Japan, was shot down by North Korea over the Sea of Japan. Thirty-one members of the crew were killed.

During the Pueblo incident, which coincided with the attempted North Korean infiltration of Seoul and other coastal areas, the United States stated that there was no firm reason to believe that North Korea would initiate a conventional military attack. South Korea viewed the infiltration attempt quite differently, however, and the lack of concern on the part of the U.S. caused a crisis in United States and South Korean relations. For South Korea, this crisis could be resolved only by a firm commitment on the part of the United States to supply up-to-date F-4 Phantom jets, heavier tanks, and above all, American troops to resist infiltration. After considerable consultation, an uneasy agreement was concluded on February 15, 1968, in which the United States agreed to engage in ''immediate consultation'' with South Korea if heavy infiltration threatened the security of that nation.

From the above examination of the relations between the United States and South Korea, it becomes obvious that although American willingness to become directly involved in the day-to-day skirmishes between North and South Korea had diminished greatly, the short-run policy goal of the United States in Korean between 1961 and 1968 had changed little from the policy pursued during the Eisenhower years, that is, to build a strong, stable government in South Korea. Reunification of Korea, as a policy, was perceived as an ideal, but one that would have to be approached incrementally over a long period of time.

---

[30] *Ibid.*, pp. 53-54.

From the early days of the Vietnam War, South Korean government officials began to seek reassurance of the U.S. commitment to South Korea in case of a North Korean attack. From the Korean point of view, the existing mutual defense pact between South Korea and the U.S. was unreliable and unsound at best. This was because the Treaty specifically stated that the United States "would act to meet the common danger in accordance with its constitutional processes." Given the current climate of American public opinion and the strong neo-isolationist tone of the American Congress, it would be most unlikely for any American president to commit land forces to the Korean peninsula should a new war break out. In contrast, a mutual defense pact between North Korea and China, as well as North Korea and the Soviet Union, clearly indicated an automatic and immediate commitment on behalf of North Korea. It read as follows:

> Should either of the contracting parties suffer armed attack by any state or coalition of states, and thus find itself in a state of war, the other contracting party shall immediately extend military and other assistance with all the means at its disposal.[31]

Interpreting this pact as giving a distinct advantage to North Korea in any outbreak of hostilities, the South Korean government officials sought a new mutual defense treaty with the United States, patterned on a NATO-type commitment to South Korea. This was to guarantee an automatic commitment on the part of the United States, thus neutralizing the North Korea-China-U.S.S.R. pacts. South Korea sensed that the best time to bargain for such a pact was during the period when America was not only negotiating for a reduction of its troop commitment to South Korea, but was attempting to get international support, such as Korean troops, for its actions in Vietnam as well. The Johnson administration, however, declined to revise the original mutual defense pact. Instead, his administration promised to increase the military and economic commitment by the U.S. and to aid in modernizing the South Korean military forces. American Ambassador Winthrop B. Brown, in a memorandum sent to the South Korean Foreign Minister citing a joint communique between President Park and President Johnson of May 1965, attempted to reassure Korean leaders that this position presented no danger to

---

[31] People's Republic of China, *Collection of Friendship Treaties* (Peking, 1965), p. 45.

South Korean security. The Communique reaffirmed "the determination and readiness of the United States to render forthwith and effectively all possible assistance including the use of armed forces, in accordance with the Mutual Defense Treaty of 1954, to meet the common danger occasioned by an armed attack on the Republic of Korea." President Johnson then said that, "The United States will continue to maintain powerful forces in Korea and will assist in maintaining Korean forces at the level sufficient, in conjunction with U.S. forces, to insure Korean security."[32] Reassured, South Korea sent its troops to South Vietnam with the belief that the United States would definitely keep its part of the bargain.

In 1969, with the announcement of the Nixon Doctrine, first enunciated by the President on Guam in that year, South Korean leaders began to lose confidence in the American commitment to South Korea. As Professor Edwin O. Reischauer rightly pointed out, "Unfortunately, the doctrine has been made to sound like a concept applying to an Asia that is so alien to the United States that it is not worthy of defense at the cost of American lives." "Asian boys should fight Asian wars" and presumably the Koreans should not count on American defense commitments. To implement this doctrine in 1970, the Nixon Administration began negotiating in Seoul for the withdrawal of a large part of the American forces within two or three years,[33] By the end of 1971, the U.S. had withdrawn one of the two American divisions remaining in Korea, although the move met with the vehement protest of the South Korean government. In an attempt to compensate the Koreans, the Administration sought an appropriation of a billion dollars, spread over five years to modernize the South Korean army. One implication of a give-and-take policy of this type is that the U.S. may have been planning to buy its way out rather than simply to leave Korea. The modernization program apparently was aimed at assuring South Korea a defensive capability against the North, but not an offensive capability. On the other hand, it was suggested that the cost of military modernization would be more than offset with the withdrawal of the remaining division from Korea, the maintenance of which was requiring $500 million a year. As a last ditch effort, South Korean leaders urged that the U.S. relocate its

---

[32] Se-Jin Kim, *Documents in Korean-American Relations* (Seoul, 1976), p. 289.

[33] Soon S. Cho, "The Changing Pattern of Asian International Relations: Prospects for the Unification of Korea," *Journal of International Affairs*, Vol. 27, No. 2, (1973), p. 217.

Okinawa bases in South Korea, should Okinawa revert to Japan, and at the same time threatened to withdraw all Korean troops from South Vietnam. The Nixon administration, however, seemed determined to withdraw American troops from Asia and to follow a policy of disengagement, thus negating all Korean attempts to assure the long-term presence of U.S. troops on South Korean soil.

These events were followed by a series of shocking international changes in the Asian scene. The admission of Communist China into the U.N., Kissinger's secret trip to China, and Nixon's own trip to China, all announced without consultation with Japan and Korea. Also we find a new economic polemic developing between the U.S. and Japan, the result being that Japanese exports into the U.S. were curtailed. This limitation was equally applied to South Korean exports into the United States. These events intensified a long-standing fear entertained by Korean leaders that the U.S. and Japan might arrange a rapprochement with China and Russia without their knowledge, leaving Korea isolated from the rest of Asia. July of 1971 thus appeared to be the realization of a nightmare for the Korean leadership, for it had always been gravely concerned with security, and now its precarious political existence was dependent on whatever form the "new identity" imposed on the Korean leadership might take in Korea-U.S. relations. Especially alarming to Korean policy makers was the possibility that Korea could be left a helpless island in Asian politics, since the President's trip to Peking would only serve to weaken Taiwan's role in U.S. strategy in Asia; the India-Pakistan War nearly decimated the already weakened SEATO; the reversion of Okinawa to Tokyo threatened the availability of U.S. air cover to the Peninsula; and, to top it off, the possibility of U.S. forces leaving South Vietnam might well end the commitment of American forces in Asia altogether. President Nixon himself stated:

> We must remember the only time in the history of the world that we have had any extended period of peace is when there has been balance of power. It is when one nation becomes infinitely more powerful in relation to its potential competitor that the danger of war arises. So I believe in a world in which the United States is powerful. I think it will be a safe world and a better world if we have a strong, healthy United States, Europe, Soviet Union, China, Japan, each balancing the other, not playing one against the other, an even balance.[34]

---

[34] *Ibid.* This remark was made by Nixon in his interview with the managing editor of

Even for the South Korean leaders it was now clear that the world was changing from the politics of bi-polarization to one of a multi-balance of power. They remembered that the situation of today as being very similar to the period from 1894 to 1905 when China, Russia, Japan and, to a lesser degree, the United States, were contending with one another to include Korea within their respective spheres of interest. At that time, the United States was the first to desert from Korea, proving, in the eyes of the Koreans, its unreliability as an ally.

South Korean leaders now had to chart a new strategy to cope with a new Asian international situation. Domestically, the change of Asian politics at the international level had affected their long-standing unification policy making it increasingly untenable. Since 1947, South Korea had continuously maintained that unification ought to be achieved through a general election throughout Korea under the supervision of the United Nations. But with the admission of Communist China to the United Nations, it now appears that U.S. and South Korean governments could no longer exclude North Korea from the U.N. debate. In August of 1970, President Park declared that South Korea would not object to the invitation of North Korea to attend the U.N. provided the North Koreans agreed to accept "the competence and authority of the United Nations."[35] Then he expressed his willingness to open a channel of trade and communication with communist nations such as the Soviet Union and Yugoslavia. In August 1971, South Korea also proposed to North Korea that Red Cross talks be initiated to exchange information on persons displaced during the Korean War.[36] North Korea immediately accepted this proposal, since it was in line with their long-standing policy supporting the exchange of personnel, goods, mail, etc. Thus, the first official contact between North and South began only after the announcement of Nixon's trip to China.

From the North Korean point of view, the world situation seemed to be moving to her advantage. The bitter disputes with Communist China during the period of the cultural revolution were over, and American troops were gradually being withdrawn, not only from

---

Time. See the issue of 3 January, 1972.

[35] Park Chung Hee, *Toward Peaceful Unification* (Seoul, 1976). Address delivered on August 15, 1970. pp. 18-23.

[36] *Ibid.,* pp. 39-42.

South Korea, but also from the Asian Continent. The Japanese were now more flexible toward North Korean trade and its security was as stable as it had been for a number of years. The only real problem left to face was that the increasing penetration of Japanese capital into the South Korean economy might hinder the future reunification of the Koreans. While North Korean economic development had become rather stagnant due to the great demands of the military budget and the decline of aid from the USSR and China, the situation was not desperate. On the other hand, the economic growth rate of South Korea, which averaged 16 per cent per annum since 1967, had become a threatening element. This rapid growth was mainly due to the inflow of Japanese capital and American economic assistance. While Japan-South Korean trade reached one billion dollars in 1970, Japan-North Korean trade amounted to only $50 million. Thus North Korea, needing comparable capital and technical know-how of the Japanese to keep abreast of the South, was reported to be seeking a long-term loan of $900 million for the import of Japanese industrial plants.

Because of this situation, it would be to the advantage of North Korea to end its long period of isolation and take a more flexible position toward South Korea, Japan, and even the United States. Consequently in August 1971, Kim Il-sung proposed that he might be open to talks with the South Korean ruling party, and in December 1971, he gave his first interview to an American correspondent. In an interview with Harrison E. Salisbury and John M. Lee of the New York Times, Kim reiterated the necessity of U.S. withdrawal from the South, and pointed out the necessity of the dissolution of UNCURK, the United Nations Commission for the Unification and Rehabilitation of Korea. He argued that the Korean question must be left to Koreans to solve without outside influence, and, that it must be based on national self determination. As a first step to unification, Kim proposed, as he had before, a kind of confederation in which a Supreme National Committee would consult and discuss matters of common concern while the North retained its communist system and the South its capitalist one.[37] The North Koreans seemed eager to convince themselves that the United States eventually must withdraw its military presence from the South and that the Southern regime was in danger of being sacrificed for solely U.S. interest.

---

[37] *New York Times,* 31, May, 1972. See also Kim Il Sung, *For the Independent Peaceful Reunification of Korea* (New York, 1976), pp. 117-143.

Under these circumstances the South Korean CIA Chief secretly went to North Korea and brought back a historic agreement for possible unification. As a result, on July 4, 1972, both the North and South announced their agreement on the principle of the reunification of Korea. The principles for reunification were as follows:

> (1) Unification shall be achieved through independent Korean efforts without being subjected to external imposition or interference.
> (2) Unification shall be achieved through peaceful means, and not through the use of force against each other.
> (3) As a homogeneous people, a great national unity shall be sought above all, transcending differences in ideas, ideologies and systems.

To facilitate the unification in accordance with the above principles the two governments further agreed "not to slander or defame each other, not to undertake armed provocations, and to take positive measures to prevent inadvertent military incidents." Furthermore, they agreed to establish a hot line between Seoul and Pyongyang as well as to organize a North-South Coordinatng Committee cochaired by Lee Hu-Rak, Director of the South Korean Central Intelligence Agency, and Kim Yong Ju, director of the Organization and Guidance Department of the Korean Worker's party and a younger brother of Premier Kim Il-sung.

This seemingly impossible development amazed not only the Korean people, but also their neighbors and allies as well. The major world powers, including the United States and Communist China, initially expressed strong support for the development in the hope that the increased communications would ease tensions between the North and South and eventually defuse a dangerous powder keg in Asia. The U.S. government was apparently pleased with this development as it had urged this kind of North-South dialogue for some time.[38]

The United States, however, subsequently developed strong skepticisms about the prospect of Korean unification in the wake of a number of drastic reforms initiated by Park Chung Hee. Park used the negotiation with the North as reason for more tight government control and vigilance in the South. After declaring martial law, the South Korean government utilized "extra-constitutional means" to abolish the direct election of the President by a major restructuring of

---

[38] Robert A. Scalapino, *Asia and the Road Ahead* (Berkeley, 1975), pp. 221-225.

government which in effect perpetuated his regime in power. In addition, a new constitution provided almost unlimited power to the President by eliminating any significant restraints on the executive by either the legislature or the judiciary. These developments came as a complete surprise to U.S. officials because there was no prior consultation with the American government. Officially, the United States could muster no more than "vague" criticism of these reforms, a lack of effective response which was necessitated by the fact that had the United States intervened, it would have incurred increased responsibility for the U.S. in a part of the world where the American public and Congress were seeking a much reduced role.[39] In short, the availability of policy options for the U.S. vis-a-vis South Korea were extremely limited, especially in the view of the newly emerging pattern of Asian international relations.

It must be remembered that the United States had long supported the unification of Korea, and its unification policy had been so closely coordinated with that of the Republic of Korea that it was difficult to distinguish between the unification policies of the two countries. Disagreements had, at times, arisen between the two governments, but they had not been longstanding nor disruptive to friendly relations. Now the South Korean government unilaterally initiated a new unification policy, again, without "prior consultation" with the American government. The accord reached secretly between the two Korean governments implied that South Korea thereafter would not seek as close a coordination of policy with the United States as before. The agreement clearly stated that "unification shall be achieved through independent Korean efforts without being subjected to external imposition and interference." Thus, allegedly moving to prepare for Korean unification, President Park announced the imposition of martial law as well as a new constitution. As a justification for his action the President referred to the "profound changes" that had occurred in the international situation and the need to guard "against the possibility that the interests of the third and smaller countries might be sacrificed for the relaxation of tension between the big powers." The immediate, publicly expressed position of the American government was mild. A State Department press officer briefly commented on the situation by saying. "We were not consulted about the decision and quite obviously

---

[39] U.S. Congress, *Investigation of Korean-American Relations*, p. 41.

are not associated with it."

The Korean government had now taken a bold step toward unification. Although Korea still remained in the orbit of U.S. influence, it
had become increasingly independent in its foreign and domestic
policy orientation; a shift which in short, generated a new turning
point in American-Korean relations. Although the United States
became increasingly disenchanted with Park's dictatorial policy, the
South Korean government was in considerable favor in Washington
because of its remarkable economic achievements and its positive
attitude toward the negotiations with the North. Therefore, Washington
adopted a policy of non-interference. President Nixon reiterated
the policy when he told Prime Minister Kim Jong-phil in January
1973: "Unlike other Presidents, I do not intend to interfere in the
internal affairs of your country."[40]

Meanwhile, the North-South dialogue did not progress as originally
hoped. From the beginning, South Korea was determined to adhere to
the principle of finding practical solutions to simple non-politcal
problems and then proceed to more complex and politically involved
questions in a step-by-step fashion as mutual trust and confidence
were built up between the two sides. South Korea thus preferred a
form of gradualism similar to the functional approach in the theory
of international integration. On the other hand, the North Koreans
chose to take a rigid stance of insisting on an immediate solution of
political and military questions. Thus, they proposed that the South
Koreans sign a peace treaty formally ending the Korean War which
would replace the existing cease fire agreement of 1953. They also
called for a mutual troop reduction of Korean armed forces to
100,000 and the complete dissolution of the United Nations Command and UNCURK. The North Koreans insisted that it was necessary to create a North-South Confederation "in order to realize a
many-sided collaboration between the North and the South." In
order to facilitate the organization of a confederate state, they urged
the convening of a consultative conference of all political parties and
social groups in both Koreas. Actually none of these proposals were
new, similar ideas having been advanced by North Korea since the
early 1960's. South Korea immediately refused all these suggestions
viewing any acceptance of such proposals as seriously endangering its
own security. Since the beginning of 1973, relations between North

---

[40] *Ibid.,* p. 39.

and South had once more become strained. Abusive language was again appearing in newspaper articles and radio broacasts in both Koreas. Finally, using the kidnapping of Kim Dae-jung (the opposition leader of South Korea) from Japan as a pretext, the North Koreans suspended the dialogue indefinitely in August 1973.

In 1971 and 1972 there were no debates at the United Nations on the Korean questions. When the dialogue broke down in 1973 the United Nations once again took the case of Korea for its agenda.

Before the 28th Session of the General Assembly, President Park, in order to take a diplomatic initiative, declared a seven-point declaration for Peace and Unification on June 23, 1973; the South Korea government proposed United Nations membership for both the ROK and the DPRK and announced that the ROK would not object to DPRK participation in the U.N. debate on the Korean question prior to its entry into the U.N. It also declared that the ROK would open its door to all the nations of the world on the basis of the principles of reciprocity and equality. At the same time, he urged those countries with ideologies and social institutions different from South Korea to open their doors to her.[41] These new policies were a drastic reversal of its previous position for reunification. However, these new proposals were immediately rejected by Kim Il-sung on the grounds that the dual entry would cause permanent division of the two Koreas. On the other hand, the South Korean government decided on a new U.N. strategy based on the voluntary dissolution of UNCURK as well as dissolution of the U.N. Command "subject to creation of an alternate arrangement for maintaining the 1953 Korean Armistice agreement." North Korea, however, did accept an invitation to participate in the UN debates and sent an observer delegation to New York in November 1973. By supporting this action, the United States now seemed to be shifting away from encouraging efforts at reunification through North-South dialogue, and toward a de facto recognition of separate states, even though it continued to nominally endorse eventual reunification of the two Koreas.

This policy of maintaining a status quo rather than creating a condition for Korean reunification has continued without much variation to the present day. In 1976, Secretary of State Henry Kissinger proposed a Four-power Conference on Korea.[42] According to this

---

[41] Research Center for Peace and Unification, *Korean Unification* (Seoul, 1976), pp. 338-340.

[42] *Ibid.*, pp. 416-418.

proposal the United States government was prepared to meet with South Korea, North Korea and the People's Republic of China during the coming session of the U.N. General Assembly to discuss the Korean questions. At the same time, he stated the four principles of the United States position with respect to Korea. These four principles were: First, the United States urged a resumption of serious discussions between North and South Korea. Second, if North Korea's allies were prepared to improve their relations with South Korea, then and only then would the United States be prepared to take similar steps toward North Korea. Third, the United States continued to support proposals that the United Nations open its door to full membership for South and North Korea without prejudice to their eventual reunification. Finally, the United States was prepared to negotiate a new basis for the armistice or to replace it with more permanent arrangements in any form acceptable to all the parties. However, this proposal was also rejected by North Korea as an old imperialistic device to create a permanent division of Korea. The same four principles were also reiterated during President Carter's administration and reaffirmed in the Joint Communique issued at the Conclusion of Meeting with President Park on July 1, 1979. The only new development under the Carter administration was that the United States and South Koreans called for a Tri-lateral Conference among the three governmental authorities, that is, the representatives of South Korea, North Korea and the United States, to discuss the reunification of Korea. This proposal of 1978 was similarly rejected by North Korea who insisted that Korean reunification should be achieved among the Koreans themselves without interference of the four powers and that the United States should deal with North Korean authorities directly without participation of South Korea.

Facing the adamant positions of North Korea, the United States now became primarily concerned with the security of South Korea rather than the immediate reunification of the Korean peninsula. The United States had sought to withdraw its troops from South Korea so that they would not fight another Vietnam War in East Asia while maintaining the security of South Korea. To this end, the reduction of 20,000 troops was completed by March 1971 and American Congress agreed to appropriate $1.5 billion over the 5 year period to modernize South Korean forces. It was, however, not until 1977 that Congress fulfilled the administration's modernization commitment, two years after the scheduled completion date. Furthermore, the amount of non-grant aid was lower than the $3 billion to $4 billion it desired. Thus, the nervous Korean government resorted to illegal lobbying in order to stop further withdrawal of American troops and to acquire the funds for its troops modernization programs. This illegal lobbying and the gross human rights violation in South Korea created more unfavorable reactions in the United States. While campaigning in June, 1976, Presidential candidate Jimmy Carter called for the withdrawal of all ground troops "on a phased basis over a time span to be determined after consultation with South Korea and Japan." He also put human rights into the troop withdrawal equation by stating that "it should be made clear to the South Korean government that its internal oppression is repugnant to our people and undermines the support for our commitment there."

The Carter administration decided in 1977 on a phased withdrawal of American troops in three steps; in the first, one brigade would be removed by the end of 1978; in the second stage, the support troops; and in the third, the last combat brigades and U.S. headquarters. While Carter's campaign pledge had called for a total withdrawal of ground forces by 1980, he later set 1982 as the new date. However, President Reagan recently cancelled Carter's troop withdrawal plan and assured President Chun that the United States has no plans to withdraw its ground combat forces from the Korean peninsula and pledged to secure the peace and security of the region.

We have seen the Korean reunification policy of the United States evolves into five distinctively different phases. First, immediately after the end of the Second World War to September 1947 when the United States presented the Korean issue to the United Nations, there was genuine desire and sincere effort on the part of the United States to reunify Korea. Second, after the establishment of the two rival governments in Korea in 1948, the hope for an immediate reunification evaporated. Thus, the United States turned its responsibility over to the United Nations to decide the fate of Korea. Third, the Korean War solidified the division more than ever before; although, there was a brief period in which the United States tried to unify Korea by military means. This effort ended in disaster. Fourth, after the Korean War to early 1970, the United States once more resorted to the United Nations for the reunification of Korea even though it became apparent that the international organization did not have the power and ability to deal with the issue effectively. Fifth, after President Nixon's trip to China and the emerging mood of detente between the Soviet Union and the United States, the United States urged reunification through peaceful dialogue between North and South leaving the solution of the Korean questions for themselves.

With the rapid change of the Asian international system and the emergence of multi-balance of power situation in Asia the primary concern of the United States has been the security of South Korea and maintenance of peace in Asia.[43] Thus, security concerns have been central to Korean-American relations since 1965. The United States as a world power has tended to view development on the Korean peninsula within a global context while the South Korean government has viewed development in terms of a North-South confrontation. These differing perspectives have often led to differing and at times conflicting responses to issues that arose in the 1960's and 1970's. To the South Korean leaders, American responses to North Korea have been inadequate and unsound while to American leaders the South Koreans were exaggerating the threat, sometimes for political purposes.[44] Although all of the American presidents have pledged to deter and defend against aggression from the North, South Korean leaders have become increasingly skeptical about American promises. The repeated warnings of American troop withdrawal since 1970 and the halfhearted attitude toward the modernization of South Korean forces have deepened ambivalent feelings toward the United States.

The United States and South Korean governments seem to believe that the early reunification is an illusion, far removed from a realistic appreciation of the present world situation. For the sake of peace in Korea and Asia they believe that the co-existence of the divided nation is inevitable for the time being.[45] Thus, they support a resumption of a constructive dialogue with North Korea in order to ease tensions and build the framework for peaceful reunification of the two Koreas. In order to facilitate this dialogue and mutual contact they support the dual entry of North and South Korea into the United Nations and maintain that all the powers should recognize both Koreas simultaneously. The United States has insisted that any unilateral steps toward North Korea which are not reciprocated toward South Korea by North Korea's principal allies will not be conducive to

---

[43] Ralph N. Clough, *East Asia and U.S. Security* (New York, 1975), pp. 158-181.

[44] Franklin B. Weinstein and Fuji Kamiya, *The Security of Korea* (Boulder, 1980), pp. 1-51.

[45] Franklin B. Weinstein, ed., *U.S.-Japan Relations and Security of East Asia: The Next Decade* (Boulder, 1978), pp. 189-227.

promoting stability or peace in the areas. As such, the United States adamantly refuses to have a bi-lateral talk with North Korean authorities. In short, today's United States policy is the maintenance of a status quo in Korea rather than the creation of an atmosphere for the reunification of the two Koreas.

At this time of precarious balance of power in East Asia, no great power seems to be sympathetic toward unification as each state is afraid of what the unification will bring. China and the Soviets do not want a non-communist unified Korea due to the geographic proximity of Korea to both the states. Neither would like a unified Korea which aligned with either one of the powers against the other. The United States and Japan also do not want to see a unified Korea, notwithstanding their official support for the eventual unification. The fall-out following unification might be as follows: any conflict would bring in large powers. Japan would probably rearm given its traditional concern over Korea.[46] A Sino-Soviet squabble over a unified Korea might bring the United States more determinately on one side or the other, thus risking poor relations with the United States. Finally, Korea might become militarily active, thus destabilizing the area.

There are other reasons why Japan is concerned with unification. A unified Korea would present an economic threat to Japan, if not a military threat. The United States also believes that a unified Korea would represent a complete retreat from the Asian continent. Such a withdrawal, in American eyes, would destabilize the region. They also wishfully think that even Communist China will welcome the presence of American ground troops in Korea as they become an important deterrent to the Soviet military expansion in East Asia. However, Communist China officially supports North Korea's position that Unitd States forces in Korea is the main factor hindering the early unification of Korea. This position was again repeated by Prime Minister Zhao Ziyang of Communist China in his recent visit to North Korea. Thus, the security of Korea is ultimately tied up in a number of relations: those between North and South Korea, China, the Soviet Union, Japan, the United States and, more generally, the East and the West.[47]

---

[46] Taketsugu Tsurutai, *Japanese Policy and East Asian Security* (New York, 1981), pp. 137-174.

[47] William J. Barnds, *The Two Koreas in East Asian Affairs* (New York, 1976), pp. 167-205.

Is this policy of maintaining status quo in Korea the best policy option for the security of the United States in Asia? Admittedly, we may today have the situation in which the possibility of another Korean War has substantially diminished due to the tight balance of power situation between the United States, the Soviet Union, China and Japan. But, once this balance of power situation is broken, Korea may again become a dangerous powder keg in East Asia. Therefore, all the great powers neighboring Korea should strive for the reunification of Korea at the earliest possible date so that it would defuse this powder keg permanently. Furthermore, the United States should seek a way out from this hopelessly deadlocked situation. It could call another summit conference such as the Moscow-Conference of 1945 to deal solely with the Korean questions. Even though Kissinger's call for the four-power conference and President Carter's call for a trilateral conference were both heard with a deaf ear, the United States, in close cooperation with its own allies, should earnestly search for ways to achieve reunification. The United States should also call a conference to establish a nuclear-free zone in Korea in relation with the future unification of Korean peninsula as the threatening nuclear weapon controversy intensifies with the deployment of SS-20 in East Asia. In conclusion, we know that the Korean reunification as an issue is closely tied to the changing nature of Asian international relations. This does not mean that the unification of Korea will be resolved solely by international development, but rather by a complex combination of international and national factors. The major force for reunification must come first from the inner energy of the Korean people. The leaders of the two Koreas, especially, should bear the major responsibilities for the continued division of their fatherland. They should strive for the unification, whenever the opportunity arises, with a lofty sense of self-sacrifice and patriotism. After all, the United States can only assist but cannot force the reunification of the Korean people if their leaders and peoples are not earnestly seeking this goal. Thus, all the Korean people should never cease to demand the creation of a unified, democratic Korean government.

CHAPTER 5

AMERICAN-KOREAN DIPLOMATIC RELATIONS, 1961-1982

Chong-Ki Choi

I. Introduction

Korea's political history has been shaped by its strategically vital geographical relationship to three major Asian powers: China, Russia and Japan. Because of Korea's location between the islands of Japan and the Asian continent the three powers have always regarded it as essential to their security. It is thus not surprising—after Soviet and American forces occupied Korea in August 1945—that the two governments were unable to agree on a unified Korea.[1]

Both Korean regimes are strongly committed to ultimate reunification, but they have confronted each other with hostility and fear ever since the 1950-53 Korean War. Since 1953 the United States has been formally committed by treaty to help defend South Korea, and Washington now regards this as essential to maintain the credibility of its pledge to defend Japan. Since 1961 both China and the Soviet Union have been formally committed by treaty to help defend North Korea and today they compete strongly for influence over its regime.[2] Today, Korea is one of the few places in the world where hostilities involving one or more of the great powers could conceivably break out at any moment.[3]

---

[1] Stephen P. Gebert, *Northeast Asia in U.S. Policy* (The Washington Paper 71, Sage Publications, London, 1979), p. 37.

[2] A. Doak Barnett, *China and the Major Powers in East Asia* (The Brookings Institution, Washington, D.C., 1977), p. 307.

[3] Joseph A. Yager, ed., *Nonproliferation and U.S. Foreign Policy* (The Brookings Institution, Washington, D.C., 1980), p. 47.

The United States, however, is some 6,000 miles away. American military forces deployed in Northeast Asia constitute a "surrogate" presence or, as recent American presidents have been fond of noting that U.S. troop presence ensures that the United States is and will remain a Pacific power.

If the balance in Asia does indeed require the maintenance of the four-nation interactive system, then American political willingness to continue to be a Pacific power is indeed crucial.

On the Korean peninsula two rival states, each possessing formidable military machines and each laying claim to the whole of the peninsula, confront each other over armistice rather boundary lines. What are the essential elements of current South Korean foreign policy? Three primary themes are prominently displayed. First, the cornerstone of the Republic's foreign policy continues to be the alliance with the United States, especially as this relates to security matters. Second, relations with Japan, normalized in 1965 after stormy internal struggles, have steadily become more important, particularly in the economic field. Third, South Korea has made a determined effort in recent years to expand its relations with a wide range of states and has even begun to relax the rigidity characterizing her earlier attitude towards all Communist states.[4]

Korea has long had a strategic importance out of proportion to its size. Great powers have interest in Korea and reflect their respective national self-interests. However, while the changing international environment in this decade has lessened the potential for violence, none of these powers can exercise "control" over the policies of their Korean ally. Too often, Americans think of Korea only in a vacuum, emphasizing only the military balance between North and South Korea. The crucial point, however, is that developments in Korea affect all of East Asia involving several powers and are potentially destabilizing to the present international equilibrium.[5]

The purpose of this paper is to describe, analyze and evaluate Korea-U.S. relations from the military revolution in 1961 to the present from a South Korean perspective. U.S. relations with South Korea have been close but not always smooth. Rapid economic

---

[4] Robert A. Scalapino, "Korea and Vietnam," in Wayne Wilcox, Leo E. Rose, Gavin Boyd, eds., *Asia and the International System* (Winthrop Publishers, Inc., Cambridge, 1972), p. 150.

[5] *The Republic of Korea: A Report to the Committee on Foreign Relations*, United States Senate, Jan. 9, 1978, p. 7.

growth in South Korea during the latter half of the 1960s and improvements in the South Korean armed forces, which sent two divisions to fight in Vietnam during this period, convinced President Nixon that the United States could safely withdraw from South korea in 1971 one of the two combat divisions it maintained there. The South Korean government at first objected strongly, but eventually acquiesced in exchange for a promise by the United States to provide a large amount of equipment to modernize South Korean forces. Delay in completing this program created skepticism among South Koreans that the military equipment proposed by the Carter administration as compensation for the withdrawal of the remaining U.S. ground force would be provided as scheduled.[6]

The Mutual Defense Treaty of 1954 is the central document binding the United States and the Republic of Korea, that treaty stipulates that an armed attack upon either country would cause each to "act to meet the common danger in accordance with its constitutional process."

The commitment of the United States to the defense of South Korea remains the primary link between the two countries. However, economic relations are growing rapidly in importance as South Korea's economy expands. Twenty-seven percent of South Korea's U.S.$46 billion foreign trade in 1981 was with the United States. Already South Korea has become the 14th largest trading partner of the United States, buying nearly U.S. $1 billion in agricultural commodities each year in addition to purchasing civilian aircraft, military equipment and other high technology products. American private firms have invested some U.S. $950 million in loans and equity in South Korea.[7] Korea received U.S.$5.27 billion in military assistance from the U.S. from 1950 to 1980.

Korea, however, has not only been receptive but also anxious to buy from the United States; the balance of trade deficits must be placed squarely on America's low productivity, inflation, failure to adopt a viable energy policy and U.S. government constraints on export sectors. Korea, its security tied to American willingness to furnish arms, military training and to deter aggression through its military presence, wants Korean-American trade to flourish and

---

[6] Ralph N. Clough and William Watts, *The United States and Korea: American Attitudes and Policies* (Potomac Associates, Washington, D.C., 1978), p. 6.

[7] *Ibid.*, p. 6.

hopes to reduce its trade surplus with the United States so that economic disagreements will not have the effect of weakening mutual security ties. For, however valuable the American market, it is the security relationship upon which Seoul necessarily places the highest value. To understand this, it will be helpful to place the Korean-American security relationship in historical perspective.[8]

II. The Evolution of Korean-American Relations

A. The Military Revolution of 1961

The Chang Myon interregnum that followed the rule of Syngman Rhee which abolished the presidential system and replaced it with a parliamentary system, was the democratic period in South Korea's political history. Newspapers proliferated, politicians scrambled for position, and political demonstrators marched daily through the streets of Seoul.

Under such circumstances, the adoption and execution of effective policies were impossible. Industrial production declined, unemployment increased and prices rose rapidly. Dissatisfaction mounted, especially within the armed forces, until the military brought down the Chang government by a military coup in May 1961, after only nine months in office. The ineffectiveness of the Chang government and the self-serving behavior of politicians further discredited party politics in the eyes of many Koreans—already disillusioned by politics under Syngman Rhee—and made them receptive to the pledges of the military leaders to bring order and progress to the nation.[9]

The United States Embassy in Seoul issued a statement on Tuesday, May 16, expressing strong support for the "freely elected and constitutionally established Government" of Premier John M. Chang.

The statement came after a military revolutionary group announced it had seized power from the Premier. In Washington responsible Government officials said that the coup in South Korea was not supported by the United States.

---

[8] Gebert, *op. cit.*, p. 37.
[9] Clough and Watts, *op. cit.*, p. 7.

Gen. Carter B. Magruder in his capacity as Commander-in-Chief of the United Nations Command, called upon all military personnel in his command to support the only recognized Government of the Republic of Korea (ROK) headed by Prime Minister Chang.

The statement in Seoul, made public by the United States Embassy's charge d'affaires, Marshall Green said; "The Position taken by the commander in chief of the United Nations Command in supporting the freely elected and constitutionally established government of the Republic of Korea is one in which I fully concur."

"General Magruder expects that the chief of the Korean armed forces will use their authority and influence to see that control is returned immediately to the lawful governmental authorities and that order is restored in the armed forces."

United States soldiers and civilians were told to remain in their quarters. A spokesman for General Magruder said; "All stations throughout Korea have been placed on an alert for protection from being involved in the present difficulties of the Korean Government. The United States Army is watching the situation."[10]

The revolutionary committee announced a six-item statement, in which it emphasized anti-communism and the promotion of friendly relation with the United States.[11]

The State Department said only that the two Americans' statements in Korea "were made within the scope of their authority in their posts." This implied support for the statements, but it was taken generally as something less than a ringing endorsement.[12]

There was a tendency in some Administration circles to criticize the action of the United States Embassy in Seoul and Gen. Carter B. Magruder, the United States military commander there, for having issued statements on May 16 in support of the Chang Government and critical of the military officers who seized power. The main question appeared to be not what they had said so much as why they had issued statements without clearing them first with Washington.[13]

Officials in Washington were hopeful on May 18 that political authority in South Korea would be returned quickly to civilian hands. In Seoul, Gen. Chang Do Young, head of the junta, reported a stepping up of

---

[10] *The New York Times,* May 19, 1961.
[11] *The Hankook Ilbo,* May 17, 1961.
The Korea Times, May 17, 1961.
[12] *The New York Times,* May 17, 1961.
[13] *The New York Times,* May 19, 1961.

anti-Communist efforts with the arrest of 930 persons on suspicion since the military seized power on May 16.

The news that Premier John M. Chang and his Cabinet had resigned reached Washington in the early hours of May 18. The Premier's move was regarded here as an inevitable development, but one not in the best interests of the U.S. from Washington's standpoint.

The biggest worry in the U.S. was that the intrusion of military men into civilian affairs would become an established pattern in South Korea. The tradition of separation of the army from politics had been cultivated assiduously in South Korea by every United States military commander there since the establishment of the Republic in 1948.

The State Department expressed deep "regret" on May 22 over the suspension of normal democratic processes in South Korea. Lincoln White, State Department spokesman, asserted; "We deeply regret that this group found it necessary to suspend temporarily the democratic and constitutional processes of the Republic of Korea." The Department said that the United States representatives in Seoul were conferring with leaders of the junta and were "exploring the most appropriate and effective means by which the United States could continue to support the Korean people" in their anti-Cummunist struggles.

There was also some conflict between military junta and the United States authorities here including the disruptive effect of the revolution on the military command. The United Nations Command was dangerously close to being ruined.

Marshall Green and General Magruder appealed to President Yoon Po Sun to use what power he had to end the coup and to get the military forces involved in the coup back into their barracks. President Yoon refused, however, and thus assured that the coup would succeed without bloodshed.[14]

In the early stages of the coup (simply referred to in Korea as "5.16" connoting the date of the coup May 16th), the United States was suspicious of the political ideology of Major General Park Chung Hee, the leader of the coup,[15] since his brother had been a communist and he himself had been involved in a communist-inspired putsch in

---

[14] *The Joong Ang Ilbo,* February 10, 1982.

[15] *The Joong Ang Ilbo,* February 19, 1982, Interview with Kim Jung Yol (Former Minister of Defense).

Yosu several years ago.

The arrival of new American ambassador Samuel D. Berger on May 24 signaled a change of policy on the part of the United States towards the military government.[16] Two days later on May 26, the military junta and the UNC issued joint communiques stating that Korean military forces would return to the command of the United Nations.[17] On June 28, Ambassador Berger called on General Park and met with ex-Premier Chang in prison, then reconfirmed the continuing support of the United States for the Republic of Korea.[18]

Talks between Chairman Park Chung Hee and President Kennedy were termed as "friendly and constructive exchange of views on the current situation in Korea and the Far East . . . .". The two leaders reaffirmed "the strong bonds of friendship traditionally existing between the two countries and their determination to intensify their common efforts toward the establishment of world peace based on freedom and justice."

Chairman Park emphasized the positive steps taken by the government for social reform, economic stability and in strengthening the nation against communism and in eliminating corruption and other social evils. In addition, he reiterated his solemn pledge to return the government to civilian rule by the summer of 1963.

The President reaffirmed the determination of the United States to render forthwith and effectively all possible assistance to Korea, in accordance with the Mutual Defense Treaty between the Republic of Korea and the United States of America signed on October 1, 1953, including the use of armed forces, if there should be a renewal of armed conflict.[19] During his visit Kennedy also broached the subject of the possibility of sending Korean troops to Vietnam for the first time.[20]

Chairman Park, embroiled in an internal power struggle among the members of the military revolutionary regime and pressure from the United States, was forced to change his stand on the return of the government to civilian rule several times. On February 18, 1963 Park stated that he would not serve as head of a civilian government in the future.[20] However, on March 16 of the same year he declared that he

[16] *The Hankook Ilbo*, February 28, 1982.
[17] *The Hankook Ilbo*, May 27, 1961.
[18] *The Hankook Ilbo*, June 29, 1961.
[19] *The New York Times*, October 14, 1961.
[20] *The Hankook Ilbo*, March 17, 1963.

would extend the period of military rule from 2 back to 4 years.[21]

The United States began to pressure Seoul to reinstate civilian rule. Chairman Park responded that such pressure from the American government for a transfer of power would greatly incense military leaders against the United States.[22] Ambassador Berger countered by warning Chairman Park that any anti-American movement or action would not be treated lightly by American authorities.[23]

At this time, the possibility of a counter-coup against the Park regime became great. Fearing open conflict and the overthrow of the new regime, over 150 senior military officers gathered in Seoul to show their support for the regime. This was done without the permission of the United States Command.[24]

The United States than decided to try to increase its influence over the Korean military leaders by gentle assuasion. Washington extended invitations to several top military men to visit the U.S., thereby helping to promote their prestige back in Korea. The end result was that the United States was able, with the help of pressure by civilian leaders, to persuade Park to hold general elections and transfer power to a civilian government on December 26, 1963.[25]

The American Embassy in Seoul strongly encouraged the transfer of power to civilian hands, asserting that such a move was necessary for stability in Korea. Korean military leaders, however, believed that the U.S. could not back up its urgings and demands. Although the American government threatened to cut down the amount of military and economic aid supplied to the Seoul government should the transfer not take place, Korean officials felt that the strategic importance of Korea to the U.S. would preclude such a move and, thus, considered the American threats to be empty.[26]

American pressure resulted in the holding of presidential elections on October 15, 1963 which Park Chung Hee won by a narrow margin over former President Yoon Po Sun. The United States then encouraged President Park to follow the example of his predecessor

---

The New York Times, March 21, 1963, Editorial: "Dilemma of Gen. Park."

[21] *The Joong Ang Ilbo,* Feb. 26, 1963, Interview with Kim Jae Chun (Former Head of KCIA).

[22] *The New York Times,* April 3, 1963.

[23] *The New York Times,* April 3, 1963.

[24] *The New York Times,* April 5, 1963.

[25] *The New York Times,* April 7, 1963.

[26] *The New York Times,* April 9, 1963.

Yoon Po Sun in constructing a democratically representative government.[27]

III. The Honeymoon Period between Korea and the U.S.

Secretary of State Dean Rusk met with President Park in Seoul and on January 29, 1964 issued a joint communique which strongly encouraged the normalization of relations between Korea and Japan.[28]

At the invitation of U.S. President Lyndon B. Johnson, Park Chung Hee visited Washington on May 17, 1965 for a ten-day state visit. The two men reviewed and reaffirmed the vital importance of defense ties between the United States and the Republic of Korea. President Park reviewed the negotiations between Korea and Japan for an agreement to establish normal relations, the components of which had already been initiated and were being drawn up in treaty form. President Johnson praised this achievement and expressed the expectation that this agreement, when completed, would not only strengthen the free nations of Asia but further the mutual interests of the two countries immediately involved. He continued that U.S. military and economic assistance to Korea would continue to be extended as set forth in paragraph 9 of the treaty after normalization of Korean-Japanese relations. President Johnson specifically stated that it was the intention of the United States Government subject to applicable legislation, appropriation and AID policies to help Korean efforts to achieve stable economic growth by (a) continuing supporting assistance for Korea's economic stability; (b) making available to Korea $150 million in Development Loan funds by the United States Government; (c) continuing technical assistance and training; and (d) providing substantial assistance in agricultural commodities. Ratification of the treaty normalizing relations with Korea and Japan was passed by the National Assembly without the participation of opposition politicians, who boycotted the proceedings on August 14, 1965.[29] The ratified treaty was then formally initialled by the two countries on December 19 of the same year.[30]

---

[27] *The New York Times,* October 21, 1963.
The New York Times, October 25, 1963.
[28] *The Hankook Ilbo,* January 30, 1964.
[29] *The Hankook Ilbo,* August 15, 1965.

As American military involvement in Vietnam expanded President Johnson decided to request the sending of Korean troops to Vietnam. A message to that effect was sent to President Park on July 25, 1965.[31] Park responded on July 29 that Korea was willing to send troops[32] and that the National Assembly, again without the participation of opposition legislators, approved the move on August 13, 1965.[33] The normalization of relations with Japan and the dispatch of Korean troops to Vietnam, moves welcomed and encouraged by the U.S., helped to improve the relations between the two countries, a situation which continued until the end of the 1960's. Korea was the only country to send combat troops to Vietnam besides the United States.

At the invitation of President Park, President Lyndon B. Johnson of the United States arrived in Seoul on October 31, 1966, for a state visit of Korea. President Johnson and President Park reaffirmed the strong ties of friendship traditionally existing between the Korean and American people.

The United States Government reassured Korea that it was secure and stated that Vietnam represented a second front for the Republic of Korea with direct consequences for Korean security. Ambassador Winthrop P. Brown was authorized to send a memorandum to Korea that the United States was prepared to take the following measures to see to it that the integrity of Korea's defense is maintained and strengthened and Korea's economic progress is further promoted.[34]

The military assistance clause stated that the United States would provide over the next few years substantial items of equipment for the modernization of the Republic of Korea forces to equip as is necessary and finance all additional won costs of the additional forces deployed to the Republic of Vietnam, to release additional won to the Korean budget equal to all of the net additional costs of the deployment of these extra forces and of mobilizing and maintaining activated reserves; in Korea and to increase technical assistance to the Republic of Korea in the field of export promotion.[35] A second memorandum

---

[30] *The Hankook Ilbo,* December 20, 1965.

[31] *The Dong A Ilbo,* July 25, 1965.

[32] *The Dong A Ilbo,* August 14, 1965.
Korean cabinet meeting had decided one combat division of Army to sending Vietnam on July 2, 1965.

[33] *The Hankook Ilbo,* August 14, 1965.

[34] American Ambassador to Korea, Winthrop P. Brown (from on August 1964 to May 1967).

[35] *The Hankook Ilbo,* March 5, 1966.

on March 7, 1966 stated that the United States would maintain a strong military presence in Korea in support of Korean national defense.[36] A third memorandum on March 8, 1966 reassured the strong commitment of the U.S. to Korean security.[37] The Brown memorandums went a long way towards persuading top Korean officials to send troops to Vietnam, but the one problem remaining was the lack of confidence in the American people.[38]

A joint communique issued by President Park and Mr. Cyrus R. Vance, special envoy of the President of the U.S. in Seoul on February 15, 1968, stated that the two men fully exchanged views concerning the grave situation that had arisen as a result of the increasingly aggressive and violent actions of the North Korean communists over the past fourteen months in violation of the Armistice Agreement and most recently the attack directed at the official residence of the President and the illegal seizure of the USS Pueblo in international waters. The two men recognized the need for continuing modernization of the Armed Forces of the Republic of Korea.

A summit conference between Park and Johnson in Honolulu in 1968 further improved friendly relations between the two nations. President Johnson reaffirmed the resolve of the United States to act promptly to fulfill its responsibilities under the Mutual Defense Treaty between the U.S. and the R.O.K. The two leaders also agreed on measures to deal with the seizure of the USS Pueblo by North Korea as well as agreeing to hold an annual meeting of the defense experts of the two countries.

IV. The Nixon Doctrine

When President Nixon took office in 1969 he was aware of growing congressional and popular dissatisfaction in the U.S. with containment in general, and with the role of the United States as "world policeman" in particular. The result was the famous "Guam Doctrine," late known as the "Nixon Doctrine," which signalled the beginning of a process that was to significantly affect America's military

---

[36] *The Hankook Ilbo,* March 7, 1966.
[37] *The Hankook Ilbo,* March 9, 1966.
[38] *The Hankook Ilbo,* July 3, 1976.

posture in Asia.[39] During the summit conference held in San Francisco in August of the same year, Nixon and Park announced that a new era was beginning in Asia marked by the increasing strength and prosperity of most Asian countries and that American forces stationed in Korea must remain strong and alert. The two leaders reaffirmed the determination of their governments to meet and repel an armed attack against the Republic of Korea in accordance with the Mutual Defense Treaty. They also agreed that allied nations should continue to work towards securing an honorable and lasting peace in Vietnam. President Nixon affirmed the readiness of the United States Government to continue to extend technical cooperation for further development of science and industry in the ROK.[40]

Permitted to run for a third term as President, Park was re-elected in 1971[41] by the constitutional amendment he rammed through the National Assembly in 1969, but by a narrower margin than in 1967. Likewise the government party, the Democratic Republic Party (DRP), was returned with a majority in the National Assembly but was no longer a two-thirds majority. Other developments posed new uncertainties for Park's government. The United States withdrew one of its two combat divisions from South Korea and President Nixon's pursuit of detente with the Soviet Union and his sudden announcement that he would visit Peking disturbed both North and South Korea. In October 1972, President Park declared martial law, suspended certain articles of the constitution and dissolved the National Assembly. Drastic constitutional changes were then adopted through a national referendum in November 1972, providing for the election of a National Conference for Unification composed of popularly elected non-party delegates who would choose the President for a six-year term. Park was duly elected President by this body for another six years in December 1972.

President Gerald R. Ford visited Korea on November 22 and 23, 1974, affirmed the readiness of the U.S. to continue to render appropriate support to the further development of defense industries in Korea and they agreed that the two countries should continue to foster close economic cooperation for their mutual benefit.[42]

The problems of human rights violations in Korea along with the

[39] Gebert, *op. cit.*, p. 41.
[40] *The Hankook Ilbo,* August 23, 1969.
[41] *The Hankook Ilbo,* April 28, 1971.
[42] *The Hankook Ilbo,* November 24, 1974.

so-called "Tongsun Park Scandal" caused Korean-American relations to take a turn for the worse. The accession to the Presidency of Jimmy Carter in 1977 saw relations between the two nations become even more troubled. Beginning in the autumn of 1976 the ramifications of what came to be called "Koreagate" dominated reporting on Korea in the American press. Stories ranged from the financial operations of Reverend Sun Myung Moon's Unification Church and Korean CIA activities in the United States to allegations that President Park Chung Hee himself in 1970 had ordered the massive campaign to win support for South Korea from senators and representatives through lavish entertainment and sizeable gifts of cash. The "Koreagate" revelations strained relations between the United States and South Korea.

On July 21, 1977, President Jimmy Carter sent a message to President Park, the United States Government's position on American ground force withdrawal plans and security commitment to the ROK.

Richard Holbrooke addressed himself to the problems in Korean-American relations in a speech before the Far East-American Council in New York on December 6, 1978. In his speech, Mr. Holbrooke delineated the "triple-crisis" in Korean-American relations; (1) misunderstandings over American troop withdrawal policy; (2) the set of scandals often referred to as "Koreagate"; (3) the problem of human rights in Korea. He remarked, "While our security cooperation is of crucial importance, many other interests bind us together as well. This new reality is one in which we expect to cooperate as allies and friends on an even more mutually beneficial basis than the past."[43]

President Carter during a state visit to Korea in 1979, noted the existance of strong bonds of friendship and cooperation and assured President Park that the U.S. would continue to support the efforts of the Government of Korea to maintain peace and stability and sustain economic and social development. The two Presidents agreed that Korean-American cooperation in maintaining a high degree of strength and combat readiness to deter and defend against possible aggression was an important contribution to peace and stability. The two Presidents noted the importance to all nations of respect for internationally recognized human rights. President Carter expressed the hope that the process of political growth in the ROK would

---

[43] *The Hankook Ilbo*, December 7, 1978.

continue commensurate with economic and social growth of the Korean nation. He also affirmed that the United States would continue to maintain an American Military presence in the ROK to ensure peace and security. Upon his return to Washington he announced a freeze on the withdrawal of U.S. ground combat troops from South Korea until 1981.[44]

Secretary of Defense Harold Brown told senior South Korean military officials on October 18, 1979, that the United States would increase the firepower of American forces here and help South Korea develop its defense industry. At the same time, he delivered to President Park a letter from President Carter in which he again expressed displeasure over South Korea's continued repression of political activity and human rights.

President Park was assassinated by Kim Jae Kyu, the KCIA director in Seoul, on October 26, 1979. Prime Minister Choi Kyu Hah was named acting President after a Cabinet meeting early on the morning of the 27th of October.

Washington repeated its pledge for ROK security, saying that the greatest concern of the United States in South Korea was the security problem. Hodding Carter, spokesman for the U.S. State Department, reiterated on October 30, 1979, that the security commitment to the Republic of Korea was firm. North Korea, in response to U.S. statements reaffirming faithful observance of its defense commitment to the ROK, denounced "the U.S. imperialists who are scheming to maintain the "Yushin (Revitalizing Reform) System" in South Korea.[46]

Some opponents of the late President were hoping for heavy American pressure to push the interim government toward an immediate amendment of the constitution. The Secretary of State was careful to point out on November 2, 1979, that the United States had overlapping interests in stability and security as well as democratic processes of the long-term Asian ally.[47] Vance urged South Korean leaders to move in the direction of political reform but would not suggest that they make sharp changes immediately. The South Korean National Assembly unanimously adopted a motion at the evening of

[44] *The Korea Times*, July 21, 1979.

[45] *The Washington Post*, October 27, 1979.

[46] *The Korea Herald*, October 31, 1979.

[47] *The Washington Post*, November 3, 1979.
Vance was head of the America delegation to the funeral of President Park.

December 1, 1979 calling on the Government to rescind Emergency Decree 9, which President Park Chung Hee's Government used to control its critics.[48] South Korea's martial law commander, Gen. Chung Sung Hwa was arrested December 12 and held for questioning in connection with the assassination of President Park, officials announced in Seoul on December 13, 1979. However, that the South Korean government acted only after the defense security commander, Gen. Chun Doo Hwan, apparently acting without civilian authority, deployed troops against Gen. Chung and other ranking officers who had been widely rumored to be implicated in Park's assassination. By this account, Defense Minister Ro persuaded the force to halt their action when he forced Gen. Chung to resign and placed him and several others under arrest pending an investigation. With that act, South Korean generals broke a long-standing agreement with American forces by withdrawing front-line troops to assist in their internal power struggle on December 12. Any troop movements were supposed to have been authorized by the U.S.-Korea combined Forces Command. The American side was informed only after the fact.[49]

The Carter administration's main concern was to get across two messages to the South Korean military; the first being that the United States would strongly oppose any moves to set back the trend toward responsible political leadership; the other being to remind the South Koreans not to permit a situation to develop that would give the Communist regime in North Korea any reason to believe that it could stage a successful invasion.[50] Ambassador William Gleysteen met with South Korean officials to deliver the sharp U.S. warning, made public at the State Department in Washington on December 12, 1979, against military intervention in the civilian government.[51] When old technocrat Choi Kyu Hah was inaugurated as South Korean President on December 24, 1979, President Carter, in a letter to Choi, underlined his long-standing desire for the country to become more democratic, wishing the new President success "as you preside over constitutional change and the development of a broader political consensus in Korea." The Americans were insisting that the country not slop back into repression.[52] Upon the resignation of President

---

[48] *The New York Times*, December 2, 1979.
[49] *The Washington Post*, December 16, 1979.
[50] *The New York Times*, December 16, 1979.
[51] *The Washington Post*, December 14, 1979.
[52] *The New York Times*, December 21, 1979.

Choi Kyu Hah, the National Conference for Unification elected Gen. Chun Doo Hwan the new President of South Korea on August 27, 1980.[53]

V. Relations with the Reagan Administration

At the invitation of President Ronald Reagan, the President Chun made an official state visit to Washington, D.C. from February 1 to 3, 1981. The two Presidents reviewed the world situation and reaffirmed the critical importance of maintaining peace on the Korean peninsula and in Northeast Asia. President Reagan assured President Chun that U.S. ground combat forces would not be withdrawn from the Korean peninsula and the two leaders agreed that they would resume immediately the full range of consultations between the two governments including the ROK-U.S. Security Consultative Meetings.

VI. Conclusion

Relations between the United States and Korea depend not only on the underlying realities, but also on the views of the American people. The views of Americans towards Korea may be summarized as follows:

Not unexpectedly, in view of "Koreagate" and considerable media attention to reported violations of human rights in the Republic of Korea, Americans are restrained in their warmth toward and support for their ally on the Korean peninsula. Views toward North Korea are far more negative, however. Americans rank both countries relatively low in terms of their importance to American global interests.[54] Americans are not well informed about a number of specific issues concerning Korea, especially the relative economic development of both North and South, and the extent of trade between the United States and South Korea.

With American opposition to the May 16, 1961 military coup,

---

[53] *The Yomiuri Shimbun* (Tokyo), August 28, 1980.
[54] *Clough and Watts, op. cit.,* p. 18.

relations between the two nations became strained. However, with the realization by the U.S. that real power in Korea had always been wielded by the military, the U.S. recognized the defects in her policies. The U.S. government began to try to bring about the transfer of power from military to civilian control through the use of American aid as a policy tool. The U.S., in recognizing the strategic and security importance of the Korean peninsula finally compromised ideals for the sake of reality and came back to a position of strong support for the government of Korea.

Korean dependence on American defense and security assistance made inevitable that she would have to accept American advice and pressure. Such was the case with the normalization of Japanese-Korean relations in 1965 and the introduction of Korean combat troops to Vietnam in 1966. Thus, the period of the Johnson Administration was the one in which Korean-American relations were the closest.

With the promulgation of the "Nixon Doctrine" in 1969, Korean fear of a total withdrawal of American forces and, thus, abandonment by the United States increased dramatically. To deal with changes in the international and domestic situation President Park took several steps, including suppression of dissent, tightened government controls over the mass media and cracked down on student activities. The period from the promulgation of the Nixon Doctrine through the Carter Administration represented the most difficult period in Korean-American relations. Should Jimmy Carter have been elected to a second term in 1980, it is possible that mutual relations could have become even worse.

The United States took prompt action to ensure the security of Korea after the assassination of Park Chung Hee on October 26, 1979. This prompt and strong response to the emergency situation was appreciated by all Koreans.

Shortly after the inauguration of newly-elected President Reagan in 1981, President Chun made a state visit to Washington which represented a turning point in U.S.-Korean relations. Reagan's pledge to freeze all withdrawals of U.S. ground forces and his reaffirmation of the United States' commitment to South Korea's defense were welcomed not only by the Korean people, but by America's other Asian allies as well.[55]

---

[55] *The Washington Post*, November 4, 1979.

The geostrategic context of Korea gives added importance to the U.S. alliance with the Republic of Korea. Realistically, the Republic of Korea has nowhere to turn but to the United States for her security needs. However, since Korea is a proud and sovereign nation, she will constantly assert her independence and insisit on her own priorities. Therefore, in the period ahead Americans must continue to deal with their allies in Korea as equal partners.[56]

The anxiety felt by the South Korean officials during the early years of the Carter Administration gave rise to the realization that U.S.-Korean relations were too heavily dependent upon the changing policies of each American administration and that South Korea should be prepared for the contingency that U.S. security assistance might not be as readily forthcoming as it has been.

However, to say that there has been a change in the nature of the Korean-American alliance is not to mean either that the continued validity of the alliance is being questioned or that the relationship between the two countries will develop into one of near symmetry. South Korea will continue to require American army air and naval support and intellegence and strategic assistance. A substantial portion of Korea's trade will continue to be carried out with the United States. For the United States, Korea will remain a strategically important area in its overall military posture in Asia and the Pacific.[57]

Korea has to become a vivacious liberal democracy with economic affluence to match. Korea has to move itself successfully out of the state of war in which it has been trapped for the past three decades. The threat of another war has to be reduced as much as possible, if not eliminated altogether. Free democracy is not possible without civic discipline and sustained economic development. Political stability and continuing improvement in the standard of living are the essential requisites for national security and political development. The more political and economic development Korea manages to achieve, the greater will be the importance of Korea to the national interests of the United States. This is the only way by which Korea can attain the status of a truly equal partner in a relationship characterized by reciprocal benefit, commonality of interests and mutual

---

[56] *The Korea Herald*, January 27, 1982.
Ambassador Richard Walker's speech at the American Women's club in Seoul on January 26, 1982.

[57] Han Sung-Joo, "South Korea and the United States' Past, Present and Future," *The Journal of Asiatic Studies*. Vol. XXV, No. 1 (1982), p. 299.

respect.[58]

We Koreans trust in the American commitment to the security of our country, but wonder why the United States continually emphasizes that a military presence in Korea is necessary for the defense of Japan. In addition, we find it impossible to forget the tragic case of South Vietnam and the more recent severing of diplomatic relations with Taiwan. The United States must keep her comitments with sincerity and confidence as a great power. History is the eternal witness; therefore, the United States must respect history as the mirror of her conscience.

---

[58] Hahm Pyong-choon, "*Korea U.S. Share Commonality of Ideology,*" *The Korea Herald,* January 7, 1982.

APPENDIX

Korean Export and Import

Year	1980	1981
Export	$17,505,000,000	$20,993,000,000
Import	$22,291,663,000	$26,132,012,000
For U.S. Export	$4,607,000,000 (26.3%)	$5,561,000,000 (26.5%)
From U.S. Import	$4,890,248,000 (21.9%)	$6,050,199,000 (23.2%)

Korea-U.S. Summit Conference

	Korea	United States	Period	Place
1st	Syngman Rhee	Dwight Eisenhower (President elected)	Dec. 2, —Dec. 5, 1952	Seoul
2nd	Syngman Rhee	Eisenhower	July 25—Aug. 13, 1954	Washington, D.C.
3rd	Huh Chung (Acting President)	Eisenhower	June 9—June 20, 1960	Seoul
4th	Park Chung Hee (Chairman)	Kennedy	Nov. 11—Nov. 25, 1961	Washington, D.C.
5th	Park Chung Hee	Johnson	May 16—May 26, 1965	Washington, D.C.
6th	Park Chung Hee	Johnson	Oct. 24—Oct. 25, 1966	Manila, 7 nations' Summit Conference
7th	Park Chung Hee	Johnson	Oct. 31—Nov. 2, 1966	Seoul
8th	Park Chung Hee	Johnson	Dec. 20—Dec. 23, 1967	Canberra (Australia) Funnel of Premier Holt
9th	Park Chung Hee	Johnson	April 17—April 20, 1968	Honolulu
10th	Park Chung Hee	Nixon	Aug. 20—Aug. 23, 1963	San Francisco
11th	Park Chung Hee	Ford	Nov. 22—Nov. 23, 1974	Seoul
12th	Park Chung Hee	Carter	June 29—July 1, 1979	Seoul
13th	Chun Doo Hwan	Reagan	Feb. 1—Feb. 3, 1981	Washington, D.C.

Korean Ambassadors to the United States

	Name	Period	Duration
1st	Chang Myon	Feb. 2, 1949—Feb. 1951	2 years
Charge d'Affairs	Kim Sei Sun	Feb. 1951—April 1951	2 months
2nd	Yang Yoo Chan	April 1951—April 1960	9 years 17 days
3rd	Chung Il Kwon	May 1960—Sept. 1960	3 months 6 days
4th	Chang Yee Wook	October 1960—June 1961	7 months 16 days
5th	Chung Il Kwon	After Military Coup in 1961 June 16, 1961—April 29, 1963	1 year 10 months
6th	Kim Jung Yul	April 29, 1963—November 2, 1964	1 year 6 months
7th	Kim Hyun Chul	November 12, 1964—October 5, 1967	2 years 11 months
8th	Kim Dong Jo	October 5, 1967—December 3, 1973	6 years 2 months
9th	Hahm Pyong Choon	December 31, 1973—May 1977	3 years 5 months
10th	Kim Yong Shik	May 13, 1977—May 30, 1981	4 years 17 days
11th	Yoo Byung Hyon	June 10, 1981—Present	

American Ambassadors to Korea

	Name	Period	Duration
1st	John J. Muccio	August 23, 1948—Sept. 1952	4 years 1 month
2nd	Ellis O. Briggs	November 1952—May 1955	2 years 7 months
3rd	Williams S.B. Lacy	May 1955—July 1956	1 years 2 months
4th	Walter C. Dawling	July 7, 1956—Oct. 2, 1956	3 years 3 months
5th	Walter P. McCanaghy	Dec. 1959—April 1961	1 years 5 months
Charge d'Affairs	Marshall Green	April 1961—June 1961	2 months
6th	Samuel D. Berger	June 24, 1961—July 10, 1964	3 years 1 month
7th	Winthrop P. Brown	August 1964—May 1967	3 years 1 month
8th	William J. Porter	August 1967—August 1971	4 years
9th	Philip C. Habib	October 1971—Aug. 19, 1974	2 years 10 months
10th	Richard L. Sneider	Sept. 7, 1974—June 21, 1978	2 years 9 months
11th	William H. Gleysteen	July 16, 1978—June 10, 1981	2 years 11 months
12th	Richard L. Walker	July 31, 1981—Present	Only Political appointee

Annual U.S.-ROK Defense Ministerial Conference

	Period	Place
1st	May 27—28, 1968	Washington
2nd	June 3—4, 1969	Seoul
3rd	July 21—22, 1970	Honolulu
4th	July 12—13, 1971	Seoul
5th	June 26—27, 1972	Colorado
6th	September 12—13, 1973	Seoul
7th	September 23—24, 1974	Honolulu
8th	August 26—27, 1975	Seoul
9th	May 26—27, 1976	Honolulu
10th	July 25—26, 1977	Seoul
11th	July 26—27, 1978	San Diego
12th	October 18—19, 1979	Seoul
13th	April 29—30, 1981	San Francisco

PART II

U.S.-KOREAN CULTURAL AND SOCIAL RELATIONS

CHAPTER 6

NATIVE CONTRIBUTIONS TO THE SUCCESS OF AMERICA'S MISSIONARY EDUCATIONAL WORK IN KOREA

Sang Ho Lee

I. Introduction

This paper is focused upon the following question: Did Korea's self-awareness have any significant role in contributing to the success of America's mission-initiated educational enterprise there? The fact that America's missionary work in the field of education in Korea has achieved unusual success is widely acknowledged. While this may well be true, one question still remains. Why have their activities flourished in Korea to a greater extent than elsewhere on the Asian mainland? What is the historical basis for this uniqueness? Only recently a few Korean scholars began to ask. Lee Kwang Rin has argued that Korea's indigenous enthusiasm for learning might have been the major factor behind the missionary's success.[1] Son In Soo makes a similar case.[2] The present paper attempts to see whether there is enough historical evidence to support their views.

Although the study covers the past century, it limits its focus to the following: 1) Korea's self-awareness of the need for modernizing education; 2) Korea's enthusiasm for modern learning during the early period of Japanese intervention; 3) Korea's national-consciousness since the March 1st Independence Struggle and its drive for learning; and 4) the educational policy of the Republic of Korea after World War II.

---

[1] 李光麟著, 韓國開化思想 (Lee Kwang Rin, *Studies on the Ideas of Enlightenment in the Later Yi-Dynasty*), 서울, 1979, pp. 249 ff.

II. Korea's Self-Awareness of the Need for Modernizing Education (1882-1910)

1. Consequences of Traditional Education

For many centuries Koreans have set a high value on learning, having adopted both the system of, and reverence for, education from China. As early as the time of Three Kingdoms, Koreans employed the curricula in use in China. Thus for nearly fifteen centuries Korean education was dominated by the traditional Chinese model, one composed mainly of the Chinese classics. Since the reign of King Sun-Dok (640 A.D.) in Silla, Korean education has been largely dominated by the philosophy of Confucius. The spirit of Hwarang-do, emphasizing loyalty and filial piety, was derived from the study of Chinese classics. China's influence culminated at the time of King Shin-Mun in 682 A.D. Korean scholars trained in China were very successful in spreading Buddhist teachings and Confucius philosophy throughout their homeland.[3]

Koryo Dynasty (918-1392) explicitly adopted the Chinese educational system. The government established Guk-Ja Kwan (in 992 A.D.)—later known as Sung Kyun Kwan during the reign of Sung Jong. The state schools designed to prepare students for the civil service examinations included Gugjahag, Taehag, and Jammunhag at the time of In Jong's rule. The curriculum was based on the age old Chinese classics of Dae Kyung, Yeki, Chun Chu, Long Yang, and Chung Kyung. An-Ku, together with distinguished scholars, also introduced I Ching. Buddhist literature of Koryo Dae Jang Kyong, originally developed in China, also had a significant impact on Korean culture. Dong Seo Hag Dang, a kind of State school later known as Obuhagdang, was established by King Won Jong in 1272. It taught almost nothing other than Confucian philosophy.[4]

The Yi dynasty virtually took over Koryo's traditional school system in 1392 A.D. Seong Gyun Gwan of Tae Jong's time (1398) was simply a new name for the already existing school of Guk Ja Gam. A

---

[2] 孫仁銖, 韓國近代教育史, (Son In-Soo, *History of Modern Education in Korea*), 서울, 1971.

[3] 車錫基, 申千湜, 韓國教育史 , (Cha Suk Ki & Shin C.J., *History of Korean Education*), 1969. 三國史記 卷6, 卷8, 高句麗本紀, 新羅本紀.

[4] Cha & Shin, *op. cit.*, p. 59.

number of schools scattered throughout the provinces called Seodang and Sowon focused primarily upon the Confucian classics, though some included indigenous Korean literature. Thus for many centuries Korea's education was dominated by the Chinese model and was characterized by the latter's devotion to the study of the humanities.[5]

There were a few attempts to study scientific issues as early as the Silla dynasty. Mathematics and astrology were taught in some schools. Practical science was occasionally recommended during the Yi Dynasty. The great King Se Jong showed an unusual interest in improving the living standards of his subjects—and toward that end invented a Korean alphabet ("Hangul") which would make it easier for the common person to learn to read and write. Sil Hak, a school of pragmatism, was active for a short period. One of its representatives was Chung Yak Yong who believed that planting fruit trees was more valuable than scribbling a few phrases from the classics.[6] With these few exceptions Korea's traditional educational system focused primarily upon the study of the Chinese classics, neglecting in the process the study of science and technology.

The high status granted detailed study of the classics was of little or no benefit to the illiterate masses. Women in particular suffered, since classical education was reserved for men. The latter used it almost entirely as but a means for personal success rather than to improve societies.

2. The Move toward Enlightenment in the 1880's.

At about the time of the Korean-American treaty of 1882 the Korean government began to show its awareness of the need for new learning by taking initiatives to promote modern Western education. In 1881 more than a hundred of young students headed by Kim Yoon Shik were sent to China to learn Western technology and the weapons it had developed. In 1882 sixty additional observers including Hong Yong Shick were sent to Japan to familiarize themselves with Japan's adoption of a Western system of education. Park Yung Hyo and Kim Ok Kyun, together with 61 students (including the brilliant So Jae Pil), were sent the following year. Kim Ok Kyun also approached R. S. Maclay with a request that missionary work begin in Korea. Delegates under the leader-

---

[5] *Ibid.*, p. 157.
[6] Sohn, Kim & Hong, *The History of Korea*, Seoul, 1970, p. 178.

ship of Min Young Ik were also sent to the United States.[7]

Eagerness for the contact with the West was very obvious in the King's attitude toward the foreign visitors. When R. S. Maclay sought out the monarch in 1884, King Ko-Jong welcomed him and granted permission for missionary educational and medical activities. S. J. Gale later stated that the King always loved the people of England, while D. A. Bunker observed that there has never been a moment he was without the King's gracious care.[8]

Indeed, the King himself had founded the Royal school in which Bunker was invited to teach, thus personally initiating the new era of modern education in Korea.[9] The government also established the first foreign language school, Yook Yong Kong Won, in 1883 where American missionaries were given an opportunity to teach. The first missionary school, operating under the leadership of Dr. Allen, began in the government hospital, Kwang Hye Won. The founding of Bae Chai (1885), Ewha (1886) and Kyung Shin (1886), and a number of other mission schools followed. Underwood was promised with $30,000 as a capital fund and an additional amount for school expenditures in the revitalization of the royal school.[10] As G. Paik has noted, "The Korean government had already taken the first timid steps toward the inauguration of a modern educational program."[11] Had there not been a great interest on the part of the royal family and the government, the missionaries would have never gained such easy entry into the Korean educational system.

Taewongun's earlier isolation policy and the Dong-Hak Revolt (Eastern learning against the Western) may have given the impression that Korea was not willing to adopt Western learning. The revolt was indeed opposed to contact with outside nations, but it focused primarily on the threat of Japanese intrusion. Domestically Dong-Hak leaders were quite progressive. They prepared such reforms as the banning of corruption, the liberation of slaves and permission for

---

[7] Lee Kwang Rin, *op. cit.*, p. 222, Paik, L. G. G., *The History of Protestant Missions in Korea*, Seoul, 1970, pp. 82-3.

[8] 尹周求編, 純宗實紀, 壽一博士 "王家와 西教."

[9] 純宗實紀, 듸·에·ㅅ벙커 – (D.A. Bunker) " 外人의 殊恩感激 " *The Shin Min*, No. 98.

[10] 呉天錫, 韓國新教育史 , (O Chun Suk, *History of Modern Education in Korea)*, 1964, p. 65, L. H. Underwood, *Fifteen Years among the Top-Knots*, New York, 1904, p. 119.

[11] Paik, p. 125.

widows to remarry. "Chuck Sa Pa," a conservative group of Confucian scholars, were also opposed to the introduction of Western religions at the time of the Korean-U.S. treaty. All were aware of the superiority of foreign products, but afraid that importing them might devastate the domestic market.[12]

3. A Nation-wide Campaign for Modern Education

However, many far-sighted Koreans, inspired by contact with the West through China and Japan, actively undertook a nation-wide campaign to open the country to the West. They held that the only way to protect Korea from falling behind economically was to learn the West's advanced knowledge by revamping the country's educational system. Park Yong Hyo argued that the strength of the nation depended on the new learning. Yoo Kil Joon was the most outspoken campaigner. Awakened by studying in Japan, and stimulated further through visiting many countries in the West, Yoo emphasized the need of modernizing education through his famous "Suh Yu Kyun Mun." He was convinced that the strongest and richest nations in the West had achieved their goals through education. Lee Kun stressed that the nation's future power demanded the renovation of education. Pak Un Shik, a proponent of mass education, insisted that of first priority was the training of a large number of teachers. So Jae Pil propagated the need of new learning through publishing the "Independent" (1895-98). Kang Wee encouraged contact with the West primarily through the United States, since its commitment to national and international justice would make it unlikely that America would seek to exploit Korea in an imperialistic manner.[13] It is significant at the very time that the missionaries began opening modern schools, Korean intellectuals were passionately engaged in campaigning for their acceptance and full use. It was during this period (1894-1909) that additional major mission schools were founded. The 34 mission schools included Chong Eui (1894), Sung Shil (1897), Kye Sung (1906), Shin Sung (1906).

Another obvious indication that the Koreans' eagerness to pursue the new learning has been a contributive factor to the success of

---

[12] Sohn, et al., *op. cit.*, p. 211, cf., Lee, *op. cit.*, p. 213, 韓㿥壽著, 近代韓國民族主義研究, 서울, 1977, p. 71.

[13] Lee, *op. cit.*, p. 24, 孫仁銖, 韓國開化教育研究 (Son In-Soo, *Studies in Modern Education in Korea*), 1980, p. 24.

mission education is shown in the fact that a large group of Korean students pursuing the new knowledge in Japan voluntarily converted to Christianity. Ri Intei was, according to some sources, one of those students. He in fact played a great role in stimulating the churches in America to open their mission work in Korea. The enthusiasm of Koreans for modern learning clearly led to their acceptance of Christianity as well.[14] McKenzie reported: "Tens of converts grew to tens of thousands. They started by reforming their homes, giving their wives liberty, and demanding education for children." "Koreans themselves (were converting to Christianity)··· in distant communities where no white men had ever been seen."[15] Fisher also made note of the fact that Koreans realized their need for modern scientific methods and that there were not enough schools to meet their needs.[16] It appears safe to conclude that the passionate desire on the part of Koreans for modern education was growing precisely at the time that missionaries were promoting Christianity through the founding of educational institutions which would help fill the Koreans' felt needs.

III. Enthusiasm for Modern Learning during the Early Japanese Intrusion.

1. Emergence of Modern Schooling among Koreans

The year 1906, and particularly the year 1910, are marked as the beginning of great tragedy for Korea: the Japanese intrusion upon Korea's sovereignty. The Portsmouth treaty not only affirmed Japan's right to colonize Korea, but it was supported by President Theodore Roosevelt. Thus began Japan's exploitation of Korea's economy for her own, rather than the Koreans', interest. Japan established the office of Resident-General in 1906 and Government-General since 1910, to carry out their colonial policy. Korea's education was under their overall control.[17]

Still, there can be no doubt that many mission schools came into existence during this time. McKenzie's statement that "Almost the

---

[14] Paik, *op. cit.*, pp. 77-79.
[15] F.A. McKenzie, *Fight for Freedom*, Seoul, 1969, pp. 208-09.
[16] J.E. Fisher, *Democracy and Mission Education in Korea*, Seoul, 1970, pp. 8-10.
[17] Sohn, et al., *op. cit.*, pp. 234-35.

whole of the real modern education of Korea was undertaken by the missionaries, who were maintaining 778 schools" appears to have been an exaggeration. Underwood asserted that, as of 1910, 666 were Protestant, a figure which may have included many schools operated by Koreans. The Japanese Government-General claimed that there were 5,000 private schools in 1908,[18] though the figure is suspect since the schools were not classified according to their level. We have no formal government statistics because private schools were not required to register until Japan took over responsibility for educational policy.

It is also clear that the majority of modern private schools were founded by Koreans. Pak Chong Wha, one well-known writer, observed that a popular phrase of that time was that "only learning is power" and that there were as many great teachers in Korea as there were stars in the heaven. Though their activities were cruelly repressed by the Japanese, Hwang Hyun reported that there were more than 20 schools in as small a county as Yong Chun Gun.[19] Some described the students rushing in like waves from the ocean.[20] Clearly thousands of schools were established by Koreans. Among the more distinctive were "Hung Hwa" (1895), Nak Yons (1896), Suh Woo Teachers (1907), "O Sung" (1907), "Kee Ho" (1908), Dae Sung (1907), O San (1907) and Jin Myung (1906).

A More significant fact is that most of the founders of these private schools were nationally known figures endowed with charisma and patriotism: Min Yong Hwan, a former diplomat, An Chang Ho, Lee Sung Hun, Lee Young Ik, Nam Gung Hyuk, Lee Shin Young, Lee Bong Rhae, Min Young Hee, and Kim Ku among many others.[21]

Their desire for new knowledge is clearly visible in their introduction of radically new curricula. Hung Hwa Institute included land surveying and engineering in addition to foreign languages. Many of these private schools sought to produce future teachers trained in such modern disciplines as geography, physics, chemistry, biology and mathematics. The shift from the old system was even more apparent in the high priority granted physical education and music. The emphasis on physical education was strengthened by the military officers who had previously served in the Korean army, thus guarantee-

---

[18] Son, *History of Modern Education*, p. 86.

[19] *Ibid.*, p. 34, O, op. cit., p. 250.

[20] Son, *op. cit.*, p. 33.

[21] O, *op. cit.*, pp. 110 ff.

ing the continuation of Korean national consciousness. One of the most representative of the new schools was Dae Sung, where the classical ordering of discipline was reversed to emphasize health above virtue and virtue above intelligence. Among the radical innovations was the establishment of a girls' school (Yang Kyu) in 1907. Coeducation was introduced as well.[22]

The continued link between the Korean desire for modernization and the activity of missionary educators is suggested by the fact that the latter were most successful in the provinces where Koreans themselves showed a special eagerness for modern education. Mission schools flourished in those northwestern provinces where the greatest enthusiasm for modern education was to be found.[23] People in these provinces were more acutely aware of advanced foreign technology as well as more resentful of the deep-rooted discrimination they had faced from those southern provinces which had been centers of traditional classic education.[24]

2. Japan's New Educational Policy

The Japanese office of Residential-General and more particularly that of the Government-General soon introduced policies which sought to exercise a new educational policy to suppress educational zeal of Koreans on the assumption that it was associated with Korean nationalism. A great number of schools founded by Koreans were ordered closed, Chung-Nyun Hak Won in 1914, Hwang Sung and Bong Myung in 1912, Jung Ri Sa in 1913, Dae Dong in 1916, and Yang San in 1910.[25] Many others threatened with closure. Numerous founders and heads of schools were imprisoned or removed from their positions. Many mission schools suffered a similar fate, for they sheltered many students opposed to Japanese rules. rules. The total number of private schools dropped from 2,080 in 1910 to 742 in 1919. Japan also sought, through the office of Government-General, to lower the level of Korean schools in order to enfeeble Korean national consciousness.

Takahashi issued a regulation to promote "practical" education,

---

[22] Son, *op. cit.*, pp. 29 ff.

[23] *Ibid.*, p. 35.

[24] 純宗實紀, 李昇薰, "西北人의 宿怨新慟 " p. 203, Lee, *op. cit.*, pp. 239 ff.

[25] Son, *op. cit.*, p. 252, Two hundred schools were closed between 1915-1917, O, *op. cit.*, p. 275.

hoping it would aid in decreasing political interest in Korea.[26] Terauchi, the government general, issued an educational act in 1911 along with an imperial edict for Japanizing Koreans so as to gain control over the private schools. The revised edition of Regulation of Governing private schools in 1915 served the purpose of reducing Korea's private schools.[27] A small number of public shcools on the high school levels were established mainly for Japanese. Very few Koreans were permitted to attend them. Saito in 1919 appeared to be easing the pressure by shifting from Hasegawa's policy of military oppression to the promotion of cultural activity and revised the school curricula drastically. But the real purpose was to discriminate against the education of Koreans. Yet an Act in 1922 appeared to provide for greater equality of Korea's educational system vis-à-vis Japan's and increased the school years relatively close to that of Japan. In contrast a campaign for "Kokugo choyo" (daily use of Japanese) was designed to hamper the use of the Korean language. In 1927 Yamanashi revived the earlier policies of Terauchi.[28] Ugaki, in 1931, stressed labor education in order to secure enough manpower to further exploit the Korean economy. In 1938 Minami went so far as to use military force to mobilize manpower for the anticipated war with the U.S. Minami promulgated the 3rd revised educational action in 1938 to assimilate Koreans as "royal citizens" of the Japanese empire. This enabled him to replace all Korean school administrators of schools by Japanese and reduce the teaching of English. The 4th educational act in 1941 reduced the number of required years of schooling. Part of the curriculum was replaced by military training. Throughout this period the Japanese promoted policies which would lower the level of Korean's private schools and limit the study of Korean language and history.[29]

3. The Missionary Policy

Some missionary educators in the early period of Japanese occupation were very sympathetic to the national spirit among Korean students. G. S. McCune, the principal of Shin Sung Istitute, not only encouraged his Korean students to fight bravely against Japanese

---

[26] Son, *op. cit.*, p. 79.

[27] *Ibid.*, p. 251.

[28] O, *op. cit.*, p. 287.

[29] *Ibid.*, p. 229 ff., Son, *op. cit.*, pp. 55, 166, 241.

colonialism, but also participated in the March 1st movement.[30] Missionaries protested the Government General's policy whenever they believed it would harm their evangelistic programs. However, in most cases the missionaries tolerated Japanese rules and took a neutral attitude toward Korea's opposition to Japanese rule. Fisher stated:

> In the first place, it can be announced that missionaries have no intention of overturning Japanese and authority in Korea. . . . . They have no power to make any move in this direction and they would not use it if they had. . . . . It would be very evident to all intelligent and fair-minded Koreans that to expect any assistance from foreign missionaries, which might involve direct interference in the political affairs of the country, would not only be futile, but that such expectations and activities which might grow out of them would seriously hamper the missionaries in their legitimate and proper educational enterprise. . . . . Missionaries declared that they would be neutral in political matters.[31]

Grajdenzeb sees this neutrality as a failure of the missionary enterprise. He believes that they should have been more helpful to those Koreans who were endeavoring to shift from their feudalism to America's democracy.[32]

Because of their neutrality and their relative cooperation with Japanese authorities, mission schools may have been less severly restricted than Korean schools. The decrease of the numbers of Korean private schools should not be interpreted as evidence of a decrease in the educational enthusiasm of Koreans. Their suppression in fact inflamed the students' national consciousness and maintained their faith in the advantage of education.

IV. Educational Consciousness after March 1st Independence Struggle

1. Students in the Uprise

The earlier nation-wide uprising on March 1st of 1919 symbolized the nation's struggle for independence from the Japanese. Many

---

[30] *Ibid.*, p. 81.
[31] Fisher, *op. cit.*, p. 100.
[32] A.J. Grajdanzeb, *Modern Korea*, (韓國의 現代史論, 李基白譯), Seoul, 1944, p. 278.

Christian leaders and missionaries were involved. F.W. Schofield, G.S. McCune, R. Gierson, and E.M. Mowry participated.[33] When Japanese troops imprisoned 30 Korean villagers in a Christian Church in Suwon, closed all the windows, and set a fire to the building, killing all (including women and infants) and burned 317 more houses in the vicinity, some missionaries helped Koreans to disclose the Japanese atrocities to the world.[34] Because of this incident the missionaries' opposition to the Japanese was often exaggerated.

The primary opposition to the Japanese came not from the mission students but from the better informed Korean students abroad in Tokyo. The student movement was not confined to the mission schools but was nation-wide. Students from Christian and non-Christian schools, including Buddhist and Chondoist founded schools and Koreans from the public schools were united in the uprising. Choi Un Hee, the first student arrested, belonged to a public school. In fact many of the participants were from non-missionary private schools.

After being subdued by the Japanese military forces, the heart of the united movement of independence was converted into many small groups of students. Again, these activities were not limited to the schools of Christian mission. Head masters in charge of Korean private schools first organized Korea's Education Society (Chosun Hak Hwe) chaired by Lee Sang Jae in 1920. More than a thousand students from Christian, non-Christian private schools, and public schools gathered and organized the Chosun Student's Federation in 1924. Kun U Hwe and a few other underground circles were organized in 1927. The Kwang Ju incidence in 1929 merely rekindled a sense of national unity among students and turned them into a new driving force to encourage learning.[35]

2. Effort to Raise the Standard to University Level.

Many private school leaders united in an attempt to raise the standard of Korean's private education by raising their institutions to the university level in 1920. Japan denied their request and instead established Kei-Jo Imperial University in Seoul for their colonial

---

[33] Son, *op. cit.*, p. 136.
[34] Sohn, et al., *op. cit.*, p. 264.
[35] Son, *op. cit.*, pp. 200 ff.

purpose. Only a limited number of Koreans had access to this university: 12% in the natural sciences and 37% in humanities and social sciences. "Korean youth were virtually deprived of the opportunity to receive higher education."[36] Some of the missionaries managed to elevate their schools to Junior College level. Yon Hee, Ewha, Sung Shil, and Severance Medical schools were registered as Junior Colleges. They termed themselves "colleges" in English and continued their efforts to elevate them to the university level. Avison and Underwood are to be credited for making enormous effort for this task through their fund-raising campaigns. But their dream was not fulfilled during Japan's domination of Korea.

It should be noted that Koreans made a similar effort. As early as during the initial independence movement, the Chosun Educational Association started an action-committee as a move toward founding a Korean University. A number of Korean publications and journalists gave them full support. Despite the unfavourable economic situation—including famine and Japan's land exploitations—the fund-raising was unable to reach its goal. Even if it had, the project probably would not have been realized because of the severe policy of educational suppression on the part of Japan. Nevertheless the funds raised became an important basis for maintaining and strengthening Korean Bo Sung civilian college. The school has now grown to Korea University, one of the largest and highest qualified universities in Korea. The move toward elevating the school level among the Korean private schools continued in many high schools by setting up specialized departments within the schools.[37]

3. Mass Enlightenment Movement

As Japan's colonial policy hampered Korea's private schools, Korea's enthusiasm for education took on a new form: the mass enlightenment movement. A number of awakened students from all types of schools were united to demonstrate their eagerness to teach by engaging in mass education, believing that the new knowledge would be the best foundation for building the nation's economy and national spirit. Students from Christian and non-Christian schools alike joined in the movement for a self-supporting economy (Ja Jak

---

[36] *Ibid.*, p. 285.
[37] *Ibid.*, pp. 177 ff.

Hwe) in 1922 to increase the interest in domestic products: a movement against the "colonial economic shackles." The study of economics for the national interest became a central attraction among students.[38] A Cooperative Society was organized by students in Tokyo such as Chun Jin Han. Kyung Sung Students introduced socialism. Students were not only interested in social reform and national welfare but even in women's liberation. All these movements toward enlightenment were the result of Korean national consciousness. It must not be viewed as merely the fruit of the external influence of Mission schools. It was a universal phenomenon among all Korean private schools.

Another significant movement is found in the intensification of the study of Korean history, culture, and language among Koreans themselves. The Government-General's sly attempt to distort Korean history and culture was seen in its establishment of the Korean Language Research Institute and the Korean's History Compilation Society. These organizations were aimed at distorting Korean viewpoints through the perspective of Japanese scholars in order to downgrade Korea's national confidence in its ability to obtain independence. Many Korean scholars refused to compromise with these Japanese distortions and began their own studies by themselves. Chu Si Gyung revived the intensive study in Korean language and Hangul (a journal started by Lee Yun Jae) appeared in 1923. Many prominent scholars from mission and non-mission schools came to be devoted in the study of Korea through the organization of Cho Son O Hak Hwe, a research society, in 1921.[39] Chu Si Gyung's publications on Korean grammar and phonetics, Choe Hyun Bae's Korean dictionary and Urimalbon, and Kim Eun Gyung's works are a few examples of efforts of that period. The wide range of devoted scholars will clearly indicate that they were not inspirated merely by mission schools but by all factions opposed to Japanese oppression. A few names of the noted Korean scholars involved are: Chu Si Gyung, Chang Chi Young, Yi Pyonggi, Kwon Tak Kyu, Yi Sang Chun, Shin Myung Gyun, and Kim Eun Gyung, Choe Hyun Bae. Likewise the historians among Koreans were no less eager to protest Japanese fabrication of Korea's history. Pak Un Sik, Sin Chae Ho, An Chae Hong, and Chong In Bo are a few notable names among them. It is apparent

---

[38] *Ibid.*, p. 202.
[39] Sohn, et al., *op. cit.*, p. 301.

that their motivation for eager study has a direct link with their national consciousness[40] and not directly with the mission education. Korea's sense of national identity was further demonstrated by the wide support of Korea's daily newspapers operated by Koreans. The newspapers in turn supported the efforts of "Vnarod" squads organized by students to stamp out illiteracy beginning in 1930.[41]

As the Japanese colonial policies were intensified, missionaries also faced a serious conflict with Japan's policy requiring the worship at Shinto Shrines and the exclusion of bible study from school curricula. Finally all missionary initiative in educational activities was put to an end between 1937-41. Japan took over the mission schools. Still the fervent desire of learning among Koreans kept burning despite all the efforts of Japan to quench the flames of Korean nationalism. Korean scholars went through severe torture and imprisonment. Yet they have never surrendered their devotion to national studies. They kept the flame of learning burning—passing the light of Korean studies to the new dawn of the Republic of Korea after liberation. This nationalist fervor among Koreans must be taken into account in any assessment of educational activities in Korea.

V. Struggle for Self-Identity after Liberation (1945-   ) as Reflected in the Government's Educational Policy

1. First Republic of Korea

With the victory of the U.S. over Japan, Korea was liberated in 1945. The U.S. military government in 1945 marked a new era as a great opportunity for the U.S. to provide a maximum influence on Korea. Yet the U.S. military government in Korea was not prepared to alter Korean education. Captain E. L. Lockerd was appointed to be in charge of Korea's education but had little knowledge of its history. He soon wisely turned his responsibility over to the Korean Committee on Education composed of leading Korean educators who had survived the Japanese colonial policies by at least minimal cooperation with them. Although their guideline was to adopt de-

---

[40] *Ibid.*, p. 304.
[41] Son, *op. cit.*, p. 223.

mocratic principles, their spirit of national independence and en-
deavor to identify themselves with the ideology of nation's pre-
Japanese tradition frequently submerged democracy in the waters of
tradition.[42]

In 1948, the government of Republic of Korea was established in
accordance with the principle of American democracy. Despite the
strong emphasis on the fairly new idea of an elective Republic, An
Ho Sang, the head of the Ministry of Education, came up with a
modified nationalism as the basic goal of education. The Educational
Law in 1949 reasserted the age-old traditional idea of *Hong Ik In Gan*
i.e., maximum service to humankind or the common prosperity of
mankind (a traditional Korean view of democracy).[43] The idea was
presented during South Korea's lengthy battle to defend itself against
the threat of communist domination from the north. The Education
Ministry constantly revised the objectives of education during and
after the Korean War. George Paik set forth the theme of Il-In Il Ki,
(one skill for the individual) as the goal of education, along with an
emphasis on human service to achieve industrial prosperity.[44] Since
the destruction of the nation's economy during the Korean War, the
country's economic buildup has always been the government's
primary concern. Choe Kyu Nam accordingly stressed the primacy of
technological skills to increase the nation's productivity. Choe Jae
Kyu put his emphasis on improving science and technology. Long
range educational ideals were necessarily subject to shorter run
economic priorities.

2. Second Republic of Korea

Although democracy has always been a basic principle of Korean
education, it has never been achieved in practice. The student uprising
in 1960 served temporarily to halt political corruptions and to provide
an opportunity to exercise democratic rules in the government. Unfortunately, it also enabled many to raise the spector of communism
as a threat to a relatively unstable government. Americans arranged
economic assistance through UNKRA and UNESKO to rehabilitate
the war-ruined schools. But democracy has never found a way to root

---

[42] 서울신문사편, 주한미군30년, 서울.

[43] 한국교육문제연구소편, 文教史 , 문교부편, 문교개관, 서울, 단기 4291, pp. 17-22,
p. 141.

[44] 自樂瀋著, "新文教政策" 韓國教育과 民族精神, 서울 단기 4292, p. 51.

itself deeply in Korea's soil.[45]

3. Third, Fourth Republic of Korea

Park's government was conscious of its immediate needs. A government report said: "Korean education intensively addressed itself to the development of technological know-how beginning in the early 1960's." Democracy as understood in the United States was not applied as unfitting in the emerging situation. According to government issued documents education was to be linked primarily to economic needs rather than political representation. This policy was put into effect with the enactment of Industrial Education Promotion Law in 1963. Many measures have been enacted to assure strict control over schools so that they follow the government policy. Min Kwan Shik, the head of the Ministry of Education, endorsed the forceful policy of Yu-Sin education initiated in 1972 by justifying it in terms of the need for national security and economic development. Since then, the government has claimed the need for a special democracy within a Korean context and stressed an education that would support both it and a flourishing economy.[46]

VI. Conclusion

The study has now revealed much of the facts known to Korean scholars. The most important one is that there has always been an overwhelming desire among many far-sighted Koreans for a shift from the traditional towards the Western system of education. To some extent, this desire served as an initiative in inviting American Protestant missionaries' activities into Korea. The active work of the missionaries has been paralleled with the labor of many ardent Koreans who were dedicated to facilitating the introduction of modern Western education.

Another significant fact demonstrated in this review, is that the

---

[45] 한국교육문제연구소 , *op. cit.*, p. 439, 대한어머니회, **韓國教育30年史** , 서울 , 1968, p. 305.

[46] 한국교육문제연구소 , *op. cit.*, p. 552, Ministry of Education, Republic of Korea, *Education in Korea*, Seoul, 1977, p. 25, On "Yu-Shin Education," see 대한어머니회 , *op. cit.*, p. 273.

enthusiasm of Koreans was not caused primarily by the stimulation from missionaries but by their national consciousness. Under Japanese rule, when most avenues towards independence were closed, their national feeling for independence increased their passion for new learning. Their desire for modern learning and their devotion for their national studies were expressions of concern for long-term preparation for strengthening their nation by way of adopting the Western system of learning modern technology and science.

Upon these factual bases the study concludes that the awareness of Koreans themselves of their need for new learning, coupled with a strong national spirit has been the driving force behind the success of missionaries' educational work. Overlooking this awareness among Koreans would not do justice to the part they played in the startling success of missionary sponsored education in Korea.

BIBLIOGRAPHY

車錫基, 申千湜, **韓國教育史硏究**, 서울, 載東文化社, 1969.

鄭相昏編著, **韓國新教育百年史料**, 서울, 民主與論社.

대한 사립 중고등학교장회, **韓國의 私學**, 서울, 民衆書舘 , 1974.

Fisher, James Earnest; *Democracy and Mission Education in Korea*, Seoul, Yon Sei University Press, 1970.

Grajdanzeb, Andrew Jonah, *Modern Korea*,
    韓國의 現代史論, 李基白譯 , Seoul Institute of Pacific Relation 1944.

韓興壽, **近代 韓國民族主義硏究**, 서울, 연세대출판부, 1977.

한국교육문제연구소편, **文教史**, 서울, 1968.

韓基彦, **韓國教育史**, 서울 博英社, 1963.

金元姬, **韓國의 改化教育思想**, 서울, 載東文化社, 1979.

金千鎰, 金炳廈, **韓國西洋教育史**, 서울, 영설출판, 1977.

李光麟 , **韓國開化思想硏究**, 서울, 一潮閣, 1979. (Lee, Kwang Rin, *Studies on the Ideas of Enlightenment in the Later Yi-Dynasty*)

McKenzie, F.A., *Korea's Fight for Freedom*, Seoul, Yon Sei University Press, 1969.

문교부편, 문교개관, 서울, 대한문교서적 닦기 4791

Ministry of Education, Republic of Korea, *Education in Korea*, Seoul, National Institute of Education, 1977.

吳天錫 , **韓國新教育史**, 서울 , 현대교육총서출판사, 1964. (O, Chun Suk, *History of Modern Education in Korea*)

Paik Lak-Geoon George, *The History of Protestant Missions in Korea*, Seoul, Yon Sei University Press, 1970.

Sohn, Pow-Key, Kim, Chol-Choon, Hong, Yi-Sup, *The History of Korea*, Seoul, Korean National Commission for UNESCO, 1970.

서울신문사 편저 , **駐韓美軍 30년** 서울 , 否林出版社, 1979.

孫仁銖 , **韓國 近代 教育史** , 서울 , 연세대출판부, 1971. (Son, In-Soo, *History of Modern Education in Korea*)

孫仁銖 , **韓國開化教育硏究** , 서울, 一志社, 1980. (Son, In-Soo, *Studies in Modern Education in Korea)*

Underwood, H.H., *Modern Education in Korea*, New York, International Press, 1926.

尹周求 , **純宗實紀** , *The Shin Min.* No. 98 서울 , 大正 15년.

CHAPTER 7

AMERICAN IMAGE OF KOREA IN 1882:
A BIBLIOGRAPHICAL SKETCH

Shannon McCune

In 1882 most Americans had never heard of Korea, nor would they have been embarassed by their ignorance. They had many national concerns and were not interested in a distant, strange peninsula. A few Americans had some superficial knowledge of the existence of the Hermit Nation somewhere near China; their interests were mainly in the potential of Korea as a market for surplus American products. The exclusiveness of Korea seemed to have intrigued a handful of American scholars, but they had few books and source materials available to satisfy their curiosity.[1] Though the state of American knowledge of Korea has improved considerably in the intervening century, there is still ignorance and an American image of Korea that has many distortions.

By 1882 the United States had recovered economically from the Civil War and was in a period which has been over-generalized, in Mark Twain's words, as The Gilded Age.[2] The ill-advised and vindic-

---

[1] There are a number of bibliographies on Korea which give references to the literature on Korea available to American scholars. The Bibliography given in William Elliot Griffis, *Corea, The Hermit Nation*, Charles Scribner's Sons, New York, 1882, pp. xix-xxv, along with his bibliographical notes on "Study by Europeans" of the Korean language and on "Cartography" are interesting. Two very useful bibliographies are G. St.G. M. Gompertz, "Bibliography of Western Literature on Korea from the Earliest Times until 1950", *Transactions of the Korea Branch, Royal Asiatic Society*, Volume XL, Seoul, 1963, ii, 263 pages, and Han-kyo Kim, Editor, *Studies on Korea, A Scholar's Guide*, The University Press of Hawaii, Honolulu, 1980, xxi, 438 pages.

[2] 1882 was an interesting but not very definitive date in American history. The general histories of the United States are apt to give very short notice to this period after the Civil War and before the exciting times of Theodore Roosevelt. Four modern

tive Reconstruction which paralyzed the South had come to an end. Industrialization had made major advances in the Northeast and Mid-West of America. Associated with this industrializaton were the growth of cities and the building of railroads. Pioneer lands were being opened in the West. California was considered an El Dorado. Great numbers of European immigrants were flowing through New York to provide workers for expanded industries and farmers for newly opened lands. The Republican Party was in control of the national government though, because of splits among the Republicans, the Democratic Party with its uneasy alliance of the Solid South and the Northern city bosses would be able to elect Grover Cleveland President in 1884.

The New Commonwealth, as it was called by the eminent American historian—John A. Garraty, was well started by 1882. He writes that ". . . between 1877 and 1890 the character of American civilization underwent a basic transformation. . . . The change took the form of a greatly expanded reliance by individuals upon group activities. Industrialization with its accompanying effects—speedy transportation and communication, specialization, urbanization—compelled men to depend far more than in earlier times on organizations in managing their affairs, to deal with problems collectively rather than as individuals."[3] Among these American organizations were Protestant churches, dedicated to the spreading of Christian beliefs, particularly in Asia. These missionary bodies coupled beliefs in conservative and militant Protestant Christianity with dynamic American democracy. They provided a strong emphasis on the expansion of American interests abroad, though they were not able effectively to penetrate

---

books which are relevant to the period but which give only passing mention to the Korean-American Treaty of 1882 are: John A. Garraty, *The New Commonwealth, 1877-1890,* Harper & Row, New York, 1968, xv, 364 pages; Ray Ginger, *Age of Excess, The United States from 1877 to 1914,* The Macmillan Company, New York, 1965, x, 386 pages; Margaret Leech and Harry J. Brown, *The Garfield Orbit,* Harper & Row, New York, 1978, xi, 369 pages; and David M. Pelcher, *The Awkward Years, American Foreign Relations under Garfield and Arthur,* University of Missouri Press, 1962, xvi, 381 pages. Pelcher's book discusses Korea in a rather pedestrian way on pages 205-214. The novel by Mark Twain and Charles Dudley Warner, *The Gilded Age, A Tale of Today,* American Publishing Company, Hartford, Conn., 1888, 574 pages, was published in many editions; it is rather convoluted but gives an interesting picture of the period.

[3] Garraty, *op. cit.,* p. xiii.

Korea until after 1882.[4] In addition to the missionary contacts, American trading and business companies were eagerly seeking markets for American industrial products.

As early as 1845 Congressman Zadoc Pratt of New York had urged that "immediate measures be taken for effecting commercial arrangements with the Empire of Japan and the Kingdom of Corea."[5] However, the mission of Commodore Matthew C. Perry in 1853 and 1854 limited itself only to signing treaties with Japan and the Liu Chiu Kingdom. American traders and whale fishermen had expanded their activities in the ill-charted Far Eastern waters. Because of the hazards of shipwrecks, attempts were made to rescue seamen and to open trade with Korea. Notable was the *General Sherman* incident of 1866 when an American trading vessel consigned to a British company went up the Taetong River to P'yongyang on an exceptionally high lunar tide, swollen by heavy summer rains, only to be stranded. Provoked by actions of the polyglot crew, Koreans set fire to the ship and killed its owner, master, crew and passengers, including a Protestant missionary.[6] Subsequently in 1871, an American naval expedition attacked and destroyed the antiquated forts on

---

[4] The Protestant Christian missionary movement in Korea has been described and discussed in many books and articles. References may be found in the standard bibliographies. One of the best books on the early period is L. George Paik, *The History of Protestant Missions in Korea, 1832-1910*, Union Christian College Press, P'yongyang, Korea, 1929, reprinted by the Yonsei University Press, Seoul, 1970, 470 pages. The almost symbiotic relations between missionaries, business interests and governments is well described in Fred Harvey Harrington, *God, Mammon, and the Japanese: Dr. Horace N. Allen and Korean-American Relations, 1884-1905*, University of Wisconsin Press, Madison, 1944. A useful general book is Allen D. Clark, *A History of the Church in Korea*, Christian Literature Society of Korea, Seoul, Rev. Ed., 1971, 479 pages.

[5] Quoted from Griffis, *op. cit.*, p. 390. Zadoz Pratt was Chairman of the House of Representatives Committee on Naval Affairs who introduced a proposition for the extension of American commerce on February 12, 1845.

[6] The *General Sherman* incident is well recorded in some of the books on Korean-American relations listed in *Studies on Korea*. A rather interesting early American investigation of the incident is noted in a report dated July 24, 1885, in George M. McCune and John A. Harrison, *Korean-American Relations, Documents pertaining to the Far Eastern Diplomacy of the United States, Volume I, The Initial Period, 1883-1886*, University of California Press, Berkeley, viii, 163 pages, in particular pages 44-50. I recall as a high school student in the late 1920's seeing the iron anchor chains of the *General Sherman* hanging in loops along the second tier of the Taedong (or East) Gate in P'yongyang. I presume that they were destroyed during the Korean War.

Kanghwa Island near the mouth of the Han River leading to Seoul. The Americans withdrew after inflicting heavy casualties, just as the French had from their expedition against Kanghwa in 1866. These withdrawals gave credence to the effectiveness of the exclusionary policy of the Taewon'gun, the Korean regent. An American newspaper, the *New York Herald,* called the American Naval action: "Our Little War with the Heathen," but there was little American reaction or concern.[7]

Though some interest has revived recently in these early episodes of Korean-American relations, in 1882 the United States was only mildly concerned with Korea.[8] There was a segment of American naval stra-

---

[7] It would be of value to make a study of the contemporary newspaper accounts of the American expedition of 1871. Since 1950 interest has been aroused over both the American action as well as that of the French of 1866. The attacks on the Korean forts on Kanghwa Island have been well described in Ching Young Choe, *The Rule of the Taewon'gun, 1864-1873, Restoration in Yi Korea,* Harvard East Asian Monographs, No. 45, Harvard University Press, Cambridge, 1972, xviii, 269 pages. A very well referenced study, broader in scope than its title indicates, is Robert Swartout, Jr., "Cultural Conflict and Gunboat Diplomacy: The Development of the 1871 Korean-American Incident," *Journal of Social Sciences and Humanities,* The Korean Research Center, Seoul, No. 43, June, 1976, pp. 117-169.

[8] There has been a resurgence of scholarly inquiry into the events of the last years of the Yi dynasty and of Korean-American relations. This research is well summarized in an essay and an annotated bibliography by Young Ick Lew, "The Late Yi (Choson) Dynasty, 1876-1910," *Studies on Korea,* pp. 80-101. In addition to the study by the late Ching Young Choe, *The Rule of the Taewon'gun,* other doctoral dissertations by scholars in American universities have appeared in book and monograph form. Four of them are especially interesting: James B. Palais, *Politics and Policy in Traditional Korea,* Harvard University Press, Cambridge, 1975, 300 pages; Martina Deuchler, *Confucian Gentlemen and Barbarian Envoys, The Opening of Korea, 1875-1885,* University of Washington Press, Seattle, 1977, xiv, 310 pages; In K. Hwang, *The Korean Reform Movement of the 1880's, A Study in Transition in Intra-Asian Relations,* Schenkman Publishing Company, Cambridge, 1978, x, 163 pages; and Harold F. Cook, *Korea's 1884 Incident, Its Background and Kim Ok-kyun's Elusive Dream,* Royal Asiatic Society, Korea Branch, Seoul, 1972, 4 pages. Dr. Cook has also written some interesting articles such as one on "Early American Contacts with Korea," *Transactions, Royal Asiatic Society, Korea Branch,* Volume 55, 1980, pp. 85-107.

One young American scholar was killed in an accident in 1968 before completing his Ph.D. dissertation, but some of his lecture notes were assembled into a small and very readable book: George A. McGrane, *Korea's Tragic Hours, the Closing Years of the Yi Dynasty,* Taewon Publishing Company, Seoul, 1973, 85 pages. Two recent books are Robert Swartout, Jr., *Mandarins, Gunboats, and Power Politics: Owen Nickerson Denny and the International Rivalries in Korea,* The University Press of Hawaii,

tegists, following the theories of Mahan and others, that wished to expand American interests in the Pacific, "the American lake." But their influence was not great outside a limited circle.[9]

In the period immediately preceding 1882 James G. Blaine, Secretary of State under President James A. Garfield, had been very active.[10] Blaine had sought to develop American interests in Korea by instructing Commodore Robert W. Shufeldt, who was then in the Far East to

---

Honolulu, 1980, and Key-Huik Kim, *The Last Phase of the East Asian World Order: Korea, Japan and the Chinese Empire, 1860-1882,* University of California Press, Berkeley, 1980, 441 pages.

[9] The influence of American naval strategic thinking on Japan and other areas of the Pacific Ocean has been the subject of some recent studies. Charles Oscar Paullin in his *Diplomatic Negotiations of American Naval Officers, 1778-1883,* The Johns Hopkins Press, Baltimore, 1912, 380 pages, quotes on page 302 from a letter from Commodore Robert W. Shufeldt to Secretary of the Navy Thompson written on October 13, 1880. In this letter there is this phrase: ". . . the Pacific Ocean is to become at no distant day the commercial domain of America." This is typical of American naval beliefs of the period. There has been little research on this influence on American relations with Korea, yet it should be a very interesting topic for study.

[10] Histories and biographies of the leading American political figures of the day are notable for their almost complete lack of mention of the Korean-American Treaty of 1882. This appears to be considered by these historians and writers as a matter of no importance in the lives of the leading figures of the time. In Thomas C. Reeves, *Gentleman Boss, The Life of Chester A. Arthur,* Alfred A. Knopf, New York, 1975, xvii, 500 pages, Korea is only mentioned in a parenthetical comment and a footnote. Willis Fletcher Johnson, *Life of James G. Blaine, "The Plumed Knight,"* Atlantic Publishing Company, Philadelphia, 1893, 578 pages, is an effusive biography with no reference to Korea. Charles Edward Russell, *Blaine of Maine, His Life and Times,* Cosmopolitan Book Corporation, New York, 1931, 446 pages, is a newsman's life of James G. Blaine with due notice of Blaine's weaknesses, including graft and corruption, but with almost no mention of Korea. Alice Felt Tyler, *The Foreign Policy of James G. Blaine,* University of Minnesota Press, Minneapolis, 1927, 411 pages, includes a chapter, pp. 254-269, on American interests in the Far East but notes that "upon all matters relating to the Far East, he (Blaine) appears to have had little knowledge and less interest." The Korean-American Treaty of 1882 is noted on pp. 261-269 but with the Comment that "negotiations with Korea which Blaine in 1881 authorized Commodore Shufeldt to make were undertaken at the desire of Shufeldt himself, who had become interested in the Orient, and not because the Secretary of State had any particular concern in the matter." There is relatively little biographical material on Secretary of State Frelinghuysen; one brief, useful chapter is Philip Marshall Brown, "Frederick Theodore Frelinghuysen, Secretary of State, December 19, 1881 to March 5, 1885," *The American Secretaries of State and Their Diplomacy,* Alfred A. Knopf, New York, Vol. VIII, 1928, pp. 3-43; the discussion of the Korean-American Treaty is on pp. 35-39, but is very routine. Frelinghuysen evidenced no enthusiasm for the Treaty, perhaps because it had been started in negotiation by his predecessor, Blaine.

arrange a treaty with Korea. It is interesting to note that the Department of State in 1880 had only 51 persons on its executive and clerical staff in Washington and only 25 Ministers and 5 Charge d'Affaires, largely in Europe and South America. The United States had some 300 consulates abroad, but these were usually unsalaried positions held by Americans or business men of other nationalities.[11] The United States, thus, depended for special tasks such as negotiations for a Korean treaty upon Naval officers.[12]

Commodore Robert W. Shufeldt was very interested in expanding American interests in the Far East.[13] He was also personally interested in the possibilities of obtaining employment as a foreign advisor to China, Japan or Korea if the opportunity arose or could be created. Shufeldt had been in command of an American naval vessel, the *Wachusett,* which in January, 1867 had been sent to Korea to investigate the *General Sherman* incident. He had been unsuccessful in this in part because he had, perhaps mistakenly, gone to a bay in Hwanghae Province instead of the ice-blocked bay at the mouth of the Taetong River! In 1880 as the last part of a trip around the world, Shufeldt stopped in Japan where he requested Japanese assistance in making contact with Korean authorities. The Japanese had signed a treaty with Korea in 1876 and had just opened a consulate in Pusan.

---

[11] These statistics on the small size of the Department of State are derived from Reeves, *Gentleman Boss,* p. 283. It is interesting to note that in 1982 those persons interested in Korea in the Department of State probably number more than the entire Department in 1882.

[12] The American Navy at this time was in rather pitiful shape with too few outmoded ships and too many super-annuated officers. It was starting to revive as is noted in Leon Burr Richardson, *William E. Chandler, Republican,* Dodd, Mead & Company, New York, 1940, xiii, 758 pages. Chandler, a New Hampshire politician, was Secretary of the Navy in President Arthur's administration, but in this biography there is little mention of Korea.

[13] Commodore Robert W. Shufeldt was the key figure in the making of the Korean-American Treaty of 1882. There are many article, theses, dissertations and chapters in books on Shufeldt. These are listed in standard bibliographies and in some of the books already cited. Oddly, there appears to be no single book specifically on Shufeldt's actions concerning Korea. Such a book should include a description of his visit in 1867 on the *Wachusett* to what the named Wachusett Bay and an analysis of Shufeldt's time waiting in Nagasaki expecting to be appointed an advisor to the King of Korea in the late 1880's. A useful summary written many years ago, Chester Oscar Paullin, "The Opening of Korea by Commodore Shufeldt," *Political Science Quarterly,* Vol. XXV, No. 3, September 1910, pp. 470-499 was used as the basis for a chapter in Paullin's book, *Diplomatic Negotiations,* pp. 282-328.

Shufeldt went to Pusan, but the American's request, forwarded through the Japanese consul, was not received by the Koreans. Later, Shufeldt went to China where he received a cordial welcome from Li Hung Chang, the Chinese Viceroy. Shufeldt returned to the United States in the late fall of 1880 and after consultations in Washington was sent back to China with the nominal title of Naval Attache to negotiate a treaty with Korea.

In 1882 the gentlemanly political boss of New York, Chester A. Arthur, was President of the United States. He had reached this pinnacle of his career because of the assassination in 1881 of President James A. Garfield. President Arthur was not too concerned with foreign policy and relied heavily first on Blaine and then Blaine's successor as Secretary of State, Frederick T. Frelinghuysen. Commodore Shufeldt, on his return to China, had been instructed to negotiate a treaty with Korea and had been sent a letter signed by President Arthur to present to the King of Korea. After lengthy delays, Shufeldt finally in the winter of 1882 negotiated the draft of a Korean-American treaty with Li Hung Chang, with some small input from Korean envoys who had been sent to China for the negotiations. The completed treaty was signed on Korean soil near Inchon on May 22, 1882. A letter from the King of Korea to President Arthur indicating the dependency of Korea on China was also given to Commodore Shufeldt. Thus, Korea was opened to American trade and commerce.[14]

It took a long time for the Korean-American Treaty to be approved

---

[14] I am expecting that as a result of the centennial celebration of the Korean-American Treaty of 1882 in 1982 there will be a spate of articles, monographs and books on the subjects of Korean-American relations. I hope that some of these will bring fresh and new insights to bear on this event of a hundred years ago. It is hoped that some of the early research will not be forgotten, for example, that of Tyler Dennet of a half century ago. His book, *Americans in Eastern Asia: A Critical Study of the Policy of the United States with Reference to China, Japan and Korea in the Nineteenth Century,* Macmillan Company, New York, 1922 and some of his articles such as "American 'Good Offices' in Asia. *American Journal of International Law,* Vol. XVI, 1922, pp. 1-24; "Early American Policy in Korea, 1883-7, The Services of Lieutenant George C. Foulk," *Political Science Quarterly,* Vol. XXXVIII, No. 1, 1923, pp. 82-103; and "American Choices in the Far East in 1882," *American Historical Review,* Vol. XXX, 1924, pp. 84-108, were important scholarly contributions. A series of interesting, recent papers was included in *The United States and Korea, American-Korean Relations, 1866-1976,* Edited by Andrew C. Nahm, The Center for Korean Studies, Western Michigan University, Kalamazoo, 1979, 262 pages.

in Washington. In part this was due to the issue of Chinese emigration to California, unfortunately linked to the Korean Treaty though it was not strictly applicable. President Arthur noted in his second Annual Message to Congress in 1882 that the Treaty had been sent to the Senate. In his third Annual Message to Congress in 1883, after the ratification of the Treaty, President Arthur expressed the view that "Korea, as yet unacquainted with the methods of Western civilization, now invites the attention of those interested in the advancement of our foreign trade, as it needs the implements and products which the United States are ready to supply. We seek no monopoly of its commerce and no advantages over other nations, but as the Chosenese, in reaching for a higher civilization, have confided in this Republic, we can not regard with indifference any encroachment on their rights."[15]

Though urged by President Arthur not to regard Korea "with indifference," Americans in 1882 still had little political interest in Korea. The Korean-American Treaty that had been negotiated with Chinese authorities (though signed by Koreans) was quite American-centered, with little concern over what the consequences might be for Korea. This Treaty was followed quickly by Korean treaties with other Western nations and Korea, the Hermit Nation, was opened to the intrigues and pressures of outside powers, particularly Russia, Britain, Japan and China.[16]

In 1882 Americans had little background information concerning Korea. The peninsula was distant and remote. Some English compilations of travel accounts were available in libraries. The usual reference in encyclopedias, travel literature and geographical atlases was in the English romanization: Corea or "the Corea," as if it were like "the Levant." After 1735, European and American world and regional maps showed Korea in its peninsular form with some degree of accuracy.[17] In 1818 a noted British travel account of a voyage along

---

[15] Quotation is from James D. Richardson, *A Compilation of Messages and Papers of the Presidents*, Washington, 1896-1927, Volume VIII, page 274.

[16] There are many articles and books on the post-1882 situation of Korea among the powers, some of these are noted in *Studies on Korea*. A most useful book is C. I. Eugene Kim and Han-kyo Kim, *Korea and the Politics of Imperialism, 1876-1910*, University of California Press, Berkeley, 1967, x, 260 pages. In the process of publication by the University Presses of Florida is a massive, two-volume work by the late George A. Lensen, *Balance of Intrigue: International Rivalry in Korea and Manchuria, 1884-1899*.

[17] There has been little study of the Western cartography of Korea, comparable to the

the West Coast of Korea was published in Philadelphia in a pirated edition, reportedly the first book pertaining to Korea published in the United States.[18] In this account Basil Hall wrote disparagingly of Korean hospitality. The British expedition had stopped at islands off Hwanghae Province now called the *So-do,* but named by Hall after his father—The Sir James Hall Group. Basil Hall also spent an hour on the shores of Piin Bay in south-western Korea, but learned little of Korea.[19] Other members of the British Expedition also published books on Korea, but these were rather superficial travellers' tales, characteristic of most of the material on Korea available to American readers.[20]

Fortunately, the few Americans keenly interested in knowing about Korea in 1882 had available three books published in 1880 and 1882. Though these books are now generally forgotten, they deserve to be better known and should be more widely available. None of these books were widely distributed in 1882 and probably were only on the shelves of libraries and bibliophiles. Each of these books was aimed at the general, interested reader. Each was written by outsiders, only one of whom had been inside Korea and that for only short lengths of time. The first, that of John Ross, was written from the perspective of Korea as seen from Manchuria.[21] The second, by Ernest Oppert,

excellent studies of Korean cartography such as Chan Lee, *Old Maps of Korea,* The Korean Library Science Research Institute, Seoul, 1977, 249 pages. I discussed some of the Western maps in two papers: Shannon McCune, "Some Korean Maps," *Transactions, Royal Asiatic Society, Korea Branch,* Vol. L, 1975, pp. 70-102, and "The Korean Cartographic Tradition: Its Cross-Cultural Relations," *Papers of the 1st International Conference on Korean Studies,* The Academy of Korean Studies, Seoul, May 15, 1980, pp. 724-740.

[18] Basil Hall, *Account of a Voyage of Discovery to the West Coast of Corea and the Great Loo-Choo Island,* John Murray, London, 1818, xvi,222 pages, appendices. This was reprinted with an Introduction which I wrote cv the Royal Asiatic Society, Korea Branch, Seoul, 1975. Its designation as "the first bc ,k published in the United States which referred directly to Korea" was made by *Korea: An Annotated Biblipgraphy of Publications in Western Languages,* Library of Congress, Washington, 1950.

[19] I visited Piin Bay in 1976 and wrote an article discussing Basil Hall's visit: Shannon McCune, "Korea is Transformed," *The Geographical Magazine,* London, Vol. XLIV, No. 10, July, 1977, pp. 643-647.

[20] One of these is John M'Leod, *Narrative of a Voyage in His Majesty's Late Ship Alceste to the Yellow Sea along the Coast of Corea. . .,* John Murray, London, 1817, 288 pages. This was reprinted with an Introduction which I wrote: John M'Leod, *The Voyage of the Alceste to the Ryukyus and Southeast Asia,* Charles E. Tuttle Company, Tokyo and Rutland, Vermont, 1963.

[21] John Ross, *History of Corea, Ancient and Modern, with Description of Manners*

was written from the perspective of Korea as seen from Shanghai.[22] The third author, William Elliot Griffis, wrote on Korea as seen from the perspective of Japan.[23]

Each book depended on previously published sources and on translations from Chinese and Japanese writings. References are made to such literature in the texts, though only Griffis' book has a separate bibliography. This bibliography illustrates very well the materials on Korea available to an American scholar seeking such information in American libraries.

John Ross was a Scotch Presbyterian missionary in Manchuria. He had contacts with Koreans and was particularly interested in studying the Korean language, for he wished to translate the Bible into Korean. His *History of Corea, Ancient and Modern* was published in Paisley, Scotland in 1880. Ross includes in his book a great deal of material on Chinese and Manchu history drawn from Chinese sources. In his Preface he recommends that "the reader begin with Chapter X, and to become somewhat familiar with the Korean people, before beginning their past history." This last fourth of his book deals with what the sub-title of the book calls a "Description of Manners and Customs, Language and Geography." This random assortment of doubtful information is drawn from the author's contacts with Koreans in Manchuria and translated from an unidentified Korean book. There is an overly lengthy section on funeral customs and a rather peculiar section on Korean literature which might better be labelled as a list of ancient Chinese classics available to Korean scholars. There are three rather crudely drawn maps and a number of inset pages with brightly colored sketches of Korean costumes "by an indifferent Corean artist." The emphasis in Ross' book upon wars and invasions of Korea by successive Chinese and Japanese forces, described at some length, does correctly note the difficulties imposed on Korea by its peninsular location in the heart of the Far East. However,

---

and Customs, Language and Geography, J. and R. Parlane, Paisley, 1880, xii, 404 pages. There was a second printing in 1891. Allen D. Clark in the Revised Edition of *A History of the Church in Korea,* includes some material on John Ross, pp. 64-67 and pp. 79-87, based in part on the research of the late Yang-Sun Kim.

[22] Ernest Oppert, *Ein Verschollenes Land: Reisen nach Corea,* Leipzig, 1880, xx, 313 pages. The English translation was *A Forbidden Land: Voyages to the Corea,* G. P. Putnam's Sons, New York, 1880, xix, 349 pages.

[23] William Elliot Griffis, *Corea, The Hermit Nation,* Charles Scribner's Sons, New York, 1882, xvii, 442 pages. This went through nine editions, the latest in 1911; it was reprinted by the AMS Press, New York in 1971.

the American reader in 1882 would likely have skipped over much of this succession of accounts of tribal struggles and military battles of the distant past and place. The reader's overall impression would have been that Korea was an appendage of Manchu China with some peculiar local customs, costumes and language.

Ernest Oppert was a trader and wheeler-dealer in the international community of Shanghai in the 1860's. His book, *A Forbidden Land, Voyages to the Corea,* was originally written and published in German; it was translated into English and published in England and the United States in 1880. Oppert was a North German citizen, but he had various associations with American, British, French and Chinese business interests in Shanghai and on the China coast. He made three voyages to the west coast of Korea in 1866, 1867 and 1868. His last voyage was a bizarre episode in which Oppert plotted with a French Catholic priest, formerly a clandestine missionary to Korea, to rob a grave or depository where the Taewon'gun, the Regent of Korea, had supposedly hidden some valuable family relics. The far-fetched idea was that if these could be obtained, they could be held for ransom to stop the anti-Catholic persecutions of the Taewon'gun and serve, incidentally, to open trade with the Western world. Oppert had even composed a Treaty in French and English versions which was to be signed by the King of Korea. An American, Frederick Jenkins, accompanied the polyglot group of adventurers. During the course of a skirmish on Kanghwa Island a Manilaman, or Filipino, was killed.

When the unsuccessful expedition returned to Shanghai the Spanish Consul, because of the death of the Manilaman, urged the American Consul-General, George F. Steward, to put Jenkins on trial in a U.S. consular court. During the trial the details of the plot and of the peculiar expedition were forthcoming, but since the Chinese sailors refused to testify the court had to acquit Jenkins. It seems, however, that Oppert on his return to Germany was given a prison term for his part in this incident or for some other offense. Perhaps it was at this time of imprisonment that he, a la Marco Polo, wrote his book on Korea. The series of voyages had their ludicrous moments and merit further study.[24]

---

[24] Ernest Oppert has been much maligned, but actually his general observations on Korea and the accounts of his three voyages, including the last disastrous journey, are interesting reading. Some years ago my daughter, now Antoinette Bement of Shelter Island, New York, wrote a paper on Oppert, but could not obtain the necessary German materials on his imprisonment. Reprints of the German and of the English edi-

Because of this "Body-Snatching Expedition," Ernest Oppert has been given little credence and his book received adverse reviews. The first half of *A Forbidden Land* is devoted to a rather general account of Korea. Within it are some rather peculiar ideas, for example, that Koreans are of two races, the upper class Caucasian and the lower class Mongolian; sketches of individuals are included to give credence to this. Oppert quotes at length from Father Regis' accounts of Korea given in Du Halde's *Description Geographique. . .de l'Empire de la Chine* of 1735.[25] He mentions three old Japanese works to which he had access. His sketch of the Korean language is based on materials he obtained from a person he identifies as J. Hoffman who had "served as assistant to Col. Siebold in Nagasaki." Oppert also quotes from Siebold's comments on Korea in Siebold's work on Japan. Oppert scoffs at Protestant missionary work in China but is sympathetic to the plight of the Catholic missionaries who along with their converts were martyred in Korea under the policies of the Taewon'gun. He does not seem to have used Dallet's *Histoire de L'Eglise de Coree* which was published in Paris in 1874 and might have been available to him.[26] He does note that as a result of the French attack on Kanghwa in 1866 over 400 Korean volumes, including many local district records, were captured and sent to the Bibliotheque Imperiale in Paris. Oppert derides Korean historiography in these words: "The few native writings, pretending to supply historical accounts, contain in truth nothing whatever that might throw light on the subject."[27] This comment may well represent the attitude of the day in Shanghai and among the foreign community. Oppert, in keeping with his desire to open Korea to trade, puts in italics his

tions with Introductions by Eckart Dege, the German geographer who has done research on Korea, would be of value.

[25] A summary of Father Jean-Baptiste Regis' contribution to Western knowledge of Korea is given in Shannon McCune, "Geographical Observations on Korea—Those of Father Regis Published in 1735," *Journal of Social Sciences and Humanities*, Korean Research Center, Seoul, No. 44, December, 1976, pp. 1-19.

[26] Ch. Dallet, *Histoire de L'Eglise de Coree*, Victor Palme, Paris, 1874, Two Volumes, cxcii, 383 pages and 595 pages. Father Charles Dallet of the Society of Foreign Missions in Paris compiled the accounts of the French missionaries who had visited Korea and in some cases been martyred there. His 192 page Introduction provided much general information about Korea. This Introduction has been translated and published under a rather misleading title, *Traditional Korea*, Behavior Science Translations, Human Relations Area Files, New Haven, 1954. The two volume work was reprinted by the Royal Asiatic Society, Korean Branch, Seoul, in 1975.

[27] Ernest Oppert, *A Forbidden Land*, p. 78.

conviction "that no other country on the whole Asiatic continent approaches Corea in mineral wealth."[28]

Oppert's major contribution to Western knowledge of Korea are the accounts of his voyages to the islands and coastal areas of west central Korea. He claims that he was well received by local officials and he seems to have enjoyed his contacts with them. The Taewon'gun, not the Korean people, was Oppert's villain. Included in the book are numerous sketches of Korean people and places and of Korean hats which he had collected. Because of the adverse reviews and because this area of Korea was already comparatively well known, as a result of the French and American attacks of 1866 and 1871, Oppert's descriptions were probably not too widely accepted by American readers in 1882. Yet they are still interesting reading and give a non-missionary slant to early views on Korea. The book was reprinted in 1891 showing that it had a continuing interest to some American readers.

William Elliot Griffis wrote the most popular and most useful book on Korea in 1882. It was published while the Korean-American treaty was under consideration and may have contributed to the ratification of the treaty by its sympathetic attitude toward Korea. Griffis was a teacher in Japan in 1870-1874 and for the rest of his long life was a prolific writer and speaker, interpreting Japan to American audiences.[29] While in Japan he gathered material for his major work, *The Mikado's Empire,* which was first published in 1876 and went through many editions. The book had a profound influence on the American view of Japan. Encouraged by the success of his Japan book, Griffis turned to Korea. He had not travelled in Korea though he had met some Koreans and had read various works on Korea as indicated in the bibliography in his book. (Parenthetically, he did visit Korea in 1926 when he was 83 years old!) A methodical researcher and writer, while serving as pastor of the Dutch Reformed Church in Schenectady, New York, he wrote the first draft of his book on Korea between 1877 and 1880. He may have brought the book to completion in the fall of 1882 because of the signing of the Korean-American Treaty on May 22nd. In later years for new editions of the book he added

---

[28] *Ibid.,* p. 172.

[29] A useful, brief account of William Elliot Griffis' life in Japan and of his influence as an American writer and speaker on the Far East is given in Edward R. Beauchamp, *An American Teacher in Early Meiji Japan,* Asian Studies at Hawaii, No. 17, University Press of Hawaii, Honolulu, 1976, xiii, 154 pages.

chapters on the events taking place in Korea to up-date the book.

Perhaps because he had been criticized for the lack of attributions to materials used in his book on Japan, in his compilation on Korea Griffis placed in his Preface many acknowledgements to other scholars, a lengthy Bibliography and an Appendix noting materials on particular topics such as language and cartography.[30] In the Preface he makes special mention of the help he received from the Librarian of the American Geographical Society of New York. As he was writing his book Griffis published a number of articles on Korea in popular magazines and encyclopedia; these are listed as the last seven items in his Bibliography. Notable among them was an article for the Journal of the American Geographical Society.[31]

Griffis' *Corea, The Hermit Nation* is a well-organized and smoothly written book. The first section is an account of Korea's Ancient and Medieval History with an inordinately lengthy account of the Japanese invasion of 1592-1598. This emphasis upon Japanese actions is understandable in view of the author's dependence upon Japanese source materials. The third section, on Modern and Recent History, also has much emphases upon Japanese actions and detailed accounts of the French and American attacks on Kanghwa. He even includes a chapter on Oppert's adventures entitled "A Body-Snatching Expedition."[32]

Between the two historical sections of Griffis' book is a 150 page section on Political and Social Corea. This includes many details of Korean life drawn from various sources but lacks any unifying theme. There is even a chapter on The Korean Tiger as exemplified in paintings and banners. Starting this section is a lengthy chapter on the geography of the eight provinces of Korea with small, clear, place-name maps of each; each province is taken up separately, but again there is no unifying theme or comment. This chapter may have been drawn from

---

[30] Griffis' Bibliography is placed after his Preface, pp. xix-xxv. His bibliographical notes on Korean language and cartography are given in the Appendix of his book.

[31] William Elliot Griffis, "Corea, The Hermit Nation," *Journal of the American Geographical Society,* Vol. 13, 1881, pp. 125-132. In this paper read to the Society on December 21, 1881, Griffis refers to a map, seven feet square, which he used to illustrate his talk. He read another paper to the Society in 1895, "Korea and the Koreans: In the Mirror of Their Language and History," *Bulletin of the American Geographical Society,* Vol. XXVII, No. 1, 1895, pp. 1-20. He also wrote other books on Korea in later years; these are listed in *Studies on Korea.*

[32] Griffis, *Corea, The Hermit Nation,* pp. 396-402.

a Japanese source or from a Japanese translation of a Korean descriptive geography. It is useful in giving an impression of the geographical diversity of the Korean peninsula.

Certainly Griffis' *Corea, The Hermit Nation* was a valuable introduction to Korea for American readers in 1882. The author, in his words, had "sought information from sources from within and without Corea, in maps and charts, coins and pottery, the language and art, notes and narratives of eye-witnesses, pencil-sketches, paintings and photographs, the standard histories of Japan and China, the testimony of sailor and diplomatist, missionary and castaway, and the digested knowledge of critical scholars."[33] It is interesting to note that in writing his work on Japan Griffis was very contemptuous of the arm-chair writer in the library, but in his work on Korea he defends his role as a compiler who "if able even in part to control his authorities . . . may be able to furnish a hand-book of information more valuable to the general reader . . ." than that of a traveller.[34] Though generally sympathetic to the Koreans, Griffis gives the impression that he believed Korea was too small a political entity to be viable and that it would be best for it to be a protectorate of emerging Japan. His personal views are also evident in a number of places where he expresses the hope that Protestant missionary activity be successful in making Korea a citadel of Christianity in the Far East. The book went through nine editions by 1911 and has been considered "by far the most widely read book on Korea in English prior to World War II."[35]

These three books available to the American reader were views of Korea by outsiders using generally non-Korean source materials. Unfortunately no books were written solely from the standpoint of the Koreans and using the extensive Korean source materials which existed in Korea. To take one example, Kim Chongho had compiled his excellent map of Korea, the *Taedong Yojido,* and had printed it by wood blocks in 1861 and again in 1864, yet no reference is made to this cartographic landmark in these books.[36] Though one may criticize

---

[33] *Ibid.,* p. XV.

[34] *Ibid.,* p. XV.

[35] *Studies on Korea,* p. 42 under 03-007.

[36] Griffis, *op. cit.,* in a note on Cartography in the appendix of his book incorrectly states that "the first map of Cho-sen made by a native Korean . . . was made by Andrew Kim." Only a few sentences before he noted that the map in the Jesuit Atlas, which he dates as 1707 rather than the correct date of 1718, was copied from "a man

these early writers for not using Korean source materials, such a criticism may also be leveled at present day American scholars, myself included, who do not use Korean materials as much as they deserve.

In spite of these three books and some newspaper and magazine articles published on Korea, the Hermit Nation was still little known by the American people in 1882. An interesting, short account of what was readily known about Korea in America in 1882 is the "hasty abstract" of a lecture given by William Elliot Griffis to the American Geographical Society of New York early in 1882 before the Korean-American Treaty was negotiated. Griffis concluded his lecture with "the hope that before many years the relations of friendship and commerce may be amicably established between our country and this last of the hermit nations."[37]

American ignorance of Korea was reflected in the tentative and cautious actions taken by the United States government at the time. It was over a year before the Korean-American Treaty of 1882 was ratified and then rather hesitantly. The American image of Korea was a hazy one of a distant, isolated peninsula, caught between China, Japan and Russia, and with a quaint people living in an area of considerable geographical diversity under a feeble, autocratic government. This image served America poorly. Inadequate images of Korea continue to persist in the United States even to the present day and hinder a thorough understanding of Korea's problems and potential.

---

kept in the palace at Seoul." Though I have not been able to identify the map copied by the Jesuit missionary-cartographers, there are many maps of Korea made by Koreans throughout the Yi Dynasty.

Griffis includes a folded, colored map in his book which he writes was reduced from a map made by the Japanese War Department in 1877. In its legend it is noted that this Japanese map was "based on Corean maps, and Japanese, American and European surveys, and corrected by the Corean scholar Kin Rinshio." The Japanese map of 1877 was probably based largely on Kim Chongho's *Taedong Yojido* of 1864.

[37] Griffis, "Corea, The Hermit Nation," *Journal of the American Geographical Society,* Vol. 13, 1881, quotation on page 132.

CHAPTER 8

KOREANS IN AMERICA: PAST AND PRESENT

Jai Poong Ryu

I. An Overview

Korean immigration to America had its known beginning in the arrival of two Koreans in Hawaii on January 15, 1900. Soon thereafter the emigration of 7,291 Koreans to Hawaii for the 1903-1905 period was the first officially authorized emigration of Koreans to a foreign country in Korean history (Choe, 1978). In June 1905, however, Korean migration to the United States practically stopped. This stoppage was largely due to the policies of the Japanese government that did not want a presence of a large number of Koreans in Hawaii for the protection of the already sizable Japanese community in the islands (Patterson, 1974; Choe, 1978). Although the Japanese annexation of Korea did not take place till 1910, Japanese had power to dictate Korea's foreign policy matters following her triumph in Russo-Japanese War of 1904-1905.

Even without the Japanese interference, however, the flow of Koreans to America was not to continue very long. The beginning of Korean immigration coincided with the growing resentment of white Americans toward the Chinese and Japanese, who had been growing in large numbers since the 1850's. Koreans became incidental victims of the 1924 Act establishing the national-origin quota system which was designed primarily to restrict the Eastern European and other two Asian groups. The early constraints from colonialism and the 1924 Act inhibited the Korean migration and the number of Korean residents in the U.S. was only around 7,000 as late as 1950.

The end of World War II terminated the colonial administration's restrictions on Korean emigration. American military government durng the 1945-1948 period and the Korean War of 1950-1953 brought about the increasing awareness of the United States in the minds of Koreans. This was reflected in an increase of Korean residents in the U.S. For 1950-1965 period, 17,382 Koreans were classified as immigrants and 7,947 became citizens through naturalization (H. Kim, 1977).

1970 Census: It was the 1965 Act (P.L. 89-236), however, that increased the number and growth rate of Koreans to an unprecedented level. The act especially opened the doors of migration to those Koreans with types of occupations which were classified by the United States Department of Labor. In response to the growing size of the Korean American population, the 1970 Census counted Koreans for the first time as a distinct ethnic group. This census enumerated 70,598 Koreans, recognizing them as the fifth largest Asian group, following the Japanese, Chinese, Filipinos, and the Hawaiians. The majority of the 1970 Koreans were recent migrants, as indicated by the fact that 55 percent of them were born outside the United States.

The foreign-born Koreans in 1970 accounted for 0.4 percent of all foreign-born in the United States and 6 percent of all foreign-born who were neither black nor white.

Table 1.   *Asian Population in the U.S. by Nativity and Sex, 1970.*

	Koreans	Japanese	Chinese	Filipinos	Total
1970 Estimates					
Total	70,598	588,324	431,583	336,731	1,427,236
Male	28,491	271,453	226,733	183,175	709,852
Female	42,107	316,871	204,850	153,556	717,384
Foreign-Born	38,145	122,500	204,232	178,970	543,847
Percent					
Foreign-Born	54.0	20.8	47.3	53.1	38.1

Source: U.S. Bureau of the Census, PC (1)-D1

Growth in the 1970's: The flow of migration that began in significant numbers in the 1960's accelerated into the 1970's. Number of Korean immigrants as reported by the U.S. Office of Immigration and Naturalization is as shown in Table 2.

The rapid growth shown in Table 2 reflects the general immigration

Table 2. Korean Residents in America by Immigration Status, 1950-79.

Year \ Type	Immigrants	Nonimmigrants	Naturalized
1950	10	335	3
1951	32	183	1
1952	127	808	2
1953	115	1,111	46
1954	254	1,270	243
1955	315	2,615	295
1956	703	3,552	155
1957	648	1,798	112
1958	1,604	1,995	168
1959	1,720	1,531	416
1960	1,507	1,504	651
1961	1,534	1,771	1,031
1962	1,538	2,112	1,169
1963	2,580	2,803	1,249
1964	2,362	4,068	1,369
1965	2,165	4,717	1,027
1966	2,492	5,076	1,180
1967	3,956	6,206	1,353
1968	3,811	9,309	1,776
1969	6,045	12,478	1,646
1970	9,314	13,171	1,687
1971	14,297	17,617	2,083
1972	18,297	23,473	2,933
1973	22,930	23,075	3,562
1974	28,028	30,377	4,451
1975	28,362	30,554	6,007
1976	30,803	35,843	7,450
1977	30,917	44,951	10,446
1978	33,421*	53,447*	12,575
1979	36,128*	63,548*	16,209*
1980	39,054*	75,559*	20,893*
1970-1980	291,551	411,615	88,296
Total	325,069	476,857	102,198

Source: *Annual Reports*, 1970-1979, INS.

* These eight figures were not directly supplied in the INS Annual Reports. They were derived by applying the annual growth rates for 1973-77 period for the first two columns and 1973-78 period for the last. The annual rates were 8.1%, 18.9%, and 28.9%, respectively.

patterns since 1965 when immigration from Asia rose drastically while Europe's share dropped substantially. As mentioned before, immigration quotas prior to 1965 had excluded Orientals throughout the century.

Between 1965 and 1977, for example, the proportion of immigrants from Asia increased from 7 percent to 34 percent of the annual total. In 1977, immigration from the Phillipines totaled 39,100; from Korea 30,900; from China and Taiwan, 19,800; and from India, 18,600.

This pattern of admissions by continents is shown in Table 3.

Table 3.   Distribution of Admissions: 1965-1977

	1965 Total 296,657	1977 Total 462,315
Oceania	0.5%	0.9%
Africa	1.1%	2.2%
Asia	7.0%	34.1%
South America	10.4%	7.1%
Europe	38.2%	15.1%
North America	42.7%	40.5%

Source: INS *Annual Reports,* 1965 and 1977.

1980 Census: The latest census counted more than 3.5 million persons from Asian countries and Pacific Islands, showing a considerable increase over the 1970 figure of 1.5 million.[1]

The growth pattern of individual groups within the Asian and Pacific Islander population varied, reflecting different levels of immigration during the decade. Table 4 briefly sums up the changed pattern from 1970 to 1980.

Koreans thus emerge in 1980 as the fourth largest Asian group[2] representing the third largest numerical increase and the fastest growing group among the four main Asiatic groups in the United States.

Distribution of Korean-American Population: The regional distribution of Korean Americans show a pattern of greater dispersal than their fellow Asian groups. In the Western region, where only 19.1

---

[1] Part of this increase represents changes in census definition rather than an actual increase in population. For example, Asian Indians were included in the Asian and Pacific Islander category in 1980 but were classified as White in 1970.

[2] When Asian Indians are included, Koreans are the fifth largest Asian group. In 1980, Asian Indian population was estimated at 361,544.

Table 4.   *Asian Population in the U.S.: 1970 & 1980.*

	Koreans	Japanese	Chinese	Filipinos
1970	70,598	588,324	431,583	336,731
1980	354,529	700,747	806,027	774,640
Increase	283,931	112,423	374,444	437,909
Percent Increase	402.2	19.1	86.8	130.0

Source: U.S. Bureau of the Census, HC (7)-9, 1970; and *Race of Population by States,* PC 80-51-3, 1980.

Table 5.   *Regional Distribution of Asian Americans: 1970 & 1980.*

		Northeast	North Central	South	West
Koreans:	1970	20.1	19.1	18.2	42.6
	1980	19.2	17.5	19.9	43.4
Japanese:	1970	6.6	7.2	5.2	81.0
	1980	6.7	6.3	6.4	80.6
Chinese:	1970	26.6	9.0	7.9	56.5
	1980	27.0	9.0	11.3	52.7
Filipinos:	1970	9.2	8.1	9.3	73.4
	1980	9.7	10.3	10.7	69.3
U.S. General:	1970	14.1	27.8	30.9	17.1
	1980	21.7	26.0	33.3	19.1

Source: U.S. Bureau of the Census, HC (7)-9, 1970; and *Race of Population by States,* PC80-51-3, 1980.

percent of the U.S. population resides in 1980, all Asian groups showed a heavy concentration both for 1970 and 1980. This was true of Korean Americans, 42.5 percent and 43.4 percent of whom resided in the West in 1970 and 1980, respectively. Compared to other Asian groups, however, the degree of Western concentration is considerably less in case of Koreans.

Distribution by states, however, shows a bit more concentration. In 1980, 50 percent of Koreans lived in four highly urban states of New York, Illinois, Maryland, and California.

The degree of concentration in these four major states appears growing, for only 40.8% of the Koreans lived there in 1970.

Table 6. Korean Population of Selected States: 1980 and 1970

	1980	1970	Change, 1970 to 1980		Percent Distribution	
			Number	Percent	1980	1970
United States	354,529	70,598	283,931	402.2	100.0	100.0
Northeast	68,152	13,908	54,244	390.0	19.2	20.1
Massachusetts	4,655	1,318	3,337	253.2	1.3	1.9
Connecticut	2,116	656	1,460	222.6	0.6	0.9
New York	34,157	6,607	27,550	417.0	9.6	9.6
New Jersey	12,845	2,349	10,496	446.8	3.6	3.4
Pennsylvania	12,503	2,454	10,049	409.5	3.5	3.5
North Central	62,149	13,172	48,977	371.8	17.5	19.1
Ohio	7,257	2,070	5,187	250.6	2.0	3.0
Indiana	3,253	857	2,396	279.6	0.9	1.2
Illinois	23,980	3,673	20,307	552.9	6.8	5.3
Michigan	8,700	2,125	6,575	309.4	2.5	3.1
Wisconsin	2,643	872	1,771	203.1	0.7	1.3
Minnesota	6,318	956	5,362	560.9	1.8	1.4
Missouri	3,519	970	2,549	262.8	1.0	1.4
Kansas	2,627	510	2,117	415.1	0.7	0.7
South	70,375	12,594	57,781	458.8	19.9	18.2
Maryland	15,087	2,139	12,948	605.3	4.3	3.1
Virginia	12,550	1,777	10,773	606.2	3.5	2.6
North Carolina	3,581	883	2,698	305.5	1.0	1.3
Georgia	5,970	921	5,049	548.2	1.7	1.3
Florida	4,673	1,147	3,526	307.4	1.3	1.7
Louisiana	1,729	337	1,392	413.1	0.5	0.5
Oklahoma	2,698	475	2,223	468.0	0.8	0.7
Texas	13,997	2,090	11,907	569.7	3.9	3.0
West	153,853	29,456	124,397	442.3	43.4	42.6
Colorado	5,316	760	4,556	599.5	1.5	1.1
Arizona	2,446	488	1,958	401.2	0.7	0.7
Utah	1,319	236	1,083	458.9	0.4	0.3
Washington	13,077	1,738	11,339	652.4	3.7	2.5
Oregon	4,427	1,085	3,342	308.0	1.2	1.6
California	103,891	15,756	88,135	559.4	29.3	22.8
Hawaii	17,948	8,656	9,292	107.3	5.1	12.5

Source: U.S. Bureau of the Census, HC(7)-9, 1970; and Race of Population by States, PC80-51-3, 1980.

Naturalization of Korean Americans: Another interesting demographic feature related to migration is the naturalization of Koreans.

As Table 2 indicated, the number of Koreans who have become naturalized citizens of the United States has increased steadily since 1950. The total number of naturalized citizens of Korean descent for 1950-1980 period was estimated at 102,098 persons.

Table 7. *Naturalization of Koreans by Age, Sex, and Naturalization Provisions**

Year	Total	Per cent of Immigrants	Per cent Female	Percent 18 Years and Over	Provisions*	
					Wife of U.S. Citizen	Children of U.S. Citizen
FY 1965	1,027	47.4	79.0	68.3	51.9	32.0
FY 1966	1,180	47.3	78.6	67.1	52.7	32.9
FY 1967	1,353	34.2	78.7	69.3	54.2	31.0
FY 1968	1,776	46.6	76.7	74.8	49.0	25.0
FY 1969	1,646	27.2	77.0	74.6	49.0	24.8
FY 1970	1,687	18.1	80.9	76.7	52.8	23.2
FY 1971	2,083	14.6	81.3	78.7	52.5	17.2
FY 1972	2,933	15.5	74.0	84.0	43.2	16.5
FY 1973	3,562	15.5	76.4	82.5	43.6	18.2
FY 1974	4,451	15.9	75.2	79.1	39.9	21.5
FY 1975	6,007	21.2	74.1	60.7	39.0	18.9
FY 1976	7,450	24.2	70.3	81.9	29.4	18.3
FY 1977	10,446	33.8	65.2	81.0	19.8	18.6

Source: INS, *Annual Reports* 1965-1977.

* also in per cent.

If we were to include U.S. citizens by birth to parent(s) of Korean origin, the number would be a lot greater. The ratio of naturalized to the annual total of immigrants steadily declined to 1974 and started to increase since 1975. This reflects the increasing size of immigrant Koreans, from which the ranks of the naturalized citizens come generally.

Several interesting facts emerge upon close examination of Table 6. Of all the naturalized Korean Americans in 1980, roughly 82 per cent of 84,000 were 18 years or older. All of these individuals were potential voters and some of them may have become candidates for public offices. Since this category of Koreans is likely to increase further, there may be some ways to utilize this potential political power for the betterment of this minority group.

Another interesting fact is the proportion of wives and children of U.S. citizens of the total naturalization volume each year. Up until 1975, this group constituted the dominant majority. The combined proportion of these two groups, however, steadily declined from 84% in 1965, through 76% in 1970 and to 38.4% in 1977. Naturalization based on other provisions has been rising proportionately. While the American military presence in south Korea would keep this group as a significant portion of naturalized citizens, their proportional representation appears to be steadily declining.

Composition of Korean Americans: No demographic analysis is complete without the discussion of structural composition of a group under investigation. My experience has been that the most interesting and revealing perspectives on Korean Americans appear in the analysis of composition along the lines of sex, age, marital status, income, education, occupation, and housing.

Unfortunately, however, this is not possible at present. Census publication of *Characteristics of the Population, General Population Characteristics, PC80-1-B* series has been delayed beyond the scheduled time of early Fall 1981. Further, the INS's *Annual Reports* for 1980 has not been published. The Annual Reports for 1978 and 1979 does not contain any ethnic information except the number of immigrants and nonimmigrant visitors and that of the Korean aliens reporting under alien registration system.

For the purpose of the present paper, therefore, compositional analysis including up-to-date data has to be postponed. All we can do is to project certain trends from the data available in the 1970 Census and immigration statistics. In the case of Koreans, however, this is a serious handicap, for the fast growth of Korean population outdates the earlier statistics quite rapidly.

II. A Limited Statistical Profile of Korean Americans

As mentioned above, neither a up-to-date nor a comprehensive analysis of Korean is presently possible. Based on some outdated and limited data, however, an attempt is made to provide certain rudimentary statistical profile of Korean Americans here.

Sex Composition: The sex ratio of Korean Americans has favored the females. The sex ratio, according to the 1970 Census, was 56 males per 100 females. For 1970-1974 period it was 61 and for 1975-1977 period it was 67. Thus, it appears, the sex ratio is becoming increasingly even, although it remains lop-sidedly female-dominant (Table 8).

The greatest unevenness is found for the 20 to 29 years of age category, with the sex ratio of 29 and 36 for early 1970's and late 1970's, respectively. This is largely explainable by the great number of Korean women married to U.S. servicemen. It is my observation, however, that the unevenness is not fully explained by this particular category of women. Even when we discount these females, the sex ratio still remains uneven in favor of females. (Ryu, 1977).

Other unevennesses are found for the age brackets of "under five years of age." This might be explained by the great number of Korean children adopted by the U.S. citizens who tend to profer female children over males (H. Kim, 1975). The smaller number of male elderly may be due to the differential life expectancy which tends to be longer for females.[3]

Age Composition: In 1970, the median age of Korean Americans was 26.1, older than blacks with 22.5. Among Asian groups, it was considerably younger than the Japanese with 32.4 while it was more or less comparable to the Chinese and the Filipinos.

(1) Children—The proportion of children of the total Korean American population in 1970 was 12.4 per cent, higher than the U.S. with 8.4 and even black with 10.7. It was higher than that of all other Asian groups as well. Since 1970, moreover, the proportion has been increasing even more, reaching 15 per cent and 19 per cent for 1970-1974 and 1975-1977 periods, respectively.

A study of Koreans in Chicago revealed that, coupled with this high proportion of children, there was a great tendency for Korean mothers to work outside the home. Researchers reasoned that this accounted for the great importance give to day-care facilities by the Korean group in Chicago (Kim and Condon, 1975).

There also exists a high proportion of children under twenty years of age. Of all Korean immigrants, 37 per cent were under twenty in

---

[3] In 1975, average expectation of life at birth in Korea was 66 for males and 70 for females (*Korea Week*, January 15, 1976).

Table 8. *Age and Sex Distribution of Korean Immigrants: FY 1970-1974 and FY 1975-1977.*

Age Group	Sex Ratio*		Age Group Percentage of Total Immigrants	
	1970-1974	1975-1977	1970-1974	1975-1977
Total	61	67	100% (93,445)	100% (90,082)
Under	65	69	15	19
5-9	93	99	9	11
10-19	78	85	13	17
20-29	29	36	32	24
30-39	94	85	22	17
40-49	109	107	6	7
50-59	65	74	2	3
60 & Over	48	51	2	3

Source: United States Immigration & Naturalization Service, *Annual Reports,* 1970-1977.

* Sex ratio refers to the number of males per 100 females.

1970-1974 period. It increased more to 47 per cent for 1975-1977 period. The implications of this for the educational and other burdens their parents must share should be studied.

(2) Aged—Due to the lateness of Korean immigration, the proportion over sixty years of age has not been significant. In 1970, it was 4.6 per cent, compared to 14.2 for the United States, 10.3 for blacks, 10.5 for the Japanese, and 10.9 for the Filipinos. Actually, this portion has been declining since the 1970 Census (Table 8). This low proportion, however, should not be taken for its face value. Owan states that, from 1969 through 1970, Asian Americans did not receive a single federal dollar for Project for the Aged (1975). Even the recent allocation from 1972 to 1974 showed just a "minor increase." Even though the proportion is minimal, this group of Koreans seems almost totally dependent on their adult children for livelihood due to the lack of other sources. The need for greater attention to the problems of the elderly will confront the Korean community in the near future.

(3) Dependency—Table 9 illustrates the changing dependency

Table 9.   *Young and Old Dependency Among Korean Immigrants, FY 1967-1977.*

(In percent)

Year	Age 0-19	Age 20-59	Age 60+
1967-1968	27.4	71.3	1.2
1969-1970	29.3	69.5	1.2
1971-1972	33.0	65.5	1.5
1973-1974	40.2	57.6	2.2
1975-1976	44.8	52.8	2.5
FY 1976-1977*	42.6	53.8	3.7

Source: United States Immigration & Naturalization Service, *Annual Reports, 1967-1976.*

* Due to the fact that INS's 1978 *Annual Reports* did not include data on age, the figures for this row was for 1 year period ending in June 30, 1977. All other figures in this table are 2-year figures collapsed into one.

Table 10.   *Korean Immigrants by Sex and Marital Status, 1965-1972.*

(In percent)

Year	Total	Male			Female		
		Single	Married	Other	Single	Married	Other
1965-1966	100	13.3	9.0	0.1	18.5	58.1	0.9
1967-1968	100	15.4	14.5	0.2	19.8	48.9	1.2
1969-1970	100	17.4	14.4	0.2	21.8	44.8	1.3
1971-1972	100	18.5	18.5	0.2	22.9	38.5	1.4
Total	100 (59,928)	17.5	16.4	0.2	22.0	42.7	1.3

Source: U.S. Bureau of the Census, *Marital Status*, PC (2)-4C.

burdens borne by Korean Americans between twenty and sixty years of age.

The proportion aged between 20 and 59 for 1967-1977 period was not unusually low. Actually, it tends to be higher for the Koreans than other ethnic groups in the United States. The trend is, however, that of decline. It has been steadily declining since 1967. This declining labor force population should have important implications for the general living standards of Korean Americans.

Marital Status: As a group, married women have been the dominant group among the Korean Americans, although they have been declining. As mentioned above, this has been due to the great number of Korean women married to American servicemen among the Korean immigrants. As the proportion of married women is declining, the proportion of single persons has been rising for both sexes and also the proportion of married men. At present, however, single females seem to far outnumber single males. The sex ratio for immigrants from 1965 to 1972 was 79.6 per cent males per 100 females. What this implies for the patterns of marriage and family among Korean Americans will be of considerable interest to many researchers.

Another notable pattern of marital behavior among Korean Americans has to do with the great portion of Koreans marrying non-Korean nationals. Although the data in Table 11 is confined to Hawaii, which displays many atypical demographic features, the Korean pattern seems too unique to ignore.

Educational Composition: Under the heading of "education," three areas will be examined: mother tongue, school enrollment, and the school years completed.

(1) Mother Tongue—In 1970, 76 per cent of all Koreans enumerated stated Korean as their mother tongue. The proportion was, of course, higher for the foreign-born with 91 per cent while 58 per cent of the native-born Koreans reported Korean as their mother tongue. Given the relative lateness of Korean immigration to the United States, this high proportion is understandable, compared to 76 per cent for

Table 11. *Asian Marriage Within Own Subgroups in Hawaii, 1970.*

		(In per cent)
Groups	Male	Female
Koreans 50	50	
Japanese	93	85
Chinese	71	71
Filipinos	72	85
Hawaiians	62	59
Whites	84	87

Source: U.S. Bureau of the Census, PC (2)-4C. 1970.

Chinese, 62 per cent for Japanese, and 64 per cent for Filipinos, who have a longer history in this country and have had other reasons why they should speak English.[4]

This linguistic handicap has, however, been worsening, due mainly to the increasing volume of Korean immigration in recent years. It is reasonable to assume that an overwhelming proportion of the recent migrants speak Korean as this mother tongue, and the 76 per cent of the 1970 Census figure might very well be too gross an underestimate to be used at present.

This linguistic difficulty has many implications for the general status of Korean Americans. A DHEW study concludes (1975) "English language facility is a major problem for all Koreans, hampering the ability to obtain a job commensurate with their education as well as the performance of children in school." Kim and Condon (1975) remark from a study of Asian Americans in Chicago, "the Chinese and the Korean groups perceived and experienced most difficulties in the areas of language and life style differences." In their survey, only 11.8 per cent of male and 4.8 per cent of female Korean respondents reported that they speak English fluently (Kim and Condon, 1975, Table 3.109). This self-evaluation score was much poorer than that of most other Asian groups.

(2) School Enrollment—As the upper panel of Table 12 shows, the per cent enrolled in school of Korean Americans is higher in all categories except for females aged between 18 to 24 years. The proportion of Korean females in this category is not only lower than that for whites, but also only half of the same age Korean male category. This may be due to differential Korean attitudes toward the education of daughters versus sons. It may also be due to early marriage on the part of females or to the high incidence of Korean women of this age group marrying American servicemen who tend to have a lower level of education.[5]

The most salient difference, however, was found for the 25 to 35 year age category. While only 5.8 per cent of white Americans of this age bracket are enrolled in school, the figure for Korean Americans is 14.4 per cent. This shows a percentage point difference of 8.6 per cent, and means that Koreans of this age bracket are 148 per cent more

---

[4] I am referring here to the historic relationship between the United States and the Philippines, beginning in 1898.

[5] Sil Kim's study of Korean wives of American servicemen shows that these women have had only 7.6 years of schooling, on the average (1975).

likely to be enrolled in school than their counterparts among white Americans. This high level of enrollment, continuing into relatively old age, appears to be one of the most conspicuous features of Korean American eduction.

The high aspiration for education this statistic reflects is apparently continuing among more recent Korean immigrants. Kim and Condon found that 35.5 per cent of Korean male and 13.4 per cent of Korean female respondents in Chicago gave "educational opportunity" as their primary reason for immigrating to the United States. This 35.5 per cent for males is the most frequently cited among nine possible reasons of immigration among Korean males, while 13.4 per cent for females was next only to "better work opportunity" with 17.7 per cent. For both groups, a higher proportion cited "educational opportunity" as the prime reason than most other Asian groups.

This high proportion of school enrollment for the 14-34 age bracket, however, may not continue at the same level into the future. In Honolulu, where Korean immigration is of long-standing, only 10.1 per cent of this age group enrolled in school. As Korean immigration to the Mainland continues for as long as it has in Hawaii so far, this proportion may well decline somewhat.

(3) School Years Completed—The lower panels of Table 12 give certain comparative statistics on median school years completed for the United States population, whites and Koreans. In the country as a whole, 52.3 per cent of all adults have completed high school. Among Korean Americans, 71.1 per cent have (over 80 per cent in Los Angeles and New York). Thirty-six point three per cent of all Korean adults have had college education, while only 10.7 per cent of the United States have had college education. This means that the proportion college graduates for Koreans is 240 per cent greater than that of white Americans. Along with the high enrollment figures mentioned above, this reflects the unusually high level of educational aspirations of Koreans both in Korea and America.

In Honolulu, however, the unusually lower proportion of College graduates should be noted. Only 13.7 per cent of Korean adults were graduated from college. Although this is considerably higher than the total United States population or for the whites, it is greatly lower than for Korean Americans in general. The Hawaiian case may point to the reasons that the college graduate proportion for Korean Americans in general could decline in the future.

At present, however, the enrollment, college graduate proportion,

Table 12. *School Enrollment and Years of School Completed for the United States, White and Korean Americans of the United States, 1970.*

Per cent Enrolled		United States	White	Korean
14 to 17 Years Old:	Male	92.1	92.8	93.1
	Female	91.6	92.2	93.1
18 to 24 Years Old:	Male	36.8	38.1	50.7
	Female	26.7	27.1	25.5
25 to 34 Years Old:		5.7	5.8	14.4
Years of School Completed				
Total Population		100.0	100.0	100.0
		(110 mil.)	(98 mil.)	(38,000)
No School Years Completed		1.6	1.4	2.8
Elementary:	1-4 Years	3.9	3.1	2.8
	5-7 Years	10.0	9.1	8.0
	8 Years	12.6	13.0	5.5
High School:	1-3 Years	19.4	18.6	9.7
	4 Years	31.1	32.2	22.7
College:	1-3 Years	10.6	11.1	12.1
	4 or More Years	10.7	11.3	36.3
Median School Years Completed		12.7	12.1	12.9
Per cent High School Graduates		52.3	54.4	71.1

Source: U.S. Bureau of the Census, PC (1)-D1; PC (2)-1G.

and median level of education are much higher for Koreans than other ethnic groups in the United States. The only notable exception may be the Jewish population, though the lack of Jewish data precludes demonstrating this.

Occupational Composition: Under the heading of "occupation," three general areas will be dealt with: employment status, occupational characteristics, and business activities.

(1) Employment Status—Of 47,000 Koreans who were sixteen years old or older in 1970, 75.5 per cent of all males and 41.5 per cent of all females were in the labor force. Interestingly, these are almost identical with the percentages for the total United States population or the white population. Similar comparability was found in unem-

ployment statistics. Due to the current recession, however, these statistics may be outdated. Given this nature of available data and the fact that the Korean statistics did not reveal anything visibly atypical, we will not spend more space here on this subject.

(2) Occupational Characteristics—Of all Koreans who reported an occupation when they arrived in the United States from 1965 to 1975, 67 per cent stated that they had highly skilled backgrounds in professional, technical and managerial occupations. The Figure for 1975-1977 period showed a decline to 51 per cent.

This high proportion of professional and kindred workers among Korean immigrants is one of the most salient features of the Korean American occupational pattern. It appears, however, that this proportion has recently shown a downward trend. In 1971, 73.0 per cent had this type of occupation, followed by increasingly smaller proportions thereafter. It was 64 per cent in 1972, 50 per cent in 1973, and 42 per cent in 1974. It appears, therefore, that this unusually high proportion of professional workers is gradually giving away to other types of occupations.

The most unfortunate aspects of the analysis of occupational characteristics of Korean Americans from a researcher's standpoint are that we only have data at the time of immigration and that data from the census on the jobs Koreans obtained after they entered the United States are lacking.

Recent surveys, however, show the general tendency of downward mobility of considerable significance for professional and managerial workers. These mobility patterns among Koreans were noted by comparing the respondents' current jobs with those held previously in their home country (Kim and Condon, 1975, Table 3.2-4). Cordova and Lee further elaborated on the downward mobility among health professionals of Korean origin in the Seattle area (1975).

(3) Business Activities—As Table 14 indicates, business activities by Korean Americans in this country have not been very prominent up to 1972, relative to other Asian groups. There were only 0.012 firms per capita among Korean Americans, while it was 0.03 for Japanese, and 0.28 for Chinese. Only the Filipinos trail behind with 0.006.

It appears that the average size of Korean establishments, indicated by dollar receipts per firm, is more or less competitive with that of Japanese and Chinese businesses, while it surpasses that of Filipino firms significantly. There seems to be an urgent need to more thoroughly study small entrepreneurs of Korean origin in the United

Table 13. *Occupational Distribution of Korean Immigrants at Time of Entry, FY1965-1974; FY1975-1977, and that of the U.S. Population in 1970.*

(In percent)

Occupational Categories	Korean Immigrants		U.S.
	1965-1974 100% (29,000)[a]	1975-1977 100% (23,094)[b]	100% (80 million)
Professions, Technical and Managerial Workers	67.0	51.2	22.6
Clerical and Sales Workers	7.5	14.2	24.9
Craftsmen and Operatives	15.1	24.0	31.9
Laborers, Farm & non-Farm	1.3	3.6	7.8[c]
Service Workers, Including Domestics	9.1	7.0	12.9

Source: U.S. Immigration and Naturalization Service, *Annual Reports* 1965-1977.

[a] This figure represents 26 per cent of all Korean immigrations for 1965-1974 period. The remainder either did not have an occupation or did not report one.

[b] This figure represents 25.6 per cent of all Korean immigrants for 1975-1977 period.

[c] This includes farmers and farm managers.

States, for their numbers seem to have been increasing since 1972.

Income Composition: It is considerably more difficult to establish income characteristics than other socio-economic features of the Korean Americans. Almost no reliable data on it exists beyond the 1970 Census. Given the heavy immigration of Koreans since 1970 and the general economic turmoil in the United States from recession, unemployment and energy crisis, any projection based on 1970 data should be viewed with great caution.

Even from the 1970 Census, data with any research utility are rare. Existing published materials are either too general or tabulated with inconsistency to make any comparison possible. For these reasons, this section will be general and the analysis will be based on only the personal income.[6]

In 1970, the income levels of Korean Americans of both sexes were close to national levels. The median income of Korean males was about $650 less than that of U.S. males in general, while that of the

---

[6] Family income or income of the unrelated individual will be more useful for our purpose. The writer, however, has been unable to find any published materials on it.

Table 14.   *Business Ownership of Asian Americans, 1972.*

	Koreans	Japanese	Chinese	Filipinos
Total Population[a]	103,771	597,538	470,935	394,578
Number of Firms	1,021	17,837	13,070	2,237
Firms per Capita	.012	.030	.028	.006
$ Receipts ($1,000)	$64,839	$1,038,887	$1,186,907	$34,641
$ Receipts per Firm ($1,000)	54	58	91	15

Source: United States Bureau of the Census, MB 72-3.

[a] Total population of each group was computed by adding the 1970 Census figure and the immigration of the group to the United States in 1971 and 1972.

Table 15.   *Characteristics of Personal Income of The United State Total Population and Asian Americans, 1970[a]*

	United States	Koreans	Japanese	Chinese	Filipinos
Per cent Under $4,000					
Male	31	43	30	41	40
Female	68	81	58	65	56
Per cent $10,000 and Over					
Male	25	25	33	24	12
Female	3	3	5	5	

Source: U.S. Bureau of the Census PC (1)-C1; PC (1)-D1; PC (2)-1G.

[a] Percent of persons 16 years and over.

females exceeded their U.S. counterpart by $260.[7]

The proportion of those earning more than $10,000 for both sexes was identical with those of the United States, although doubt remains about the differences when the graduation was made at a higher level,

---

[7] These median income figures, however, are somewhat misleading. Median income for Koreans was computed for individuals sixteen years of age and over, while that of the U.S. was for eighteen years and over with income. Thus, the Korean figures might be a little higher.

The higher income of Korean females over the U.S. females may be more a function of over-time pay, full-part time job continuum, and the nature of hourly wages than reflecting a genuine difference in income for similar kinds of work. At present, however, this is mere speculation.

say, about $20,000. Fewer Korean females belong to this income category than their counterparts in other Asian groups.

For income category of under $4,000, however, the males and females of Korean origin were not only greater in proportion than the United States population, but also the greatest among Asian groups. The causes and consequences of this high proportion of Korean Americans in this category merit investigation by students of miniority groups. Also, in spite of the comparable median income level mentioned above between Korean Americans and the United States population, the earnings of Koreans are in fact much lower than those of the total United States population, when their high proportion college educated and professional workers are considered.

Table 16 shows that the high level of education among Korean Americans has not paid off in high income.

Table 16. *Ratio of Persons Earning $10,000 or More to Persons with a College Education, 1970.*

United States	1.4
Koreans	.8
Japanese	1.2
Chinese	.7
Filipinos	.4

Source: U.S. Bureau of the Census, PC (1)-D1; PC (2)-1G.

This imbalance appears prevalent among Asian groups with a notable exception of the Japanese Americans. The median school years completed and the proportion college graduates are, however, highest for the Koreans than for other Asian groups (DHEW, 1975). The imbalance, therefore, may affect the greater portion of Korean Americans than the other Asian groups. The question as to whether this imbalance will persist or, if it does, how it would affect the high educational aspirations of the Koreans remains a research interest.

Household and Housing Characteristics: The proportion of Korean American families headed by females in 1970 was 14.7 percent, which was considerably higher than its national proportion of 10.8. While few married persons reported themselves as divorced, separated, or widowed at the time of immigration (see section on "marital status"), this high proportion of female-headed households may indicate increased level of family instability after immigration. No definitive statements, however, can be made at present due to a lack of reliable divorce and other statistics.

These female-headed families tended also to have children. A quarter of the female-headed Korean families had children under six in the metropolitan areas of Honolulu, New York, and Los Angeles. Outside these areas, 47 percent had children. This phenomenon seems to point again to the urgent need for day care facilities.

In 1970, 43.4 percent of Korean-occupied housing units were owned by Korean Americans, quite comparable to that of the other Asian groups.[8]

A further look at Table 17 shows certain interesting features about the housing of Korean Americans.

Korean Americans tend to live in more crowded surroundings than their fellow Asians. Average number of persons per housing unit was 4.8 for Koreans while other Asians showed lower proportions. Nearly 30 percent of all Korean occupied housing units had 1.51 persons or more per room. Other Asians appeared to live in far less crowded units.

In purchasing homes, Korean Americans seem to spend less money relative to their income than other Asians. Thirty-seven percent of Koreans owning their homes in 1970 brought them at a value less than 1.5 times of their annual income, while 37 percent of Japanese and Chinese and 35 percent of the Filipinos bought them at a value between 1.5 to 2.4 times of their annual income. This general difference, however, may have changed considerably since 1970.

In renting houses or apartments, Koreans appear to be more conspicuous in spending. In 1970, 38 percent of Koreans living in rental properties were paying 25 to 34 percent of their income for rental fees, highest among Asian groups.

The implication of this differential between buying and renting behavior of Korean Americans should be of interest to researchers of many fields.

---

[8] A survey of Koreans in Chicago revealed that 88.6 percent of the respondents lived in rented houses or apartments (Kim and Condon, 1975). The figure of 43.4 percent based on 15 percent sample in 1970 appears somewhat of an overestimate.

Table 17. Housing Characteristics of Asian Americans, 1970.

	Korean	Japanese	Chinese	Filipino
Total Population[a]	98,794	486,675	433,469	336,823
All Occupied Housing Units	20,675	167,268	120,920	89.901
Percent Owner Occupied	43.4%	56.3%	43.9%	39.3%
Persons Per Housing Unit	4.8	3.6	3.6	3.7
Percent Housing Units W/1.51 Persons or More Per Room	29.9%	2.3%	8.5%	12.4%
Median Household Income: Urban	$8,500	$11,000	$8,900	$8,300
Rural	$4,300	$9,200	$10,700	$6,700
Housing Value-Income Ratio[b]:				
Percent Less Than 1.5	37.0	23.0	22.0	26.0
1.5-2.4	27.0	37.0	37.0	35.0
2.5-3.9	19.0	23.0	24.0	22.0
4.0-or more	14.0	16.0	16.0	15.0
Gross Rent as Percentage of Income:				
Percent Less Than 15.0	23.0	30.0	28.0	35.0
15.0-24.0	27.0	27.0	28.0	27.0
25.0-34.0	13.0	12.0	13.0	12.0
35.0-or more	25.0	22.0	24.0	18.0

Source: U.S. Bureau of the Census.

[a] This table is constructed on 15 percent sample and thus the population figures are at about 20 percent variance with other figures of the census publications.

[b] This is based on "specified" owner occupied units which exclude some units which did not specify the requested information. Also, this is limited to one-family homes on less than ten acres and no business on property.

Summarizing Remarks:

We have seen in this brief paper that the Korean American population is one of the most rapidly expanding groups in this country. Aside from its phenomenal growth rate, this Korean group has many other unique characteristics, the investigation of which may contribute much to the field of demography in general, as well as other branches of sociology. The disparate sex ratio, dispersed settlements, the high rate of exogamy, the high educational attainments and the other social and economic characteristics of the Korean

American population lend themselves greatly to potentially fruitful research. The problem was, and is, that the kind of reliable detailed data that is needed is not yet available. Beginning with the 1980 Census, I believe that the increasing quantity and quality of information on Korean Americans will make such potentially valuable research possible.

III. Emerging Patterns of Adjustment

The process through which patterns of assimilation and exclusion of a migrant ethnic group emerge is a dialectic one. Such patterns are a product of a dynamic interplay between the definition of the situation made by the migrant group of individuals and the definitions which the host society has provided for them.

As can be noted from these remarks, the principal concept employed for this paper is "the definition of the situation," conceptually developed and empirically validated in a study of Polish migrants by Thomas and Znaniecki (1920).

The purpose of this portion of the paper is to reflect this concept against available data on Korean Americans to see what patterns of assimilation and exclusion may be identified.

More specifically, we will entertain the following three sets of questions:

1. Do the available data suggest any dominant patterns in the manner with which Korean Americans define their situation?
2. Do the available data suggest any dominant patterns in the manner with which native Americans define the situation relevant to Korean Americans?
3. If such dominant patterns may be identified, are these two definitions in harmony or in conflict? If they are in conflict, can any predictions be made about the ways in which these conflicts may be resolved?

Data and Methodology: In order to establish various definitions of the situations by *The Polish Peasant in Europe and America* (1920), Thomas and Znaniecki advocated the use of the "life history," the detailed personal narrative and the exhaustive study of the individual case as the methods appropriate to their materials. They made major firsthand assemblages. As the sociological methodology developed in sophistication, however, it became clear that the life history is only a technique and not a self-sufficient method. It is equally clear, however, that a similar study of life histories may shed a significant light on some unique patterns of adaptation Korean Americans display in this country.

This study deviates from the classic mode in that it does not employ life histories of Korean Americans. In the first place, meaningful life histories are rare, for Korean immigration to America reached a significant volume and growth rate only recently (H.C. Kim, 1974; Ryu, 1976). Further, studies of life histories often take many years and necessitates some transoceanic travels, the luxury this writer can scarcely afford at present.

The data utilized for this study, therefore, will be empirical findings of recent demographic (H.C. Kim, 1974; Ryu, 1976) and survey (B.L. Kim, 1975; Hurh, 1976) monographs on Korean Americans.

The empirical findings of these monographs will be juxtaposed against the typology developed for identification of the dominant "definition of the situation."

The following sections will largely follow the lines of the three questions listed earlier.

A. Korean Definition of the American Situation

Students of ethnic minorities developed a host of typologies on patterns of minority responses. Wirth (1954) distinguished among pluralist, assimilationist, secessionist, militant and others. Rose's (1964) typology contained submission, withdrawal, avoidance, and integration. Simpson and Yinger (1972) drew lines along acceptance, avoidance, and aggression.

A careful review of these literature shows, however, that these typologies require sufficiently refined data for their employment in research. Data on Korean Americans are indeterminate. So far, we have only one census information on Korean Americans, i.e., 1970 census which enumerated Koreans for the first time as a distinct ethnic group. Survey research attempts have been limited to studies on small samples drawn from a single locale like Chicago or Los Angeles (B. Kim, 1975; Cha, 1975). This void in useful information on Korean

Americans made the editors of *The Journal of Social Issues* (1973, Vol. 2, No. 3) lament that "other groups such as the Filipinos and Koreans have not been studied thoroughly; we regret that they thus cannot be included (in the volume devoted exclusively to the study of Asian Americans) (Kitano and Sue, 1973:4)."

At present, therefore, a simpler typology enabling utilization of incomprehensive data will have to be developed for an analysis of Korean Americans. There are many indications, however, that the present situation will improve substantially in the near future.

This study thus employs simple dichotomies for typing of Korean Americans: (1) traditionalist versus integrationist, distinguished primarily by individuals' attitudes toward earlier realities (pre-migration days, i.e., Korea) and the present realities (post-migration days, i.e., America); and (2) organizationist versus individualist, distinguished mainly by migrants' attitudes toward organizations or individuals as major instruments to solve their problems in the new country.

Traditionalist Versus Integrationist: Berger and Luckman (1967: 173-183) imply that there may be many different identities in an individual but only one subjective world is really open to an individual. Most individuals are, of course, sufficiently complex to warrant an assumption that no single culture system may encompass the totality of a person. In the case of Korean Americans, however, the notion of Berger and Luckman seems to deserve a note.

Korean immigrants, perhaps excepting their offspring, have two compelling sets of culture systems to cope with: Korean and American. Each of the two systems have developed during many centuries complicated systems of beliefs and rules of behavior. When the two such all-encompassing systems clash in a person, an individual is offered a difficult choice. Although the choice may not be perceived to be either/or type, Berger and Luckman tell us that an individual rarely has more than an either/or choice.

Cognitive dissonance generated by choosing to live simultaneously under the two systems may be too much for most to bear. Creative integration of the two systems for individual growth and cultural enrichment may be possible for a few creative individuals but not for most immigrants.

For these reasons, I think that most Korean migrants may be characterized either as a traditionalist or as an integrationist, taking certain risks of oversimplification.

Traditionalists are those who may formally accept the American realities, but whose only "really" meaningful realities are those of the earlier period before they left Korea. In a new culture, they do not seriously go through the reprimary socialization process. Their earlier commonsense realities may be somewhat modified, but the impact of this is generally minimized. The traditionalist may even try to pass as an insider in a new culture without really intending or being capable of membership.

Integrationists are those whose only meaningful realities are present American realities, and whose earlier realities are increasingly displaced from his subjective world. As Berger and Luckman put it, this is "a cutting of the Gordian knot of consistency and reconstructing reality de novo (1967:162)." An integrationist may give lip services to traditional values or even attempt to pass as a traditionalist, but all his behavioral manifestations indicate the integrationist tendency from mild acculturation to all-out conversion.

The empirically discernable trends today is that integrationists are proportionately increasing among Korean Americans.

1. Migration statistics show that an increasing number of Koreans are coming with the intention of staying.

(a) The number of Koreans who have become naturalized citizens of the United States has increased steadily since 1965 (See Table 7). Citizenship, or decision not to return may not by themselves indicate that the "traditionalist" component among Korean Americans is declining. The fact that these decisions are increasingly reflected statistics indicate, however, that an increasing number and proportion of Korean Americans have decided to accept the new American realities for their own.

(b) The number of Koreans who have obtained the status of permanent resident (immigrant) has also drastically increased since 1965. (See Table 2). This rate of increase is unprecedented for Korean Americans and represents the highest growth rate among all Asian Groups including Japanese, Chinese, and Filipinos.

(c) Survey research findings indicate that only a miniscule proportion of Koreans in America are showing interests in returning to Korea. In a sample of 225 Koreans in Chicago in 1975 which included some non-immigrant Koreans, only eight individuals or 3.6 per cent of the sample indicated a plan to return to Korea (B.L. Kim, 1975: 61). Although a significant 64 individuals or 28.4 per cent of the sample indicated that they were uncertain or even regretful of their decision to emigrate to America, they entertained no plan to return to Korea.

   2. *There is other statistical information that indicates the significance of "integrationist" components among Korean Americans:*

   (a) A greater proportion of Koreans are marrying non-Korean nationals than any other Asian group in this country. Although the data in Table 11 is confined to Hawaii, which displays many a typical features, the Korean pattern seems too unique to ignore. It appears safe to say, however, that the rate of mixed marriages among Korean Americans is high. This appears also to be a behavioral indication that the "integrationist" component among Korean Americans is significant.

   A preliminary review of a survey research in Chicago further demonstrated this. A significant 27.5% of males and 31.1% of females interviewed indicated that they have a "favorable attitude toward interracial marriage" (Hurh, 1976: 49).

   (b) A significant proportion of Korean Americans seem to reject outright certain "traditionalist" views. In a Chicago survey, 45.1% of Korean males and 46.6% of females expressed their attitude that "some Korean customs need to be discarded (Hurh, 1976: 49). This seems to be indication that the "integrationist" attitude is taking a strong hold on Korean Americans.

   (c) There are also strong indications that Korean Americans have high aspirations for integration. Table 12 shows that a significant gap exists between those who reported their English fluency as either fluent or adequate and those who cited language as a serious problem.

   It is interesting to note that, only a small fraction of the Asian Immigrants with the exception of the Chinese Americans perceived language as no problem while a significant proportion of the same sample evaluated their English as either fluent or adequate. Doubtlessly, there may be many different interpretations of this.

   What this should indicate for everyone, however, is that a significant portion of Korean Americans and a few other Asian groups have come to perceive fluency and/or adequacy in English language is not good enough. The question is "not good enough for what?" The answer appears to be that it is "not good enough for integration." Can this be interpreted as a testimony that there is a strong current of

Table 18.   Self-evaluation of English Fluency & Perception of Language as
Problem.

(In percent)

	Korean		Fililpino		Japanese		Chinese	
	M	F	M	F	M	F	M	F
English, fluent or adequate (a)	65	48	93	96	69	46	21	11
Language presents no problem (b)	11	11	52	58	16	11	20	11
Difference (a)—(b)	54	37	41	38	53	35	1	0

Source: B.L. Kim, 1975: 35 & 59.

(a) Proportion of ethnic migrants who evaluated their own English as either fluent
or adequate. The percentages in this row were obtained by collapsing two rows
in Table #3. 109 (B.L. Kim, 1975: 35).

(b) Proportion of ethnic migrants and citizens who did not mark "language" as a
"problem area associated with immigration (B.L. Kim, 1975: 59)." The percentages in this row were obtained by subtracting from 100% the proportion of
those who did mark language as problematic. Other problem areas presented
to the interviewees were homesickness, lack of ethnic person contacts, food
differences, weather differences, and life style/cultural differences.

integrationist sentiment among Korean Americans? Our answer is a
tentative "yes."

Organizationist Versus Individualist: Our second typology has to
do with strategy types employed by migrant groups in coping with
their problems associated with immigration. All individuals and
groups have problems to cope with. Some respond to the problem
situation by seeking organizational channels while others rely mainly
on self, family, and a circle of intimate friends.

The empirically discernable trend today is that the predominant
number and proportion of Korean Americans are *individualists* in
strategy orientation. The following facts may document this claim:

*(1) Distributive patterns of Korean Americans show the indication
of individualist tendency.*

(a) The regional distribution of Korean Americans displays a
unique pattern as shown in Table 5.

Koreans in America

Table 19.   *Urban-Rural Distribution of Asian Americans, 1970.*

(In percent)

	Korean	Japanese	Chinese	Filipino
Total Population	100	100	100	100
Urban	67.0	89.2	96.6	85.5
Rural	33.0	10.8	3.4	14.5
Inside SMSA's	61.8	86.3	93.7	85.0
Outside SMSA's	38.2	13.7	6.3	15.0
In Central Cities	33.3	48.4	68.8	48.1
In Suburbs	28.5	39.9	25.0	37.0

Source: U.S. Bureau of the Census, HC (7)-9, 1973.

Korean Americans thus display the most dispersed settlement patterns regionally among all Asian groups. Although this fact by itself may not indicate any individualist tendency, it certainly demonstrates that Korean Americans are not inclined for ethnic concentration which may create conditions conductive to organizational responses to collective ethnic problems.

(b) The Korean Americans are also more dispersed than their fellow Asian groups in the urban-rural landscape of the United States. As Table 19 shows, Korean Americans are far more rural than other Asian groups.

This atypical feature also holds true of Koreans even inside the SMSA's. Although the proportion suburban of Korean Americans is lower than for that of Japanese and Filipinos, fewer Koreans in proportion to their numbers in the SMSA as a whole live in central cities than do all their fellow Asian groups. A significant 46.2 per cent of Korean Americans in SMSA's live in suburbs, compared to 28.6 for Filipinos, 44.0 for Japanese, and 26.6 per cent for Chinese. All in all, the general tendency among minority immigrants to concentrate in urban-metropolitan-central city area is considerable less for Koreans than for their fellow Asian groups.

Korean Americans are clearly more rural, suburban in residence than the other Asian groups. This dispersed pattern may further reinforce our previous observation that Korean Americans are not inclined toward ethnic concentration and thus display individualist orientation.

(2) Survey findings show that a significant proportion of Korean Americans are skeptical about the efficacy of organizations in helping them solve their problems.

(a) A recent survey of Asian Americans in Chicago shows that 36.1 per cent of Korean immigrants did not seek organizational help because they believed "organizations can not help," or they didn't want "others to know," or they didn't know "where to go." Table 20 below presents the data in a greater detail:

This question was asked of only those respondents who did not seek help. Additionally, these respondents could give more than one response to this question, thus the numbers at the bottom line do not represent the number of respondents but responses. B.L. Kim's table broke this data down by sex which is collapsed for the purpose of this paper.

The proportion of Korean Americans who expressed some degree of anti-organizationist view ("organizations can't help" or "didn't want others to know") was greatest among the four and other places show that they tend to be in perennial financial crises or staffing problems. In short, viable ethnic organizations representing Korean Americans are currently almost non-existent. This does seem to reinforce the previous observation that the confidence in organizational efficacy among Korean Americans is extremely low. This may be both the causes and consequences of the individualist tendencies already described.

Concluding Remarks on Typology: Empirical data on Korean Americans are rare and limited when they exist. The present state of available information makes it difficult to employ refined typologies for establishment of trends. When simpler typologies of traditionalist-integrationist and organizationist-individualist types are reflected on existing facts, however, there emerge certain indications of general trends.

The overall trend appears to be that a significant proportion of Korean Americans are increasingly taking an *integrationist-individualist* behavioral orientation. If further research can establish the validity of this hypothesis more definitely than this paper has, an even more fruitful study may then be made about establishing the causes of this tendency.

Some of the testable factors may be: (a) an elite migration tendency among the recent Korean Americans; (b) the fact that Korea-to-

Table 20.   Reasons Cited for Not Seeking Help

(In percent)

Reasons for not seeking help	Koreans	Filipinos	Japanese	Chinese
No problem or Not serious	22.9	46.1	41.7	20.2
Solve by self or with family	35.7	44.1	38.5	22.5
Org. can't help	11.3	2.6	4.2	7.0
Didn't want others to know	6.4	.1	2.1	.1
Language Barrier	5.3	.1	5.2	14.7
Didn't know where to go	18.4	5.9	8.3	34.9
Size of responses	266 (100%)	152 (100%)	96 (100%)	129 (100%)

Source: B.L. Kim, 1975: 82.

America migration tends to be urban-to-urban migration; (c) increasing tendency that whole families are migrating today instead of individual migrants of previous years; (d) occupational, status, income structure of the Korean American community that work against organizationist orientation; (e) analysis of culture traits of Korean groups that might shed light on their adjustment patterns; (f) and so on and so forth.

B. American Definition of Korean (American) Situation

As was the case with the patterns on minority responses, there exists a host of literature on majority responses. Outstanding among them is Gordon's assimilation model (1964), which distinguishes such types as cultural, structural, identificational, attitude-receptive, behavior-receptive and others. There have also been attempts to generate theoretical hypotheses, such as Allport (1958) and Blalock (1967) on prejudice and discrimination, Shibutani and Kwan (1965) on ethnic stratification, or Van Den Berghe (1967), Schermerhorn (1970), and Kinloch (1974) on inter-ethnic relations.

Once again, however, a simpler typology than the ones suggested in the relevant literature will have to be utilized in the case of Korean Americans. Again, this is generally due to the fact that a significant immigration of Koreans to the United States has been a recent phenomonon and thus few opportunities have been made available for students of Korean Americans to conduct a comprehensive analysis.

Our typology will, therefore, take a simple dichotomy to total-receptivity and partial-receptivity. We may likewise conceive of non-receptivity. The fact that immigration of a sizeable volume has been allowed itself will, however, largely preclude such a possibility.

Total receptivity will be construed in a case when there exists an equal opportunity to Korean Americans as to other Americans. Of course, no existing society permits an equal opportunity even to all of its own citizens.

Socially approved passages toward wealth, power, and prestige tend always to contain exclusive features along the lines of age, sex, race, and others. For the purpose of this paper, however, total-receptivity will be declared existent if lack of opportunities is not grounded on race/ethnicity of the Korean Americans. Partial-receptivity will be noted when native Americans are shown to be selective in their receptiveness toward the Korean Americans.

The empirically discernable trend today is that native Americans tend to be highly selective in their receptivity towards the Korean American, thus displaying partial-receptivity. The following findings may substantiate this claim:

(1) A great felt racial-distance was found to exist between Koreans and Korean Americans on the one hand and the majority of Americans on the other hand.

As Table 21 illustrates, Koreans and Korean Americans have been noted for displaying one of the greatest racial distances.

Koreans were ranked at 27th and 30th in 1966 and 1976, respectively. Korean Americans were ranked at 26th in 1976. The general picture from Table 21 is mainly two-fold: (a) that the racial distance

Table 21. Bogardus's Racial Distance Scale for 1966 and 1976

Racial/Ethnic Groups	1966*		1976**	
	Scale	Rank	Scale	Rank
Americans (U.S. White)	1.07	1	1.11	1
English	1.14	2	1.41	2
Canadians	1.14	3	1.49	4
French	1.36	4	1.51	5
Irish	1.42	5	1.59	7
Swedish	1.42	6	1.48	3
Norwegians	1.50	7	1.70	11
Italians	1.51	8	1.58	6
Scots	1.53	9	1.61	8
Germans	1.54	10	1.63	9
Hollanders	1.54	11	1.69	10
Finns	1.67	12	2.00	16
Greeks	1.82	13	1.80	12
Spanish	1.93	14	2.09	17
Jews	1.97	15	2.14	18
Poles	1.98	16	1.96	14
Czechs	2.02	17	2.36	20
Indians (American)	2.12	18	1.96	13
Japanese Americans	2.14	19	2.40	23
Armenians	2.18	20	1.98	15
Filipinos	2.31	21	2.53	27
Chinese	2.34	22	2.54	28
Mexican Americans	2.37	23	2.32	19
Russians	2.38	24	2.37	22
Japanese	2.41	25	2.47	25
Turks	2.48	26	2.42	24
Koreans	2.51	27	2.59	30
Mexicans	2.56	28	2.37	21
Negroes	2.56	29	2.60	31
Indians (from India)	2.62	30	2.54	29
Korean Americans			2.52	26
Arithmetic Mean	1.92		2.02	
Range	1.55		1.49	

Source: *Bogardus, 1968: 152, based on a study of 2,605 selected persons throughout the United States.

**Hurh, 1976: 12, based on a study of 120 students enrolled in an introductory course in sociology at Western Illinois University at McComb, Illinois.

felt by the average American toward Koreans and Korean Americans is extremely big and of long standing; and (b) that the distance felt is overshadowed by "race," an unalterable, permanently fixed trait of the Korean Americans. For this paper, these findings are interpreted to mean that "total receptivity" towards Korean Americans is not to be expected.

(2) Comparison of job levels between the United States and Korea of the Korean immigrants reflects a general downward occupational mobility and/or underemployment.

Table 22 is the result of B.L. Kim's attempt to "determine whether the present job indicates underemployment for respondents who had been gainfully employed prior to emigration, these persons were asked to compare their current job level with those of jobs held in their native country. (B.L. Kim, 1975: 43)."

While the Japanese and Chinese Americans are showing general upward mobility, Korean and Filipino Americans display a downward mobility and/or underemployment. This is reflected in the inability of the Korean Americans with professional/managerial experiences to obtain the jobs of these categories. Presumably, many of these individual Korean Americans are employed for skilled, semi-skilled, and unskilled occupations of various kinds. For this paper, this finding has been interpreted to mean that the American occupational structure is highly selective in its hiring practices regarding the Korean Americans.

Table 22. Comparison of Job Levels Between the U.S. and Native Countries of Respondents & Spouses

Ethnic Groups	Professional	Managerial	Skilled/ White Collar	Proprietors	Semi-Unskilled
Koreans	−12.1	−3.4	+ 14.9	+ 4.2	+ 25.8
Filipinos	−11.5	−3.8	+ 27.0	−1.1	+ 1.7
Japanese	−4.3	+ 10.1	+ 14.0	+ 5.1	+ 12.7
Chinese	+ 0.6	+ 0.2	+ 30.1	+ 8.9	+ 13.7

Source: B.L. Kim, 1975: 45.

(3) Apart from the racial distance felt toward and downward occupational mobility experienced by the Korean Americans, however, a general receptivity is noted in other findings.

(a) Of 47,000 Koreans who were sixteen years old or older in 1970, 75.5 per cent of all males and 41.5 per cent of all females were in the labor force. Interestingly, these are almost identical with the percentages for the total United States Population or the white population. Similar comparability was also found in unemployment statistics (U.S. Bureau of the Census, PC (L)-Cl; PC (2)-1G).

(b) In 1970, the income levels of Korean Americans of both sexes were close to national level. The median income of Korean males was about $650 less than that of the U.S. males in general, while that of the females exceeded their U.S. counter part by $260.

(c) Although certain methodological questions exist on the Census Bureau's sampling procedures on Asian housing data, in 1970 43.3 per cent of Korean-occupied housing units were owned by Korean Americans, quite comparable to that of the other Asian groups.

(4) Overall patterns in the American definition of the Korean (American) situation is, therefore, one of partial receptivity.

Korean Americans have not been accepted as "our kind" by the majority of Americans as evidenced by long-standing racial distance felt toward the Korean Americans mentioned before. In the areas of employment, income, and housing, however, the overall majority response has been one of general receptivity.

The findings on downward mobility and/or underemployment of the Korean Americans, however, raise a possibility of what may be called a "selective discrimination." This hypothesis of selective discrimination has been further corroborated by different degrees of discrimination felt in different areas by the Korean Americans. In B.L. Kim's study of Asians in Chicago, 14.5 per cent of the Korean Americans stated that they experienced "definite or probable discrimination" in housing. While only 1.3 per cent experienced discrimination in keeping the jobs, a significant 27.3 per cent of the respondents stated that they passed over promotions due to discrimination (B.L. Kim, 1975: 67). Although only a tentative statement can be made at present, the probability is high that selective discrimination exists against those Korean Americans in professional/managerial positions or higher-than-average income bracket.

Incomprehensive our data may be, therefore, the general pattern of majority response toward Korean Americans is that of partial-receptivity.

C. Interplay between the Two Definitions of the Situation

As we stated at the outset, the process through which patterns of assimilation and exclusion of an immigrant group emerge is a product of a dynamic interplay between the definition of the situation made by the migrant group and the definitions which the host society has provided for them.

A preliminary analysis of the available demographic and survey findings suggests that the Korean definition of the situation is characterized by *integrationistic-individualistic* tendencies while that of the majority response to it is characterized by *partial-receptivity*.

Even if these interpretations of our facts are proven valid, however, these definitions are not static or impermeable to change. Whereas the pattern of mutual adjustment is a product of clashing definitions, the definitions themselves will undergo significant alterations with the interplay.

The two definitions are not presently in a harmonious state. One is at least a partial negation of the other. Psychological theories of group dynamics (Lewin, 1948 and others) and sociological theories of equilibrium (Ogburn, 1950) or exchange (Homans, 1974: Blau, 1967) would postulate that this partially but mutually negating propositions will tend to move toward a resolution.

Although none of sound mind would attempt to make a definite statement about the nature of such a future resolution, however, certain predictions of low level may be possible.

1. Although there exist two definitions, the two are not of equal strength. While the *integrationistic-individualistic* definition of Korean Americans are feebly supported by less than a quarter of a million Korean Americans and their limited experiences in the new country, the *partially-receptive* American definition is supported by many tens of millions and their historical experiences of having dealt with divergent groups of immigrants. As the definitions go through the process for mutual accommodation, therefore, it is likely that more

profound changes will occur in the Korean component of the two definitions.

This is not to say that a sheer numerical strength or years of experience will always settle the courses of various definitions. What it means is that any significant changes in the American definition of *partial-receptivity* in any foreseeable future is highly improbable. For instance, a transformation of the American definition to *total-receptivity* would require disappearance of the racial distance. For racial distance to disappear, however, there should be either an extensive miscegenation as in Hawaii or basic changes in perception of racial/ethnic differences as in Brazil. Not only is realization of such prospect unlikely, but also contrary to currently dominant trends toward racial/ethnic identity and pride.

2. If such circumstantial forces are to induce changes in the Korean definition, it may be also foreseeable that the presently strong current of integrationistic-individualistic tendencies is to be weakened or modified. As to how such a modification will take place, however, it can only be speculated.

What may be safely speculated, however, is that the Korean American community will become more diversified. As the volume of Korean immigration has increased in recent years, so has the probability that the immigrants are bringing with them increasingly diverse back ground in culture, socio-economic experiences, and so on. Further, as Korean Americans are more dispersed in settlement than other groups, they may also be subjected to more diverse set of circumstances in the United States.

It is likely, therefore, that the present dichotomies of *traditionalist versus integrationist* or *organizationist versus individualist* will become inadequate to describe the patterns as assimilation and exclusion of the Korean Americans.

As Korean Americans undergo this process of diversification and as more and better facts are revealed about them, therefore, social scientists are going to be called upon to undertake a more refined typological analysis than the one employed here.

Why, it may even be possible to undertake a study of scope undertaken by Thomas and Znaniecki in their study of *The Polish Peasant in Europe and America* (1920). Anyone for *The Korean Elite in Asia and America?*

REFERENCES

Allport, Gordon W.
1958 *The Nature of Prejudice* (Garden City, N.Y.: Doubleday).
Berger, Peter L. and Thomas Luckmann
1966 *The Social Construction of Reality: A Treatise in the Sociology of Knowledge* (Garden City, N.Y.: Doubleday)
Blalock, Hubert M., Jr.
1967 *Toward a Theory of Minority-Group Relations* (New York, Wiley).
Bogardus, Emory S.
1968 "Comparing Racial Distance in Ethiopia, South Africa and the United States," *Sociology and Social Research* (52: 149-156).
Choe, Yong-ho
1978 "The Early Korean Immigrants to Hawaii: A Background History," in M. Shin & D. Lee (Eds.), *Korean Immigrants in Hawaii: A Symposium on Their Background History, Acculturation and Public Policy Issues* (Honolulu: Beau Press) pp. 1-17.
Cha, Marn J.
1975 "Ethnic Political Orientation as Function of Assimilation: with Reference to Koreans in Los Angeles," *Journal of Korean Affairs*, 5:14-25.
Cordova, Dorothy L. and Ick-whan Lee
1975 "A Study of Problems of Asian Health Professionals," unpublished monograph, Seattle: Demonstration Project for Asian Americans.
Department of Health, Education and Welfare
1975 "A Study of Selected Socio-Economic Characteristics of Ethnic Minorities Based on the 1970 Census: Asian Americans," prepared by Urban Associates, Inc., for DHEW. HEW Publication No. (OS) 75-121.
Gordon, Milton M
1964 *Assimilation in American Life: The Role of Race, Religion and National Origins* (New York: Oxford).
Hauser, Philip M. and Otis D. Duncan
1959 *The Study of Population.* Chicago: University of Chicago Press.

Hurh, Won Moo
    1976 "Comparative Study of Korean Immigrants in the United States," a paper presented at the 1976 meeting of Korean Christian Scholars in North America, Chicago.

Kim, Bok-Lim C. and Margaret E. Condon
    1975 "A Study of Asian Americans in Chicago: Their Socio-Economic Characteristics, Problems and Service Needs: Final Report," NIMH-DHEW.

Kim, Hyung-chan
    1975 "Some Aspects of Social Demography of Korean Americans," *The International Migration Review:* 23-42.

Kim, Sil D.
    1975 "An Analysis of Problems of Asian Wives of U.S. Servicemen," unpublished monograph, Seattle: Demonstration Project for Asian Americans.

Kinloch, Graham C.
    1974 *The Dynamics of Race Relations: A Sociological Analysis* (New York: McGraw-Hall).

Kitano, Harry L. and Stanley Sue
    1973 "The Model Minorities," *The Journal of Social Issues,* (29:1-9).

Korea Week (weekly newspaper published in Washington, D.C.)
    September 3, 1975.
    December 13, 1975.
    January 15, 1976.

Owan, Thomas
    1975 "Asian Americans: A Case of Benighted Neglect and Bilingual-Bicultural Service of Delivery, Implications to Spanish Speaking Americans and Native Americans," paper presented at the 1975 National Conference on Social Welfare, San Francisco.

Patterson, Wayne
    1974 "The First Attempt to Obtain Korean Labors for Hawaii, 1896-97," a paper delivered at the Columbia University Seminar on Korea, May 17, 1974.

Rose, Peter I.
    1964 *They and We* (New York: Random House).

Ryu, Jai P.
    1976 "Koreans in America: A Demographic Analysis," in H. C. Kim (Ed.), *The Korean Diaspora* (Santa Barbara, Calif.:

ABC-Clio) pp. 205-228.

Siegel, Jacob S.
  1973 "Estimates of Coverage of the Population by Sex, Race and Age in the 1970 Census," paper presented at the 1973 Annual Meeting of the Population Association of America, New Orleans. Mr. Siegel works for the U. S. Bureau of the Census.

Simpson, George E. and J. Milton Yinger
  1972 *Racial and Cultural Minorities: An Analysis of Prejudice and Discrimination* (New York: Harper).

Thomas, William I. and Florian Znaniecki
  1920 *The Polish Peasant in Europe and America* (Chicago: University of Chicago Press).

U.S. Bureau of the Census (from *1970 Census of Population* publications):

1. *General Population Characteristics, United States Summary,* PC(1)-B1.

2. *General Social and Economic Characteristics, United States Summary,* PC(1)-C1.

3. *Detailed Characteristics, United States Summary,* PC(1)-D1.

4. *Subject Reports:*
   a. *National Origin and Language,* PC(s)-1A.
   b. *Marital Status,* PC(2)-4C.
   c. *Japanese, Chinese and Filipinos in the United States,* PC(2)-1G.
   d. *Housing of Selected Racial Groups,* HC(7)-9.

5. *Minority-Owned Business: Asian Americans, American Indians, and Others,* MB 72-3.

U.S. Immigration and Naturalization Service
  1965-
  1977 *Annual Reports.*

CHAPTER 9

AMERICAN PROTESTANT MISSIONS TO KOREA AND THE AWAKENING OF POLITICAL AND SOCIAL CONSCIOUSNESS IN THE KOREANS BETWEEN 1884 AND 1941

Young Il Shin

Since the first American missionary arrived in Korea in September 1884, many others followed him quickly and soon began their work in varied fields. Their activities in all fields were well received by the Koreans from the very beginning and by the time the Japanese absorbed Korea into their expanding empire in 1910, there were "altogether 807 churches, 200,000 converts, over 400 Korean pastors, 257 foreign missionaries, 350 schools directly attached to Christian missions, 15,000 students receiving instruction from Christian missionaries, and 15 hospitals under mission management."[1]

The successful planting and nurturing of Protestantism in Korea by American missions owe largely to the following three supportive elements that existed almost from the beginning of their work.

When the country was forced open its doors to the rest of the world, first, by the Japanese in 1876, then, even wider by the United States in 1882, the aging and impotent government of Korea found itself powerless in the game of imperialist power politics and totally unprepared to guide the shocked nation into politics and totally unprepared to guide the shocked nation into a new world of violently different order.

While the ruling class members, both in and out of government service, were politically divided, confused, and feuding among

---

[1] *The Missionary Review of the World* (Citied hereafter as *MRW*) XXIII, March 1910, p. 231.

themselves in their frantic search for a new direction for their country, Korea's ignorant and voiceless masses were left neglected to subsist barely in abject poverty. There were neither religious nor cultural traditions truly powerful enough for the people to look up to for assuring signs of hope and promise in the days of rapid change and uncertainty. The whole nation was waiting for something fresh and powerful from somewhere to come in to lift her spirit up from the state of despair. The Chrisitian religion and its American carriers found an eager and genuinely interested audience in Korea.

The second supportive element was the government of Korea. Though the government was fully aware of the uncivilized appetite for material gains of all imperialists powers which had made their presence in Korea uninvited, it was most favorably disposed toward the Americans over all other imperialists and showed its particular eagerness to establish a special relations with them ever since the U.S.-Korea treaty was signed in 1882. It must have heard from various sources about the Americans in Asia as a whole as less vicious, more humane and square dealing than other "barbarians" from the West. In fact, even before 1882, the governmet was informed by an observant Chinese that the Americans as less dangerous barbarians, having no territorial ambition in Asia, than the Japanese and others from the West.

When Dr. Horace N. Allen, officially physician to the American Legation in Seoul but actually the first Protestant missionary appointed to Korea by the Presbytarian Church of the United States, saved the life of Prince Min Young-Ik, the queen's nephew, who was gravely wounded in the abortive coup of December 4, 1884, which was carried out by a radical reformist group opposed to the Min faction then in power, Dr. Allen was "honoured by being made medical officer to the court and maritime customs service, and was provided with a hospital in which to treat the thousands of natives who had conceived the most exaggerated ideas of the virtues of Western medical and surgical science, because of the fact that their prince had been saved thereby."[2] Dr. Allen's special relations so established with the ruling royal family was to benefit greatly the works of American missionaries from the beginning.

The third supportive element for the success of the missions in

---

[2] Horace N. Allen, *Things Korean* (New York: Fleming H. Revell Company, 1908), pp. 71-72.

Korea was the quality of the missionaries. Almost all pioneer missionaries were liberally educated in America's ranking colleges and had additional professional training in medicine, theology, and other fields. Also, perhaps, having learned some important lessons from the experiences of the missions in China and Japan, they were in general more imaginative, liberal, and pragmatic in dealing with problems, although their theological views were conservative.

Starting in the summer of 1884, the missionaries were admitted into the country, although the ban on the propagation of Christianity was not yet officially lifted until 1888. It appears that the government of Korea wanted specifically the "Americans" to do some of the urgent works for the modernization of the country, which included Western medical and educational works.

Doctors and nurses were wanted at the government hospital in Seoul, which was founded in early 1885 at Dr. Allen's recommendation. In the spring of 1885 the government of Korea requested its American counterpart to select three teachers to start a government school in Seoul to train future diplomats and officials not only in Western languages but also in other disciplines of the West. The qualified doctors, nurses, and teachers did come, and they were all missionaries at the same time. It is interesting to note that these missionaries accepted the call to work for the Koreans in the secular institutions, such as hospitals and schools, in the country where the preaching of Christianity was prohibited.

More missionaries were admitted into the country. They worked in the government schools for a while, then, set out to organize schools of their own. The first two mission schools were founded in Seoul in 1886: the Ewha Girls' School, the first school ever in Korea for girls, and the Paejae Boys' School. These two were quickly followed by 22 others and by 1904 there were 24 mission schools and 11 of them were for girls.

One of the aims of these girls' schools was explained by the founder of one of them as follows:

> They, the girls, are not being made over again after our foreign way of living, dress, and surroundings, because it occasionally appears from home and even in the field that we thought to make a change in all ways. We take pleasure in making Koreans better Koreans only. We want Korea to be proud of Korean things, and more, that it is a perfect Korea through Christ and his teaching.[3]

The aim of education of the boys' schools was "to make liberally educated men" to serve as "Christian and secular teachers for Korea."[4] The young men and women of all socio-economic classes came to these schools for Western education and they were not tuition-free institutions. The Paejae Boys' School, for example, had the self-support program to provide on-campus jobs for the needy students "to make the pupil feel that no aid will be given him unless he makes a return for it. The founder of the school further stated that "Everybody paid tuition and nobody was given money unless he earned it."[5] When the first and only mission press in Korea had its printing shop installed in the school, it was able to offer more jobs to the self-supporting students. In short, the ultimate goals of mission school education were not merely to teach Western curriculum, but more importantly to restore in the Koreans the sense of racial pride for being Korean, to help develop the sense of pride and accomplishment by earning their own education through manual work, and to train them to be Christian workers for their own people.

I. Dr. So Che-pil and His Activities in Korea between 1896 and 1898

Almost all historians agree with this writer that Dr. So Che-pil was the first man who did the most for the awakening of the political and social consciousness in the Koreans.

In 1884, So Che-pil, a twenty one year old young scholar with an official rank in the government and ambitious radical reformist, took part in the abortive coup against the Min faction of the government. When the coup collapsed after only three days, he fled to Japan and then to the United States in 1885. There he obtained his U.S. citizenship and American education. A brilliant student both in high school and college, he went on to medical school acquiring his M.D. degree in 1893. In the following year he married an American and just opened his own clinic, when the Korean government, now under the

---

[3] George L. Paik, *The History of Protestant Missions in Korea: 1832-1910* (Pyong Yang, Korea: Union Christian College Press, 1929), p. 119, quoting from the *The Gospel in All Lands for 1888*, p. 373.

[4] *Annual Report of the Board of Foreign Missions of the Methodist Episcopal Church for 1892*, p. 285, quoted in Paik, *op. cit.*, 121.

[5] Same *Report* as above *for 1890*, p. 272, also quoted in Paik, *op. cit.*, p. 121.

radical reformist control, nominated him as Vice Minister of Foreign Affairs. He was not interested and the nomination was withdrawn. Then, in the course of a year he changed his mind, and returned to Korea in late December 1895 to work for the country with the education he had received in the United States. Without question, So Che-pil was the best and most highly educated Korean at that time.

Although he was appointed as an advisor to the Privy Council by the government upon his return, his workload was light and his reformist ideas on political matters were unsettling to those in power. Unable to influence the government still controlled by the conservatives, he decided to devote his energies to the education of the masses which he felt Korea needed most urgently. To do this, he chose to publish a newspaper, THE INDEPENDENT. In an article "What Korea Needs Most" in the KOREAN REPOSITORY, a periodical published by the Methodist Mission (North) with H.G. Appenzeller as one of its editors, Dr. So wrote:

> My purpose in this paper is not to discuss politics, but to endeavor to bring before the public my ideas as to how to bring about the solution of this grave problem. The government must know the condition of the people, and the people must know the purpose of the government. The only way to bring about mutual understanding between the government and the people is the education of both parties . . . Without education the people will never understand the good intentions of the government and without education the government officers will never make good laws. . . My idea may seem ridiculous to some—the solving of such an urgent problem by gradual education of the people, whereas the condition of the country requires immediate relief. But the relief-work has not yet commenced so far as I can ascertain. There may be several methods of relief, but education is one of the most effective and permanent means.[6]

In the editorial of the October 7, 1897 issue of THE INDEPENDENT he wrote:

> At the time we first began publication, our basic intention was to inform the Korean people about world happenings. To this end, we decided to carry articles dealing with world conditions as well as informative accounts dealing with scholarly matters and economic issues. We also decided that these articles should be readable by women as well as men.

---

[6] Lee Kwang-Rin (1), "The Enlightenment Thinking of So Che-pil," *Social Science Journal*, Vol. VII, 1980, p. 65.

Moreover, we decided that the articles appearing in our paper should deal with both the right and the wrong things people do so as to bring censure down on those who do wrong and to commend those who do right. Finally, we decided to carry accounts of those things which become common experience both at home and abroad.[7]

As the above quotes indicate, THE INDEPENDENT was not only to inform the masses of the things happening in the world, but to make them think actively on the matters of political and social concern and urge them to come out of apathy.

THE INDEPENDENT was not Korea's first newspaper, but it was the first newspaper published for the masses. The first three pages of this four pagepaper were written totally in the plain Korean language and alphabet of the masses and the fourth page was in English to provide the foreign residents in Korea with more accurate news of the things happening in the country. He explained his reasons for publishing the newspaper in the Korean language in the first issue of THE INDEPENDENT as follows.

Our paper does not employ Chinese characters but is written in the Korean language so that people of all social stations can read it. Publishing news items in our own language in this way makes them easy to read and ensures that their content will be grasped clearly. . . Comparing our language with Chinese, there are serveral obvious reasons why it is better to write in our own language and alphabet. In the first place, our own alphabet is very easy to learn which is certainly not true of Chinese characters. A second point is that all Koreans, regardless of their stations in life, can immediately understand something written in Korean since it is the language they speak, provided only that the Korean alphabet rather than Chinese characters be employed. What a pity it is that the Korean people in fact seem to understand something written in Chinese more readily than something written in their own language since they have become thoroughly accustomed to writing in Chinese characters and ignoring their own writing system.[8]

If we remember his Korean education which was totally in the Chinese classics and he had used Chinese characters as a government official, the decision to use the Korean alphabet and language for his newspaper was, indeed, revolutionary and nationalistic.

In its 43 month long life of THE INDEPENDENT, its chief-editor

---

[7] *Ibid.*, p. 66.
[8] *Ibid.*

So Che-pil wrote most of its 776 editorials himself. Among the topics discussed in his editorials were: political topics 271 times, social topics 147 times, educational topics 98 times, economic topics 59 times, and cultural topics 36 times.[9] Through these editorials So Che-pil taught that all men were created equal by God, that the existing inequality in Korea was, therefore, against the will of God, that the individual human rights enjoyed by the Westerners were the rewards they earned through struggle, and that the Koreans, too, must struggle to earn the same rights.[10]

The paper was issued three times a week in its first year, every other day in its second year, and every day in its third year on until it was forced to shut down in 1895 with its December 4th issue. It was popular with increasing number of readers all over the country and had circulation depots set up in several major cities to meet the demands. One of the reasons for its forced demise was that it had accumulated good many enemies for the political and social consciousness and revolutionary spirit THE INDEPENDENT was implanting in the minds of the masses. Its incisive criticism at the government that had no positive policies to handle domestic and foreign affairs and at the Western powers exploiting Korea's resources with their proven efficiency in the nation's political vacuum, became the cause of its own end.

Before concluding this section of the study, we should not forget the visible and invisible support generously given to Dr. So and his paper by the missionaries. In fact, the first and early issues of THE INDEPENDENT were printed by the Methodist Mission's Trilingual Press in the Paejae Boys' School.

II. So Che-pil and the Debating Society at Paejae Boys' School

In 1896, the Paejae Boys' School was almost ten years old and had some 160 students with two missionaries and five Koreans on the faculty, but the projected Western education had not been going well due to the language barrier and the lack of appropriate teaching

---

[9] Lee Kwang-Rin (2), *Lectures in Korean History* (in Korean). 李光麟著, 韓國史講座 v. (近代篇). (서울: 一潮閣 , 1981), p. 413.
[10] *Ibid.*, p. 415.

materials. Soon after his return to Korea, So Che-pil was invited by Dr. H.G. Appenzeller, the founder and principal of Paejae Boys' School, to give a series of lectures to the students of his school. Dr. So accepted the invitation and inaugurated his celebrated lecture series to the students on May 21, 1896. His lectures on world geography, European history, and politics were an instant success. The excitement and popularity created by this special educational treats were so great that Dr. So proposed the organization of a debating society to keep the spirit for learning alive.

The Hyopsong Debating Society was organized by the students and teachers of the school and its first meeting was held on November 30, 1896. The rules to make a debate an educational experience were adopted from H.M. Robert's mannual of Rules of Order for Parliamentary Assemblies. The Society offered the students the opportunity to develop the skills in public speaking and the operation of public meetings.

To the students who had been taught to remain respectfully passive in learning, the debating society was the most revolutionary thing that ever happened to them. The topics chosen for debates were mostly on pressing problems of the time and each debate was to show the possibility of solving problems in an orderly and productive exchange of thoughts. The membership of the Society was open to the public, which included the students of other mission schools in Seoul and it grew to 200 by the end of 1896 and to 300 by March of the following year.

As its membership swelled and the fame of the Society spread, many leading citizens of various regions of the country came to witness the workings of the Paejae meetings. When they returned home, they organized their own debating clubs and societies to enlighten their own people. Dr. So suggested the members of the Society to publish its own news letter, the *Hyopsonghoe Hoebo,* and its first issue of the weekly newsletter came out on January 1, 1898. Within four months, it turned to a daily newspaper calling it *Maeil Sinmun.* Its first issue, which was published on April 9, explained the change in the editorial.

> Since New Year's Day of this year we have published a paper every Saturday. The thirty-four issues which have appeared so far have carried news of the affairs of this society, domestic and international developments and discussions of scholarly topics with the intent of contributing

what we can to the progressive development of our nation's civilization. With God's help and thanks to the devotion of the members of the society, the paper now has a circulation in excess of 1,000 copies. We are grateful to our subscribers for their support of our paper. Now, mindful of the impatience with which our readers must be waiting for each new issue of the paper, a few learned members of the society have worked hard to make the paper a daily and, supported by donations from all the members of the society, today's issue marks the launching of the publication of a daily to be known as the *Maeil Sinmun*. We will continue to print domestic and international news as well as articles beneficial to the people. It is with devotion and love for the nation that we send this greeting to the people.[11]

Here again Dr. Appenzeller and his missionary colleagues were behind the students at Paejae, who were learning to exercise their rights to assemble, express themselves, and print what they wanted in a free and responsible way.

III. So Che-pil's Independence Club

Encouraged by the tremendous success of THE INDEPENDENT and his lecture series which resulted in the birth of the Hyopsong Debating Society at Paejae, Dr. So now decided to do something similar with the influencial Koreans with power and money. He organized a social club called *Independence Club* with over a dozen influencial Koreans in the summer of 1896. They had two patriotic projects in their mind: one was the construction of an arch called *Independence Gate* and the other, a recreational park, in commemoration of Korea's newly acquired independence from China's political domination after the Sino-Japanese War of 1894-95. It must be noted that at the laying of the corner stone of the arch, Dr. Appenzeller was invited to offer prayer.[12]

The Club had as its members many prominent government officials in and out of office, who had been to or served in various official capacities in foreign countries. Many of them were friends of the United States and some of them were Christians. At any rate, the

---

[11] Lee Kwang-Rin (1), p. 74.

[12] Edwin M. Bliss, *The Missionary Enterprise—A Concise History Of Its Objects, Methods and Extension* (New York: Fleming H. Revell Company, 1908), p. 320.

members met regularly on Sunday afternoons to enjoy the company of their equals in conversation and recreational activities. Then, in August 1897 the Club decided to extend its membership to students, merchants, and other citizens who wished to join. This change of the membership policy was the work of the younger but increasingly influential members of the Club, such as Yun Chi-ho, Yi Sang-jae and Namgung Ok, who wished to make it a democratic organization. As the membership grew, the nature of the Club, too, changed quickly. It ceased to be a leisurely social club of the elite, but became an organization intent to do something positive for the nation and its people.

Under the leadership of the above mentioned three men and others, the Club organized a debating society of its own in the model of the Paejae prototype and held its first meeting on August 29, 1897 with some 70 members participating. By November the size of attendance grew to over 500, although not all of them were the members of the debating society. The topics selected for debate were all current problems Korea had to cope with sooner or later. Unlike the Paejae Debating Society, the aim of which was to give the participants and general audience an educational experience, the Independence Club's was to take positive actions to bring changes in the government, international relations, and in the attitude of the people toward all matters of national concern.

The weekly sessions, which gathered over 500 on Sunday afternoons, were awakening the people of all walks of life to their nation's political, social, and economic realities for the first time in the country's history. Dr. So, who endorsed the debating society for educational reasons, seemed mildly disturbed by this turn of development, but did not intervene. His wishes for the society were:

> to discuss matters concerning national improvements and customs, laws, religions and various pertinent affairs of foreign lands. The main object of the Club is to create public opinion which has been totally unknown in Korea until lately. The Club is really the center of distributing useful information. It is therefore more of an educational institution than a political wigwam as is supposed by some. These weekly meetings produce wonderful effects upon the thoughts of the members. They begin to realize the superiority of western civilization over that of eastern civilization; they are gradually becoming imbued with the spirit of cohesion, nationalism, liberality of views and the importance of education.[13]

---

[13] Lee Kwang-Rin (1), p. 82.

Stung by the mounting criticism directed at the government in the popular debating sessions of the Independent Club, the government marked Dr. So as the chief instigator of an inflammatory movement against the established authorities and fired him from his advisory post in the Privy Council in December 1897. Although most members of the Club were liberal and reformist oriented in their political outlook, many of them, especially those who had government connections, left the Club seeing that the time was not ripe for a radical reform.

Early 1898 the two historically significant political actions were planned by the Club. One was to submit petitions to the Emperor and the other was to stage mass rallies to press their demands for a swift implementation. The Club presented its first petition to the Emperor on February 21 and staged its first mass rally on March 10. Some 8,000 people participated in the rally and many of them were students of Paejae and other mission schools in Seoul. Among the speakers were the students of Paejae and other schools and they spoke up for the nation and the people. Unfortunately, the Emperor and his government were not yet ready to listen to the voice of the people that demanded the recognition of basic human rights, social justice, national independence, and clean and caring government for the people. In the petition the government was criticised for mismanagement of domestic and foreign affairs, the corruption in high places, and tardiness in carrying out reform programs. It presented, at the same time, some concrete suggestions and proposals for a new Korea.[14] The first rally or *Manmin Kongdonghoe* was without incident, but the subsequent rallies were marred by violence provoked by the thugs hired-for-pay by the government. The angry supporters of the Club began to retaliate with violence and the rallies during the month of November in particular "had gone beyond the control of the Independence Club," declared by Yun Chi-ho, the Club's chairman.[15]

The Club was officially outlawed by the imperial edict on December 25, 1898. Many key members of the Club and those who had been active in the mass rallies were arrested and thrown into prison and others disappeared to wait out the hopeless times.

Thus came to an end a political party whose aims were of the highest

---

[14] Clarence N. Weems, ed., *Hulbert's History of Korea*, Vol. II (New York: Hillary House Publishers Ltd., 1962), pp. 319-320.

[15] *Ibid.*, p. 323.

character, whose methods were entirely peaceable but whose principles were so far in advance of the time that from the very first there was no human probability of success. But, as Mr. Yun Chi-ho said, though the party dies the principles which it held will live and eventually succeed.[16]

Here we must be reminded that of the leading members of the Club imprisoned in December 1898 and afterward, some were already Christians and many others became Christians while serving their terms, influenced by Christian literature including the Bible, which were made available in the prison library, and by the Rev. A.D. Bunker, a Methodist missionary, who visited the prisoners every Sunday. And also the activities of the Club were closely watched and carefully documented by many missionaries. It was they who provided the information of the Korean's struggle for survival as a nation to the outside world.[17]

In theory, Korea was still an independent nation between 1895 and 1905, but the government was torn by the conflicting advices of the Japanese and the Russians. After the Russo-Japanese War, the government was no longer of the Koreans.

IV. Korea between 1900 and 1920

What was the policy of the United States towards Korea when the Japanese were openly intent to swallow up the nation of Korea in the first decade of this century? "We cannot possibly interfere for the Koreans against Japan," wrote President Theodore Roosevelt in January 1905.[18] Dr. Horace N. Allen, the first American missionary doctor, who later served the United States as the Secretary of the American Legation in Seoul (1890-96), Minister Resident and Consul General (1897-1900), then, Envoy Extraordinary and Minister Plenipotentiary (1901-05), wrote:

Our treaty with Korea of May 22, 1882, in its first article, makes the

---

[16] *Ibid.*, p. 324.

[17] Kim Ryang-sun, *History of Korean Protestant Christianity* (in Korean). 金良善著, 韓國基督教史 (改新教史), 韓國文化史大系 . 12 (宗教. 哲學史), (서울 : 高大民族文化 研究所, 1970, 1979), p. 597.

[18] Dennett, T. *Roosevelt and the Russo-Japanese War*, pp. 104-105 quoted by Paik in his book, *op. cit.*, pp. 258-259.

following promise:

'If other Powers deal unjustly or oppressively with either government, the other will exert their good offices on being informed of the case, to bring about an amicable arrangement, thus showing their friendly feeling.'

We paid no heed to this solemn pledge at the critical time of the Portsmouth convention and must accept the odium attached to such violation of sacred covenants.[19]

"Since that war (the Russo-Japanese War of 1904-05)," Dr. Allen wrote in the same book, "the Koreans have seemed to have no one but the missionaries to whom they may turn for sympathy, and incidentally it may be mentioned, that many awkward questions have been put to our people regarding the conduct of our own government in turning a deaf ear to Korea's plea for the kindly offices promised them in our treaty."[20]

Homer B. Hulbert, a veteran missionary educator for some forty years since 1886 in Korea and the author of *The History of Korea, Comparative Grammar of Korean and Dravidian,* and *The Passing of Korea,* wrote to his fellow Americans in 1906:

The treaty-making power is vested in Congress and not in the executive. The latter cannot add a single word to a treaty between the United States and a foreign power. It follows that the executive cannot abrogate, or drop a single word from, an existing treaty. Is it not pertinent, then, to ask by what authority our treaty obligations to Korea were so summarily impaired?

. . . We were the first Western power to conclude a treaty with her, and in making that treaty we guaranteed to keep a watchful eye upon her safety and interests. For twenty-five years American representatives and other residents in Korea reiterated the statement that we stood for the 'square deal,' for the ascendency of right as against mere brute force, and Korea had a right to regard our government as the one above all others which would demur at any encroachment upon her independence. But when the time of difficulty approached and America's disinterested friendship was to be called upon to prove the genuineness of its oft-repeated protestations, we deserted her with such celerity, such cold-heartedness and such a refinement of contempt that the blood of every decent American citizen in Korea boiled with indignation. . .

How can we, the American people, prove to the Koreans that we were

---

[19] Allen, *op. cit.,* p. 8.
[20] *Ibid.,* p. 170.

not accessory to this act which was so contrary to the principles we have professed to hold? There is only one way,—by helping them to the one thing that will enable them to hold together as a nation. . . That one thing is education.[21]

Seeing objectively the futility of political activities by the Koreans against the Japanese, the missionaries advised the Koreans in essense, as worded by F. A. McKenzie:

> Submit and make yourselves better men. You can do nothing now by taking up arms. Educate your children, improve your homes, better your lives. Show the Japanese by your conduct and your self-control that you are as good as they are, and fight the corruption and apathy that helped to bring your nation to its present position.[22]

Their political consciousness awakened and restless, the Koreans now resolved to wage a new kind of campaign to enlighten the masses through education and other self-strengthening programs. Numerous patriotic organizations, both Christian and non-Christian, were formed during this period, but only one organization was able to survive more than a year under the repressive government controlled by the Japanese.

In February 1907, some of the ex-leading members of the Independent Club together with the leading Christians of the North-western provinces of Korea formed a secret society, named Shin-minhoe (New People's Society). The aims of the society were:

1. To instil the sense of national dignity and the spirit of independence into the minds of the people,
2. To discover and gather like-minded men and women to carry out national campaign of self-strengthening of the nation,
3. To encourage education of the youth by establishing schools, and
4. To finance the Society's activities and elevate the living standard of the people by creating commercial and industrial enterprises.[23]

The Society's activities were geared to give the people the sense of their own power through education and economic independence, and ultimately to qualify themselves to claim Korea for the Koreans.

---

[21] Homer B. Hulbert, *The Passing of Korea* (New York: Young People's Missionary Movement of the United States and Canada, 1906), pp. 426-465.

[22] F.A. McKenzie, *Korea's Fight for Freedom* (New York: Fleming H. Revell Company, 1920), p. 211.

[23] Kang Jae-un, Korea's Enlightenment Thoughts (in Korean). 姜在彦 著 - 鄭昌烈 譯 . 韓國의 開化思想 · (서울 : 比峰出版社), 1981, p. 373.

Inspired by the Society's lofty aims, prominent Church leaders and Christian businessmen, teachers, writers and students joined it. With their own money and the money donated by the people, the members of the Society founded schools, a publishing house, bookstores, and a porcelain factory, while enlisting more members through their provincial and county level chapters. For almost three years between 1907 and 1910 the works of the Society flourished in spite of developing factionalism with the leadership.

Determined to eliminate all anti-Japanese and nationalist activities from the country now annexed officially to Japan, the Governor-General of Korea invented a fabricated charge against 123 Korean Christian leaders in the Northwestern provinces of Pyong-an and Hwang-hae, where the Society's activities were mostly concentrated. The charge was that the Korean Christians conspired to assassinate the Governor-General during his trip to Shinuiju in December 1910. A mass arrest of some 700 Koreans, which included almost all leading members of the Shinminhoe, was carried out by the police. After almost over a year long interrogation and torture, 105 of them were convicted and sentenced to prison terms ranging from five to ten years, although the assassination plot was never proved. The entire leadership of the Society so unjustifiably eliminated, the New People's Society or Shinminhoe was forced to dissolve by the summer of 1912.

The Japanese even attempted to implicate a number of American missionaries, such as Dr. George McCune of Sun-chon, Dr. Samuel A. Moffett of Pyong-yang, Dr. Horace G. Underwood of Seoul, and even the pro-Japanese Methodist Biship M.C. Harris, but failed to prove their involvement in the plot which never existed.[24]

The infuriated missionaries protested to the Japanese and let the world know about the Japanese cruelty and injustice against the Korean Christian leaders, who were tortured for the crime they did not commit, but it did not make any noticeable impact on the Japanese policy. To rouse the public outcry of Western nations against the Japanese injustice was the only thing they could do for their suffering friends of Korea.

---

[24] Kim Ryang-sun, *op. cit.,* p. 612, also McKenzie, *op. cit.,* p. 222.

V. The March First Independence Movement of 1919

Though hopelessly subjugated by the Japanese, the Koreans expected a miracle in the early months of 1919, the actual liberation from the Japanese. Stimulated by the Wilsonian doctrine of "self-determination," which was enunciated in January 1918 at Paris, the Korean nationalists carefully planned in utmost secrecy a well co-ordinated nation-wide mass demonstration to break out on March the First of 1919.

The Independence Movement so successfully launched at Seoul on March the First spread rapidly to all over the country and it lasted at least two months. There had never been a nation-wide popular uprising of this scale against the ruling authority participated by men and women, the old and young of all walks of life, in the history of this nation. To many young Koreans, the Movement was their first awakening experience to political consciousness. "This was my first awakening to political consciousness, and the power of mass movement shook me to the very roots of my being," recalled a Korean Communist revolutionary active in China in the 30's.[25]

Taken by surprise, the Japanese reaction was violent and ruthless. Although the demonstration was to be peaceful, violence errupted both in Seoul and other cities and villages. According to a government report, for the period from March 1 to April 30, 1919, there were 848 incidents (332 with violence, 516 without); 26,713 were arrested; 553 Koreans were killed; and 1,409 injured. According to the statistics from Korean sources covering the longer period from March 1, 1919 to March 1, 1920, 7,645 were killed and 45,562 injured.[26]

Of the thirty-three signers of the Declaration of Independence, 16 were Christians, 15 the followers of Chondogyo, and 2 Buddhists. Almost all Christians, numbering about 200,000 out of 13 million Koreans in 1919, took part, and the students, teachers, and graduates of the mission schools were leaders of the demonstrations especially in the countryside. After all, only religious groups had an effective machinery of communication on a national scale. Unlike other up-

---

[25] Nym Wales and Kim San, *Song of Ariran*—A Korean Communist in the Chinese Revolution (San Francisco: Ramparts Press, 1941), p. 78.

[26] Henry Chung, *The Case of Korea* (New York: Fleming H. Revell Company, 1921), p. 346.

risings, such as the Tonghaks of 1894-1895 and Righteous Armies of 1895-1912, the March First Movement was truly national for every segment of the society participated.

Two other things need to be mentioned here for their particular significance. One was that a very large number of students of public high schools and colleges involved themselves in the movement, proving that the Japanese colonial education to Japanize the youth of Korea had not worked. The other was that for the first time in the country's history, several thousands of women of Korea participated in the movement, showing the whole world that from now on they would be dedicated partners with their men in the struggle for the national freedom and independence.

Some Japanese, including the police, doubted the possibility of a complete success in colonizing the country, and some other Japanese, especially Christians and intellectuals, disapproved the attempt to colonize Korea altogether. The *Fukuin Shimpo* (Gospel Daily), published in Tokyo, on May 15, 1919, had an article by a Japanese minister, which read in part:

> This disturbances will be suppressed. What cannot be suppressed is the spirit of the Chosenese, their anti-Japanese thoughts. What should be done about these thoughts and feelings? . . .
>
> Chosenese are human beings. They have their national pride, their love of native land. Japanese have no monopoly of patriotism. With our shameless swagger and brandishing of "Japanism" how can we quiet their opposition? If we do not get rid of this spirit and take our stand upon conduct growing out of the love which "loves the neighbor as oneself," I do not think we can long hold our position as lord of the East.[27]

Although the missionaries kept their neutral position throughout the movement, the Japanese authorities at first accused the missionaries and Christians to be responsible for the uprising. Director of Judicial Affairs of the Government-General, issued the following statement to clarify the missionary position in the movement.

> Rumors have been rife that foreign missionaries incited the disturbances, or, at least, showed sympathy with the rioters. These rumors owe their origin to the fact that among the leaders of the rioters, there have been found Christian pastors and students of mission schools, so it is not to be wondered that they gained currency. But that they are entirely groundless

---

[27] *MRW*, XXXII, September 1919, pp. 611-663.

has been established by the result of investigations into the matter conducted by the authorities. The authorities have carried out thorough and strict inquiries concerning it and are satisfied that there is not trace whatever that foreigners instigated the disturbances. Nor is there any evidence that they knew beforehand of the occurrence of the trouble or gave support to the rioters. It is wrong to harbor suspicion against foreigners without justifiable grounds. It is still more to be condemned to spread through the press false reports and baseless accusations against foreigners, fabricating such reports and accusations out of mere suspicion. Such acts will excite the ill feeling of foreigners against Japan and may cause trouble in international relations. Should any foreigners be found guilty of sedition or similar offense, the authorities will have no hesitation in prosecuting them; but, as none have been found to be responsible for the recent trouble, people at large should cast away whatever doubt they may still entertain against them.[28]

The missionaries could not and did not join the Koreans in the movement, but their sympathy towards them and their approval of the non-violent movement were unanimous. Dr. Robert E. Speer, Secretary of the Board of Foreign Missions of the Presbyterian Church of the U.S.A. articulated the universal feeling of the missionaries as follows.

The national resentment of Korea at the domination of Japan is due to her dread of the extinction of her national autonomy. The new order is vastly superior to the old, and the men who have been at the head of the Japanese administration of Korea have been of the highest political principle, but the Koreans had looked forward to the opportunity to develop their national character and destiny as an independent political personality, and are even yet unwilling to surrender what they regard as their right to free statehood.

This spirit of nationalism is inevitable and it is invaluable. It is not in conflict with the ideal of a united humanity. It is essential to its realization. The same God Who made of one blood all nations of men, assigned them also their racial and national character and destinies to the end of a perfect humanity. The development of state consciousness, stage conscience, state ambition, state duty, is a development in the will of God for man, and the true world citizenship will recognize this and build the unity of mankind, not upon any speculative theory of humanity, nor upon any sand-heap of individual units, but upon corporate nationalities such as God has always dealt with and built upon in human history.[29]

---

[28] Hugh Heung-Wo Cynn, *The Rebirth of Korea* (New York: The Abingdon Press, 1920), pp. 61-62.

The neutral position taken by the missionaries was not without criticism from some Korean Christians, but, had they physically taken part in the movement, the Japanese could and would have either forced them out of the country or obstructed their works by all means at least 20 years earlier than it actually happened between 1938 and 1941.

The mere presence of the missionaries as witnesses of the events then developing in Korea was itself valuable for both the Koreans and the world, and of course, the maintenance of the mission schools, hospitals, and other socio-cultural service organizations were very important for the Koreans in the long run. However, the missionaries were not mere observers of the events. It was they who were chiefly responsible for reporting to the world of the events, successfully solicited international outrage against the Japanese for their cruelty to the Koreans, and forced the colonial government to introduce the reform measures after 1919.

VI. Korea between 1920 and 1941

After 1919, no organized political activity of any sort was possible within Korea. Feeling betrayed by the West and the United States in particular, and seeing futility of further struggle for independence within Korea, many Christian and non-Christian nationalists left the country to carry on their anti-Japanese activities elsewhere. Those who stayed in the country embraced once again the idea of national self-strengthening and poured their energies into various service oriented works to raise people's socio-economic respectability. Numerous educational and social service organizations were formed by non-Christian Koreans during this period, but only a very few of them survived in the hostile atmosphere created by the Japanese authorities.

The Korean Y.M.C.A., which was founded by the missionaries in 1903, was one of the few social organizations the Japanese could not easily crush. It provided many valuable educational, social, and spiritual services besides recreational and sport programs for the

---

[29] Robert E. Speer, *Christianity and the Nations* (New York: Fleming H. Revell Company, 1910), pp. 117-118.

young men of Korea. In the cities, they operated night school for those who could not attend regular schools and vocational training centers, where the students learned carpentry, printing, iron work, photography, and other industrial and commercial skills. In the rural areas, seminars and workshops on modern farming methods and public health were conducted by the trained Y-workers.

One of the ablest leaders in the rural work program was Dr. Francis O. Clark, the Agricultural Adviser of the National Council of Korean Y.M.C.A. He was sent by the organization to every mission station of all denominations to secure the co-operation of interested missionaries in a nation-wide effort to raise the economic level of the farming population. Under his leadership twenty-one tenday farm schools were held in many places throughout the country between December 3, 1929 and April 10, 1930, to which the real "dirt farmers" were invited. Dr. Clark reported the following results of this project.

> These schools were very practical. One-half of the time was spent in lectures, one-fourth in question and answer discussions, and one-fourth in demonstrating how to prepare soil, make and use simple farm machinery, select the best seed, judge stock, etc. Lutz, Bunce, Kim and Pak started on school, while Clark, Avison, Hong, and Lee began the other. At the end of 5 days, we exchanged schools. By this system it was possible for each instructor to perfect his work and discuss topics which he was most thoroughly prepared to demonstrate. Mr. Lutz and party specialized on dry-farming, soils, fertilizers, crops, horticulture, bee keeping, etc. The other group discussed animal husbandry, as applied to Korea, and the various phases of farm management, financing, marketing, home industries, etc.
>
> All the missions of the Federal Council in Chosen are co-operating in this farm school movement and the mission workers, together with the Korean church leaders, are largely responsible for the attendance at sessions of the farm schools.
>
> . . . The influence of the missionaries and the Christian church is great, and a united effort will make these schools more successful and prepare the way for a large number of demonstration farms. . . At the cost of $100 a year for 3 years (for equipment, seed and fertilizer) a group of ten or twelve men, trained in agriculture, may be able to train Korean leaders and in ten years can turn over the main part of the program to them. . . The mission forces should take the lead and supply the necessary men, women, and means to make this demonstration of applied Christianity. The church must prove to the people that it really cares for their human welfare as well as for their spiritual life.[30]

Other Christian organizations, especially those of women, were active with their campaign against smoking, drinking, and prostitution. The schools for the blind, the deaf and mute, the orphanages, the leprosariums, and the nursing homes founded by pioneer missionaries in the earlier decades, rendered their important services almost uninterrupted during the 20's and 30's.

The Western medicine, first introduced to Korea by Dr. Allen who was also the first Protestant missionary to reach the country, was one of the most important and respected curative arts the missionary doctors used to serve the suffering Koreans throughout the colonial period. By 1930 there were over fifty mission hospitals and dispensaries all over the country and many of these institutions and the Severance Union Medical College were responsible for training Korean Christian doctors and nurses whose professional competence was that of the highest quality.

Many of these service institutions and organizations, though founded by various Protestant missions, soon became financially independent and distinctly Korean institutions and organizations. From the beginning, one of the great emphases in institutional work was placed on self-support and self-management to make the church and other Christian institutions truly of the Koreans, by the Koreans, and for the Koreans.

Countless number of Koreans were taught and trained by the missionaries to be self-sacrificing, self-reliant, self-respecting, and responsible individuals. Serving the people through Christian organizations, the Koreans also learned to do things in democratic ways. They were also "being parepared, all unconsciously, for the storm which would remove from them their Occidental missionaries and cut off financial aid from the West."[31]

VII. The Shinto Shrine Issue and the Exodus of Protestant Missions

When Japan began to expand her empire by military conquest in the 30's, the Japanese authorities in Korea, too, began to accelerate

---

[30] *MRW*, XLIV, October 1931, pp. 736-739.

[31] Kenneth Scott, Latourette, *A History of the Expansion of Christianity* (New York: Harper and Brothers Publishers, 1945), Vol. VII, p. 405.

their programs of assimilation by eliminating the Korean language instruction in all elementary and secondary schools, making the Koreans to change their family names to Japanese forms, forcing loyalty pledge to the emperor, and insisting upon the attendance of Koreans, particularly of the students, Shinto shrines.

In the early days, the Shinto shrine issue was seldom raised for Christian organizations, such as churches and schools, but starting around 1935, all members of every Korean organization—commercial, social, or religious—were required to go to the shrines at least once a month to display their loyalty to the Japanese emperor and his ancestors. By enforcing this pseudo-religious Shinto program, the Japanese succeeded in splitting up the only nation-wide Korean organization, the Church, shut down almost all mission schools and other Christian organizations, eliminated physically almost all prominent Christian leaders from their works for refusing to perform the ritual, and eventually drove almost all foreign missionaries out of Korea by 1941.

In 1941, at least to some, it seemed as though the Japanese had finally succeeded in putting an end even to the people's desire to exist as Korean and Christian in their own land. But, had they?

VIII. Conclusion

In 1882, the Koreans as a whole had no 'political consciousness' as we understand the term today. If we can define the term as a state of mind in which the individual feels that everyone owes his supreme loyalty to the nation-state and is endowed with certain natural rights to take part in the life of that state and perform certain duties for the well-being of the same, the Korean had no such consciousness yet when the Americans came.

For centuries the Koreans were ruled by a small group of Confucian scholar-officials, who assisted the king whose mandate was to govern his subjects in 'benevolent despotism.' Whether the king was benevolent or not, the people were taught to submit to his dictate. Certainly there had always been a small number of Koreans in governing circles, who were politically active, but their activities were always for the purpose of protection or promotion of their particular interest. In other words, political activities were exclusively for the

Confucian degree holders and the people were left untrained to take any part in such activities.

When the Westerners started coming to East Asia with their big guns, first to China and then to Japan, the Korean government was naturally alarmed and in utter chaos began to prepare itself to confront them. In 1876 the Japanese forced their entry first into Korea and the people in a larger number were alarmed, but in the absence of political and national consciousness in them they were helpless to resist the determined Japanese, whose territorial ambition to take the peninsula was nothing new to the Koreans.

After one victory in the war with China in 1894-95 and another with Russia in 1904-05, the Japanese grip on Korea was now complete. The government of the United States didn't do anything in spite of their treaty agreement to intervene in Korea's behalf, "if other Powers deal unjustly or oppressively with either government."

Although the American missionaries, who were firsthand witnesses to all these rapid changes, were genuinely angered by their own government's inaction against Japanese injustice towards the Koreans, they were unbiased observers enough to realize that the Koreans were not at all prepared to protect and assert their country's political and territorial integrity. The missionaries saw, under the existing circumstances, that the only thing they could do for the Koreans was to awaken their socio-political consciousness and teach them its attendant responsibilities. By introducing the dynamic Protestant Christianity, Western style education, the spirit of social service, and democracy to the Koreans, the missionaries helped the people to become autonomous individuals with dreams for themselves and for their country.

No one can dispute the fact that the Korea's first generation of nationalists, both Christian and non-Christian, were profoundly inspired by the missionaries especially from the United States and learned much from them the ways to express their political and social consciousness in their active lives.

Without giving due recognition to the Korean Christians, who played vital leading roles, it is, indeed, impossible to recount such historically important organized activities as of the Independence Club, the New People's Society, the mass rally of 1898, the March First Independence Movement of 1919, and countless other service organizations which served the people well throughout the period covered in this study. And without giving due recognition to the devoted works of the missionaries, the emergence of so large a number of Korean Christians in so short a period is unimaginable. It is amazing to note that the Koreans were not only able to organize and launch a nation-wide mass demonstration demanding international justice before the Chinese, but, in fact, inspired them to stage a similar demonstration, mostly by students in Peking, two months later, although its impact was widely felt after a time.[32]

---

[32] Nym Wales and Kim San, *op. cit.*, p. 87.

PART III

U.S.-KOREAN RELATIONS:
THE MILITARY-SECURITY DIMENSIONS

CHAPTER 10

U.S.-KOREA SECURITY RELATIONS

Tae-Hwan Kwak

I. Introduction

Korea was divided into two zones by the U.S. and the Soviet Union at the 38th parallel, which was originally conceived as a temporary, military line to receive the Japanese surrender in Korea in August 1945. It, however, became a permanent, political line between the two Koreas. The United States, which proposed a dividing line, did not have a coherent, long-range policy or plan for a solution of the Korean problem as a result of the division of Korea. The Korean leaders themselves attempted to solve the Korean problem, while for two years the two occupying powers at the Joint American-Soviet Commission failed to bring about a negotiated settlement of the Korean question.

The U.S. finally brought the Korean question to the United Nations. In May 1948, general elections were held only south of the 38th parallel under the U.N. supervision. The Republic of Korea (ROK) was established in August 1948, and shortly thereafter in the north, the Democratic People's Republic of Korea (DPRK) was created in September 1948 under the sponsorship of the Soviet Union. Thus, the two Koreas were born in the Korean peninsula, and each looked for opportunities to unify all of Korea on its own terms.

When the DPRK invaded South Korea on June 25, 1950, to unify Korea by the use of military force, the U.S. immediately sent its troops to defend South Korea from North Korean aggression. Ever since, the U.S. and the ROK have been trustworthy alliance partners, and the U.S. has become the ultimate military guarantor of South Korean security against a North Korean attack, although U.S.-Korean security relations has undergone gradual changes in recent years.

The nineteenth-century British Prime Minister Lord Palmerston remarked, "Her Majesty's Government has neither permanent friends nor permanent enemies but only permanent interests." In spite of its often moralistic rhetoric, the U.S. has carried out its foreign policy according to this maxim. U.S.-Korean security relations went under great strains in the late 1970's. The patron-client mentality between the two has still lingered. America's cold war mentality toward South Korea and South Korean dependence on the U.S. have slowly adapted to changes in the international strategic environment. In view of the continuing debate over Korean security and unification issues, it is significant to reassess Korea-U.S. security relations and the changing U.S. policy toward the Korean peninsula in the coming decade.

II. U.S. Security Interests and Objectives in Korea

The U.S. security interest in Korea has evolved from an American "Japanocentric" strategy which has sought to maintain an effective and stable balance of power and credible deterrent force to contain Sino-Soviet expansion in East Asia. As a link of this strategy, U.S. policy-makers have perceived the Korean peninsula as a buffer zone for the defense of U.S. core/security interests in Japan and the Western Pacific region, primarily because of Korea's geo-strategic position vis-a-vis Japan and U.S. bases in the Western Pacific.[1]

In the cold war bipolarity, the U.S. strongly asserted its ideological core interest, i.e., defending non-Communist states from Communist aggression. This interest became a predominant determinant of U.S. security policy toward Korea. Since the U.S. intervened to defend the

---

[1] Core interests may be defined as those interests which are determined by decision makers as being so vitally important to the existence of the nation-state that if those interests are threatened, the existence of that state itself is threatened. The concept may be used as an analytical tool in the study of international politics and foreign policy. For further details, see Tae-Hwan Kwak, "The Use of the Concept of Core Interests in International Political Analysis," *Proceedings of The Fourth Joint Conference of The Korean Political Science Association/The Association of Korean Political Scientists in North America* (Seoul, The Korean Political Science Association, 1981), pp. 23-31.

ROK from North Korean aggression in June 1950, the U.S. has asserted its core interests in the ROK and has sought to achieve the following policy objectives and goals. First, it has assisted the ROK to maintain its security and stability and to improve the general welfare of the Korean people. Second, it has deterred renewed North Korean aggression by providing the military and economic assistance to the ROK. Third, it has encouraged South Korea in regional cooperation to promote security, stability and living standards. Fourth, it has prevented any single power from dominating the Korean peninsula, thus maintaining a balance of power in Northeast Asia, which would contribute to peace and stability in East Asia. Finally, it has continued to support Korean reunification by peaceful means as a long range goal by promoting favorable conditions for Korean political integration process.

U.S. strategic objectives and goals in Korea may be divided into two categories: short-range and medium/long-range goals. The short-range goal of U.S. policy in Korea may be identified as the protection of South Korean territorial integrity and political independence. The medium/long-range goal may be the promotion of favorable conditions for Korean reunification by easing tensions in Northeast Asia, particularly by creating an international climate conducive to inter-Korean *détente*. The U.S. government has used various policies and actions to attain these goals since the birth of the ROK in 1948.

III. The Korean War and Security Commitment

Let us take a brief look at U.S. strategy in Korea in 1947-49 with reference to U.S. disengagement from Korea. The U.S. government in 1947 concluded that it had little strategic interest in maintaining its troops and bases in the Korean peninsula.[2] This had become an established U.S. military policy prior to the outbreak of the Korean war. The U.S. decided to withdraw its troops from South Korea by June

[2] For a further evaluation of U.S. military and civilian leaders' views on the strategic position of Korea in the event of a total war in Asia, see *Korea: Report to the President by General A. C. Wedemeyer* (Washington, D. C., 1951), pp. 24-25; Harry S. Truman, *Years of Trial and Hope* (New York, 1956), pp. 325-28; *Military Situation in the Far East,* Joint Senate Committee on Armed Services and Foreign Relations Hearings, 82nd Congress, 1st Session (Washington, D. C., 1951), pp. 1988-90.

1949 without considering the long-term strategic effects and implications for U.S. policy toward Asian countries.

Because the U.S. was unwilling to make any military commitment to the ROK, it failed to provide the ROK with a sufficient deterrent force against North Korea. The total withdrawal of U.S. forces from the ROK in 1949 was then considered necessary and appropriate in view of a manpower shortage and the perceived strategic insignificance of the Korean peninsula in the event of total war in the Asian continent. Meanwhile, North Korean leaders perceived such American action as an invitation to aggression, which they launched in June 1950. As a result of total war strategic considerations, U.S. leaders failed to perceive Korea's strategic importance in case of limited war in the Korean peninsula. Thus, it can be argued that U.S. policy makers misjudged the strategic value of Korea vis-a-vis Japan and U.S. bases in the Western Pacific in the event of limited war in Korea.

When North Korea invaded the South, Washington changed its views of Korea's strategic value in Northeast Asia.[3] Since 1950, U.S. policy makers have recognized the importance of the geo-strategic location of Korea in the event of limited war and they have also recognized that a Communist Korea could pose a grave threat to U.S. security/core interests in Japan and the Western Pacific.[4]

The 1954 Mutual Defense Treaty between the U.S. and the ROK has been a cornerstone of U.S.-South Korean security relations. In this treaty the U.S. has been firmly committed to the defense of South Korea. Article 3 of the treaty reads as follows:

> Each party recognizes that an armed attack in the Pacific area on either of the parties in territories now under their respective administrative control, or hereafter recognized by one of the parties as lawfully brought under the administrative control of the other, would be dangerous to its own peace and safety and declares that it would act to meet the common danger in accordance with its constitutional processes.[5]

---

[3] For a detailed core interests analysis of U.S. military intervention in the Korean war, see Tae-Hwan Kwak, *United States-Korean Relations: A Core Interest Analysis Prior to U.S. Intervention in the Korean War* (Ph. D. Dissertation, Claremont Graduate School and University Center, 1969), pp. 226-266.

[4] See Ralph N. Clough, *East Asia and U.S. Security* (Washington, D. C.: The Brookings Institution, 1975), pp. 170-72.

[5] U.S. Congress, Senate Subcommittee on United States Security Agreements and Commitments abroad of the Committee on Foreign Relations, *United States Security and Commitments Abroad: Republic of Korea*, Part 6, 91st Congress, 2nd Session (Washington, D. C., 1970), p. 1717.

During the Vietnamese war in the mid-1960's, the ROK government sought reassurance that the U.S. would defend the security of South Korea should a new war occur in Korea. From Seoul's standpoint, the existing defense treaty provided an insufficiently strong American commitment to Korean security. The treaty does not provide a NATO-type guarantee of American automatic commitment to South Korea in the event of a North Korean *blitzkrieg,* but simply prescribes that the U.S. government "would act to meet the common danger in accordance with its constitutional processes." This means that the U.S. government would decide what measures to take on the basis of American perceived national interests in consultation with the Congress should such a war occur in Korea.

Since 1965, the U.S. government has reaffirmed its determination to use U.S. ground troops to defend the ROK. It has done so through joint U.S.-ROK communiques.[6] Notwithstanding these assurances, ROK policy-makers have asked U.S. leaders time and again: "In view of the present public and U.S. congressional mood, would the U.S. once again use its ground troops to defend South Korea?"

In the late 1960's, the U.S. began to reassess its security interests in the world primarily because of what may be called the "Vietnam syndrome" caused by a protracted and frustrating war in Vietnam and by American domestic difficulties, including inflation, a balance of payments deficit, embittered public opinion and a hostile Congress. On July 25, 1969, President Nixon expressed his desire to reduce the U.S. military presence in Asia and to reassess U.S. policy toward Asian countries so as to avoid future Vietnams. The President stated that future U.S. policy in Asia would seek to avoid military intervention which could involve the U.S. in situations like Vietnam. The U.S. would encourage Asian states to assume greater defense responsibilities, would place greater emphasis on the concept of self-help and self-reliance, and would create a partnership between the U.S. and Asian states for the region's economic development.

President Nixon emphatically restated the concept of self-help and self-reliance when he met President Park Chung Hee in San Francisco in August 1969. Nixon reaffirmed U.S. treaty commitment to defend the ROK against Communist aggression, but he also warned that "all the aid in the world will not help the people who are unable or unwill-

---

[6] See Joint Communiques of 1965, 1966, 1968, 1969 in *United States, op. cit.,* pp. 1718-1725; See also *Dong-A Ilbo,* February 6, 1971; *The Korea Times,* August 28, 1975.

ing to help themelves.''[7]

The Nixon doctrine was implemented in U.S.-ROK security relations which underwent profound changes with incremental decisions in the early 1970's. The U.S. removed 24,000 troops from South Korea by December 31, 1973. Although the reduction of U.S. forces in Korea was inevitable and appropriate in view of U.S. domestic difficulties, the U.S. has kept its existing commitment to the security of the ROK by providing military and economic assistance. Washington declared that in the event of armed aggression the U.S. would defend the ROK.[8] South Korean leaders, however, have concluded that U.S. policy toward South Korea would be flexible according to changes in international and American domestic political environments as far as the involvement of U.S. ground troops in a renewed conflict is concerned.

The U.S. as a Pacific power attempted to build a strong, stable, and credible deterrence force in the ROK in 1971—77 under the $1.5 billion modernization program.[9] As a result of the modernization program, President Park said in 1977 that "in terms of combat capabilities, the Republic of Korea is almost on a level with North Korea."[10]

Events in the spring of 1975, including the debacle in Vietnam and Kim Il Sung's sudden visits to China and other socialist countries, shocked South Korean leaders. Kim's move was perceived by the South as aggressive, and thus, the ROK strengthened its security system internally as well as externally. The U.S. reaffirmed its determination to stand firm against a North Korean attack, and the Ford administration and the Congress warned Kim not to mistake American determination to stand firm against a Northern invasion despite U.S. disengagement from Indochina.

Former Secretary of Defense James Schlesinger stated that if South Korea were invaded by the North, "it is necessary to go for the heart of the opponent's power; destroy his military forces rather than simply being involved endlessly in ancillary military operations."[11] He expressed the possibility of using tactical nuclear weapons in Korea in the event of a North Korean attack by stating that "The U.S. cannot foreclose any option to use nuclear weapons or introduce more

---

[7] See *United States Security Agreements and Commitments Abroad,* p. 1724.

[8] *Dong-A Ilbo,* May 23, 1974.

[9] *The Korea Times,* January 12, 1977.

[10] *The Korea Herald,* January 28, 1977.

[11] *U.S. News and World Report,* May 26, 1975.

ground troops.[12]

In the late 1970's the ROK considerably strengthened its defense capability by purchasing military hardware from the U.S. In 1974-75, the U.S. sold $219 million worth of military hardware to South Korea, and in 1975-76, $509.5 million worth of military equipment, missiles, and aircraft.[13] In 1976-77, the ROK ordered 24 OV-10 aircraft for $58.2 million, 421 M-48 A-1 tanks for $37.7 million, and 733 Side-winder air-to-air missiles for $20.8 million.[14] In 1978, the U.S. Congress approved a $1.2 billion military assistance program for the ROK, including an $800 million military equipment transfer program. The ROK air force also received additional F-4E Phantom jets in 1978-79. There were also plans for a $1.2 billion sale by the U.S. of 60 F-16 fighters to the ROK within the next few years.[15] The arms sales and military assistance program were intended to maintain the military balance between North and South Korea.

South Korea is now moving toward nuclear power status. The ROK has one nuclear power plant (Kori no. 1) in operation, and two power plants are being built by a U.S. company. These power plants would produce plutonium weapons-grade nuclear material. President Park stated in June 1975 that "South Korea would and could develop its own nuclear weapons if the U.S. nuclear umbrella is withdrawn."[16] However, on January 29, 1977, Park declared that South Korea would not develop nuclear arms.[17] The U.S. government was very critical of French and Canadian sales of nuclear technology to South Korea.[18] The U.S. did not want the ROK to become a nuclear power, and South Korea's acquisition of nuclear weapons could trigger a new arms race between South and North Korea.

---

[12] *Korea Week,* June 30, 1975. According to Rep. Donald V. Delums (D.-Calif.) the U.S. kept about 1,000 tactical nuclear weapons in South Korea, *ibid.*

[13] *Korea Week,* October 31, 1975.

[14] *Korea Week,* October 18, 1976.

[15] Han Sungjoo, "South Korea and the United States: The Alliance Survives," *Asian Survey,* Vol. XX, No. 11 (November 1980), p. 1080.

[16] *The Korea Times,* June 13, 1975.

[17] *The Korea Herald,* January 29, 1977.

[18] *The Washington Post,* November 6, 1975; *The New York Times,* October 29, 1975.

IV. The Strained Alliance: The U.S. Troop Withdrawal Issue

In the 1960's and early 1970's, the U.S. was firmly committed to the defense of the ROK, and provided a credible, stable deterrent force against a renewed North Korean attack. With the inauguration of the Carter administration, the U.S. government decided to withdraw U.S. ground forces from South Korea. In South Korean eyes, the withdrawal policy would likely weaken a deterrent force on the Korean peninsula.

The original objectives of keeping U.S. forces in Korea were to deter a North Korean attack and to prevent Chinese and/or Soviet military intervention in the event of recurrence of war in Korea. By defending the security of South Korea and preventing a renewed war in the Korean peninsula, the continued presence of U.S. forces provided stability and peace in Northeast Asia, thereby defending U.S. interests in Japan and the Western Pacific.[19]

The military justification for the continued presence of U.S. ground forces in Korea was questioned in view of the changing international environment, developing Sino-American *détente* and Soviet-American *détente*. Chinese and Soviet leaders were unlikely to promote a war in the Korean peninsula. Moreover, South Korean forces could defend against a North Korean attack. Seoul and Pyongyang maintained a rough balance of military power by 1978, although South Korean airpower was relatively inferior.[20] Thus, the military role of the U.S. was to redress the imbalance in air power between the two Koreas, and the imbalance could be eliminated by providing South Korea with additional aircraft to overcome Pyongyang's advantage in the air. Hence, the military rationale for the presence of U.S. combat forces appeared weak.

The official rationale for the U.S. military presence has become primarily political and psychological in nature. The presence of U.S. ground forces in Korea symbolizes its determination to keep its defense commitments to South Korea and Japan in the event of a renewed war in Korea.

Even before the fall of the South Vietnam government in April

---

[19] See Ralph N. Clough, *Deterrence and Defense in Korea: The Role of U.S. Forces* (Washington, D.C.: The Brookings Institution, 1976).

[20] The International Institute for Strategic Studies, *The Military Balance*, 1978-79 (London: The IISS, 1978).

1975, there was a great debate over reduction and total withdrawal of U.S. forces in Korea in U.S. Congress. It was seriously argued by some members of U.S. Congress and witnesses at congressional hearings that the U.S. should reduce the level of U.S. troops and even withdraw its commitment to Korea primarily because of budgetary constraints and the South Korea internal political situation.

In a press conference in his Georgia home on December 21, 1976, President-elect Carter made the first formal remarks on troop withdrawal from Korea after his election victory. "My stance on the Korean withdrawal will be a very slow, a very methodical, a very careful withdrawal of the ground forces after consultation with South Korea and Japan is carried out."[21] Although his statement contained an element of ambiguity, Carter made it clear that the U.S. would withdraw its ground forces from Korea in four or five years. The South Korean government strongly opposed the U.S. troop withdrawal plan.

According to Carter's original withdrawal schedule in the 1977 report, the Carter administration would withdraw about 26,000 ground troops from Korea in three phases by July 1982, leaving air force, navy and army support units numbering about 16,000 men in Korea after 1982. The first phase was originally planned to be completed in 1978 when 6,000 troops including one infantry brigade (2,400 men) of the 2nd Division and elements of 1st Signal Brigade and 2nd Transport Company would be withdrawn. During this stage a dozen F-4 Phantom aircraft would be added to the U.S. tactical fighting wing in Korea and a new joint U.S.-ROK command would be established to improve operations efficiency. The second phase would involve primarily support troops of 9,000 men by the summer of 1980. The third phase would involve the last two combat brigades of the 2nd Infantry Division and its headquarters which would be withdrawn by July 1982.[22]

The U.S. troop withdrawal policy of the Carter administration was based upon the six premises according to a testimony of Michael Armacost, Deputy Assistant Secretary of Defense, before the Senate Armed Services Committee on March 6, 1979.[23] The administration's

---

[21] *The New York Times*, December 21, 1976.

[22] *The Korea Herald*, February 14, 1978.

[23] U.S. Congress, Senate Committee on Armed Services. Department of Defense Authorization for Appropriations for Fiscal Year 1980. Part 4: Manpower and Personnel. Hearings. 96th Congress, First Session, 1979, pp. 1454-60.

premises may be summarized as follows: First, South Korea was capable of repelling an attack by North Korea without the assistance of U.S. ground combat forces, provided the U.S. afforded air, naval, and logistic support to the ROK. Second, the four major powers— the U.S., Japan, the Soviet Union, and China—had a common interest in preventing a renewed war on the Korean peninsula. Third, South Korea's dynamic economic growth shifted the balance of power in the ROK's favor. Fourth, the U.S. would modernize the ROK army with carefully prepared withdrawals over a period of four or five years. Fifth, the U.S. would keep an effective deterrent through continued deployment of air power in Korea after U.S. ground troops had been completely withdrawn from Korea, leaving some residual ground units to perform logistic, communications, and other functions. Sixth, in the light of the "Koreagate" investigations then unfolding, the Carter administration's failure to develop a long-term plan for adjusted U.S. troop levels in Korea could invite congressional action to legislate redeployments. In that event, U.S. troop withdrawals might not have been the result of a U.S. strategic evaluation but rather would have appeared to be a by-product of executive-legislative struggle.

The Carter administration had several unstated rationales and objectives for the withdrawal policy.[24] Carter's withdrawal policy was certainly influenced by American public mood in the post-Vietnam war period, the "no more Vietnam syndrome," the changing structure and process in Northeast Asian international system, and the idiosyncrasy of President Carter. The most important unstated rationale for the withdrawal policy is that in view of the "no more Vietnam syndrome" in the American society, the Carter administration was less willing to get involved in an Asian land war. Presidential Review Memorandum (PRM) 13, the Carter's basic policy document on the withdrawal plan, stated that U.S. ground troop withdrawal, especially the 2nd Infantry Division located just south of the demilitarized zone, would remove the "trip wire" of automatic American involvement in ground combat in the event of a renewed war on the Korean peninsula.[25]

The Carter's policy based upon strategic miscalculation and indefensible premises could disrupt the military balance between the two

---

[24] For other unstated rationales, see Larry A. Niksch, "U.S. Troop Withdrawal From South Korea: Past Shortcomings and Future Prospects," *Asian Survey*, Vol. XXI, No. 3 (March 1981), pp. 326-28.

[25] For a detailed account of PRM-13, see *Mainichi Shimbun*, March 7, 1977.

Koreas which had been accepted as a minimum requirement for stability and peace on the Korean peninsula, thereby weakening an effective, credible deterrent force against a North Korean attack.

The South Korean leaders needed their psychological adjustments to the Carter's withdrawal plan. The ROK government resolutely insisted that U.S. ground forces in Korea should be kept at their 1977 levels until the military modernization of the ROK was fully accomplished by 1981. Before U.S. forces would be withdrawn in four or five years, the ROK government put a great emphasis on strengthening its credible, self-reliant forces for national defense. South Korean leaders feared that the withdrawal of American forces would weaken U.S. commitment to the security of the ROK and increase the danger of war by the unpredictable Kim Il Sung, and would cause China and the Soviet Union to perceive less cost and risk in support of another Kim's adventure.

President Park declared on January 12, 1977, that the ROK would not oppose the withdrawal of U.S. forces from Korea if a nonaggression agreement were concluded between South and North Korea.[26] His statement was generally interpreted as warning North Korea against renewed aggression by showing South Korean confidence in self-reliant forces, and it also alluded to the Carter administration that the ROK government clearly would object to the total U.S. troop withdrawal unless there was a guarantee on South Korean survival. Park's statement symbolized South Korean fear of the seemingly weakened security commitment of the U.S. to the ROK.

The Japanese government also opposed the U.S. troop withdrawal from Korea, stressing that U.S. forces in Korea have been linked to their security. Tokyo has supported the continued presence of U.S. forces in Korea, which is essential to stability in the Korean peninsula, which in turn, would contribute to peace and security in Northeast Asia.[27] The Japanese government also believes that the U.S. military presence in Korea promotes favorable conditions for Japanese trade and investment in South Korea by diminishing the risk of war in the Korean peninsula. Finally, the presence of American forces provides a firm base for the coordination of U.S. and Japanese policies toward South Korea, and, furthermore, strengthens the credibility of the U.S. commitment to the defense of Japan.

---

[26] *The Korea Times,* January 12, 1977.
[27] See Clough, *Deterrence and Defense in Korea.*

Carter's troop withdrawal plan as described in the 1977 report had to be significantly modified due to a number of international developments and American domestic political process. U.S. congressional and military leaders' strong opposition to Carter's plan prompted him to revise the withdrawal schedule on April 21, 1978.

According to Carter's revised schedule, the first phase of the withdrawal schedule involving 6,000 men, which was originally planned to withdraw in 1978, was scheduled to be implemented in 1979. By the end of 1978, 3,400 men were withdrawn, including 800 combat troops from the 2nd Infantry Division. The remaining 2,600 men involved in the first phase were scheduled to withdraw from South Korea in 1979. The authorized combined U.S. troop levels in South Korea by January 1, 1980 would be 36,000 men.

As U.S. ground troops in Korea were reduced, U.S. air force strength in Korea was increased by 20% in manpower and number of aircraft. In November 1978, the 497th U.S. Air Force Tactical Fighter Squadron comprising 12 F-4D Phantom jets moved into South Korea, and a U.S.-ROK Combined Forces Command was established for joint operational decision-making. In August of the same year, U.S. Congress approved a $1,167 million military assistance program for the ROK, including an $800 million military equipment transfer program.

In early 1979, however, the military balance between South and North Korea was drastically shifted in favor of North Korea. The new U.S. intelligence data in January 1979 indicated that North Korea had its ground forces at between 600,000 and 700,000 men, rather than the 440,000 previously estimated, comprising over 40 combat divisions instead of the prior estimate of 29 divisions. North Korea had 2,600 tanks, 600 more than the previously estimated 1,950.[28]

This intelligence report inevitably led to a new evaluation of the U.S. troop withdrawal plan which would be completed by 1982. On February 10, 1979, President Carter announced that "right now we are holding in abeyance any further reduction in U.S. ground combat troop levels in South Korea until we can assess the new intelligence data on the buildup of North Korean force levels, the impact of normalization with China and the new peace proposals or discussions for peace that have been put forward by both South and North Korean govern-

---

[28] *The New York Times,* January 4 and 21, 1979; *The Washington Post,* January 14, 1979.

ments.''[29]

President Carter visited Seoul from June 29 to July 1, 1979, for a Carter-Park summit meeting, and he announced his decision not to make any further troop withdrawal until 1981 at which time the situation on the Korean peninsula was to be reassessed in order to determine whether to proceed with further withdrawals.[30] This suspension became permanent in a statement issued on July 20, 1979, in which Carter gave up plans to withdraw U.S. ground forces from South Korea by 1982. Thus Carter's troop withdrawals planned for 1979, 1980, and 1981, totaling about 26,000 men were suspended.

Several factors should be considered to understand Carter's decision to suspend the U.S. troop withdrawal plan. First, Japan and South Korea strongly opposed the withdrawal policy from the beginning. Second, American public and congressional leaders expressed their misgivings about Carter's unilateral withdrawal policy. Third, American foreign and defense officials questioned the wisdom of Carter's decision. Fourth, the new intelligence data indicated that there was no military balance between South and North Korea. Under these conditions of imbalance, the maintenance of U.S. ground forces was more appropriate than further withdrawals. The planned removal of U.S. ground forces from South Korea could have weakened a deterrent force against another North Korean attack. Thus, Carter had no choice but to suspend the U.S. troop withdrawal program. In Korean eyes, the U.S. troop withdrawal issue, a major irritant in Korea-U.S. security relations, was temporarily resolved. Presently, South Korean leaders recognize that U.S. forces in Korea will not stay there indefinitely, but they insist that the timing of the withdrawal is crucial. Seoul and Washington will have tough negotiations over when and under what conditions a partial and/or total withdrawal of U.S. forces can be implemented in the near future.

Let us now turn to South Korean attempts to build up self-reliant defense capabilities. The $1.5 billion modernization plan of the South Korean armed forces was financed through the U.S. military assistance program. This plan was originally scheduled to be completed in 1975, but the U.S. fulfilled only 69% ($1,034 million) of its aid program in the 1971-1975 period.[31] The remaining portion was fulfilled in 1976-1977.

---

[29] *The New York Times,* February 10, 1979.
[30] *The Korea Herald,* July 3, 1979.
[31] *Joong Ang Ilbo,* November 1, 1977.

In mid-1975, South Korea initiated its own expensive five-year Force Improvement Plan (FIP) in the 1976-1980 period. The FIP includes substantial increases in aircraft (F-4E and F-5E); air defense improvements; an upgraded tank force; acquisition of TOW anti-tank missiles; domestic production of artillery and small arms (e. g., M-16 rifles); and an enhancement of logistics and war reserve munitions. The South Korean government hoped that by 1980 South Korea would develop a military force capable of defending against a North Korean attack with U.S. logistical support only.[32] In November 1979, the FIP was revised for the sixth time, making it a six-year plan, and it was finally completed at the end of 1981. The total $7.6 billion was allocated for the first Force Improvement Plan during the 1975-1981 period. However, the considerable military imbalance between the two Koreas still remained. Therefore, South Korea has drawn up a second Force Improvement Plan in 1982-1986, emphasizing artillery, armor, anti-tank weapons, and reserve munitions for ground forces, modern aircraft (F-5E and F-16) for the Air Force, and anti-submarine warfare equipment and small ships for the Navy.

South Korean President Chun visited Washington to meet President Reagan in early 1981. In the Joint Communique released by the White House on February 2, 1981, President Reagan assured President Chun that the United States had no plans to withdraw ground combat forces from the Korean peninsula and reaffirmed that the U.S., as a Pacific power, would seek to ensure the peace and security of the region.[33]

V. The Role of the U.S. in Korean Reunification

Let us now turn to American medium- and long-range goals for easing tensions in the Korean peninsula and for promoting favorable conditions for Korean reunification.

Two major factors should be taken into consideration as stumbling blocks to a smooth journey to Korean unification. One is stark reality on the Korean peninsula; there exist two incompatible values, ideologies, political-economic systems, and mutually exclusive unifi-

---

[32] *The New York Times,* August 21, 1975.
[33] *The New York Times,* February 3, 1981.

cation approaches. The other factor is the constraints of the four great powers concerned with Korea, where their interests intersect. Their conflict of interests makes it more difficult to reunify Korea unless there are adjustments and concessions among these powers. Under existing conditions, the U.S. does not, and will not, allow the unification of Korea by military means. The U.S. has supported South Korean unification policies since 1948.

The United States has attempted to reduce tensions and promote more durable arrangements for peace on the Korean peninsula by proposing an international conference among the U.S., China, North and South Korea to discuss the dissolution of the United Nations Command while preserving the 1953 Korean armistice agreement. The U.S. is willing to consider other measures to reduce tensions, including a wider international conference to negotiate more fundamental arrangements for peace and reunification in the Korean peninsula.

Former Secretary of State Henry Kissinger made a speech before the Economic Club of Detroit on November 24, 1975, in which he reiterated the U.S. commitment to the security of South Korea based on the U.S. historic relationship with the Korean people, "a bond forged by common sacrifice" in the Korean war. Recognizing that the security of Japan is "directly linked to the security of Korea," Kissinger emphatically stated that the U.S. "will resist with determination any unilateral attempt to change or upset the equilibrium" on the Korean peninsula. He stated further:

> We will not acquiesce in any proposals which would exclude the Republic of Korea from discussions about its future. And we will not allow our military presence, which derives from bilateral agreements, to be dictated by third parties. But we are prepared now to transform the armistice arrangements to a permanent peace.[34]

Kissinger also made it clear in the same speech that the U.S. would be willing to talk to North Korea about the future of Korea, provided that South Korea be present. In July 1979, President Carter in Seoul proposed direct talks among the U.S., North and South Korea.

President Ford declared a new Pacific doctrine of the U.S. on December 7, 1975, in which he clearly expressed U.S. determination to stay in Asia as a Pacific power in the post-Indochina era. Ford

---

[34] For full text, see "The Secretary of State Speech," Office of Media Services, Bureau of Public Affairs, Department of State, November 24, 1975.

once again reiterated U.S. commitments to the security of South
Korea by stating:

> . . . . Peace in Asia depends upon a resolution of outstanding political
> conflicts. In Korea tension persists. We have close ties with the Republic
> of Korea; and we remain committed to peace and security on the Korean
> peninsula, as the presence of our forces there attests.
> . . . . Today, the United States is ready to consider constructive ways
> of easing tensions on the peninsula, but we will continue to resist any
> moves which attempt to exclude the Republic of Korea from discussion
> of its own future.[35]

While the Nixon doctrine of 1969 called for the gradual reduction
of U.S. power and influence in Asia in the rapidly changing international situation in the late 1960's, Ford's Pacific doctrine was a
significant policy statement in the post-Indochina era to renew U.S.
economic, political and military participation as a Pacific power and
to defend its interests in the Pacific region by maintaining a stable
balance among the four great powers in the region.

Meanwhile, the United States continued to seek a solution for the
Korean question in the United Nations. The 30th U.N. General
Assembly adopted two conflicting resolutions on Korea on November
18, 1975.[36] The Western resolution sponsored by the U.S. and 27
other members of the United Nations was adopted by a vote of 59-51
with 29 abstentions. It called for negotiations to find alternative
arrangements for the 1953 armistice agreement by the parties directly
concerned meaning North and South Korea, China, and the U.S.,
allowing the dissolution of the United Nations Command (UNC) by
January 1976. The U.S. has contended that U.S. troops in South
Korea are there under the 1954 bilateral defense treaty between the
U.S. and the ROK and that the UNC in Korea now has only around
300 officials.[37]

The pro-North Korean resolution sponsored by Algeria, China, the
Soviet Union, and many Third World countries was also adopted by a
vote of 54-43 with 42 abstentions. It called for the immediate dissolution of the UNC, the withdrawal of all foreign troops from South
Korea, and the replacement of the armistice agreement with a peace

---

[35] For full text, see "President Ford's Pacific Doctrine," *The Department of State
News Release*, December 7, 1975.

[36] *The New York Times*, November 19, 1975.

[37] *The Korea Times*, November 20, 1975.

treaty between North Korea and the U.S. North Korea has contended that South Korea should not be included in negotiations for a peace agreement between North Korea and the U.S. to replace the armistice agreement since South Korea was not a party to the 1953 armistice agreement.

U.S. efforts to solve the Korean issue may be futile in the coming years under the present conditions in the General Assembly of the United Nations where the Third World countries now enjoy an absolute majority. The U.N. General Assembly, which adopted two conflicting resolutions on Korea in 1975, showed its weakness in dealing effectively with the Korean question. It may be better to deal with the Korean question outside the General Assembly, perhaps at the Security Council and/or an international conference comprising the four major powers and the two Koreas, where contending parties can have better opportunities to understand one another's positions on the issue so as to avoid the direct confrontation of diplomatic propaganda.

Secretary Kissinger once again made a proposal for a conference to discuss ways of adapting the armistice agreement to new conditions and replacing it with more permanent arrangements before the 31st session of the U.N. General Assembly on September 30, 1976. Kissinger proposed a three-phase approach to a resolution of the Korean question.

The first phase would be preliminary talks between North and South Korea to discuss venue and scope of the conferences. In this phase the U.S. and China could participate as "observers or in an advisory role." The second phase would be an international conference of the U.S., China, North and South Korea if the first phase proved fruitful. The third phase would be "a wider conference in which other countries could associate themselves with arrangements that guarantee a durable peace on the peninsula."[38] Kissinger reiterated that to reduce tensions and promote security, the U.S. is prepared to have the U.N. Command dissolved as long as the armistice agreement is preserved by more durable arrangements at international conferences.

Since 1977, the Korean question has not been on the agenda of the U.N. General Assembly. Meanwhile, North Korea has rejected U.S.

---

[38] For full text, see "Toward A New Understanding of Community," The Secretary of State Speech Before the 31st Session of the U.N. General Assembly, Bureau of Public Affairs, Department of State, September 30, 1976.

proposals to discuss the Korean question at an international conference and, instead, has insisted on a peace treaty between Washington and Pyongyang. Since 1975, Kim Il Sung has proposed direct bilateral talks with the U.S. to reduce tensions in the Korean peninsula, but these proposals have always been rebuffed on the grounds that South Korea was not invited. Thus, the U.S. reaffirmed its position that it will meet with North Korea only if South Korea is present at a conference. South Korea was reassured that the U.S. will not go behind its back and negotiate separately with North Korea.

VI. Conclusions: Security, U.S. Troop Withdrawal and Unification—The Triangle

The U.S. as a Pacific power has defense commitments to Japan, Korea, Phillipines, Australia, and New Zealand. America's strong determination to stand firm against Communist aggression in East Asia is still key to stability and peace in this region, thereby deterring a renewed war on the Korean peninsula.

The U.S. should continue to supply arms to South Korea to maintain the military balance between the two Koreas, and should continue to guarantee the security of the ROK by keeping U.S. ground forces in Korea in the short-run, which at present would serve as a strong, stable deterrent force against a new North Korean attack.

If the U.N. Command, which is a party to the 1953 armistice agreement, would be voluntarily dissolved, the U.S. should search for alternative arrangements in place of the present armistice agreement, and the alternative arrangement might be U.N. Security Council's guaranteed peacekeeping force and/or a non-aggression pact between Seoul and Pyongyang.

In the long-run, the U.S. should continue to seek a four-power agreement on Korea at international conferences. Although the Sino-Soviet conflict at present will make such an agreement difficult to conclude, both Chinese and Russians should learn that such an international agreement on Korea would serve their interests better by keeping stability and peace in the Korean peninsula.

In the 1980's, the United States should be prepared for the partial withdrawal of U.S. forces from Korea at the proper time in consultation with Seoul and Tokyo, and might recognize North Korea if Seoul and Pyongyang concluded a non-aggression agreement on the condition that U.S. ground troops stationed in South Korea be removed only by a step-by-step plan.

If the U.S. should withdraw its 2nd Army Division from Korea in the coming years, would the U.S. military capability to carry out its commitment to Korean security still be adequate? In the event of a renewed war in the Korean peninsula after the U.S. troop pullout, how effective would the U.S. air support be? Would the U.S. send its ground troops to defend the ROK again in the event of a renewed war in Korea? These are some of the questions South Korean leaders have asked time and again. Certainly, it is not unreasonable for them to question U.S. credibility. It became clearer that the U.S. would be unwilling to commit its combat troops to a renewed war on the Korean peninsula. However, the U.S. would likely provide economic and military assistance to the ROK after its ground troop pullout in the event of any violent conflict in the Korean peninsula.

In the coming decade, the U.S. would be prepared for a gradual, coordinated withdrawal plan without endangering peace and security in Northeast Asia. A precipitate withdrawal of U.S. forces would not be in the best interests either of the big powers concerned or of South Korea since it would like whet North Korean appetite for more aggressive behavior toward the South.

In short, a few points are reiterated again here with regard to the triangular relationships among Korean security, U.S. troop withdrawal, and Korean reunification. First, U.S. ground forces in Korea plays a balancer in the South-North Korean military equation. The presence of U.S. forces in Korea helps to achieve a military balance between the two Koreas since the military balance between the two today shifts in favor of North Korea.

Second, under the existing condition of the military imbalance between the two Koreas, it is likely that unilateral U.S. troop withdrawal would tempt Pyongyang to take violent actions against South Korea to unify all of Korea. Therefore, U.S. troop withdrawal is strongly opposed by Seoul and Tokyo. If and when a military balance is achieved between the two Koreas, U.S. troop withdrawal would not change the *status quo* on the Korean peninsula. As a result of the balance, it is unlikely that North Korea would attempt to take violent actions against Seoul.

Third, if and when a military balance is achieved between South and North Korea, the U.S. troop withdrawal issue could be, at minimum, used as a political bargaining chip against North Korea to reduce tension on the Korean peninsula and to induce Pyongyang to come to a negotiating table with Seoul. Since North Korea has insisted on the withdrawal of U.S. troops from Korea, charging the U.S. with "plotting to perpetuate the division of Korea and hamper her reunification,"[39] the U.S. troop withdrawal issue could be a key for inducing Kim Il Sung to come to a Chun-Kim summit meeting. Therefore, it is proposed that the following measures be taken by the U.S. and the ROK.

U.S. troop withdrawal from Korea without any conditions would be undesirable. Thus, the U.S. and the ROK should seek to gain some concessions from the Soviet Union, China, and North Korea, e. g., (1) cross-recognition of the two Koreas by the four major powers concerned; (2) a non-aggression pact between Seoul, Pyongyang, and Washington; and (3) a Chun-Kim summitry on the conditions that the U.S. troop withdrawal issue be discussed and that all U.S. forces in Korea be withdrawn by a step-by-step approach.

Washington and Seoul should take a little more flexible approach to the reduction of U.S. forces in Korea in order to induce Pyongyang to come to the South-North talks. Thus, it would be necessary and desirable for the U.S. to take the initiative to remove 6,000 combat troops from Korea in close consultations with Tokyo and Seoul as a good gesture of Washington-Seoul willingness to negotiate the U.S. troop withdrawal issue with Pyongyang without weakening a stable deterrent force against the North. At the same time, the U.S. and the ROK should make a proposal that a trilateral peace conference consisting of the U.S., ROK, and DPRK be held to discuss the conclusion of a peace treaty or non-aggression pact in exchange

---

[39] Kim Il Sung, *For the Independent Peaceful Reunification of Korea,* Revised Edition, (New York: Guardian Associates, Inc., 1976). For detailed discussion of South-North Korean interactions via events data analysis, see Tae-Hwan Kwak, "Patterns of South-North Korean Interactions, 1970-74: Events Data Analysis," *Asian Profile,* Vol. 4, No. 4 (August 1976), pp. 295-322; For an integrated model of Korean political integration, see Tae-Hwan Kwak, "A 'Block-Building' Approach to Korean Reunification," in *Problems of Korean Unification* (Seoul, Korea: Research Center for Peace and Unification, 1976) edited by Se-Jin Kim; "Political Conditions for Korean Reunification: Problems and Prospects," *Korean Journal of International Studies,* Vol. 8, No. 3 (1977), pp. 57-81. For U.S. role in Korean reunification, see Tae-Hwan Kwak, "U.S. Policy Toward Korean Unification." *Politics of Korean Reunification.* edited by Young Hoon Kang and Yong-Soon Yim (Seoul: Research Center for Peace and Unification, 1978).

for U.S. troop withdrawal.

What if Pyongyang rejected the proposal? What if tensions between South and North Korea rise in the interim? What if Pyongyang would not accept a three-power peace conference proposal? If North Korea still refused to come to talks after the token of U.S. unilateral withdrawal, as suggested above, it would mean that the North is not ready to seriously discuss the Korean problem yet with Seoul and Washington. It would also mean that Pyongyang will not abandon a South Korean revolution. The U.S. would then have no choice but to reaffirm its defense commitment to the security of the ROK, and the U.S. 2nd Army Division in Korea and U.S. air force units as a symbol of U.S. firm commitment to the security of South Korea should continue to stay in Korea as long as the U.S.-ROK Mutual Defense Treaty is in force.

The United States must recognize the Republic of Korea as an equal partner in the U.S.-Korean security alliance system which has contributed to the defense of U.S. security interests in Northeast Asia. The future role of the ROK in sharing the burden of Northeast Asian security by countering the Soviet military build-up in East Asia will depend in part upon further close U.S.-Korean security cooperation. It is doubtless that a continued U.S.-Korean security cooperation would best serve the security interests of the two allies. In the final analysis, the credibility of U.S. firm commitment to the security of the ROK should not be eroded. The U.S. firm commitment and ROK self-reliant defense forces only can deter a renewed war on the Korean peninsula, and can also insure stability and peace in Northeast Asia in the coming decade.

CHAPTER 11

US-KOREAN SECURITY INTERDEPENDENCE: WITH SPECIAL REFERENCE TO NORTHEAST ASIA*

Yu-Nam Kim

I. Introduction

Northeast Asia is an area whose delicate strategic balance could easily collapse over any minor disagreement between the parties of the region. This presumed disequilibrium and intra-regional fragility do not necessarily result from the geopolitical location and vital economic resources as in the case of the Middle Eastern area. Nor is Northeast Asia's potential as a flashpoint in contemporary world politics derived from buffer characteristics that lie between two rival cultures as is the case in Eastern Europe.

Peace and security problems in Northeast Asia are different from those of the Middle East and Eastern Europe in that they stem from a crossroad environment. It is one of very few areas, if not the only one, in the world today where the security interests of four powers meet and must interface. The Soviet Union, the People's Republic of China (hereafter referred to as "China"), and Japan are presented by virtue of their physical geography. The United States joins the Northeast Asian family by virtue of its global status and security interest.[1]

---

* The opinions and views expressed in this paper are those of the author and do not represent those of the Korean government or the Institute of Foreign Affairs and National Security. This paper grew out of a panel on Armed Forces and National Development at the First Wharangdae International Symposium in Seoul, September 20-22, 1981.
[1] For the US security interest, see Stephen P. Gibert, *Northeast Asia in U.S. Foreign Policy* (The Center for Strategic and International Studies, Georgetown University, 1979), pp. 7-9.

These four powers, seeing each other's vested interests in their own terms, observe the behavior of any potential adversary. The system may therefore be described as the Four-Power consortium of Northeast Asia. So long as the geographical integrity is maintained, the Soviet Union, China, and Japan will coexist in Northeast Asia, while the United States' presence rests on political decisions which will determine the extent of US involvement in the consortium. In the present situation within the four-power constellation, peace and security of the region do require a balance of the powers, and the need for the United States to remain as a Pacific power is paramount.

Even the most cursory glance at East Asia reveals the importance to the United States of maintaining the equilibrium of the four-power system and not permitting changes which would jeopardize peace in the area. Thus the power contest tends to lose some of the zero-sum game characteristics: a loss of influence by the United States, for example, will not necessarily translate into a gain by the Soviet Union and vice versa. In this multipolar situation in Northeast Asia, an individual state, i.e., the Soviet Union, cannot devise policies solely to oppose another nation but must always consider the reactions of the consortium members. This is the reason why the Russians are bound to meet with an anti-Soviet coalition as the price of unilateral expansion.

The most conspicuous new factor in the military situation in Northeast Asia is the growth of Soviet military strength. This Soviet expansion is characteristic of the past two decades throughout the world. It is outside of the scope of this paper to give an entire account of the Soviet strategic parity with the United States in the first quarter of the 1970's or of Moscow's continued drive for military superiority since the 1972 SALT agreements. However, suffice it to say, the Soviets have not been satisfied with the parity, nor with quantitative superiorities in many of the various indices of relative strength, and the Soviet Union has proven its capabilities of projecting its forces far from Russian borders.

Northeast Asia today witnesses militarily weak China, defenseless Japan, which forfeits her own security at the expense of others, and North Korea which exhibits the world's fifth largest military camp.[2]

---

[2] According to IISS Military Balance, North Korea by 1981 maintained 700,000 ground forces; 3,800 tanks/APC's; 16,500 Artillery guns/Mortars; and 700 combat aircrafts. *The Military Balance, 1981-1982* (London: The International Institute for Strategic Studies, 1982), pp. 82-83.

Seeing the regional balance of military strength in favor of the Soviets and their socialist comrades in North Korea, defensively strong South Korea, with the assistance of US military forces on the Korean peninsula and elsewhere in the Western Pacific, elevates what might be a minor consideration to one of global importance. In the absence of a NATO-counterpart in Asia, the United States, faced with a growing defense burden, urges Japan to expand her security role in the area. An additional significance to the United States move is the improved relationship with China for security collaboration to counter the Soviet expansion in the region.

The Reagan Administration, replacing an ill-fated plan of US withdrawal from South Korea with a program to strengthen its on-the-scene capabilities, is committed to building a security community of its allies and friendly powers to meet the Soviet challenge in Asia. This cooperation will create a greater defense and a total security cooperation in broader terms, but will fall short of a collective security arrangement, linking the defensively isolated regions of Southeast and Northeast Asia. The security linkage will be stretching from the Soviet Sea of Okhotsk in the north to south of the West Pacific, instituting the "Reagan Doctrine."[3]

Against this regional background, this paper contends that peace in Asia and the US-Korean security interdependence are correlative by virtue of given geostrategic locations of the regional power constellation. Moreover, the linkage perspective indicates that the future state of Northeast and Southeast Asia's security becomes increasingly fragile in the face of the Soviet presence. The Vladivostok-based Soviet Pacific Fleet, including the aircraft carrier, MINSK, has sailed into the gulf of Thailand and Soviet spyplanes maintain constant surveillance of US ship movements in the Asian area. Between the Korean peninsula and states of the Association of Southeast Asian Nations (ASEAN) is a strategically vital sea lane of communication (SLOC) of two points, basically, the straits of Malacca and the Strait of Korea. While South Korea is concerned with a possible Soviet-North Korean military arrangement for use of Najin port facilities of North Korea by the Soviet Pacific Fleet, the ASEAN states are already menaced by the Soviet use of Cam Rahn Bay in Vietnam.[4]

---

[3] For a reference to the "Reagan Doctrine," see *US News and World Report,* August 10, 1981, p. 36.

[4] "Be Realistic about Soviet Presence," *Asian Defense Journal* (Malaysia), July 1981, p. 10.

The main topics of this paper are Korea's security perspective and its future role with non-Communist nations, specifically the United States, Japan and the ASEAN countries. "Security" used in this connection is a broad one and is inclusive of politico-economic and military security measures deemed necessary for protecting the Western nations from external threat. "Threat" in this context is confined to the Soviet threat and that of Soviet-sponsored proxies, namely North Korea and Vietnam.

Accordingly, if we were to be protected from the Soviet threat, there is a need to define it in military, political, and economic terms, and especially to articulate our perception of the threat. In order to deal with the Soviet threat as such, the states in Northeast and Southeast Asia including the United States, likewise, must view security in reference to these politico-economic and military realities. It is therefore almost axiomatic to say that no nation in this world of "international ecology,"[5] even the defense-free Japan, can really prosper without relying on the security services of other friendly nations.[6]

Since this paper is designed to elicit a useful exchange of views on a new US-Korean security interdependence vis-a-vis the Soviet challenge to peace and security in Northeast Asia, the paper emphasizes (1) the Soviet Challenge in the Pacific, (2) the Japanese Reaction, and (3) the Role of South Korea. Finally, in lieu of summary, the paper presents minor propositions for an overview of security cooperation in order to provide a broad conceptual framework for usefully illustrating interactions between diverse views and issues.

II. The Soviet Challenge in the Pacific

The Soviet challenge in the Pacific is Moscow's grand plan for the year 2,000. The Soviets, with their economic and military develop-

---

[5] The term, "international ecology" is meant to be a nation's gain, i.e., security and survival is to a large extent interrelated with the external environment. See Harrold and Margaret Sprout, *The Ecological Perspective on Human Affairs: With Special Reference to International Politics* (Princeton University Press, 1965), pp. 64-68.

[6] Japan, not to mention her dependence on food, energy, resources, and security "umbrella" to the United States, relies on "safe and hospitable" passages for import and export sea lanes of transportation in Southeast Asia. For a rather sensitive argument, see Mituo Yagisawa, "America's Four-Umbrella," *Japan Quarterly*, Vol. XXVIII, No. 2, April-June 1981, pp. 172-174.

ments in Siberia and in the Soviet Far East, hope to accomplish Soviet supremacy over the entire Pacific area. If the West cannot deter the Soviet move now, it is most likely that nations in the Pacific will have to tolerate a Soviet-dominated "Pacific era" in the year 2,000. This possibility is already visible even at a superficial glance at the Soviet Siberian resources development plan, the Baikal-Amur Mainline (BAM) railroad construction, the growth of the Soviet Pacific Fleet, and its port facilities of the Vladivostok-Vostochny-Nakhodka complex in the Soviet Far Eastern maritime province.[7]

The Soviet Union is undertaking one of the greatest railway projects of the century, the Baikal-Amur Mainline (BAM), designed to open up new resources areas of Pacific Siberia for trade with the United States and with other industrial countries in the Pacific. This project, to be completed in 1983, will greatly enhance the position of the Soviet Union as a raw material supplier to the rest of the world. One basic problem in the past has been the lack of access to Siberia's still largely unexplored mineral resources, which the BAM is intended to provide in the early 1980's.[8] In short, the BAM, together with the existing Trans-Siberian Railway system, will undoubtedly facilitate the Soviet Union's "Eastward Movement" from the Urals to the Soviet eastern shore of Asia.

Siberia occupies nearly half of the territory of the USSR, throughout most of the Russian Soviet Federation of Socialist Republic (RSFSR) in Asia. This area has considerable natural resources of water, power, and timber with large deposit of oil, gas, coal, iron ore, and the ores of many non ferrous metals, basically all of the elements that are required to build a Soviet empire in Asia. Today, Siberia accounts for half of the explored iron ore deposits in the Soviet Union; 80 percent of the hydropower resources; 90 percent (about 7.6 trillion tons) of coal; and almost 80 percent of timber resources. The deposits of oil and natural gas, on the other hand, amount to more than 60 percent. The 3,200-kilometer (about 2,600 miles) railway, which will connect the very heart of the Siberian resources to the Pacific coast, brings to the fore the whole question of the Soviet Pacific outlook.[9]

---

[7] Vostochny literally means "Port of Orient." The port will be the Soviet Union's largest deep-water port when completed. For more on port Vostochny, see "The Sea Gate of BAM," *Soviet Weekly* (London), September 27, 1980, pp. 8-9.

[8] Theodore Shabad and Victor L. Mote, *Gateway to Siberian Resources—the BAM* (New York: John Wiley and Sons, 1977), pp. 45-50.

The BAM was first mentioned as a practical proposal by General Secretary Leonid Brezhnev in March 1974 at the Central Committee of the Soviet Council of Ministers. Today large sections of the mainline have been laid. It will stretch from Taishet, west of Lake Baikal, where it links with the Trans-Siberian Railway, to Sovetskaya Gavan on the Pacific. There is also a "little BAM," 260 miles long, branching off the Trans-Siberian Railway to the mainline BAM. The importance of the BAM cannot be over-emphasized. It has been called by the Sovets "the project of the century."[10] Additionally the BAM runs through undeveloped areas with abundant natural resources. These areas are the South Yakutian coalfields, the Neryngri coalfields, and iron ore of Aldan in Eastern Siberia.[11]

Some will argue that the BAM will never pay for itself and that the debts incurred during construction[12] will be excessively high. If the Soviet risks are economically great, the psycho-political benefits could be greater. Western scholars have stated that it is the manifest goal of the Soviet Union to develop its Pacific seaboard within this century. Raw materials in the heavily populated western third of European Russia are declining both in quality and quantity. Sooner or later, new raw material bases will have to be exploited; therefore, the virgin resources of Pacific Siberia provide the answer. The BAM should, in its external impact, exert influence on the Pacific areas in the last quarter of the 20th century as did the opening of the Trans-Siberian Railway to the Soviet western front in Europe. If the Soviet plan succeeds, the Soviet Union could dilute the United States influence in the Pacific area. Indeed, if Soviet authorities realize their goals in Pacific Siberia, they may obtain hegemony in the Pacific area before the year 2,000.

The Soviet Pacific Fleet has already established its presence in the Pacific and Indian oceans. Even now, the Soviet Pacific Fleet appears to exceed the United States Seventh Fleet in tonnage and exhibits a

---

[9] For a Soviet view on the BAM, see Valentin Aleksandrov, *The Wonder Land Called Siberia* (Moscow: Novosti Press Agency Publishing House, 1977), pp. 3-7.

[10] For details, see "Guaranteed Oil and Gas from Siberia," *Soviet Weekly* (London), April 18, 1981, pp. 8-9. According to the Soviet expectations, Siberia will be producing 385-395 million tons of oil and 330,000-370,000 million cubic meters of gas per year by 1985.

[11] Nikolai Yanovsky, ed., *Rasskazy o Sibiri* (Moskva: Izdatel'stvo Progress, 1975(?), p. 72.

[12] It is believed that $6 billion would be spent on the railroad proper and more than $15 billion for the entire project. Theodore Shabad and Victor L. Mote, *op. cit.*, p. 67.

high mobility with its aircraft carrier, MINSK, together with its unsinkable lond-based carrier, Cam Rahn Bay in Vietnam. Soviet seapower in the Pacific is occasioned by the Siberian resource development and a simultaneous development of the eastern seaport complex containing Vostochny, near Nakhodka, Sovetskaya Gavan, and Vladivostok. By 1984, the gateway to Siberia will be connected by the BAM with the eastern seaports. At the same time, the Soviets have been active in the Southwest Pacific to obtain visitation privileges and portcalls in Fiji, Western Samoa, and Tonga.[13] Above all, Soviet plans for the construction of the new port of Vostochny, on the Gulf of Nakhodka, represents the Kremlin's grand scheme for the era of the Soviet Pacific Siberia in the year 2,000.

Vostochny port is the sea-terminal for the BAM railway. The physical limits of Vladivostok and Nakhodka were reached in the 1970's. Access to Vladivostok's rail depot is blocked by waiting trains and the situation in Nakhodka is not much better as dozens of ships have to waste time offshore waiting for space at a pier. The congested harbor situation would be twice as bad when the BAM started delivering even more commodities. This is the reason the Soviets started laying the railway the building the new port simultaneously. The warm-water port, Vostochny, will be the deepest, most highly mechanized, and the largest seaport in the Soviet Union. The seaport will specialize in the transshipment of containers for the Trans Siberian Landbridge (TSLB) services, which will be shorter than the Panama Canal route by about 5,800 miles (Cargoes originating from Yokohama, Japan and destined for Leningrad via Vostochny-Nakhodka have to travel only 8,700 miles, as compared with 14,500 miles via the Panama Canal or nearly 17,000 miles around Africa).

Vostochny port, with the current facilities, already handles 70,000 containers a year and when the second section of the terminal is completed in 1984 the capacity will be doubled. Over the next five years, the port will get three more container terminals and automated piers for ore, grain, and coal. Port Vostochny is being equipped with a vast array of instruments, such as those used in airports including 16 computers of the latest models to control traffic. When completed before the year 2,000, the port facility will be able to handle nearly

---

[13] Soviet diplomats have recently proposed aid to Tonga in return for trawler bunkering facilities for Soviet ships. General George S. Brown, "Asia-Pacific: U.S. Military Posture," *Asia-Pacific Defense Forum*, Vol. III, No. 1, 1978, p. 19.

17.5 million tons of cargo annually at 64 piers. Additionally, port Vostochny must be viewed in military terms as the largest warm-water port facility for the Soviet Pacific Fleet in Asia.[14]

In view of the foregoing, Northeast Asia has become a setting for possible naval engagements. Today the Soviet Pacific Fleet is the second largest fleet of the Soviet navy. Moreover it is the only fleet based in the northeastern flank of the Pacific area and has extended itself as far as the Indian Ocean. The Northeast Asian naval theatre presents potential constraints for both the Soviet Pacific Fleet and the US Seventh Fleet. The Soviet ships and submarines must enter the open sea to the Pacific through relatively narrow, dangerous, if not hostile, passages of Korean and Japanese waters, while the US Seventh Fleet must also bear the risk of assault from the long-range BACKFIRE's of the Soviet naval air forces, as well as Soviet nuclear attack submarines.[15]

The "dangerous passage" concept of the naval strategy in Pacific Northeast Asia may very well be the underlying theme by which the Soviet Pacific Fleet can be examined. Development of the Soviet Pacific Fleet tends to be concentrated on area defense with headquarters at Vladivostok. It has been operating off the Soviet eastern maritime provinces, but now it deploys submarines carrying strategic ballistic missiles to the waters of the westcoast of the United States and, at the same time, leaves a permanent flotilla in the Indian Ocean. The ships stationed at Vladivostok, however, must endure restricted access to the Pacific due to the dangerous gateways ("choke points") ingressing Korean and Japanese waters, namely the Korean Strait, the Tsugaru Strait, and the Soya Strait of Japan.[16]

The Soviet Pacific Fleet's infantry strength is the largest among the Soviet fleets. Its submarine force, second only to that of the Northern Fleet, has also been increasing in numbers. The Naval Aviation Force assigned to the Pacific Fleet includes medium-range bombers (BACK-

[14] *Magistral' Veka* (Moskva: Izdatel'stvo Progress, 1977), p. 101.

[15] Seymour J. Deitchman, "Designing the Fleet and Its Air Arm," *Astronautics and Aeronautics,* Vol: 16, No. 11, November 1978, pp. 18-36.

[16] There are two other alternative passages in theory, detour out of Korean and Japanese waters, namely the Tartar Strait and Petropavlovsk on the Kamchatka peninsula. These alternatives, however, do not appear promising due to their physical limits. See Stuart E. Johnson, *The Military Equation in Northeast Asia* (Washington, D.C.: The Brookings Institution, 1979), p. 16; Col. William V. Kennedy, "Kamchatka: Non-nuclear Deterrent," *Military Review,* February 1978, p. 26.

FIRE's) with antiship missiles, reconnaissance aircraft with a combat radius of 2,500 to 3,000 kilometers, and more than 145 antisubmarine helicopters with a combat radius of 500 to 2,300 kilometers. During recent years, such units have stressed antisubmarine warfare (ASW).[17] In addition, with the assignment of the KIEV-class MINSK aircraft carrier to the Pacific Fleet, the fleet's strike force will attain a significant upgrading in its offensive capabilities.

In short, the Soviet Pacific Fleet has been changing from a coastal defense force into one designed to carry out blue-water missions. The growth and missions of the fleet show a marked propensity to support the Soviet perceptions of the global threat and response to it. After all, the Soviet Union perceives that her security is threatened by "some 2,500 US overseas bases in more than 30 foreign countries."[18] Evidence has shown on a number of occasions since 1960 in Cuba and around the Horn Of Africa, for example, that the Soviets will go to almost any length, regardless of cost, to defend against any perceived threat, no matter how far from its territorial waters.

According to the Soviet Navy Commander-in-Chief, Admiral Sergey G. Gorshkov, the Soviet path of naval development is aimed at building up capabilities not only for nuclear wars, but also for conventional wars in order to protect Soviet interests abroad. He states, "in order to do so, the (Soviet) Navy, as the main component of the seapower of the state, can counter the oceanic strategy of imperialism."[19]

III. The Japanese Reaction

Nowhere is the interrelationship between the Soviet naval build-up and its strategic expansion seen more clearly than in Japanese waters. Here the total resources of Soviet seapower, near Hokkaido, combined with those of the powerful Far Eastern Air Force based in the

---

[17] The BACKFIRE's will be able to attack ships with air-to-surface missiles at extended distances from their home bases in the Soviet Far East. For details, see *Department of Defense Annual Report, Fiscal Year 1981* (Washington, D.C.: Government Printing Office, 1980), p. 104.

[18] "Where is the Real Military Threat?," *Soviet Weekly* (London), October 27, 1979, p. 6.

[19] Sergey G. Gorshkov, *Morskaya Moschch' gosdarstva* (Moskva: Voyenizdat, 1976), p. 9.

Vladivostok area, are used to back up the expanding naval presence in the Western Pacific. Another major objective of the Soviet Navy in the area is to put political pressure on Japan at a time when Tokyo's defense spending is minimal and when the US Navy is clearly over-stretched from the Persian Gulf to the Sea of Japan (Korea's Eastern Sea). A major threat comes from Japan's "northern territories," which are the islands occupied by the Soviet Union in the closing days of the Pacific War following the 1945 Yalta agreement to give the Kuriles to Stalin as a reward for entering the war against Japan. In this process Soviet forces occupied Etorofu, Kunashiri, Shikotan, and Habomai. Tokyo, at last, seems to have killed any possible treaty with the Soviet Union unless the problem of the four islands can be solved.[20] The Soviet Union, and for its part, too, unequivocally maintains that the issue is closed, and that the islands will remain Soviet territory.[21]

There have been reports that Soviet vessels were harassing Japanese fishermen in Hokkaido waters, sometimes within the Japanese 10-mile limit. Soviet military manoeuvres in Japanese waters underline the message. In the April 1975 "Ocean II" exercises, Soviet naval capa-bility was shown by four Russian naval task forces deployed around Japan. The Soviet military build-up on Shikotan island, less than twelve miles off Hokkaido, posed a direct threat to Japan in 1979. A division-level force (about 12,000 combat troops) on Shikotan is believed to have been equipped with tanks, SAM antiaircraft missiles and about a dozen assault helicopters.[22] There are also an additional Soviet troops stationed on other Kurile islands of Etorofu and Kuna-shiri with radar stations which track the Japanese and American force movements. Ever since the Sino-Japanese Peace Treaty signed in 1978, Soviet naval manoeuvres have been an even more pointed warning to Tokyo; warships sailed through the Sea of Japan to Okinawa, and Soviet aircraft flew southward over the seas on both sides of Japan and close to the Korean Strait.[23]

---

[20] Prime Minister Zenko Suzuki had said that Japan's efforts to improve relations with the Soviet Union is out of the question due to the territorial dispute over the Soviet occupied northern islands. *The Japan Times,* July 20, 1980, p. 3.

[21] A. P. Markov, *Poslevoennaya Politika Yaponii v Azii i Kitai, 1945-1977* (Moskva: Izdatel'stvo Nayka, 1979), p. 220.

[22] "Echoes of Cuba: Other Soviets on Other Islands," *Time,* October 15, 1979, p. 46.

[23] "LDP Proposes the Soviet Military Buildup in the Northern Territory," *FBIS Daily Report* (Asia and Pacific), Vol. IV, No. 026, February 6, 1970, p. c5.

As a result of the increasing Soviet threat, the Japanese defense white paper of 1980 seems to have recognized, for the first time, the threat posed by the Soviet military build-up in East Asia in more specific terms such as the total tonnage of naval craft and the number of divisions in the Far Eastern Army of the Soviet Union.[24] The report, published by the Japanese defense agency, also has outlined a 2.4 trillion Yen budgetary request for 1981, up 9.7 per cent from the previous year. However, a great majority in Japan, including most of the press, who feel safe under United States protection, is critical of increased defense appropriations for weapons procurement. *The Mainich Daily News* and *Asahi Shimbun* both have been more than critical by saying that Japan's security options must be more political and less military.[25] In other words, an equally strong voice in opposition to a demanded increase of the Japanese defense build-up undoubtedly draws public opinion of the "peace-loving economic giant" of Japan. The government of Japan, in the meantime, is enjoying its vacilating position in the defense issue while Tokyo is plying the issue with its "omnidirectional diplomacy (or *Zen Hoigiko*).

At a glance, Japan fulfills her defense obligation under the US-Japan Security Treaty within the provision of the "Peace Constitution" framework. Today, Japan, a regional military potential with her defense expenditure which ranks seventh in the world, is under the "Guidelines of US-Japan Defense Cooperation" formulated in the fall of 1978 and is strengthening joint air and naval drills and arms development cooperation with the United States. However, Japan's defense policy is still predicated upon United States preparedness to deploy its military capabilities as a deterrent to aggression against Japan. Some major decisions made after the Soviet invasion of Afghanistan may have enhanced her defense capability, but Japan's overall defense structure is still complementary to US defense posture in South Korea and elsewhere in the Western Pacific.[26]

Some may argue that Japan's defense-related expenditure in 1980

---

[24] For details see *Nippon-no Boei* (Tokyo: Boeiho, 1980), pp. 56-60 & 125.

[25] *The Mainich Daily News,* August 3, 1980; *Asahi Shimbun,* August 30, 1980.

[26] The Maritime Japanese Self-Defense Forces took part for the first time in the joint naval exercise, RIMPAC-80 during February and March 1980. At the same time, Japan's decision to produce F-15's and P-3C's will significantly improve her air defense and antisubmarine warfar (ASW) capability. Susumu Takahashi, "Japan's Security and Public Opinion," *Japan Quarterly,* Vol. XXVIII, No. 1, January-March 1981, pp. 61-64.

was 2.23 trillion Yen, but the amount, though less than 0.9 per cent of her GNP, is equivalent to $10 billion, and is about two and an half times the South Korean defense expenditure. For her part, Japan may be arguing that for a country which is committed under the "Peace Constitution" to only self-defense, $10 billion military expense in "peace time" is not a small sum. Another issue relevant to the Japanese defense posture in question is Japan's security role within the present structure of the US-Japanese security cooperation. It is almost certain that Japan will continue to remain as one of super powers without military muscle until such a time when the United States no longer requires military bases in Japan. The point is that the Japanese know that the time will never come as long as the US-Soviet rivalry remains in the Pacific. Thus, by any imagination, the future role of the Japanese in the defense of the Pacific area against the Soviet threat seems to be totally irrelevant to the Japanese themselves.

It appears that the Japanese perception of the Soviet threat is based on US-Soviet competition and not on Russo-Japanese antagonism itself. The Japanese view seems to generate a line of reasoning that the Japanese threat perception of North Korea is also a result of Tokyo's close politico-economic relations with Pyongyang's adversary, South Korea. This kind of threat perception as such is bound to generate a defense posture of "free ride" which sympathizes with its security ally's immanent threat perception, but which is reluctant to be involved with any risky counter-measures, lest the burden won't pay off. However, the United States expects Japan to be prepared for emergency and capable of blockading the three straits along the Japanese territorial waters and assuming the responsibility of securing sea lanes of communication (SLOC) in the Western Pacific. These are the two major tasks that Japan is expected to undertake as an ally of the United States as well as an independent state for self-defense.

Article 5 of the US-Japan Security Treaty reads as follows:

> Each Party recognizes that an armed attack against either Party in the territories under the administration of Japan would be dangerous to its own peace and safety and declares that it would act to meet the common danger in accordance with its constitutional provisions and processes.

In addition, Article 6 of the treaty, which authorizes the bases to the United States, provides Japan with a positive military role. The Japanese defense role is not only restricted to the security of Japan but is, as expressed by the 1978 Defense White Paper, "for the maintenance of peace and security throughout the Far East." The securing of maritime transportation sea lanes from the Persian Gulf through the Straits of Malacca to Japan require cooperation with many maritime countries of the region. The blockading of the Tsushima Strait near by the Korean Strait involves cooperation with South Korea by virtue of its geographical proximity. However, Japan sees no direct linkage between her maritime security and that of South Korea.

The Japanese "omnidirectional diplomacy," which seeks for Tokyo's independent foreign policy of superpower status, has been one of major sources of indecisive defense policy vis-a-vis Soviet expansionism. Tokyo has been seeking an opportunity to improve relations with Moscow, which hardened after the Sino-Japanese peace and friendship treaty was signed in August 1978. Since it is impossible to please the Soviets politically, Tokyo has been prodding Japanese businessmen to come up with ideas which may assuage Moscow and give substance to Japan's avowed all-direction foreign policy. In the meantime, Soviet Foreign Minister Andrei Gromyko who attended the UN General Assembly in 1978 Charged that Japan is making "the same mistake it made before," meaning that Japan is joining an anti-Soviet bloc just as it did before World War II.[27]

If the Japanese-Soviet political relation has deteriorated, particularly since 1978, Tokyo's economic front toward Moscow is helping to restore the relation which the Soviets clearly desire and which the Japanese are more able to offer. Two powerful private business organizations, *Keidaren* (the Federation of Economic Organizations of Japan) and the Japan-USSR Economic Committee, were called into action, since technically bilateral trade is strictly a private affairs at this end, not involving the Tokyo government. In the mist of Deng Xiaoping's Tokyo visit in October 1978, a Tokyo-Moscow private business talk was going on for a long-term agreement for economic cooperation on Siberian development. As of October 1976, the total bank loan contracts amounted to as much as $2,000 million, of which $900 million was for the socalled "national projects" involving the development and export of natural resources of Siberia.[28]

---

[27] See S. Ivanov, "The 35th Anniversary of the Defeat of Imperialist Japan," *Far Eastern Affairs* (Moscow), No. 4, 1980, p. 13.

[28] Rodger Swearingen, *The Soviet and Postwar Japan* (Standford, CA: Hoover Institution Press, 1978), p. 130.

The Soviets are now on their new plan, the 11th 5-year plan (1981-1985), and as the new plan year comes into being, fund requirements pressed Japan for greatly increased amounts of semi-official bank loans. Moscow is likely to keep up the pressure on Japan and will be watching closely for any economic concessions Tokyo might give Peking, in order to demand the same for itself. The Soviets would obviously like to quicken the pace of Siberian development, notably in the long-pending Yakutian natural gas project as the BAM railroad construction is to be finished in 1983. Japan, however, may face difficulties since she cannot join this project without the United States, which has cooled towards Moscow of late, particularly after the Afghanistan invasion and the Polish interference by the Soviet Union.

Since 1965, Japan and the Soviet Union's economic cooperation in the development of Siberian resources and some in the Soviet Far East has been active under the auspices of the Japanese-Soviet Economic Cooperation Committee. Out of two general agreements, cooperation in the development of the timber industry in the Soviet Far East and the building of the first stage of the Vostochny port[29] were fulfilled in 1978. Additional agreements made between the two countries, which are yet to be materialized, are to exploit the South Yakutian coal basin, the Sakhalin shelf for oil and gas, and surveying the Yakut for gas deposits. In February 1981, Japan held a series of meetings with the Soviet authorities of the gas and oil industry for cooperation in the development of the gas and oil fields on the continental shelf around Sakhalin Island. In the meeting, the Soviets proposed a plan to transport the gas to Japan via an underwater pipeline in the Soya Strait which would connect the Sakhalin Island with Hokkaido,[30] one of three major naval choke points against the Soviet Union.

In short, notwithstanding Japan's security interest for her continuous economic expansion, Tokyo still has not defined a defense posture and continues to pursue economic gains from the same adversary who poses a direct security threat. In the meantime, the Soviets, met with Reagan's anti-Soviet policy, try hard to persuade

---

[29] Japan is also interested in a third general agreement with the Soviet Union which would include Tokyo's cooperation for developing the adjacent regions of the BAM railway and for her participation in the second stage development of Vostochny port throughout the Soviet 11th 5-year plan (1981-1985). See V. Spandaryan, "Soviet-Japanese Trade Relations," *Far Eastern Affairs* (Moscow), No. 4, 1980, p. 89.

[30] *Soviet Weekly* (London), February 14, 981, p. 3.

the Japanese that the best security guarantee that Japan can get from the Soviet Union is an "economic *détente*"[31] with Moscow. For this and other reasons, Japan seems to resist pressure from the United States in increasing her defense spending and defense cooperation with neighboring countries of the West. Japan's reluctance to beef up her security contributions to Northeast Asia may, in turn, irritate South Korea, because Seoul has made its position clear that security cooperation between Seoul and Tokyo will be the key regional arrangement for the United States' Soviet policy. Japan may, in return, see the South Korean position as a simplistic view of regional security, looking at it through "military binoculars."[32]

IV. The Role of South Korea

An American Soviet specialist once argued that North Korea could become another "Afghanistan" in the 1980's; "it could lose its independence to the Soviet Union, or become increasingly dependent on the Soviet Union and lose its ability to conduct an independent foreign policy."[33] If the North Korean scenario is a probable future outlook of the Soviet strategic view of the Korean peninsula, North Korea equally bears a "Vietnam thesis," which drew Soviet influence and then invited a subsequent Chinese invasion in 1979. North Korea, seemingly uncommitted to either side of the two military protagonists, occupies the heart of the strategic gateway both to Manchuria of China and the Soviet Pacific Siberia. That is to say, Pyongyang, fallen into either side of Peking or Moscow, would cause a vital threat to the security of the entire Pacific area.

South Korea, on the other hand, occupying the southern half of the divided peninsula, serves as a vital point of strategic importance which insulates Japan from direct pressure for an immediate need of

---

[31] V. Arkhipov, "The Soviet Union's Struggle for Peace and *Détente*," *Far Eastern Affairs* (Moscow), No. 4, 1981, p. 9.

[32] Rodney Tasker, "The Wooing of Asean," *Far Eastern Economic Review*, June 26, 1981, p. 32.

[33] Donald S. Zagoria, "North Korea: Another Afghanistan?," a paper delivered at a Conference on North Korea, Co-sponsored by Asiatic Research Center, Korea University and the Institute of East Asian Studies, University of California, Berkeley, February 23-28, 1981, p. 1.

military security. The US presence in South Korea keeps Japan nuclear-free on the one hand and reduces Japan's need to become a military power commensurate with her economic power on the other. The evidence here is a power symmetry in the regional configuration based on the geostrategic location of the Korean peninsula. Because of the Korean geostrategic location, a sudden change in the power equilibrium over the peninsula could give rise to serious instability that no regional power would like to encounter. In other words, both Koreas can play a substantial role either to keep peace or to destroy it. And the peace-keeping role, to a greater extent, can be assumed by South Korea's politico-economic and military cooperation with the United States, Japan, and friendly states of Southeast Asia.

South Korea's security contribution to the Pacific area has yet to be explored in reference to an idea that brings together members of maritime states in the Pacific for a closer cooperation in all inter-actions. There has even been a proposal for a voluntary peacetime "All-Oceans Alliance" for the region.[34] Any cooperation, which entails security linkages to counter the Soviet influence, would have to be considered security cooperation. Security cooperation in this context is seen, not through "military binoculars," but through joint activities of diplomacy for grouping a regional community with a common territory against undesirable outsiders. A security com-munity as such will be greatly benefited by examples set by the Association of Southeast Asian Countries (ASEAN). Projecting a future community of security cooperation, the visit by President Chun Doo Hwan to the five member states of ASEAN adds a signi-ficant step to the embryonic but promising idea of a "Community of the Pacific Basin."[35]

Building a Pacific community of security consciousness might be imperative if nations in this region are to realistically counter a Soviet scheme of the "Asian Collective Security System" that the Soviets proposed in 1969. After a decade of unsuccessful attempts, the Soviets, particularly after the signing of the Sino-Japanese treaty of

---

[34] Ray S. Cline, *World Power Trends and U.S. Foreign Policy for the 1980's* (Boulder, Colorando: Westview Press, 1980), p. 183.

[35] For more ideas on the Pacific Basin Community, see U.S. Congress, Senate, Committee on Foreign Relations, *An Asian-Pacific Regional Economic Organization: An Exploratory Concept Paper*, 96th Congress, 1st Sess., 1979; Pacific Basin Coopera-tion Study Group, *Interim Report on the Pacific Basin Cooperation Concept* (Tokyo: November 14, 1979), pp. 2-3.

1978 and the Sino-US normalization in 1979, resumed the "peace-offensive" towards non-Communist nations of Asia urging that "the path of security in Asia is not the path of military blocs and grouping but the path of good-neighbor cooperation among the states interested in this broad development of economic and other areas."[36] *Sistemy Kollektivnoy Bezopasnosti Azii,* as the Soviets call it, the Asian collective security system appears to be Moscow's long-term strategy to build a Soviet Pacific era incorporated with the Soviet Siberian development plan. In view of the emerging idea of the Pacific Community against the Soviet peace-offensive toward non-Communist Asian states, South Korea is able to contribute its share to the formulation of the community idea with its economic and defense experiences.

South Korea's role in security of the Pacific can be more than its military role which maintains a balance of military power in the Korean peninsula vis-a-vis North Korea. Politically stable South Korea, for example, would greatly enhance security environments in Northeast Asia. With the giant step toward democratic transition of power stipulated in the new Constitution of the Fifth Republic, President Chun's leadership will be paramount in the coming years as he wrestles with the ever-present problem of security for the Korean peoples. At the present time, some of the problems may be only shadows as North Korea is in a quasi political turmoil. An "ideological screening program" has been initiated in Pyongyang in order to consolidate the Kim hierarchy from father (Kim Il-sung) to his son, Kim Chung-il, and both of them are faced with a forthcoming 7th Party congress of the North Korean Workers' Party in 1985 for power transition. The 40-year old Kim Chung-il's leadership will most likely be challenged when the dynastic leadership of Kim Il-sung phases out from the power scene.[37]

The global reach of multinational corporation is transforming the world political economy through its increasing control over three fundamental resources of economic life; technology, capital, and market. The internationalization of production means simply that more and more of the world's goods and services (or Gross World Product) are being produced through more and more countries and

---

[36] M. S. Kapitsa, et al., *Istoriya Mezdunarodnykh Otnosheniy na Dal'nem Bostoke, 1947-1977* (Habarovskov knizhnoe Izdatel'stvo, 1978), pp. 541-542.

[37] See Zagoria, *op. cit.,* p. 29.

that the process completely ignores national boundaries. The Republic of Korea is not a country to be left behind in this internationalized economy. South Korea, along with its industrial experiences, continues to transcend its geography and at the same time widen its doors to foreign investment. Additionally, with its internationalized economic structure, South Korea will be able to contribute to the consolidation of regional ties for security. South Korea's positive role, together with that of Japan, for cooperative economic development with friendly countries in Southeast Asia not only enhances an economically beneficial community of a common market, but it can also be an accelerator for peace and stability in the region.

Militarily, South Korea can offer friendly countries of the region its defense experiences which were gained through the uneasy process of defending the nation from a Communist invasion in 1950 and its subsequent involvement in the Vietnam War with the United States. If conventional and guerrilla warfare were the governing threat to security of the Pacific region under the strategic US air and naval protection, South Korea's defense experience would be of great value to those countries without such a first-hand experience. South Korea has substantial experiences in defense industry which could also be shared with friendly states of the region. To this end, South Korea's security cooperation in terms of military exchange of personnel and views for defense planning and operation will be of major importance in understanding security problems of the region.[38]

Seminars and symposia to jointly explore security problems of the Pacific area with concerned scholars, government officials, and military personnel of the region will undoubtedly lay the foundation for specific cooperation. The office of the Commander-in-Chief, Pacific (CINCPAC), the US Pacific Command (PACOM), seems to have discussed a security forum in 1978. It has been sponsoring the "Pacific Armies Management Seminar" in order to facilitate an exchange of views on individual countries' defense experiences.[39] Seminars of this nature will definitely broaden security contacts among concerned countries for mutual interests.

In the final analysis, South Korea's military role in defense of the security in the Pacific region is technically limited to the defense of

---

[38] Yu-Nam Kim, "Prospects for the U.S.-Japan-Korea Security Cooperation," *The Defense Studies*, Vol. 23, No. 2, December 1980, pp. 185-191.

[39] "Pacific Armies Management Seminar," *Asian-Pacific Defense Forum*, Spring 1979, p. 29.

Northeast Asia by preventing an invasion of North Korea. Any North Korean military move toward South Korea will destroy the delicate balance of power presently maintained by Russia, China, the United States, and Japan. In order to fulfill this role, South Korea requires a family of security cooperation and coordination. Some friends may criticize South Korea's far-reaching concern with its security issue as "Seoul's obsession with security."[40] And the Russians, in support of North Korea, even charge that South Korea's "threat perception from north" (or *Ugroza s Sebera*) is "hysterical nightmare to justify the American troops in the Korean peninsula."[41] However, those friends and enemies should realize that South Korea, with help of the US 2nd Infantry Division, is barely defending itself from the world's fifth largest North Korean army just 25 miles north of Seoul. If South Korea is defensively obsessed, it is because the nation has a strong will to survive on the one hand and the country is concerned for the security of the entire Pacific on the other.

It is assumed that one side of South Korea's security role is to militarily defend south of the demilitarized zone (DMZ) of Korea and the other side of the role is to be diplomatically aligned with a united front against the Soviet expansion in the region. South Korea, for all practical purposes, expects to increase its diplomatic coordination with the United States, Japan, and friendly states of Southeast Asia. If nations of this region, including South Korea, were to join together under the United States leadership for building a security community, South Korea may consider that the present security arrangement with the United States should be revised in diplomatic and military areas.

Diplomatically, South Korea's relations with China, which is one of the anti-Soviet friends of the United States, needs to be seriously examined in view of the changing trend of the security dynamics in this region. If Peking were bold enough to establish even a quasi-military cooperation with North Korea's "archenemy," the United States, Peking's hesitant attitude toward South Korea would seem to be less convincing, although understandable, not wanting to provoke Pyongyang's bitterness.

Militarily, if South Korea were to strengthen its defense insitutions

[40] David Bonavia, "South Korea: Prosperity's New Problems," *Far Eastern Economic Review,* October 13, 1978, p. 20.

[41] Major General Y. Neshunov, Chief of Staff of the KGB Border Guard Troops of the USSR Council of Minister, "Na Rubezhakh Ottszny," *Krasnaya Zvezda,* May 28, 1977, p. 2.

in reference to the Soviet threat, its military forces would also have to be treated as part of the united front against Soviet expansionism. The Korean Armed Forces with elements of US Army and Air Forces stationed in Korea have traditionally been considered forces primarily to counter the North Korean threat based on the principle of the Korean-American military alliance at the end of the Korean War of 1950. If a new Korean-American alliance is to emerge with the purpose of checking the Soviet expansion, it is logical to add new requirements to the existing alliance.

V. Implications for Propositions

As long as the present leadership of North Korea continues to remain totally deaf to President Chun Doo Hwan's proposal for a meeting between the highest authorities of South and North Korea,[42] it is very doubtful that North Korea will emerge from its reclusiveness but will join the Soviet expansionism for want of unification on its own terms. North Korea's pro-Soviet "tilt" will undoubtedly increase the growing fears of Asian states. After a Communist victory in Vietnam, the United States was unable to hold the Soviet expansion in the region. Likewise, the US-China coalition against the Soviet expansionism is not likely to have a positive influence on North Korea. In view of the above, if South Korea were to join the anti-Soviet front, there seems to be little necessity to review the role of South Korea for future policy implications.

1) The United States should upgrade its military forces stationed in South Korea to counter the Soviet Far Eastern military build-up and explain to North Korea the purpose of the increased force-levels. At the same time, the United States should assist in improving the South Korean Armed Forces in order them to perform minor roles against the Soviet presence in the region.

2) Once the United States recognizes that the Korean Armed Forces are a force to deter the Soviet military manouevres in the region, it must also provide the ways and means to cope with the expansion in

---

[42] This historic proposal was made at the New Year Policy Statement issued by President Chun Doo Hwan on January 12, 1981 and a reiteration of the proposal addressed to North Korea was made on June 5, 1981. For a full text of the statement, see *The Korea Herald*, January 13, 1981, p. 5.

cooperation not only with the US forces but also with its allied forces, i.e., the Self-Defense Forces of Japan. In this tripartite defense cooperation, the Korean Armed Froces could fulfill its role in close cooperation with its counterparts since South Korea and Japan cover at least two-thirds of the common defense zone stretching from north to south. The "Guideline for US-Japan Defense Cooperation," in this regard, may be broadened to include South Korea as an observer.

3) The Korean government may desire to explore areas for defense cooperation with member states of ASEAN in order to exchange security information and military personnel for "military diplomacy." The South Korean military authorities could participate as observers in the RIMPAC exercise of the ANZUS and military exercises of the Five-Power Defense Arrangement (Britain, Australia, New Zealand, Singapore, and Malaysia) to forge a security link between the Southwest and Northeast Pacific areas.

4) If China maintains the view, as Deng Xiaoping puts it, that "it does not matter whether a cat is black or white so long as it catches mice" toward non-Communist Asian countries, it might be a prudent time for South Korea to explore avenues to convey a "Seoul Message" to Peking. After all, China must realize that Peking's "Pyongyang card" against Seoul no longer serves the interest of the Chinese anti-Sovietism, nor does it serve the US interest on the Korean peninsula.

5) The horizons of security cooperation may be broadened if South Korea can initiate a security symposium to commemorate the US-Korean Security Treaty. This will bring together Korean and American statesmen and scholars to review the treaty achievements and identify problems of the consortium for possible updating of content to meet future security requirements. An annual symposium of this nature will assist the Korean-American Security Consultative Meeting in providing and refining an agenda for policy considerations. Such a symposium can also be arranged with the Japanese counterpart, hoping to broaden it into a trilateral forum based on the format of the US-Japan Shimoda Conference.

CHAPTER 12

RIDING THE TIGER: MILITARY CONFRONTATION ON THE KOREAN PENINSULA

Gregory F. T. Winn*

The military confrontation on the Korean peninsula continues with little probability of *démarche*. This essay evaluates the military situation in Korea primarily from a North Korean perspective. Both descriptive and normative analytical objectives are addressed. The first part examines the military situation on the Korean peninsula. The second section suggests areas where both Korea's might reach accord on limiting the Korean arms race.

Realistically, there is little probability that the leaders of the Republic of Korea (ROK) and the Democratic People's Republic of Korea (DPRK) will establish a negotiation forum in order to reduce defense expenditures and/or weapons productions. But, should a change in either leadership or leadership attitudes occur, some of the ideas in this essay may prove useful in the resolution of the military confrontation on the Korean peninsula.

There are few instances in history where an escalating arms race did not lead to war. The present confrontational strategy is like riding a tiger, it is difficult to get off once mounted.

I. General Setting

During the period of Japanese occupation of Korea, and later Manchuria, anti-Japanese Korean guerrilla bands were organized under

---

* The views expressed in this chapter are solely those of the author and do not represent the U.S. government.

Chinese communist and Soviet tutelage. In the "Manchuria Guerrilla Circle" of Marxist-Leninist, anti-Japanese fighters, formed in 1932, Kim Il Sung established a preeminent leadership position. Kim Il Sung was later credited with founding the Korean People's Army (KPA).

With this military force, and with the tacit support of the Soviet Union and People's Republic of China, Kim Il Sung launched the Korean War in June 1950. The impact of this war on North Korea was particularly devastating. The extent of the devastation was indicated by the wartime comment of the head of the United Nations Bomber Command in the Far East, that "there are no more targets in Korea." P'yongyang's population fell from 400,000 to 80,000, that of the North in its entirety from 9.62 million in 1949 to 8.49 million in 1953. In all, about half a million North Korean troops were killed and the level of destruction during what the North Koreans call the "Fatherland Liberation War" left a bitter legacy of anti-American hatred.

During the war, the Chinese army had saved Kim Il Sung's forces from almost certain defeat; and the Soviet Union, while not introducing troops into the war, had supplied large amounts of weapons and material. Both nations aided in the reconstruction of the DPRK, but as relations between the PRC and USSR soured, North Korea was forced into an uneasy balancing act between allies. In 1958, China withdrew its military force.

Partly in reaction to the military coup *d'etat* in South Korea by Park Chung Hee, the North successfully concluded a "Friendship, Cooperation and Mutual Aid Treaty" with the Soviet Union on July 6th 1961 and a similar pact with the People's Republic of China on July 11th 1961. Both treaties included provisions stating that, should a concerned party be invaded, the other party would "render military and other assistance with every available means at its command."

Thereafter, North Korean relations with its communist neighbors were constantly in flux. For example, relations with the PRC have been intermittently disturbed by competing territorial claims over the Mount Paektu area of their common border. Apparently settled in 1963, the issue was re-opened in 1965 when Chinese leaders began to criticize Kim Il Sung and reasserted China's claim to the disputed territory. Border provocations occurred between 1967 and 1969. Relations improved markedly after the April 1970 visit to P'yongyang of Zhou En Lai, however, and in the 1970's Beijing agreed to supply combat aircraft and submarines to P'yongyang.

After cooling-off period in the early 1960s, the North Korean relationship with the Soviet Union improved. In 1965, Kim Il Sung convinced visiting Soviet Premier Kosygin that, in light of United States aggression in Vietnam, North Korea needed more advanced weaponry to bolster its defenses. The possibility of direct Soviet-United States confrontation, stemming from North Korean aggressive actions in 1968 and 1969, placed a strain on the DPRK-USSR relationship. In 1972, Moscow stopped providing advanced military equipment to P'yongyang. The ax murders of two American soldiers at the truce village of P'anmunjom in August 1976 apparently did little to relieve Soviet fears of North Korean unilateral adventurism.

Despite an apparant trend in the late 1970s toward closer relations with China, several international events led North Korea to its equidistant *"Juche"* foreign relations policy. Kim indicated his awareness of the problems of dependency on the PRC and the Soviet Union even before the situation had been made more complex by China's *rapprochement* with Japan and the United States. In a June 1977 interview with the editor of *Le Monde,* Kim stated,

> In the past great-power worshipping was glaring in our country, and our people had little pride in their own nation and in their independence. But now . . . no longer do our people think of depending on others. Our people are convinced that if they struggle and make endeavors by themselves and live industriously, they can surely stand on their own feet, building an independent economy and ensuring national independence and sovereignty.

Peking has some leverage over P'yongyang—partly because of North Korea's need for raw materials, capital goods, technological assistance, and military equipment. The Chinese have even indicated, according to unconfirmed reports, a willingness to reduce or cut off oil supplies to North Korea in an effort to increase their leverage over Korean military and political behavior.

Yet, Peking can not afford to antagonize P'yongyang as long as it finds itself in a confrontation with both the Soviet Union and Vietnam. Pushing North Korea into the Soviet camp would complete the Middle Kingdom's encirclement by adversaries or potential adversaries (Soviet Union, North Korea, Taiwan, Vietnam, and India). Consequently, the Chinese have supported Kim Il Sung's position on Korean reunification, and have given tacit if not enthusiastic approval for his son's ascension to the throne.[1]

Additions to the Soviet fleet (to include the aircraft carrier Minsk) and construction of new port facilities, have increased East Asian awareness of the USSR's military presence. While Kim Il Sung needs sophisticated Soviet weapons as well as Soviet tacit approval for the succession of Kim Chong Il, there is little evidence to date that Kim's equi-distant *"juche"* approach to foreign relations will allow him to trade Soviet access to North Korean ports (for example, Najin) in exchange for Soviet military and political support.[2]

II. Military Expenditures and the Arms Race

Until the mid-1970's North Korean defense expenditures clearly out-distanced those of the South. Between 1961 and 1974, North Korea spent US$1 billion more than the ROK. Between 1966 and 1967 alone, North Korea had increased its defense budget by a factor of approximately 3x, or 200 percent.

Announced military budgets continued to increase an average of 15 percent per year until 1972, when they *declined* sharply as part of Kim Il Sung's short-lived effort to bring some semblance of *détente* to the Korean peninsula. Since this 1972 reduction, the North's defense budget increased at a slower rate than the South's (from US$532 million in 1972 to US$1.37 billion in 1980 and US$1.47 billion in 1981).[3]

Evaluating the exact amount of North Korean military spending is difficult at best, in part because there is little consensus on suitable exchange rates. Many analysts assume that the DPRK hides significant defense-related expenditures—such as military weapons production, militia and para-military pay, and logistical supply expenses—under the other nondefense budget headings. United States

---

[1] The first such instance of Chinese tacit support was given at a banquet hosted by North Korean Ambassador Chon Myong-su in Beijing (October 24, 1981), when Chinese Defense Minister Geng Biao toasted both Kim Il Sung *and* Kim Chong Il.

[2] The Soviet Ambassador to P'yongyang G.A. Kriulin made the first oblique reference to the succession when he said in December 1981, "we are aware that Comrade Kim Chong Il gives direct and concrete guidance" to the programming of land reclamation (*Far Eastern Economic Review (FEER)*) Dec. 11, 1981. In February 1982, both Chinese and Soviet guests at a Kim Chong Il birthday celebration in P'yongyang made short but positive comments about the "son of the sun."

[3] *Pukhan Chonso 1945-1980* (ROK government sponsored study of the DPRK), and the *Military Balance 1981-1982*, London: Autumn 1981.

(Arms Control and Disarmament Agency Reports) and South Korean government analysts argue that the North is really spending between 15 and 25 percent *of its GNP per year on its* military development program, versus the 14 to 17 percent of *budget* reported by the DPRK.[4] Thus, the 1979 North Korean military budget was somewhere between US$1.26 billion and more than two billion. Although exact statistics remain a matter of conjecture, DPRK defense spending has increased at a brisk pace.

In comparison, the military budget of South Korea was relatively modest until 1975, with a 4% to 5% rate of annual expenditure increases. Extrapolating from the 1960's and 1970's, and based on that rate, the 1975 and 1976 ROK budgets would have been roughly US$460 and US$500 million. This, however, was not the case. In 1975 a sudden budget shift occurred in reaction to the American withdrawal from Vietnam. In that year, the ROK defense budget rose to over US$800 million, and the 1976 budget jumped to approximately US$1.5 billion. This exponential trend continued since the mid-1970's with the ROK defense budget exceeding US$2 billion in 1977, US$3 billion in 1979, and US$4.4 billion in 1981.

The general pattern of North and South Korean military growth indicates that both nations in the late 1970's and early 1980's were locked into an exponential arms race. It is not necessary to use complex mathematical techniques (Richardson or more recent differential equation models) to see that North and South Korean military spending levels match the traditional "arms race model". Korean leaders were also quite clearly aware of the situation, but few efforts have been made to break the cyclical logic of matching military escalations. In January 1976, then President Park Chung Hee of South Korea stated:

> By the time we complete the bolstering of our defense power in the five years to come, the North Korean communists will also have probably reinforced their arms. In that case, we may find it necessary to further reinforce ours again. This may lead to a sort of arms race after all. Of course this is not desirable, but we have no choice.

His prophecy proved correct. Even as early as 1969, Kim Il Sung observed that DPRK "national defense power has been gained at a very large and dear price (and that) frankly speaking our spending on

---

[4] *World Military Expenditures and Arms Transfers 1969-1978* U.S. Arms Control and Disarmament Agency, December 1980, p. 55.

national defense has been too heavy a burden for us in light of the small size of the country and its population." At that time, the heavy burden of defense spending necessitated a three year extension of the DPRK's Seven Year Plan (1961-1967). Now, in the 1980's, the North Koreans find that they are approximating South Korean defense expenditures even though their estimated GNP is 1/4th the size of the South's.

In defending substantial increases in the 1983 American defense budget, U.S. officials argued that defense spending is an "ultimate social program" in that it "stimulates investment . . . and creates jobs."[5] Others argue, and with some insight, that "no analytical studies have yet established a positive link between military expenditures and economic development in the broad sense. There is, in fact, a growing body of evidence pointing to retarding effects through inflation, diversion of investment, use of scarce materials, and misuse of human capital."[6]

Whatever the economic merits of military expenditures, it is necessary to evaluate cost in terms of threat and in light of the prevailing economic situation of the nation.[7] Calls by President Chun Doo Hwan for a "halt to the arms race" may be motivated as much by the desire to reduce tensions on the Korean peninsula as by the popular outcry for "price stabilization" and continued economic growth.[8] Kim Il Sung and his successors are undoubtedly feeling similar pressures.

III. Relative Military Capabilities

An itemized analysis of North and South Korean military capabilities is admittedly only one piece of the national security puzzle, but it is

---

[5] *Washington Post*, March 8, 1982.

[6] *World Military and Social Expenditures 1981* ed. by Ruth Leger Sivard, World Priorities Inc. Leesburg, Va., p. 17.

[7] Asked in September 1981 to identify their formost concern, 84 percent indicated "commodity price stabilization." (Jungang Ilbo Survey). In December 1981, South Koreans cited "economic difficulties" (52%) over threats to national security (25%), political stability (18%) or human rights (4%) as the major problem confronting the country. "Price rises" were cited as the heaviest burden for daily living. (Statistical Research Institute of Korea University).

[8] *Jungang Ilbo* poll—survey August 1981, and *Donga Ilbo* poll—survey December 1981.

important in two contexts: 1) the military capability of the adversary directly affects threat perceptions, and 2) programs for disarmament are of necessity linked to weapons estimates and weapons capabilities.

Comparing DPRK military capabilities in 1982 with ten other nations in the world with approximately the same population (16 to 24 million) suggests that North Korea's military posture is not primarily defensive. With the exception of East Germany which has approximately the same number of tanks, North Korea's military force is far superior to all nations of comparative size, maintaining four times the number of men in uniform, and at least three times the average number of tanks and combat aircraft.

North Korean forces in early 1982 were formidable. The army numbered some 700,000 active duty troops in 40 or 41 divisions. Ground weaponry included approximately 2,600 tanks, 1,000 personnel carriers, 4,000 to 5,000 artillery guns and howitzers, 9,000 mortars, 3,400 various range rocket launchers, and 5,000 to 6,000 antiaircraft weapons. South Korean experts argued that the North had artillery with a maximum range of twenty to twenty-five miles, and between thirty-nine and 100 FROG 5 and FROG 7 surface-to-surface missiles, with a maximum range of forty-two to fifty-six miles. The DPRK had also "dug-in" or "hardened" several of its bases and logistical supply areas in defense against aerial attacks.

In comparison to South Korean forces, the North had more than twice as many tanks, artillery weapons, and armored personnel carriers as the South. At the same time, comparisons between North and South Korea can be misleading. For example, the ROK has M-60 and M-48 tanks, while the North has T-54's and T-34's, tanks of an older vintage and probably less reliable. The same is true in sea and air: the South has destroyers and modern F-16, F-4 and F-5 aircraft; the North has a large number of coastal craft and older Il-28, MIG-15, and MIG-17 aircraft in its arsenal. Nonetheless, the DPRK has twice as many combat aircraft (even if many of these are outmoded); and in the event of war could probably control the sea lanes to South Korea with its naval forces (19 submarines, 33 large patrol craft, 318 fast attack craft, and 100 coastal and amphibious ships).

Both nations are also busy building up a munitions industry and modernizing their weapons systems. According to Stockholm International Peace Research Institute (SIPRI) reports, North Korea in 1975 had received permission for license manufacturing of the MIG 21 combat aircraft from the Soviet Union, and by manufacturing its own or taking delivery on additional advanced "third generation" MIG 21s from the Soviets, it was possible that in early 1982 North Korea had as many as 150 of these planes rather than the 120 estimated by the International Institute of Strategic Studies. At the same time, the Soviets had not furnished the DPRK with any of the more advanced MIG (Mikoyan) models such as the MIG 23, 25, or 27.

Besides the alleged assembly of MIG 21s, the North has developed a large munitions industry. Consequently, it can produce AK-47 rifles, mortars, rocket launchers, artillery, anti-aircraft weapons, personnel carriers, patrol craft, submarines, and possibly tanks. In addition to its indigenous weapons development capability, the DPRK reportedly received some US$1,055 million in military grant assistance from the Soviet Union between 1961 and 1979.[9] Further, the DPRK received in 1978 and 1979 offers of more military aid, economic assistance and oil deliveries from the Chinese.

The South Koreans have been equally busy developing their own weapons industry and aquiring more advanced weapons systems from the United States. Since the mid-1970's South Korea has produced its own M-16 automatic rifles, mortars, ammunition and artillery. They have also launched a fledgling helicopter industry, and re-building M-47/48 tanks and fast-patrol boats. Output has doubled in the past four or five years and South Korea is looking abroad for opportunities to sell its efficient, competitively priced equipment.

Export of these weapons systems in turn will help reduce the ROK's balance of payments deficit and foreign debt (US$ 30 billion in 1982).[10] Proposals for the construction of more advanced howitzers, mortars, surface-to-surface missiles and the assembly of US F-5E fighter aircraft are becoming actualities.

The United States has given the South Koreans at least US$2 billion in military aid since the Korean War, and is actively helping the ROK in the modernization of its military forces. While the Carter administration would not approve the sale of 60 F-16s to Seoul, the Reagan administration reversed that position. Although still receiving some aid from the United States, the ROK government spent US$1.5 billion alone on weapons between 1974 and 1977, and has some US$700 million earmarked through 1985 for improving its "war-fighting" capability.

---

[9] *World Military and Social Expenditures 1981,* Sevard (ed.), p. 7.

[10] "South Korea Under Chun: A New Sense of Vigor" *New York Times,* March 4, 1982.

Thus, in addition to spending exponentially greater amounts of money each year on their defense budgets, both the DPRK and ROK are actively modernizing their military capabilities, both offensive and defensive, and are developing large weapons industries. Those who argue for ever-greater defense expenditures may find additional economic reasons for constructing a military state. Rather than halt or reduce the rate of defense spending, military proponents will point to foreign weapons sales as the appropriate method for redressing economic ills.

IV. The Fundamental Threat: Geopolitics and Offensive Options

Located on a peninsula of the Asian land mass, South Koreans consider themselves the "mouse on the tail of the elephant," a mouse that the North attempted to push into the sea during the Korean War. Aided by China, North Korean forces can always retreat, whereas geography prohibits this option for the South.

Potential offensive North Korean military advantages include more combat divisions, greater ground firepower, superior naval assets, larger logistics and military weapons production, the proximity of major allies, the capability of surprise and the vulnerable location of Seoul. The United States Command in Korea has argued that the North is almost constantly in a state of offensive readiness. Other analysts point to the major DPRK effort to build industrial as well as military complexes underground as indicative of a more defensive posture. One senior United States official has suggested that North Korea's "forward defense strategy" with "defense-in-depth" rear echelon forces implies the conviction that "the best defense is a good offense." Leaving aside theoretical considerations, it is a fact that poised military forces confront each other along the DMZ in a situation which leaves North Korea with a number of offensive options.

The DMZ dividing the land mass of Korea extends approximately 130 miles from east to west to the Yellow Sea. Roughly four kilometers wide, the DMZ is essentially a peace-fire line from the Korean War. It is a no-man's land of burnt-over brush, barbed wire, mine fields and numerous guard posts zig-zagging along the zone up the middle demarcation line.

Off the coast of North Korea and northwest of Seoul, are five

"Western Islands" which are South Korean territory in accordance with Article 13(157) of the 1953 Armistice Agreement. Some of these islands are within the (originally recognized) twelve mile territorial limit of the DPRK, and all are within the 1977 DPRK "announced" 50 mile coastal zone. Foreign military planes and ships are forbidden to enter this extended military/economic zone. Thus, according to North Korea's legal perspective, they could cut logistical supply lines to the islands at any time. Or, North Korea could attack these islands, especially the farthest west island, P'aengyong-do, in a fashion similar to the PRC attack on Quemoy and Matsu in 1958.

Between 1975 and 1978, three large tunnels were discovered under the DMZ, one of which was 246 feet below the surface and near the truce village of P'anmunjom. Two possible uses cited for these tunnels were as an access channel for the infiltration of North Korean agents and as an offensive military strategem for the rapid transfer of DPRK troops in the initial stages of an invasion. Other tunnels probably existed, their exact purpose unknown.

The tunnels were discovered near the Ch'orwon and P'anmunjom-Munsan-ri areas of the DMZ—two of the three major attack corridors to Seoul. An all-out invasion of the South would probably focus on the Munsan corridor with secondary attacks through the Ch'orwon Valley and along the east coast. South Korean forces constructed a fortified "FEBA-ALPHA" line two to five miles south of the DMZ to hold such an attack. Seoul lies twenty to twenty-five miles south of this secondary defense line.

In many respects Seoul is similar to Berlin, in that it is geographically vulnerable to a "blitz" attack by advancing forces. The city is also a very desirable target. Because Seoul contains over twenty percent of the population, including much of its educated elite, and is a communications center, its destruction would effectively debilitate South Korea. If DPRK forces could advance south of the DMZ, Seoul would be clearly vulnerable to sustained artillery and rocket attacks; and even from north of the DMZ FROG 5/7 missiles could, at least initially, bombard and harrass the city. P'yongyang's leaders "might" believe that if Seoul were taken quickly, the North could then call for a ceasefire and negotiate a settlement to their advantage.

Perhaps as more likely offensive scenario would be linked to political conditions in South Korea. In Kim Il Sung's speech to the Sixth Korean Workers' Party Congress, October 10, 1980, he stated: "The tragic developments in South Korea and the disasters suffered by its people today immediately represent the distress of the entire Korean nation. . .Anyone who is of Korean blood cannot remain a passive onlooker to the unhappy state of affairs today. . .We must do away with the colonial fascist rule of the U.S. imperialists and their stooges in South Korea and reunify the country. . ." Rather than invade the South, the DPRK might emphasize amphibious landings, paratroop deployments from lowflying AN-2 aircraft or other methods and routes of infiltration.[11] The potential for subversion depends on the extent of deep-seated domestic discontent, political and economic distruption and student alienation.

V. Stimuli and Restraints on Conflict

The analyses of historical legacies, defense budgets, military capabilities, geopolitics and offensive options, lead to increased concern over the future of the Korean peninsula. Other complicating factors include hostile attitudes among North and South Korean foreign and defense policy elites, ideological and political rigidity, rigid social order, a lack of open communication and nationalist "siege mentalities."

Economic problems in North Korea including unpaid international debts, and in South Korea including a 40% inflation rate in 1980, were aggravated by enormous defense budget allocations. The possibility of nuclear proliferation, however remote, further intensifies perception of threat and needs for pre-emption "in defense."

Only recently have elites in both societies shown a degree of imagination, creativity and flexibility in dealing with conflict issues. Yet, perhaps most significantly, the view that "victory is possible" remains, allowing either side to choose military rather than peaceful methods to reunify the peninsula.

On the other hand, compared to other conflict arenas the Korean situation is less complicated and more clearly constrained. Neither Korean state is involved with armed conflict with another country, and neither presently possesses a nuclear capability. No nation claims territory from either the DPRK or ROK, the major powers clearly

---

[11] U.S. Official pronouncements in early 1982 focused upon the growth in the DPRK's commando forces and infiltration capabilities, *Korea Times,* January 31, 1982, speech by Ambassador Walker, and *Kyonghyang Sinmun,* February 9, 1982, summary of U.S. Defense Secretary Weinberger's Annual Report.

want to prevent another war between the Koreas, and neither Seoul nor P'yongyang is confronted with domestic separatist movements, ethnic strife, or indigenous terrorism.

Conflict is limited through a combination of economic and psychic deterrents. Kim Il Sung's address to the Sixth Party Congress in October 1980 clearly focused on technical engineering, basic sciences, and ways to improve economic management in the DPRK. While castigating American "imperialists" and South Korea's "military fascist rule," Kim also argued:

> Our people do not want war; they want to evade a fratricide and reunify the country peacefully at all costs. Eliminating the military confrontation between the North and the South and obviating the danger of war is the prime requisite for the peaceful reunification of the country.

Ever-escalating defense budgets are an obstacle of improving the economic conditions of the Korean people in both countries. A lack of optimism about the future may also lead to an unwillingness to work without financial incentives. According to a Japanese economic journal, Kim Il Sung observed that "some workers do not want to work"—leading the editors to conclude that there is growing opposition in the DPRK to extra labor without additional compensation.[12] The lengthy succession process for Kim Chong Il will meet with fewer obstacles if the DPRK's economy thrives under his direction.

The political fortunes of President Chun are similarly affected by economic and psychological gains. The revitalization of the Korean economy from 1980's negative growth is a positive sign, as was the selection to Seoul for the 1988 Olympics. But continued investment into escalating defense budgets may adversely affect economic growth and serve to further isolate South Korea from the non-aligned states and communist nations it would like to have participate in the Olympics.[13]

Offensive military options certainly exist, but Korean leaders may wisely choose to control and limit conflict on the peninsula, and thereby transfer on to future generations the significant economic accomplishments they have made since the Korean War.

---

[12] *Seoul Yonhap*, June 1, 1981.

[13] *Dong-A Ilbo* poll, December 1981 survey found, perhaps surprisingly, that 84 per cent agreed that there was a need to improve relations with the People's Republic of China, and even more (92%) felt that an improvement was likely.

VI. Preliminary Steps in the Evaluation of Arms Control and Disarmament (ACD) Measures

It certainly does not come as a shock to many analysts of international relations that arms control and disarmament (ACD) proposals are often little more than pious hopes or rhetorical flourishes issued for foreign and domestic consumption. Furthermore, ACD agreements are unlikely to eliminate conflict itself, but serve to reduce the probability of conflict. Despite these inherent problems, ACD agreements can work effectively to alter patterns of conflict.

Prior to initiating ACD negotiations, leaders in Seoul and P'yongyang might ask themselves several questions:

- First, what kinds of ACDs do they envision—reductions in the total number of weapons, phased disarmament, the creation of inspection systems, the introduction of third-country monitoring teams, multilateral or bilateral negotiations, etc?
- Second, what is the appropriate role for the military in the economic sector?

They would also need to determine whether military expenditures require resources which could be better utilized in the civilian economic sector. And whether reductions in the number of military personnel would lead to major unemployment problems, or perhaps serve to redress labor shortages.[14] In addition, Korean leaders would ask to what degree military imports adversely affect their balance of payments, and whether military research contributed to the civilian economy.

Having ascertained that reductions in defense expenditures would be beneficial for their economies (as this study contends), then Korean leaders would have to evaluate how defense cuts and arms reductions might potentially destabilize the military situation on the Korean peninsula.

Thus, in order to reduce arms and arms spending, the first general step is the analysis of the conflict situation with particular emphasis on weapons quantities, capabilities, and the relationship among

---

[14] In comparison to the rest of the world, North Korea ranks second (using IISS statistics) behind Israel in the ratio of soldier to civilian populations. According to the account of recent American travelers to the DPRK, North Korean leaders dispute foreign estimates of their military forces, putting the total at closer to 400,000 than 782,000—and argue that many of these soldiers are "busy in agriculture."

weapons, geography, and strategy.

The communication of a sincere interest in ACD negotiations could then lead to the exchange of information on relative weapons capabilities, quantities, and deployment. In addition, and most significantly, both sides would indicate the minimal level of military strength that each considered necessary for their security.

VII. General Proposals and Confidence Building Measures: Context

The North-South talks which had led to a joint communique in July 1972, came to a close in March 1973 partly over South Korea's refusal to establish subcommittees for the negotiation of political, military, and diplomatic issues.

The North responded stressing the importance of what they called a "four-point" agenda:

- The discontinuation of the arms race to include a ban on the introduction of new weapons,
- the mutual reduction of force levels and armaments,
- the withdrawal of foreign forces, and,
- a North-South peace agreement.

The North Koreans subsequently launched several major proposals ranging from force reductions so that both sides would have equal numbers (100,000 each), to reductions in forces leaving the existing proportion of forces undisturbed.

South Korean leaders argued that the DPRK's proposals were "sequenced" in such a way that the initial process of disarmament would lead to a clear-cut military advantage for the North. In addition, Seoul opted for the phased adoption of confidence building measures (CBMs) which would lead eventually to concrete ACD accords.

The July 1972 Joint North-South Communique included a renunciation of propaganda efforts by each party, and the installation of an emergency "hot line" across the DMZ. These actions are typical of confidence building measures designed to reduce threat perceptions and create a new psychological platform upon which additional agreements are constructed.

Ten years later, one of the seven points in President Chun's 1982 new year's address was a call for an end to the arms race and the military confrontation between the two sides, and the opening of liaison missions in both capitals. The President's proposal and a subsequent ROK 20-point Reunification Plan (February 1982), may have brought new life to the confidence building process.

Given the Korean situation, both sides have little to lose by allowing the exchange of scientists, or cultural exchanges, or allowing mail deliveries, or even linking both nations telephonically.

Other CBMs might include freer travel between nations, or failing that, allowing divided families from the Korean War to meet in some third country such as Japan. Exchange visits between P'yongyang and Seoul for military, political and party leaders could be renewed, and President Kim Il Sung of the DPRK might accept President Chun Doo Hwan's invitation to visit Seoul.

In addition, trade relations could be initiated which would be mutually beneficial—perhaps via a third country.

Over the next five years, as both sides gain confidence in conventional military parity (given the present ROK development program) they could issue a declaration opposing the first-use of nuclear weapons.[15] Subsequent joint declarations renouncing the development and/or proliferation of nuclear weapons might lead eventually to the creation of a Northeast Asian nuclear free weapons zone. Similar statements concerning the nonuse of chemical and biological weapons would also help defuse the present situation. Actions taken to reduce mutual threat perceptions might then lead to additional exchanges of information on military matters and the initiation of ACD negotiations.

VIII. Arms Control and Disarmament Proposals

As indicated, there are numerous approaches that are viable in arms control negotiations, but a preferred strategem for the Korean situation might be to first alter the "nature" of armed forces prior to actually reducing their numbers. Thus, both sides might agree to measures that would limit their relative "offensive" capabilities, which insuring adequate defenses against all potential adversaries.

---

[15] This idea was first proposed by Prof. Hiroharu Seki of Tokyo University in September 1975.

Having reduced mutual fears of offensive preemption, Korean leaders might then proceed toward actually decreasing their military arsenals and the number of active duty personnel. The following un-prioritized and non-chronological list of ACD proposals is offered as a stimulus for further discussion of this complex and important issue:

- Redeploy and/or limit the number of offensive units, such as amphibious brigades, and units with self-propelled guns, tanks and armored personnel carriers.
- Restrict the deployment of forces in certain areas, i.e. on both sides of the DMZ north of Seoul.
- Enlarge the present area of the DMZ, and preclude military forces from entering the zone. At the same time, live up to the Armistice agreements which prohibit the introduction of new weapons systems into the DMZ.
- Set up joint observation posts to monitor violations of accords, and introduce a third party—in this case members on an enlarged Neutral Nations Supervisory Commission, Sweden, Switzerland, Poland and Czechoslovakia.
- Restrict the size and location of military maneuvers in order to make it more difficult to pre-position troops for an attack in the guise of a "training exercise."
- Give prior notification for any major military training exercises.
- As proposed by the U.N. Military Armistice Commission (January 1982), invite members from the "other side" to observe military exercises.
- Make joint declarations confirming that "rules of engagement" are designed to constrain conflict and reduce the probability of accidental attack.
- Allow the deployment of large numbers of neutral troops in key areas, and create joint patrols.
- Limit the production of weapons which are considered strictly offensive, or the acquisition of these weapons.
- While limiting the production of offensive weapons, encourage the production and even deployment of such "defensive" weapons as anti-tank guns, TOW missiles, surface-to-air missiles, and even short-range interceptor aircraft.
- Establish more military "hot" lines across the DMZ to improve communications and reduce mutual threat perceptions.
- Either place a ceiling on the number of armed forces and armaments, or agree to a percentage of reduction, or to the

maintenance of similar ratios during the reduction process.

- Limit military defense budgets, first by exchanging information on budget accounting systems and total defense expenditures, and second by reducing defense expenditures.
- Initiate non-military confidence building measures.

The initial stages of rapprochement should not intensify either side's feelings of vulnerability. Two objectives should remain the central focus for intra-Korean relations during the remainder of this century: 1) the maintenance of peace, and 2) the ultimate convergence if not re-unification of the Korean people.

It is obviously very difficult to evaluate the conflict situation in Northeast Asia, particularly in light of the multiplicity of great power interests in this region. Furthermore, lists of confidence building measures or disarmament proposals are likely to remain only lists. But, the realization that military victory is no longer possible and that huge defense budgets can adversely affect national economic growth, may lead North and South Korean leaders to consider these and other alternatives to war.

CHAPTER 13

U.S. STRATEGIC DOCTRINE, ARMS TRANSFER POLICY, AND SOUTH KOREA

Yong Soon Yim

I

Ever since the Peace, Amity, Commerce and Navigation Treaty[1] established an official contact between the United States and Korea on May 22, 1882, the U.S.-Korean relationship has gone through many cycles of different lives. In the retrospect of the historical states, however, it appears that the mutual relationship has grown, like a human being, from childhood state to being an adult. While the growing pain has often been very difficult to overcome, the growth of communal relationship between them has helped to achieve a healthy development process. Particularly, after World War II, the relationship has been transformed from merely an expedient alliance to mutually interdependent community.

No relationship between these two countries has been more eminent than that of the military in the last several decades. The United States practically started the basic foundation of South Korean military forces. It also trained, equipped, and built South Korean forces which later became part of the "Combined Forces Command". Thus South Korea has become "benefically" of U.S. arms transfer policy of the last several decades. In this historical perspective, this paper will attempt to explain the impact of the U.S. strategic doctrine on the U.S. arms transfer policy toward South Korea. In order to explain this process, this paper will attempt first to explore the historical pattern

---

[1] See U.S. State Department, *A Historical Summary of the United States-Korean Relations* (Washington, D.C.: U.S. Government Printing Office, 1962).

of the strategic and arms transfer policy toward South Korea. Second, it will search the sources or perhaps reasons behind such a policy pattern. Third, this paper will attempt to answer the change of such U.S. policy on the development process of South Korea military capability. Fourth, it will then speculate the future direction of U.S. arms transfer policy to South Korea in the 1980's.

II

The United States was not known as a major arms supplier. This situation was drastically changed due to World War II. The United States began its role as a big international arms supplier about a year before she entered World War II. President Franklin D. Roosevelt proposed in 1940 that the United States lend, lease, sell or transfer not only weapons, but also food, machinery and services to nation whose defense was vital to this country. Congress finally approved in March, 1941 the so-called Lend-Lease Act. This Act provided that a country should receive aid on such terms as "the President deems satisfactory" and that repayment was to be "in land or property or in other direct or indirect benefits which the President deems satisfactory." The Lend-Lease Act was originally intended for Britain, and then extended later to every ally as America entered the war. When terminated by President Truman in August 1945, total lend-lease aid had exceeded $50.6 billion.

In the post-war years, the United States continued to distribute arms throughout the world. Unlike the previous arms supplies, the post-war U.S. arms transactions were based upon many complex motivations. The famous Stockholm International Peace Research Institute suggested three broadly defined motivation of arms transaction policy of a state. One of the motivations is an attempt to control political and military events by supplying arms. Second, transaction of arms can be motivated frequently for purely economic profits. Third, some states attempt to restrict arms flow or at least be very selective in transferring weapons to others.[2]

The post-war arms transfer policy of the United States was

---

[2] The SIPRI, *The Arms Trade with the Third World* (Stockholm: International Peace Research Institute, Inc.).

motivated with complex reasons. Its policy toward the Far East, particularly Korea, was largely motivated with political and military strategic reasons. Thus U.S. arms supply to South Korea closely followed military strategic doctrine to defend against Communism expansion. Consequently, South Korea's position in the U.S. strategic doctrine should be understood in order to evaluate the post-war arms transfer policy.

Immediately after World War II, while the prevailing mood in public opinion was that of peace, the main American strategic concern was to face the possibility of total war with the communists. American policy-makers were primarily concerned with an all-out war with the Soviet Union. Indeed, many Americans believed that "the Soviet leaders, like themselves, thought only in terms of all-out war."[3] In terms of the Far East, according to Professor Akira Iriye, this was either a misperception or a distortion of reality, due to a lack of American experience in that area.[4] Under the assumption of total war, a Soviet occupation of Korea did not raise Korean strategic significance for U.S. policy-makers.[5] The American strategic plan concluded that the Korean peninsula could be neutralized by American air and sea power. Considering the fact that America maintained, at that time, an air force and navy far superior to that of the Soviet Union, this was a convincing argument to many American policy-makers. With this superior capacity, America could effectively meet a Sovet attack with conventional forces. The Americans also perceived that since the Soviet Union outnumbered the U.S. in ground troops, in a major war the U.S. ground troops would be vulnerable to Soviet land forces. Furthermore, this situation may well lead to the trapping of U.S. forces by the Soviet army on the Korean peninsula. Since the nearest American main forces were nearly 600 miles away in Okinawa, and that forces in the Philippines were about 1,500 to 2,000 miles away, it would be very difficult for the U.S. to mobilize reinforcement quickly to the Korean peninsula. In American security thinking,

---

[3] John Spanier, *American Foreign Policy Since World War II* (New York: Praeger Publishers, 1977), p. 85.

[4] Professor Iriye makes a point that due to the fact that the U.S. had never been more than a secondary Asian, the United States' policy became strongly idealistic. See Akira Iriye, *The Cold War in Asia* (Englewood Cliffs, New Jersey: Prentice Hall, Inc., 1974).

[5] Harry S. Truman, *Memoirs, Vol. II: Years of Trial and Hope* (Garden City, N.Y.: Doubleday & Co., 1956), p. 333.

particularly, it was assumed that should a global war occur, the out-come would be decided not in Korea, not even in the Pacific area, but most likely in Europe. This kind of strategic thinking made South Korea militarily dispensable within the larger framework. The logical out-growth of this perception was the exclusion of South Korea from the American Pacific defense perimeter. That perimeter established the defensible range, running from the Aleutians to Japan, through the Ryukyus to the Philippines, but excluding Korea.

While the Truman Doctrine and the Marshall Plan were in opera-tion in this period, the United States was beginning to realize the need for military security in Europe—the increased communist activities in France and Italy, the takeover of Czechoslovakia and the blockade of West Berlin in 1948 and 1949. Americans strongly perceived that if the Marshall Plan were to be effective in containing communism, Europe needed a strong military protective shell while the economic rebuilding could be completed. This conceptual frame was later known as the theory of containment and was first made public in an article written by George Kennan.

In terms of military strategic doctrine, containment theory differed significantly from the previous doctrine of total war. Containment was a first attempt to integrate nuclear weapons into American military strategy. The major source of aggression was seen as the Soviet Union and the most probable site for this aggression was Europe. In this theory, since the U.S. military did not possess the conventional capability of the Soviet forces, particularly ground forces, NATO ground forces would defend Europe as long as possible while the U.S. atomic weapons capability would be directed against tactical targets in the field and be employed in a strategic capacity against the source of aggression. Any major conventional attack by the Soviet Union in Western Europe would be answered by American nuclear strike on the Russian heartland. However, Soviet initiatives of less-than-armed-conflict intensity would be met at the equivalent level. Subconventional conflicts, such as the Berlin blockade, would be met with firmness, but not necessarily with military force. This was an attempt to get out of the dilemma that the U.S. conventional capability was far inferior to that of the Soviet Union.

In early stages of containment, Korea was again totally neglected in American military strategy as well as its political calculation. Even after the downfall of Chiang Kai-Shek's Nationalist Government in 1949 in mainland China, the U.S. Government took an optimistic view in the Far East. Although public criticisms of the administration's handling of China were upsurging, Secretary of State Dean Acheson expressed his belief that despite the common ideological grounds of the Chinese and the Soviet Union, they would eventually clash with one another. This perception of Asia greatly contrasted with the American perception on European development. This view of the relationship between China and Russia eventually minimized the role of South Korea in American security policy. This perception changed rapidly when the North Korean communists attacked a totally unprepared South Korea on June 25, 1950. This surprise attack was a startling event in the United States. Many Americans believed that since the attack could not be carried out without the Soviet's blessing, it was considered as a part of a general plan for expansion, and even perhaps a prelude to general war. In this view, President Truman made the following speech:

> Communism was acting in Korea just as Hitler, Mussolini and the Japanese had acted ten, fifteen, and twenty years earlier. I felt certain that if South Korea was allowed to fail Communist leaders would be emboldened to override nations closer to our own shores. If the Communists were permitted to force their way into the Republic of Korea without opposition from the free world, no small nation would have the courage to resist threats and aggession by stronger Communist neighbors. If this was allowed to go unchallenged it would mean a third world war, just as similar incidents had brought on the second world war.

As this statement indicated, the survival of the once-neglected[6] South Korea suddenly became synonymous with the survival of the United States. The Korean War had a number of implications for the United States. First, Korea's strategic significance had been altered.[7] Its value could no longer be assessed in terms of its relative importance during a total war. In this regard, Korea became incorporated as a part of American containment strategy.

Second, the United States was beginning to realize the significant role that South Korea could play, not only for the sake of containing communist expansion, but also in protecting Japan politically and psychologically. Right after the North Korean attack, John Foster Dulles suggested that the attack may have been motivated in part by a

---

[6] The U.S. Congress, Senate, *The United States and the Korean Problem: Documents 1943-1953* (Washington, D.C.: Government Printing Office, 1953), pp. 29-32.

[7] Even in a report of the Joint Chiefs which stated that "from the standpoint of military security, the United States has little strategic interests."

desire to block the American effort to make "Japan a full member of the free world." He suggested that the attack may have been ordered because the communists could not tolerate the "hopeful, attractive Asiatic experience in democracy."[8] Thus the significance of Korea in protecting Japan was finally institutionalized in American defense policy.

Third, the Korean War became a testing ground of the overall containment policy with regard to the security of Europe. The Korean War had become a landmark. It illustrated to Americans that this small peninsula was intricately linked with the overall system of containment. This fact was finally institutionalized on October 1, 1953, by the Mutual Defense Treaty between the United States and the Republic of Korea. The treaty made it clear that "by self-help and mutual aid the parties (would) maintain and develop appropriate means to deter armed attack."[9] With the Mutual Defense Treaty, South Korea was officially recognized as a frontier of the containment policy.

Fourth, the early strategy of containment policy heavily relied upon other than military means, such as expressed in the Truman Doctrine and the Marshall Plan. However, along with the Soviet's first successful atomic test in the fall of 1949, the Korean conflict of 1950 changed American strategy substantially. Korea thus became a decisive factor in the militarization of containment. The scope and means of military containment were transformed and extended to a scale of almost total mobilization. By the end of 1951, total requests for defense spending had reached $74 billion. More than seventy new American military bases and support facilities were to be constructed in the U.S., North Africa, and the Middle East. The Air Force was to be placed within striking range of the Soviet Union and its strike capability was supported by the decision to deploy a new long-range bomber, the B-47. America was now committed to Korea with military power and the Chinese Communists were effectively blocked access to the Taiwan Straits by the Seventh Fleet. Furthermore, the Japanese peace treaty had included the right of U.S. military bases to be established in Japan. The United States also was determined to support the French in Indochina, the Dutch in Indonesia, and to

---

[8] Allen S. Whiting, *China Crosses the Yalu: The Decision to Enter the Korean War* (New York: Macmillan Co., 1960), p. 37.

[9] Adam Ulam, *Expansion and Coexistence: The History of Soviet Foreign Policy, 1917-1967* (New York: Praeger Publishers, 1967), pp. 517-520.

extend aid to Chiang Kai-shek in Taiwan. Thus, a full-scale plan of containment with military strength was institutionalized by the Korean War.

Fifth, the Korean War has produced for the first time in American history a strategy of "limited war." The United States recognized Russia's long-standing interest in the Korean peninsula. The American dilemma was that an increased American commitment to Korea would force an unnecessary level of Chinese dependence on the Soviet Union.[10] Therefore, American action in Korea had to be kept limited, principally by maintaining the integrity of the system of containment.

With changing international conditions came a new American military doctrine known as the "deterrence through massive retaliation." On January 12, 1954, Secretary of State John Foster Dulles, in a speech before the Council on Foreign Relations, articulated this doctrine. The speech started with a critique of previous administrations' containment policy: "We need to recall that what we did was in the main emergency action, imposed on us by our enemies."[11] Furthermore, what Americans saw as the lack of any unifying doctrine meant that the aggressor could pick the time, place and means for aggression. The consequences of this policy were constantly escalating defense expenditures and domestic economic dislocation. Dulles stated that local defense in various areas of the non-Western world was important, "but there is no local defense which alone will contain the mighty land power of the Communist World. Local defense must be reinforced by the further deterrent of massive retaliatory power."[12] Dulles concluded that America must "depend primarily upon a great capacity to retaliate instantly by means and at places of our own choosing."[13] This policy as stated by Dulles was "a maximum deterrent at a bearable cost."[14]

Vice President Richard Nixon gave his version of the policy on March 13, 1951:

> Rather than let the Communist nibble us to death all over the world in little wars we would rely in the future primarily on our massive mobile retaliatory power which we could use at our discretion against the major

[10] *New York Times* (January 13, 1954), Also see Department of State, *Bulletin* (January 25, 1954).

[11] *Ibid.*

[12] *Ibid.*

[13] *Ibid.*

[14] *New York Times* (March 14, 1954).

source of aggression at times and places that we choose. . . . We adjusted our armed strength to meet the requirements of this new concept and, what was just as important, we let the world and we let the Communists know what we intended to do.[15]

What was the role of South Korea in American massive retaliation doctrine? If indeed a massive strategic strike with nuclear warheads was a key to the U.S. deterrent policy, why was South Korea needed? There were a number of military and political rationales for the role that South Korea would play. First, as William Kaufmann points out, one of the inherent problems of deterrence is that the enemy may find it hard to believe that America means it.[16] Many Americans perceived that precisely this lack of credibility of American commitment caused the North Korean attack in 1950. The United States had concluded bilateral agreements with Taiwan, Japan, and South Korea, and had initiated a regional alliance in the Southeast Asia Treaty Organization. By committing ground troops, the U.S. intended to demonstrate its seriousness in defending the Far East against the Soviet Union and China.

Second, the existence of at least some local ground troops would function as a first-level sensory organization to detect whether there was a genuine attack or a mere false alarm. Morton Halperin stated:

> The presence of at least some local ground forces, not sufficient to deter a determined aggressor but sufficient to indicate that a war had started, might be an important component of a massive-retaliation policy. Such forces, although they could not prevent successful aggression, would at least make the aggression clearer.[17]

With such a sensory mechanism, the U.S. could avoid an accidental release of its nuclear arsenal. Thus, the presence of U.S. ground forces would allow at least some time for the policy-makers in Washington to evaluate strategic options.

Third, South Korea was to become a buffer territory for U.S. military strategy. Massive retaliation strategy emphasized more the role of the Air Force and deemphasized the role of ground forces. However, should warfare commence, ground forces were imperative until the air and naval forces could be fully mobilized. As Morton Kaplan points

---

[15] *New York Times* (March 13, 1954).
[16] Morton H. Halperin, *Limited War in the Nuclear Age* (New York: Wiley, 1963), p. 117.
[17] Morton A. Kaplan, *The Strategy of Limited Retaliation* (Princeton: Princeton University Press, 1959), pp. 6-7.

out, the strategy of retaliation is most credible when it has a well-built second-strike force.[18] Thus, when and if Western Europe or some other area were under a surprise attack, military force stationed in South Korea would be able to counter attack either the Soviet Union or China. Particularly, when local insurgent forces attempt to damage American security interests, ground troops of the United States and South Korea would act as a counter insurgency force[19] to prevent any further dislocations of the strategic balance in the Far East.

Fourth, South Korea itself would provide a substantial degree of conventional defense to compensate American troop reductions. This argument presumed that if forward conventional defense responsibilities could be left to indigenous military capabilities, then it would be possible to reduce American military manpower. South Korean troops exactly would bridge the possible strategic gap left by an American military reduction in the Far East. Furthermore, modernizing and maintaining the indigenous troops would be far less expensive compared to maintaining American troops in South Korea. This reasoning was quite compatible with the policy of economic stringency advocated by the Eisenhower Administration. To achieve these military, strategic, and economic objectives, the United States infused massive amounts of training into the South Korean defense forces.

Throughout international events, it had become quite clear that the United States could not have released its nuclear arsenal in these localized conflicts. Even though, as late as 1961, Deputy Secretary of Defense Roswell Gilpatric stated that "a nuclear retaliatory capability of 'lethal power' was considered mandatory for both general and limited war."[20] This created a serious dilemma to the strategy of massive retaliation. As illustrated in the cases of Indochina, Cuba, Berlin and others, the United States was not able to "retaliate" with nuclear weapons upon the heart of the Soviet Union. Furthermore, the U.S. realized that it could not even use the nuclear and thermonuclear weapons in local conflicts.

Furthermore, many technological developments of the Soviet

---

[18] For a study of counterinsurgency warfare, see David Galula, *Counterinsurgency Warfare: Theory and Practice* (New York: Frederick A. Praeger, Inc., 1941).

[19] James Nathan and James Oliver, *United States Foreign Policy and World Order* (Boston: Little, Brown and Company, 1976), p. 197.

[20] For an excellent work in this dimension, see Donald S. Zagoria, *The Sino-Soviet Conflict: 1956-1961* (Princeton University Press, 1962).

weapon system gave a new dimension to American policy. The Soviet Union now possessed strategic weapons delivery technology equal to that of the United States. There was also a new development in the relationship between China and the Soviet Union. A Sino-Soviet conflict was rapidly surfacing in the 1950's.[21] The Soviet Union refuses to provide necessary technology, particularly nuclear technology, for the Chinese Communists. The Chinese were bitter and denounced what they perceived as the irresponsibility of the Soviet Union. By this conflict, Americans were beginning to realize that world communism was no longer a monolith, controlled exclusively by the Soviet Union.

Furthermore, officials of the United States were also beginning to realize that many local conflicts, particularly Indochina, were initiated by indigenous communist forces, which received only indirect and limited assistance from major communist countries.[22] Furthermore, many Americans perceived that local communists were concerned more with national interests than world revolution exclusively controlled by the Soviet Union.

With these problems of military strategy and international developments, many intellectuals were beginning to wonder about the effectiveness of the massive retaliation policy. Finally, President John F. Kennedy, who was strongly in favor of strengthening American military capability, called for a reappraisal of that capability. Secretary of Defense Robert McNamara summed up the new defense doctrine:

> Our new policy gives us the flexibility to choose among several operational plans, but does not require that we make any advance commitment with respect to doctrine or targets. We shall be committed only to a system that gives us that ability to use our forces in a controlled and deliberate way.[23]

This policy was an attempt to have a wide option for American military strategy. In this context, if the Soviet Union or the Chinese employed guerrilla tactics, a conventional attack, or nuclear weapons, the United States would respond in kind. This McNamara doctrine

---

[21] See Amitai Etzion, *The Hard Way to Peace: A New Strategy* (New York: Collier Books, 1962), pp. 27-32.

[22] Henry A. Kissinger, *Nuclear Weapons and Foreign Policy* (Garden City, N.Y.: Doubleday, Anchor Books, 1958), p. 264.

[23] See Herbert P. Bix, "Japan and South Korea in America's Asian Policy," in *Without Parallel,* edited by Frank Baldwin (New York: Pantheon Books, 1974), p. 205.

was a serious attempt to avoid the dilemma of responding to local or guerrilla warfare with nuclear attack as advocated in the policy of massive retaliation or of not responding at all. Thus, the flexibility of options in responding to the enemy was the primary feature in this policy. Therefore, nuclear weapons were viewed as only one of several instruments to be employed to protect American security interests.

In order to implement this policy, the United States emphasized the development of submarines with nuclear missiles and long-range bombers, including the B-52. It also added B-47 medium-range bombers and supersonic medium-range bombers, the B-58 Hustler, plus numerous aircraft carriers and an assortment of tactical aircraft. Furthermore, there was an extensive development of the intercontinental and intermediate range ballistic missiles, the ICBMs and IRBMs. In order to fight possible guerrilla wars, anti-guerrilla forces of the Army Special Forces and other special units were extensively trained.

There were numerous ways in which South Korea played a significant role in the context of this flexible response. First, South Korea play a role as buffer territory for American security interests. American felt a "missile gap," particularly in the area of intercontinental ballistic missiles. Because of a successful ICBM test by the Soviet Union, the mainland of the United States no longer became a sanctuary from nuclear attack. A strategic implication was that the United States had to make up this deficiency with middle-range or short-range missiles of the IRBM-class. Furthermore, if communist forces should attack with a limited purpose in a local conflict, the United States had to respond with conventional forces. In this regard, the military bases in Japan, Taiwan, South Vietnam, and South Korea became essential perimeter bases.[24] Under this assumption, while attempting to develop ICBMs such as the Minuteman and submarine launched ballistic missiles such as the Polaris, the United States extensively developed Thor, Jupiter and other IRBMs in this period. Various types of bombs such as the Hustler and Valkyrie (B-70) were also developed in the American defense structure. Thus, South Korean military bases were seen as necessary to overcome a

---

[24] John F. Kennedy, "Annual Message to the Congress on the State of the Union, January 30, 1961," *Public Papers of the President, 1961* (Washington, D.C.: U.S. Government Printing Office, 1962), pp. 23-24.

perceived strategic imbalance in American security interest. From a strategic point of view, once middle-range missiles and medium-range bombers such as the B-47 and the B-58 were incorporated as important defense mechanism, the ground bases became imperative in the defense strategy.

Second, South Korea became a counter-revolutionary force. President Kennedy told the American public that "we are moving into a period of uncertain risk and commitment. . . . thus we must be able to respond with discrimination and speed, to any problem at any spot on the globe at any moment's notice."[25] Ultimately, this concept developed into the policy of flexible response. One of the problems for the Kennedy and the Johnson administrations, however, was the uneasy circumstances in the Third World. The United States had to deal with revolutionary developments in the Congo, Laos, Vietnam, Cuba and in virtually every corner of the Third World. Even in South Korea, there was turmoil in transition from the Second Republic to the Third Republic. The United States was beginning to perceive that the Third World was to be a major testing ground of communist and American will. Americans concern became, therefore, how to oppose revolutionary forces in these regions. One development was the expansion of American military and economic assistance to defeat communist efforts in the Third World. The United States launched economic assistance programs, such as the Alliance for Progress, and also trained many indigenous troops for counterinsurgency and counter-guerrilla activities. Ground forces were perceived as particularly efficient mechanisms for a deterrence policy. South Korea fit exactly into American strategy as an Asian counter-revolutionary force. American ground forces along with South Korean indigenous forces would make an effective force to deny the enemy's threat. This strategy was perceived as extremely credible: it would deter war in East Asia by threatening to defend on the ground.

Third, South Korea was again playing a key role in the defense of Japan. The United States repeatedly made it clear that Japan was essential for American security interests and Japan constantly demanded a concrete commitment from the United States. The Japanese Cabinet Investigation Office states in 1964 that "South Korea controls the entrance to the Japan Sea and is extremely important for the security of Japan. Viewed historically, not allowing South

---

[25] Nathan and Olvier, *op. cit.*, p. 365.

Korea to fall to hostile forces had become the number one goal of Japanese foreign policy."[26] Thus the strong U.S. commitment in South Korea was concrete evidence of a guaranteed security of Japan.

For a strategic point of view, American ground troops in South Korea could be quickly mobilized against any small scale conventional attack by communist forces. Because of this military flexibility, the United States was pressured to normalize relationships between Japan and South Korea. Assistant Secretary of State William P. Bundy stated on October 3, 1964, that "in the event the R.O.K. is attacked by the communist side, both the American and Korean governments, of course, and Japan too, within the limits permitted by its constitution, will assist South Korea to repel the Communist armies."[27] Thus, the United States was beginning to explore a greater role for the Japanese self-defense forces in defending the Far East and entertaining the idea of a strong triangular alliance, consisting South Korea, Japan, and the United States. In 1964, the United States pressure on both South Korea and Japan increased in proportion to the worsening U.S. position in South Vietnam. Eventually Japan and South Korea accepted the normalization treaty in 1965.[28] By this time, however, South Korean indigenous forces were detrimental to the defense of Japan, while the United States had committed its portion of the ground and air forces in Vietnam.

American strategic doctrine was gradually transformed when Richard Nixon became president. The new administration characterized its policy in terms of the Nixon Doctrine and the strategy of "nuclear sufficiency."

While Vietnam conflict was worsening, the Nixon administration was having second thoughts about its foreign policy. President Nixon declared the "post-war period in international relations had ended."[29] What Nixon emphasized was a new perspective in U.S. policy. "We are involved in the world because we have commitments; we have commitments because we are involved. Our interests must shape our commitments, rather than the other way around."[30] Thus emerged

---

[26] Quoted from Herbert P. Bix, *loc. cit.*, p. 212.

[27] *Ibid.*, p. 212.

[28] For the background of the treaty, see Kwan Bong Kim, *The Korean-Japan Treaty Crisis and the Instability of the Korean Political System* (New York: Praeger Publishers, 1971).

[29] Richard M. Nixon, *U.S. Foreign Policy for the 1970's: A New Strategy for Peace* (Washington, D.C.: U.S. Government Printing Office, 1970), p. 2.

[30] *Ibid.*, p. 7.

the Nixon Doctrine:

> The United States will participate in the defense and development of allies and friends, but. . . . American cannot—and will not—conceive all the plans, develop all the programs, execute all the decisions and undertake all the defense of the free nations of the world. We will help where it makes a real difference and is considered in our interest.[31]

This doctrine entailed various policy tenets. First, it was an attempt to move the concept of "national interests" rather than moral tenets to the center of American foreign policy. Second, it indicated that the U.S. unilaterally would not aid governments engaged in civil conflict unless American assistance was requested and unless the government under siege showed some indication of strength to survive. The doctrine attempted to rule out extensive intervention into conflicts of the scale of Vietnam. Third, although it did not exclude the need for "defense and development of allies and friends," the Nixon doctrine stressed shared responsibility for defense. American policy-makers saw that the failure in Vietnam was partly due to the lack of support from the Vietnameses people and of the lack of coordination between American and Vietnamese troops. American realized that unless it has strong support from the indigenous population and troops, it could not operate its military strategy effectively. This concept of shared responsibility, therefore, was an attempt to defend against communism but at a lower military cost to the United States.

Together with the Nixon doctrine, the concept of "nuclear sufficiency" was incorporated into American military thinking. This doctrine resulted from a reevaluation of Soviet nuclear strength.[32] During the Kennedy administration, the U.S. possessed more than 1,000 ICBMs. These land-based missiles were also supported by nuclear warheads carried aboard long-range bombers, missiles in nuclear-powered submarines, and navy short-range bombers on aircraft carriers. These systems formed more than an adequate deterrent to Soviet aggression. Furthermore, since the nuclear power possessed by the United States was far superior to that possessed by the Soviet Union, the latter pushed hard to close the gap. The Soviet Union in 1970 finally had reached a measurable parity in its overall nuclear arsenal.

---

[31] *Ibid.,* p. 6.

[32] For a detailed explanation, see Harland B. Moulton, *From Superiority to Party: The United States and the Strategic Arms Race, 1961-1971.* (Westport, Conn.: Greenwood press, 1973).

Instead of competing with the Soviet Union in building more nuclear devices to attain a superior position, the doctrine of nuclear sufficiency made clear that the United States would maintain a nuclear capability that was "sufficient" to deter the Soviet Union. This doctrine perceived that since the United States in the early 1970's possessed an overkill capacity of four times, it would have been meaningless to build additional missiles with nuclear warheads. Many Americans also were beginning to realize that should a nuclear war between the United States and the Soviet Union occur, no one would be safe. To a great degree, the Nixon administration's policy of the detente was a product of the kind of reasoning. The Strategic Arms Limitation Talks (SALT) were by and large an attempt to institutionalize   military parity under the framework of the nuclear sufficiency policy.[33]

There are several ways that South Korea played a reduced, nonetheless significant role in American defense policy during this period. First, though the Nixon doctrine called for a shared responsibility, President Nixon nevertheless made it clear that in terms of strategic policy, deterrence of war was still the main component of the American military posture and, according to Nixon, the United States would keep all of its treaty commitments.[34] In this regard, though the United States reduced its forces stationed in South Korea by one-third in 1971, American troops in South Korea were still significant in terms of protecting the traditional alliance as articulated in the 1953 Security Treaty and in deterring possible communist ambition in the Far East.

President Ford made a speech outlining a "Pacific Doctrine" on December 7, 1975, where he stated that "we remain committed to peace and security on the Korean peninsula, as the presence of our forces there attests."[35] The U.S. troops stationed in South Korea were to be a deterrent force to discourage any possible breakout of conflict which might eventually force the United States to become involved in another war in East Asia. Though the size of the American ground troops in South Korea was relatively small, discounting the strategic forces, the fact that American forces are there became in itself a deterrent factor. As Ralph N. Clough stated, "in addition to provid-

---

[33] Richard Nixon, *U.S. Foreign Policy for the 1970's: Shaping a Durable Peace* (Washington, D.C.: U.S. Government Printing Office, 1973), p. 182.

[34] *Ibid.*, p. 109.

[35] For the reprint of the speech, *Journal of Korean Affairs* (January, 1976), p. 85.

ing a hedge against military uncertainties, the presence of U.S. combat forces in South Korea demonstrates that the United States continues to take a deep interest not only in that nation's security but also, more generally, in continued peace in Northeast Asia."[36]

Second, South Korea again played a significant role in defense of Japan, one of the most important allies of the United States. President Nixon confirmed the importance of that alliance in 1973:

> For the U.S.-Japanese alliance remains central to the foreign policies of both countries. We are two major powers of the free world, interdependent to an extraordinary degree for our prosperity and our security. The United States therefore places the highest possible value upon this partnership, as it has for more than two decades.[37]

In this regard, the United States constantly pushed for the improvement of Japan's defense capability. Particularly, the Nixon administration's steady effort helped to modernize Japanese conventional military capability. Japanese security still depends upon American military capability, particularly the nuclear deterrent umbrella. Thus, while the Nixon and Ford administration pursued more shared responsibility, Japan's security still remained under American security interests. South Korean and American troops were still imperative in the defense of Japan. There was more than a simple military strategic concern. Japan was particularly concerned over the possible reduction of the American presence in the Far East. President Nixon stated that "she (Japan) has taken a special interest in the security and diplomacy of the Korean peninsula."[38] Takeo Miki, then Japanese Prime Minister, made it clear in 1972 that "the aim of both countries. . . was to avoid any chance in the military balance in Korea that could lead to any military clash. . . due to a sheer miscalculation."[39] Thus, American troops stationed in South Korea would become on the one hand a deterrent factor for American security interest, and on the one hand, relieve the fear of Japan in the midst of growing military presence of the Soviet Union and of China in East Asia. While the United States was projecting that, by the end of the 1970's, Japan's fifth Defense Build-up Program would enable the Self Defense Forces

---

[36] Ralf N. Clough, *Deterrence and Defense in Korea; The role of U.S. Forces* (Washington, D.C.: The Brookings Institution, 1976), p. 20.

[37] Richard Nixon, *op. cit.*, p. 96.

[38] *Ibid.*, p. 95.

[39] See *The Washington Post* (August 13, 1975).

to assume a primary responsibility for backing up South Korea and defending the U.S. bases on Okinawa,[40] American ground troops in South Korea were imperative until the Japanese built up sufficient capability.

Third, South Korea on a small scale played the role of a balancer in East Asia. The doctrines of Nixon and Ford perceived that Communist China would become a major factor in countering the expanding influence of the Soviet Union in the Far East. However, the United States had become aware that neither the Soviet Union nor China were able to control the behavior of North Korea. The United States had no doubt that neither the Soviet Union nor China would encourage North Korea to take any rash action against South Korea. The fact, however, that neither would be able to control North Korea created a measure of uncertainty to American security policy. Thus, South Korean forces, plus American troops became a strategic force to deter any possible military action from North Korea. To measure up this purpose, while pulling more than 20,000 troops from South Korea, the Nixon Administration made a promise to give approximately $1.5 billion in military aid from 1971 to 1975 to modernize South Korea local forces.[41] Addition military equipment would be purchased at South Korea substantially reached self-sufficiency in the production and repair of conventional weapons such as tanks, military vehicles, and ammunition by 1971. By 1975, South Korean forces were equipped with SAM battalions, medium tanks such as M-47s, M-48s, M-60s, and one battalion of artillery with Honest John surface-to-surface missiles. In addition, the South Korean navy was equipped with destroyers, and the air force with sophisticated F-4s and other military systems.[42] With this impressive development, however, South Korean defense capability was still behind, in terms of numerical and quantitative measure, particularly in naval and air forces to that of North Korea. To fill in this gap, South Korean forces were supplemented by the presence of American forces, particularly with tactical nuclear weapons.[43] Extensive military aid and

---

[40] Herbert P. Bix, *loc. cit.*, pp. 213-214.

[41] *The Washington Post* (July 1, 1971).

[42] See International Institute for Strategic Studies, *The Military Balance, 1975-1976* (London: 1155, 1975), p. 55-57.

[43] For the size and break-down of America nuclear forces in South Korea see John R. Sano, "United States Foreign Policy Towards South Korea: An Immediate Post-Vietnam View," *Korean & World Affairs* (Winter, 1977), p. 386.

training of South Korean forces would serve to fulfill the policy of shared defense responsibility in a long-term perspective. Yet the presence of American troops, no matter how small in number would serve to assure that the United States would fulfill its defense commitment in the event of renewed conflict. Thus, it was argued, the strengthened South Korean forces, plus American nuclear capability would become a balancing force in Korean peninsula.

In 1977, the new Carter Administration attempted to define and build its own foreign policy. Special Assistant for National Security, Zbigniew Brzezinski attempted to move from an "acrobatics" to an "architecture" approach in building world order. From the onset, the Carter Administration faced difficulties in carrying out its policy, especially regarding human rights, energy problems, and the Panama Canal. Particularly, in the national security strategic area, a clearly discernible policy has yet to emerge. This lack of a strategic doctrine has created confusion for the role of South Korea in American security policy and has triggered a controversy over the American troop withdrawal from South Korea.

At this stage, one can only deduce the foreign policy intention from various writings of Brzezinski and the first movements of the Carter administration. Before becoming the President's national security adviser, Brzezinski wrote more than 200 articles and 8 books ranging from Eastern European affairs to international politics. One of his theories concerns his conception of contemporary world order. In total disagreement with Nixon and Kissinger's conception of a "balance of power" world, Brzezinski argues that, in terms of military, political, and economic leverage, "the world is, and likely to remain, a bipolar one."[44] In this world, the United States will face a multiple state of triangular relation, namely, a competitive triangle of China-Russia-America and a cooperative triangle of American-Europe-Japan. In terms of global strategy, while maneuvering the China-Russia-America triangle, he emphasized the more binding community of the developed nations.

> It does seem desirable to widen as rapidly as possible those areas of international cooperation for which the preconditions already exist. Share political values as well as economic prowess clearly dictate the desirability

---

[44] Zbigniew Brzezinski, "The Balance of Power Delusions," *The Theory and Practice of International Relations,* edited by David McLelland and others. (Englewood Cliffs, New Jersey: Prentice-Hall, Inc.), p. 100.

of transforming the existing cooperation between Europe, Japan, and America into a more binding community of the developed nations.[45]

He then suggests that "an effort must be made to forge a community of the developed nations that would embrace the Atlantic states, the more advanced European communist states, and Japan"[46] In this the United States becomes the "principle global disseminator of the tech-netronic revolution," in order to transform the world environment. This strategy entails (1) strengthening relation with the traditional and more advanced European countries, plus Japan, Australia, Israel, and Mexico; and (2) cooping more advanced Eastern European countries with the influence of American technology. The underlying hypothesis is that the more communist countries become dependent upon Western technological benefits, the closer will be the relationship between Eastern European communists and Western countries. This would lead to more openness of the Eastern European countries and in the long run to the disintegration or at least to less hostility from the communist bloc. This is a more active and to some degree an offensive strategy toward communist countries—not within military weapons but with a more potent and endurable weapon, namely, American technology.[47]

There are several decisions the administration made which reflected Carter's strategic thinking. The administration's decision not to match the Soviet Union's move toward a possible-first strike capability against land-based missiles rests upon the assumption of diversifica-tion of technological abilities. Thus, even if the Soviet Union were able to destroy American land-based missiles, the United States would still have its nuclear submarine and bomber fleets to retaliate. Of course, U.S. strategic offensive forces are still based on the Triad concept of three separate and distinct types of weapons, land-based bombers, land-based missiles and sea-based missiles. However, instead of matching *pro rata* basis with the Soviet Union, the United States would attempt to develop an overall strategic compatability with superior technology. The emphasis is more on the technological quality of weapons than on numerical superiority.

---

[45] *Ibid.*, p. 102.

[46] Z. Brzezinski, "Between Two Ages: America's Role in the Technetronic Era," *American Defense and Detente*, edited by Eugene J. Rosi (New York: Dodd, Mead & Company, 1973), p. 526.

[47] *Ibid.*, pp. 526-528.

The Carter administration's decision to shift its priority to NATO forces in Europe was partly an attempt to correct the deficiencies of military capability that stemmed from the conflicts of 1973 in the Middle East and in Vietnam. This shift of priority toward Europe is providing a ground work for Brzezinski's concept of forging of the advanced European countries. Furthermore, the U.S. attempt to incorporate the neutron bomb into NATO forces illustrates the administration's drive to use technological means to guarantee the safety of Europe. Although Secretary of Defense Harold Brown stated that "We are and will remain a major force in the Pacific."[48] there is clearly a distinctive pattern emerging. While attempting to infuse more troops in Europe, the Carter administration, contrary to the increasing presence of the Soviet Union, drives to reduce American militry presence in East Asia.

In terms of the defense of Europe, the forward defense strategy is one which calls for the United States, West Germany, and other allied armies to meet the enemy as close as possible to the border, with maximum force. This strategy rejects the old concept of a fighting retreat, of giving up West Germany to buy time for mobilization and later counterattacks. This strategy recognizes the urgency of weapon technology and pursues a more aggressive defense. It is not merely an attempt to contain or balance forces. This concept is very compatible with Brzezinski's concept of the "disseminator or the technetronic revolution." In terms of nuclear strategy, US will select military installation in the Soviet Union as primary nuclear targets rather than indiscriminately attack industrial Russia cities.

The Carter administration's early decision which was averted later to pull out American ground troops from Korea and the somewhat negligent attitude of the administration toward China in the early state was again a reflection of Brzezinski's perception that China has yet to reach a military capability that is genuinely a threat to American society. It is still the Soviet Union in a loosely structured bipolar world order that can and will seriously threaten American security.[49] Recent shift of American focus on the Middle East has at least a few strategical implications for American security policy. Seeing the possibility that the Soviet Union might develop a serious shortage of oil by the end of the 1980's, the U.S. would face a serious challenge of

---

[48] *New York Times* (February 21, 1978).
[49] *Loc. cit.*, pp. 100-101.

Russian influence in the Middle East. In order to carry out a technological offense the United States needs not only a consolidation of technologically-advanced nations, but also needs to secure countries that can supply resources to support such a technological development, namely oil, chrome, copper, uranium, and so forth.[50] Particularly, since the Yom Kippur War in October 1973, the United States well realizes the implications of what these natural resources can do to American security.[51] In this regard, as appeared in Secretary Vance's statement of foreign policy decisions for 1978 before the Los Angeles World Affairs council, January 13, 1978, the Middle East and Africa have become one of this country's major American foreign policy priorities.[52] The Carter's doctrine and the development so-called Rapid Deployment Forces was an attempt to protect Middle East from the possible invasion from subversive forces. It appeared that the United States becomes more and more dependent upon technological ability for its security policy. President Carter was the first president to recognize, at least officially, arms race in space. President Carter and Defense Secretary Brown recognized the fact that the Soviet Union had developed 'hunter killer' satellites with orbital bombardment vehicles. Both the United States and the Soviet Union have experimented with laser beam weapons in space. American policy recognizes that future warfare might well be space warfare with highly sophisticated technology. Carter's decision to halt production of the B-1 bomber,[53] and, instead, to exploit the long-range cruise missile was a reflection of economic reasons. Thus it could be proposed that the more American relies upon non-conventional technological weapons for its security, the less susceptible it is to the traditional geo-political and geo-strategical implications. In this stage, the United States, of course, still recognized the strategic role of South Korea. The U.S., however, was increasingly driving to modernize the South Korean local military capability and to expand the role of

---

[50] See Frank N. Trager, Editor, *Oil, Divestiture and National Security* (New York: National Strategy Information Center, Inc., 1977).

[51] Klaus Knorr, "Foreign Oil and National Security," *ibid.*, pp. 106-123.

[52] State Department, *Foreign Policy Decision for 1978* (Washington, D.C.: Department of States 1978). Also see J. Bowyer Bell, *The Horn of Africa: Strategic Magnet in the Seventies* (New York: National Strategy Information Center, Inc., 1973). Also see Roger Pearson, *Sino-Soviet Intervention in Africa* (Washington, D.C.: Council on American Affairs, 1977).

[53] For details of the strategic weapon, see Norman Polonar, *Strategic Weapons: An Introduction* (New York: National Strategy Information Center, 1975).

Figure I. Strategic Potency of South Korea

Time Period	Administration	Strategic Doctrine	Location of Possible War	Strategic Potency of South Korea
1945-1948	Truman	Total War	Europe	Low
1949-1952	Truman	Containment	Europe Middle East	Medium-high
1953-1960	Eisenhower	Massive Retaliation	Europe Middle East Asia	High
1961-1963	Kennedy-Johnson	Flexible Response	Europe Middle East Asia	High
1969-1976	Nixon-Ford	Nuclear Sufficiency	Europe Middle East	High-medium
1977-1980	Carter	Technological Strategic Offense	Europe Middle East Africa	Medium
1981-	Reagan	Overall Strategic Superiority	Europe Middle East	Medium-high

Janpanese forces of the Far East. Furthermore, the Iranian incident and Russian invasion of Afghanistan again made Carter administration to re-evaluate the strategic importance of South Korea.

The Reagan administration's strategic doctrine has not yet emerged as a distinctive pattern. It is perhaps primarily due to the fact that not enough time has lapsed for a clear pattern in the new administration's foreign policy. From the onset, the Reagan's administration faced difficulties in carrying out its domestic programs such as reducing inflation and federal spending.

One can deduce, however, the trend of a Reagan administration's policy by analyzing various actions it has taken in the past. Many of the administration's policies were actually enunciated by previous administrations. Strengthening the "Rapid Deployment Forces" and maintaining the forward defense tactic are only two examples. There are, however, some actions taken by the Reagan Administration which clearly depart from the Carter Administration. First, unlike the Carter administration's military parity to the Soviet Union, the present administration wants to achieve overall military and technological superiority over the Soviet Union. It also emphasizes strategic and civil defense against nuclear war. Second, the Reagan administration paractically has nullified the long-negotiated SALT II. Furthermore, it makes clear that any arms control agreement which makes the United State military position inferior will not be accepted. Third, the U.S. will help its "allies and other noncommunist countries" to defend themselves against communist aggression. In this respect, the human rights policy should not become an impediment to help other countries whose military capabilities are in doubt against communist aggression.

As part of overall strategic superiority, the Reagan administration ordered the deployment of the MX missile and reinstalled the B-I bomber program. At the same time, the modernization programs of the military command and control system and conventional forces are urged to implement as quickly as possible. In other effort to achieve these objectives, the administration has substantially increased defense expenditure. It further emphasizes "hard-target counterforce capability" to disarm Soviet military targets in a second-strike.

A logical outgrowth of this military thinking is to re-state the importance of South Korea. Unlike the early period of the Carter administration, the new President invited South Korean President Chun to an official visit to the United States in order to insure stability in the Korean peninsula. The new administration will continue to maintain, even possibly increase the future, U.S. troops in South Korea indefinitely as counterforcing troops. The "Team Spirit" operation will be exercised regularly to make sure co-ordination and mobility of the military forces of the two countries.

III

As discussed, U.S. strategic rationale determined its policy of arms transfer to South Korea. Following the birth of the Republic of Korea on August 15, 1948, the U.S. officially transferred political, military, and other authorities to the newly established government. Then, its army was renamed as the Republic of Korea Army (ROKA). The ROK military forces were essentially created, trained, and equipped by the United States. As previously discussed, according to U.S. strategic doctrine, Korea was not considered very important. Consequently, U.S. military aid and arms transfer to South Korea was neither intensive nor very impressive. Without serious preparation, U.S. troop withdrawal was completed by July 1947, leaving behind an unprepared Korean army with a small military and naval mission for the training of Korean security forces.

During this early period of the young republic, U.S. military aid, as can be seen from Table 1, was relatively modest. By the summer of

Table 1. *Defense Expenditure of South Korea, 1949-1955*

(In million won: Approximately 274 won = US$ 1)

Year	Defense Expenditure	Total Budget	Counter-part Fund (US Aid)
1949	23.95	91.11	0.22
1950	132.43	242.96	13.15
1951	329.84	617.86	—
1952	946.28	2,150.76	306.95
1953	3,260.54	6,068.31	795.89
1954	5,991.81	14,239.16	4,470.43
1955	10,637.88	28,143.94	15,053.63

Source: Republic of Korea, *1962 Budget* (The Economic Planning Board).

1948, the total of the South Korean military exceeded 50,000 men. At the outbreak of the Korean conflict in June 1950, the total of the ROK army exceeded 100,000. This was much inferior to the North Korean People's Army in terms of both weapons and manpower.

Not only the US military aid to Korea was modest, but also quality as well as quantity of the U.S. weapons given to the army was not impressive. The U.S. Government transferred mostly used weapons for the World War II. Even then, many of South Korean army did not have weapons.

This was a reflection of U.S. strategic doctrine with regard to South Korea's military value in this period. This situation was drastically changed due to the outbreak of the Korean conflict. By 1952, South Korea army had exceeded more than 250,000 men. By 1954, South Korean army manpower strength reached its peak of 650,000 men. It expanded into twenty full-combat divisions and ten reserve divisions. Consequently, as can be seen from Table 1, U.S. military aid was substantially increased to meet the need. A massive transfer of U.S. arms to Korea was carried out, for its army was totally equipped by U.S. arms. Furthermore, the war itself compelled the U.S. to provide large amounts of military assistance in addition to American troops to South Korea through the regular Department of Defense appropriations.

During this period, numerous reasons served to make American leaders less reluctant to aid South Korea. First, the containment doctrine was already officiated as the military strategy to defend against communist expansion. Second, due to, as discussed, the communist takeover of China, outbreak of the Korean conflict and other external events, American public was willing again to commit large resources to military build-up for the implement of the straegic doctrine. Third, massive rearmament with large defense expenditure made U.S. Government readily available at its disposal of large arms for her allies.

With the Mutual Defense Treaty signed in November 1954, U.S. arms supply to South Korea rose even higher in the second half of the 1950's. As previously discussed with the Mutual Defense Treaty, South Korea was officially recognized as a frontier of the containment doctrine. The order to contain communist expansion in the Korean peninsula and also in protecting Japan politically and psychologically, this massive transfer of U.S. arms was quickly implemented. As can be seen from Table 2, the U.S. extended massive economic aid to build the war-torn South Korea. In 1955 alone, it provided 315

Table 2.   U.S. Economic and Military Assistance to Korea (1955-1967)

(In million U.S. dollars)

Year	Economic Aid			Military Aid		
	Total	Grants	Loans	Total	Grants	Loans
1955	315	315	—	33	33	—
1956	387	387	—	226	226	—
1957	349	349	—	262	262	—
1958	292	284	8	331	331	—
1959	274	262	12	189	189	—
1960	216	215	1	184	184	—
1961	247	241	7	200	200	—
1962	190	165	25	137	137	—
1963	181	155	26	183	183	—
1964	218	190	28	124	124	—
1965	182	134	48	173	173	—
1966	262	181	81	210	210	—
1967	178	114	64	272	272	—

Source: U.S. AID, *Overseas Loans and Grants and Assistance from International Organizations* (Washington, D.C.: Government Printing Service, 1969).

million dollar worth of economic aid to South Korea. Total of the military grant was about 33 million dollars. More importantly, military aid had quickly jumped the next year to $226 million. It reached 331 million dollars in 1958. Then it was gradually decreased to $189 million in 1959 and $184 million in the following year. Meanwhile, economic aid also steadily kept up with the military grant. The economic aid also gradually declined after 1960. Nearly 7 percent of South Korea's GNP between 1954 and 1965 consisted of economic and military aids from the U.S.[54] Furthermore, every year several hundred U.S. military advisors known as the Korean Military Advisory Group (KMAG) participated in training the South Korean army in those early periods.

This massive military aid was an attempt to counter North Korean forces directly, and as equally importantly, Communist Chinese forces. As previously discussed, the U.S. perceived that the People's Republic

---

[54] Gabriel A. Almond, *The American People and Foreign Policy* (New York: Frederick A. Praeger, Publishers, 1968).

of China had enormous potential for conventional military forces. Thus healthy development of South Korean army would become a balancing force in East Asia. This will insure the strategy of containment.

The arms flow to South Korea, however, was discernably slowed in the first half of the 1960's. As can be seen from Table 2, U.S. military aid was about 200 million dollars in 1961. It was reduced to 137 million dollars next year. It was even further reduced to 124 million dollars in 1964. Then again, it was gradually increased in succeeding years.

There were several reasons for the decline of arms transaction in the early 1960's. First the threat in Korean Peninsula was somewhat reduced due to various overtures from North Korea. Second, North Korea received almost no military supplies from the Soviet Union during this period. Third, the Korean army was by and large equipped with full capacity. Thus initial heavy investment for the new equipment was minimized. As a matter of fact, by 1965, ammunitions, parts, food, and training accounted for some 80 percent of U.S. military assistance to South Korea.[55] Fourth, the doctrine of massive retaliation was emphasizing far less on local conventional forces to protect U.S. and its allies.

This pattern, however, was again changed. The U.S. arms supply increased again sharply. As Table 2 shows, U.S. military aid was increased to 210 million dollars in 1966. Then it reached to 272 million dollars the following year. Compared to the military aid, the economic grant was increased to 181 million dollars in 1966, and then again decreased to 114 million dollars in 1967.

There were several reasons for such increase in military aid to South Korea. First, U.S. strategic doctrine adopted a new concept of flexible response. In this strategy, flexibility of options in responding to the enemy with both conventional and non-conventional capability was the primary feature. This required strengthened military capability of the forward defense areas such as Korea. Second, Soviet Union resumed arms supplies substantially to North Korea. In addition to aids from Communist China, the resumption of Soviet arms supplies was quite an unsettling event to South Korea and the U.S. Third, the U.S. promised to help South Korea to modernize the economic and

---

[55] For an excellent discussion of future Korean roles in American policy, see Roger Pearson, *Korea in the World Today* (Washington, D.C.: The Council on American Affairs, 1977). Also see William J. Barnes, *The Two Koreas in East Asian Affairs* (New York: New York University Press, 1976).

military capability in exchange for Korean troops dispatched to Vietnam. Fourth, North Korea began to step up its belligerences to the South. Constant incidents surrounding the DMZ provoked by North Korea reminded the U.S. a possibility of another war in Korean peninsula. Then the Pueblo incident and armed commando attack to assassinate South Korean president, Park Chung Hee, convinced the U.S. needs to strengthen South Korea's military capability. To meet this need, the U.S. stepped up supplying such weapons as anti-aircraft equipment, patrol boats, ammunition and phantom jets.

Military assistance to South Korea continued to accelerate and reached 389 million dollars in 1968, and topped $480 million in 1969. Military assistance through the Defense Department alone reached more than 400 million dollars in 1971. Substantial military aid to South Korea was continued up to 1973, and then gradually dwindled. This is, however, somewhat misleading on the surface. As can be seen from Table 3, while military grants were decreased, arms sales to South Korea was steadily increased. Thus the total volume of arms transaction was actually increased. Thus the declining use of military assistance to an increasing reliance on arms sales became the new trend of U.S. policy.

Table 3. *Military Assistance Program and Foreign Military Sales to South Korea 1968-1977*

(Dollars in thousands)

Year	MAP	Educ. & Training	Excess Def. Art.	FMS Agr.	FMS Del.	Commercial Exports
1968	357,270	6,599	51,377	1,504	1,428	588
1969	425,222	7,244	124,964	3,093	716	1,907
1970	313,071	4,965	34,813	—	1,934	1,033
1971	434,804	5,359	137,115	393	408	2,037
1972	285,727	4,519	226,113	8,765	371	685
1973	296,742	2,032	32,142	1,589	2,378	187
1974	92,008	1,527	19,505	100,392	13,318	1,090
1975	79,185	1,291	7,976	216,010	57,452	3,550
1976	59,817	2,058	1,153	634,625	161,260	19,909
1977	1,185	1,395	—	653,987	184,818	62,500

Source: Data taken from *Foreign Military Sales and Military Assistance Facts,* December, 1977, published by Data Management Division, Comptroller, Defense Security Assistance Agency.

The policy shift from military assistant program to military sales to South Korea came quickly and quite large in terms of the volume of arms transactions. As can be seen from Table 3 the military assistance was reduced from about 296 million dollars in 1973 to merely 92 million dollars in 1974. It was further reduced to slightly over 1 million dollars in 1977. Meanwhile, U.S. began to provide military loans to purchase arms for South Korea. It provided 15 million loans to purchase arms for South Korea. It provided 15 million dollars worth of military loans for South Korea in 1971. It was steadily increased in the following years. Military loans reached 59 million dollars in 1975.

More significantly, the military sales were drastically increased. For example, military sales to South Korea were a merely 295,000 dollars in 1967. It was increased up to 1.5 million dollars. As can be seen from Table 3, the growth rate of arms sales to South Korea was fluctuated up to 1973. It was, however, drastically changed in 1974. For example, the military sales agreement between the U.S. and South Korea mounted to $100 million in 1974. It reached more than 653 million dollars in 1977.

There were numerous reasons for such policy of arms transaction of the U.S. First, the Nixon's doctrine called for a shared responsibility of defense against communist forces. As discussed, the U.S. already demanded the West Germans and others to share the defense burden of Western Europe. The Nixon's doctrine further reinforced the concept of shared responsibility with regard to the arms transaction to South Korea. Second, the domestic factor also played a key role in inducing such a policy. The Vietnam war, the economic difficulties, deficit of balance in payments due particularly to oil from abroad and others strained U.S. defense expenditures. With these problems, the U.S. reduced its forces stationed in South Korea by one-third in 1971. Third, in this period, South Korea experienced incredible economic development. The growth of South Korea GNP was 7 percent in 1972, and an incredible 15.2 percent in 1976. With enormous domestic economic development, South Korea earned large sums of foreign currency to support arms purchase. Fourth, North Korean provocation was intensified due to its strategic attempt to unify Korea by Vietnamization[56] in the Korean peninsula. Such provocation, and later President Carter's announcement of U.S. ground troops withdrawal

---

[56] See Yong Soon Yim, *Two Koreas Unification Policy and Strategy* (Baltimore: University of Maryland, 1980).

from Korea created an enormous sense of insecurity in South Korea. This in turn created demands for arms purchases. From the U.S. perspective, arms sale was a logical step to equip South Korean military to defend against a possible North Korean attack while spending relatively small amounts of money.

The Carter Administration attempted to control arms flow to other countries. President Carter ordered a review of U.S. sale to other countries. Then President Carter established criteria for the types of arms to be sold and a ceiling on the amount of U.S. arms sales to other countries in 1977. This was an attempt to curtail transfers that exceeded legitimate defense needs. The Carter arms transfer ceiling was beset with difficulties. Various circumstances forced the Carter Administration to make exceptions for some countries such as Saudi Arabia, Iran, Turkey and others. Then the Soviet invasion of Afghanistan, and the Iranian incident changed to perception of the Carter administration on arms sales policy. Prior to this event, the Conventional Arms Transfer negotiation between the United States and the Soviet Union ended in stalemate in December 1978. The June 1980 Foreign Relation Committee report pointed out that President Carter's plan to restrict arms sale totally failed inspite of the good intention. Finally the Reagan administration totally abandoned Carter's policy of arms sales.

While arms sales policy was fluctuating between Carter administration and Reagan's presidency, U.S. arms transaction to South Korea was unimpeded. Even the Carter administration requested Congress to provide $800 million in military aid to South Korea in 1978. Particularly, the Carter administration pledged 1,500 million dollars worth of surplus military equipment and foreign military sales credit in the context of the proposed withdrawal of U.S. troops from South Korea. Then eventually President Carter reversed his decision of troop pullout. In spite of the reversed decision of troop pullout, during the Carter administration, South Korea's military orders had often been either delayed or withheld on human rights grounds and other disagreements. This situation was changed when the Reagan administration pledged to help South Korea to improve its defense capability. As part of the pledge, the Reagan administration decided to sell 36 F-16 jet fighters to South Korea, along with related equipment for $900 million in 1981.

Besides this pledge of massive sales, numerous sales of military hardware were consumated between 1977 and 1980. As can be seen

Table 4. U.S. Arms Supply to South Korea

Supplier	No. ordered	Weapon designation	Weapon description	Year of order	Year of delivery	No. delivered	Comments
U.S.A.	6	C-130H Hercules	Transport	1977			Pending congressional approval
	37	F-4E Phantom	Fighter	1977	(1979)	(19)	
					(1980)	(18)	
	14	F-5F Tiger-2	Trainer	1978	(1979)	14	Bringing total to 20
	27	Model 205 UH-1H	Hel	1977			On order
	56	OH-6A Cayuse	Hel	(1978)			On order
	37	M-109-A2	SPG	1978			Ordered Aug 1978
	200	AGM-65A	ASM	1977			On order
	600	AIM-9L	AAM	1975	1977	60	
					1978	200	
					1979	220	
					1980	120	
	1800	BGM-71A TOW	ATM	1979	(1980)	(360)	DoD notified Congress about planned sale Apr 1980; order incl 10 bombers
	112	RGM-84A Harpoon	ShShM	1975			For 7 PSMM-5 FPBs
	1	Genne Class	Destroyer	(1979)			

Source: *World Armament and Disarmament, Yearbook* (Stockholm: SIPRI, 1980).

Table 5. *U.S. Arms Sales Agreements (Fiscal Years 1975-1979)*

Saudi Arabia	$21,861,000,000
Iran	12,583,806,000
Israel	5,089,469,000
South Korea	2,119,624,000
Netherlands	1,906,878,000
West Germany	1,905,035,000
Egypt	1,630,916,000
Taiwan	1,514,747,000
Belgium	1,348,950,000
Norway	1,319,047,000
Australia	1,317,937,000
United Kingdom	1,216,762,000
Greece	925,027,000
Jordan	783,337,000

Source: Defense Security Assistance Agency

from Table 4, during this period, the U.S. helped to build the South Korean air force and other rapid military transportation systems. Thus, large quantity fighter jets, helicopters and others were delivered or ordered for future delivery. By the end of 1970's, South Korea became one of the fourth largest arms clients of the United States.

As Table 5 indicates, U.S. arms sales agreements with South Korea between 1975 and 1979 was more than 2 billion dollars worth. In this period, openly Saudi Arabia, Iran, and Israel were ahead of South Korea in terms of the volume of arms sales agreement with the United States.

More important trends emerged in U.S. arms supply policy toward Korea. The United States helped South Korea to establish its domestic arms industry. By the end of the 1970's, South Korea became capable of producing all types of equipment, from combat aircraft to small arms. Many believe that by 1980 South Korea was able to meet all the requirements of its armed forced from local sources, with the exception some highly sophisticated electronic equipment and high-technology combat aircraft. Meanwhile, some combat aircraft was produced under a licensed agreement of U.S. companies. As can be seen from Table 6, the United States allowed South Korea to produce of the F-5E Tiger-2 and other relatively sophisticated weapons. South Korean request to produce the more sophisticated F-16 was refused

Table 6.   South Korean Arms Production with Foreign Licenser

Licensers	No. ordered	Weapon designation	Weapon description	Year of licence	Year of production	No. produced	Comments
Italy	170	Type 6611	APC	1976	1977	20	Not yet in production in Italy
				1980	1978	(20)	
					1979	(50)	
						(50)	
USA	16	F-5E Tiger-2	Fighter	1980			Negotiating total costine 321–15 some lunded riaIMS asseMAS Plan
	12	F-5E Tiger-2	Trainer	1980			
	12	Model 500D	Hel	(1979)	(1979)	(50)	Some 100 delivered end 1980
					(1980)	(75)	
	18	Model 500 MD	Hel	1976	1978	(10)	
					1979	(10)	
					1980	(10)	

Source: World Armament and Disarmament, Yearbook (Stockholm: SIPRI, 1980)

Table 7. Rank order of the 12 largest Third World major-weapon exporting countries, 1977-80.

Figures are SIPRI trend indicator values, as expressed in US$ million, at constant (1975) prices.

Exporting country	Total value	Percentage of total Third World exports	Largest importer (per exporter)
1. Brazil	421	*33.1*	Chile
2. Israel	367	*28.9*	South Africa
3. South Africa	116	*9.1*	Zimbabwe
4. Libya	98	*7.7*	Syria
5. Egypt	72	*5.7*	Somalia
6. South Korea	38	*3.0*	Indonesia
7. Argentina	35	*2.8*	Chile
8. Saudi Arabia	31	*2.4*	Somalia
9. Singapore	17	*1.3*	Thailand
10. Indonesia	16	*1.3*	Benin
11. Cuba	15	*1.2*	Peru
12. India	12	*0.9*	South Africa [a]
Others	33	*2.6*	—
Total	1,271	100.0	

[a] Via a company in Spain; final destination not known to Indian government.
Source: SIPRI computer-stored data base.

by U.S. Government. According to South Korean sources, it will be ready to produce the F-16 in the near future.

Furthermore, South Korea launched its five-year Force Improvement Plan (FIP) in 1976. With an initial fund of $7.6 billion, the FIP attempted to establish various projects such as the purchase of more modern fighter bombers and TOW anti-tank missiles, upgrading air-defense and tank forces, domestic production of some artillery and small arms, and enhanced logistics and war reserve munitions.[57] After its completion, South Korea commenced another one to end in 1986. With such success of the economic and military industries, South

---

[57] Chang Yoon Choi, "South Korea: Security and Strategic Issues," *Asian Survey* (November, 1980).

Korea emerged as arms supplier to other third world countries. Table 7 shows that South Korea takes only 3 percent of the total third world arms market. This figure, however, represent the fact that South Korea occupies the sixth place among third world arms exporting countries. Should this trend continue, South Korea will eventually become competitive even in international arms markets. During the period between 1977 and 1980, South Korea sold $8 million worth of arms to Indonesia. This will increase substantially in the near future as South Korean military industry upgrades its capability.

IV

The post-war arms transfer policy of the United States to South Korea closely followed its strategic doctrine. Therefore, the logic of the strategic doctrine prompted to supply arms to South Korea. U.S. strategic doctrine has constantly been in motion. This change of doctrine changed the perception of the decision-makers on the role of South Korea in American security policy. This change of perception also changed the flow of the arms transaction between the two countries.

Post-war arms supply took various forms. The post-war arms transfer program in 1950, the principal form of assistance was government grants under the military assistance program. As Figure II clearly shows, however, arms transfers through grants-in-aid were gradually diminished. Then the Foreign Military Sales program of government-to-government sales began to replace to the grants-in-aid program. Particularly, since 1975, while the total arms transfers rose steadily, the grants-in-aid became a much less significant factor in the transaction volume. The post-war arms supply to South Korea was also followed with similar patterns with only a few years of time lapse. Thus U.S. policy toward South Korea closely followed the overall strategic, political, economic, and other requirements of the U.S.

With such trend, a few observations can be made for the perspective of U.S.-Korean relationship in the 1980's. It appears that U.S. arms supply to South Korea will continue to increase in the 1980's for several good reasons. First, it has to do with the strategic policy of the Reagan administration. As previously discussed, the Reagan

Figure II.   *U.S. Government Arms Supply*

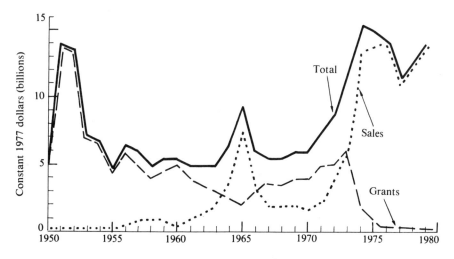

Source: Thomas Brewer, *American Foreign Policy* (Englewood Cliffs: Prentice-Hall, Inc., 1980).

administration has persued overall strategic superiority throughout the world. It has proposed a substantial increase of defense expenditure including $170 million in direct military aid this year for South Korea. Even Gen. Jones, Chairman of the Joint Chiefs of Staff proposed in a report to Congress to increase military support to Korea. Such a strategic superiority requires much improved South Korean forces in defending East Asian region. In order to strengthen the defense, the United States plans to dispatch 48 of its new F-16 fighter and a new army electronic espionage battalion. The Reagan administration also plan to transfer some of M-551 tanks and F-16s to South Korean forces. These moves certainly set a tone of the future policy. However, various public polls indicate that the public willingness to send U.S. troops to defend South Korea is very moderate.

In addition to this military aid and support, there have been annual Defense Minister's conferences known as Korea-U.S. Security Consultative Meeting, between the representatives of Korea and the U.S. since 1968. This meeting was to discuss the changing military situation and to establish common military strategies on the Korean peninsula. The first meeting was held between Korean Defense

Table 8. Sending U.S. Troops to Help Defend Western Europe/West Berlin/Persian Gulf/Poland/Yugoslavia against Soviet Invasion

	Favor	Oppose
Western Europe		
July 1981	53%	36%
February 1981	51	35
February 1980	60	27
July 1978	43	43
West Berlin		
February 1981	46	41
February 1980	54	31
December 1979	50	39
July 1978	40	47
December 1974	34	43
Sending U.S. Troops to Help Defend South Korea against Invasion by North Korea		
February 1981	20%	63%
July 1978	19	69

	Favor	Oppose
Persian Gulf		
January 1980	64%	26%
Poland		
February 1981	23	58
January 1981	25	61
Yugoslavia		
April 1980	33	53
January 1980	36	48
March 1977	13	64
December 1974	11	65
Sending U.S. Troops to Help Defend Israel against Invasion by Arab Forces		
July 1981	28%	61%
February 1981	26	58
February 1980	35	47
July 1978	21	65

Source: Alvin Richman, "Public Attitudes on Military Power, 1981," *Public Opinion* (December/January 1982).

Minister Choe Yong-hui and the Secretary of Defense, Clark Clifford on May 1968. The latest one was held between Chu Yong-bok of the Defense Minister and the U.S. counterpart Casper Weinberger on April 1982. Furthermore, the Korea-U.S. Combined Forces Command was established on Nov. 7, 1978 to co-ordinate a balanced defense partnership between the two armed forces.

As Table 8 indicates, the public remains selective regarding the countries it is willing to help defend. About half of those polled favor sending troops to help defend certain regions perceived to be vital to U.S. interests, namely Western Europe, Japan, and the Persian Gulf. No more than 20 percent of those polled however, favor sending U.S troops in defense of South Korea. In this situation, an alternative would be strengthening South Korean military capability. The logic of this strategic requirement entails a sustained U.S. arms supply to South Korea.

Second, the escalating North Korean's military capability will be again a major factor to the U.S. arms supply policy toward South Korea. Both Koreas have a large military arsenal compared to their sizes and populations. Particularly, North Korea has a larger military force compared to that of South Korea. The Navy seems to be slightly inferior, though not necessarily in terms of South Korea. Though South Korean military forces enjoy a good reputation in terms of combat capability, North Korea's overall strategic superiority even in terms of conventional military capability is undoubtedly undisputable. To support and equip a large standing army, the North Koreans have developed military industries to the degree that the country is self-sufficient in manufacturing most conventional arms such as automatic rifles, machine guns, field artillery, tanks and other weapons.

Unfortunately, such an attempt tends to alarm South Korea. In return, it will again drive South Korea to develop military forces to meet the perceived challenge of North Korea. This tends to perpetuate a vicious cycle of arms race between the two Koreas. Furthermore, various sources indicate that North Korea has spend nearly 20 percent of its GNP for military build-up. As this trend continues, South Korea will have to import various weapons from the United States to compensate its military deficiency.

Third, the continued expansion of the Soviet Union would still become an important factor to the U.S. arms transaction policy. Various sources indicate that the Soviet Pacific naval strength is of alarming proportion in comparison to the naval forces of the U.S.

Navy in every category except the aircraft carriers. The strength of Soviet Pacific air force was also increased to an alarming proportion. The total number of Soviet airplanes in this region was 1,430 in 1965. This number was increased to 1960 in 1971, and finally reached to 2,010 in 1975. This is quite alarming to Japan and the U.S. Furthermore, it would be very difficult for the United States to maintain such a large continuency of military forces in the Pacific regions. One way of overcoming such a deficiency is to help strengthen South Korean military forces. This perspective is certainly presupposed to see continuous arms supply to South Korea.

Fourth, numerous economic rationales will encourage U.S. to supply arms to South Korea in the 1980's. Arms sale deeply is involved in numerous ways the troubled American economy. First, arms sales abroad is one of major elements in "the overall balance of payments" between the United States and other countries.[58] Furthermore, many industries are involved in arms production for their business venture. To some industries, more than 70 percent of their revenue is relied upon defense contract. Meanwhile due to the economic development, South Korea will continue to provide a lucrative market for the defense industry. Second, a U.S. Department of Labor study estimated that every one billion dollars worth of U.S. arms delivered overseas provides some 52,000 American jobs. A study prepared by the Department of the Treasury found that a cut of 10 percent in orders US arms sales abroad would result in the displacement of 132,000 U.S. workers. Third, some argue that arms sales abroad would "allow American arms manufacturers to lower the per-unit cost, help pay for research and development, and in some cases make it possible for the United States to produce for its own use of weapons it otherwise could not afford."[59] Fourth, the United States should from time to time reduce its large stocks of surplus and outdated military equipment to continue to supply arms to South Korea at least in the 1980's.

---

[58] John L. Moore, *U.S. Defense Policy: Weapons, Strategy and Commitments* (Washington, D.C.: Congressional Quarterly, Inc., 1980). p. 94.

[59] *Ibid.*

PART IV

U.S.-KOREAN ECONOMIC RELATIONS

CHAPTER 14

THE DEVELOPMENT OF CONTEMPORARY U.S.-ROK ECONOMIC RELATIONS*

Ki-Hoon Kim

Historically, the development of contemporary United States-Republic of Korea economic relations was originated on May 22, 1882.[1] This year (1982) we commemorate the centennial of diplomatic ties between the two nations. This study focuses on the post-World War II era during which the odd couple established an indispensable and steadfast bilateral relationship in economic, as well as political, military, and cultural fields. Korea is now America's ninth largest trade partner and the fourth biggest importer of U.S. farm products. How has this come about?

An analysis and evaluation will follow a general description of the development of economic relations.

I. The U.S.-ROK Economic Relations

1. The Unilateral Aid Period (1945-1961)

When Korea was liberated from Japan in 1945, her economy all

---

* The author wishes to express his gratitude to Jae Yoon Kim, Young Gak Shin, Paul L. Altieri, Robert S. Rippey, Edward A. Olsen, and J. K. Lee for their help and valuable comments. Errors and shortcomings are, of course, solely the author's.

[1] *The New York Herald* reported on its September 19, 1883 issue that Korea as "a wealthy country of the Hermit Kingdom and 'the curious people, queer customs and a strange language . . . openings for American enterprise.'" It also added that the nation was rich in gold and silver. See "100-Year-Old Credentials of First Envoy to U.S. Found," *The Korea Herald*, February 2, 1982, p. 6.

Table 1.   Comparison on Output Value of Mining and Manufacturing in
          South and North Korea before August, 1945 (Per cent)

Manufacturing (1940)			Mining (1936)		
	South Korea	North Korea		South Korea	North Korea
Chemical	17.9	82.1	Gold (Sand Gold)	29.3	70.7
Metal	9.9	90.1	Gold and Silver Ore	27.3	72.7
Machine	72.2	27.8	Iron Ore	0.1	99.9
Spinning	84.9	15.1	Pig-iron	—	100.0
Ceramics	20.3	79.7	Tungsten and	21.5	78.5
Wooden Articles	65.3	34.7	Molybdenite		
Book Binding	65.1	34.9	Graphite Coal	29.0	71.0
Printing	89.1	10.9	Bituminous Coal	0.5	99.5
Foods	65.1	34.9	Anthracite	2.3	97.7
Electric Power Capacity	14.0	86.0			
Annual Average Generating Power (1945)	8.0	92.0			

Source: The Bank of Chosun, Chosun Economic Yearbook, 1948. Quoted by Hyung
Yoon Byun, "Industrial Structure of Korea," The Seoul National University Economic
Review, 1 (December 1967), p. 42.

but collapsed as more than 700,000 Japanese nationals who occupied
the top layer of economic, political, technical and cultural positions
were repatriated. Moreover, the intensive exploitation of resources
and industrial facilities in the interest of the Japanese war machine
left the former colony's railroads, factories, mines, and the agricultural
sector in almost complete disrepair.[2] The immediate problems of

[2] See Haskell P. Wald, "Use of Tax Collection in Kind to Combat Inflation in The
Republic of Korea," Public Finance, 9 (1954), p. 177; Jung Jae Park, One Hundred
Years of the Korean Economy (Seoul, Korea: The Korea Productivity Center, 1971),
p. 69; Takashi Hatata, A History of Korea, translated and edited by Warren W. Smith,
Jr. and Benjamin H. Hazard (Santa Barbara, Calif.: American Bibliographical Center
—Clio Press, 1969), pp. 131-133; John K. Fairbank, Edwin O. Reischauer and Albert
M. Craig, East Asia: Tradition and Transformation, New Impression (Boston, Mass.:
Houghton Mifflin Co., 1978), chapter 27; Woo-Keun Han, The History of Korea,
translated by Kyung-Shik Lee (Seoul, Korea: The Eul Yoo Publishing Co., 1970),
chapters 33-34; Herman Kahn, World Economic Development, 1979 and Beyond (New
York: William Morrow & Co., 1979), p. 338.

relief alone were so urgent that the U.S. military government in Korea was unable to concentrate on economic rehabilitation or reconstruction.

On top of this, the division of the 85,000 square-mile peninsula along the 38th parallel, the first in over 1,200 years, aggravated the situation. As Table 1 shows, south Korea was deprived of her major sources of coal, electricity, and virtually all heavy industry facilities; she was left only with productive capacity for light industries.[3] In fact, south Korea's total output in manufacturing after the division fell to about 15 percent of that in 1944. The war in 1950 resulted in a *coup de grace* effect on the already weak and unbalanced Korean economy.

The $3 billion property damage caused by the war destroyed the meager supplies of capital, plant and equipment as well as ruining almost the entire infrastructure, not to mention the effect on south Korea's human capital. Nearly one million civilians and 370,000 soldiers were killed. For the period 1950-53, over 5.7 million American military personnel were engaged in the Korean conflict and 54,246 lost their lives. Moreover, the resource-poor nation had to carry a heavy defense burden: military spending occupied over 40 percent of the government budget during the war. The deficit, which was financed by borrowing on overdraft at the Bank of Korea, was mounting. During the fiscal year ending March 31, 1951, for instance, total government revenues amounted to merely 30 percent of the total expenditures.

In addition, inflation, which started during World War II, spilled over into the post-war period. It was intensified by the invasion from the North. The price level increased by more than six times during the first year of the Korean war and was further worsened by poor harvests in both 1951 and 1952. Refugees from the North swelled the existing population, a problem which is ever present. As of 1975, 363 persons per square kilometer of land and 14.8 persons per hectare of farmland was among the world's highest.[4]

Herein lies the importance of foreign aid, especially from the

[3] See Hyung Yoon Byun, "Industrial Structure of Korea," *The Seoul National University Economic Review*, 1 (December 1967), pp. 41-43.

[4] In 1975 the population density per square kilometer in Japan was 294 persons, and 333 in the Netherlands. See D. C. Rao, "The Pattern of Economic Growth, 1961-76," in *Korea* (A World Bank Country Economic Report), Edited by Parvez Hasan and D. C. Rao (Baltimore, Maryland: The Johns Hopkins University Press, 1979), p. 15.

United States, which was crucial for Korea at the critical period in her history. Table 2 shows the magnitude of such aid for the period 1945-1980.[5]

A. The Foreign Aid Program, 1945-1953

Along with Vietnam and Israel, Korea has been one of the largest recipients of foreign assistance in the world. For the three decades (1945-1976), the United States' econmmic and military aid alone reached $12.6 billion,[6] or roughly $500 per capita during the same period. If we add all other aid, the figure would be $600 per capita. Table 3 summarizes the total picture.

The first aid program was implemented by the United States Army Military Government in Korea (USAMGIK) in September 1945 and lasted until 1948 when the Republic of Korea was established. This was accompanied by the GARIOA (Government Appropriations for Relief in Occupied Areas) aid program which had three major objectives: (1) Prevention of starvation and disease, (2) increasing farm output, and (3) supplementing the shortage of consumer goods. For the five-year period, the aid reached $500 million. As Table 2 shows, for the period 1945-53, all but 3 percent ($31.7 million) donated by the UNKRA came from the United States. The total of $1,011 million amounted to about $5 per capita per annum for the eight-year period, which was roughly equal to 10 percent of per capita income.[7]

In December 1948, the ROK-U.S. Agreement on Aid, an intergovernmental pact similar to the ECA program in Western Europe, was signed. The ECA program itself was extended to Korea in 1949 but all hopes of economic recovery and stabilization were shattered when the north Koreans invaded the south on June 25, 1950. The ECA had to readjust its aid plan for wartime effectiveness, mainly for relief, and the total aid during 1949-53 was $109 million. Even though the CRIK (Civil Relief in Korea) and UNKRA programs were sponsored by the United Nations, the major donor to the fund was

[5] The U.S. Agency for International Development, or AID, terminated its mission in Korea in 1980.

[6] Edward S. Mason, et al., *The Economic and Social Modernization of the Republic of Korea* (Cambridge, Mass.: Harvard University Press, 1980), p. 165.

[7] See Anne O. Krueger, *The Development Role of the Foreign Sector and Aid* (Cambridge, Mass.: Harvard University Press, 1979).

Table 2. Foreign Economic Aid Received by Korea, 1945-1980

(In Millions of U.S. Dollars)

Year	Total	United States of America				CRIK**	UNKRA
		GARIOA	ECA	PL480*	AID		
1945	4.9	4.9					
1946	49.9	49.9					
1947	175.4	175.4					
1948	179.6	179.6					
1949	116.5	92.7	23.8				
1950	58.7		49.3			9.4	
1951	196.5		32.0			74.4	0.1
1952	161.3		3.8			155.4	2.0
1953	194.2		0.2		5.6	158.8	29.6
1954	153.9				82.4	50.2	21.3
1955	236.7				205.8	8.7	22.2
1956	326.7			33.0	271.0	0.3	22.4
1957	382.9			45.5	323.4		14.1
1958	321.3			47.9	265.6		7.7
1959	222.2			11.4	208.3		2.5
1960	245.4			19.9	225.2		0.2
1961	199.2			44.9	154.3		
1962	232.3			67.3	165.0		
1963	216.4			96.8	119.7		
1964	149.3			61.0	88.3		
1965	131.4			59.5	71.9		
1966	103.3			38.0	65.3		
1967	97.0			44.4	52.6		
1968	105.9			55.9	49.9		
1969	107.3			74.8	32.4		
1970	82.6			61.7	20.9		
1971	51.2			33.7	17.6		
1972	5.1				5.1		
1973	2.1				2.1		
1974	1.0				1.0		
1975	1.2				1.2		
1976	1.7				1.7		
1977	0.9				0.9		
1978	0.2				0.2		
1979	0.2				0.2		
1980	0.4				0.4		

* A portion of the proceeds used by the United States Government from sales of surplus agricultural commodities imported under the U.S. Public Law 480 cannot be regarded as foreign aid received, but for convenience it is included here to show the total imports under the same Law.

** Civil Relief in Korea (UN).

Source: The Bank of Korea, *Economic Statistics Yearbook, 1981*, p. 241, Jung Jae Park, *One Hundred Years of the Korean Economy* (Seoul, Korea: The Korea Productivity Center, 1971), p. 384.

Table 3.   Summary of Economic and Military Assistance to South Korea from the United States

($ Million for U.S Fiscal Years)

	1946-52	1953-61	1962-69	1970-76	Total
Economic Aid	666.8	2,579.2	1,658.2	963.6	5,745.4
Military Aid	12.3	1,560.7	2,501.3	2,797.4	6,847.3
Total	679.1	4,139.9	4,159.5	3,761.0	12,592.7

Source: Edward S. Mason, et al., *The Economic and Social Modernization of the Republic of Korea* (Cambridge, Mass.: Harvard University Press, 1980), p. 182 (sic).

the United States.

Thus, the early period of U.S. aid (1945-53) was a time for adjustment for Korea, from the Japanese colonialism to an independent nation which had gone through a devastating war. The United States provided "unrequited" economic and military aid which sustained the Republic of Korea and its people.

B. The Post-War Period (1953-61)

The Korean War reinforced the U.S. ROK relations in every area In addition to national defense, Korea faced difficult yet inevitable post-war reconstruction and economic stabilization problems. Inflation and domestic capital formation were not an easy task to cope with. Again, these objectives required continuous aid from the United States which amounted to more than $2.5 billion during the 1953-61 period. This was also the time when the AID program was implemented. Total aid increased from 4.4 percent of GNP in 1954 to 10.9 percent in 1956. In spite of a war-torn economy Korea could manage an average annual growth rate of 5.1 percent in her GNP for the period 1954-59.

In general, the economic aid accomplished three objectives: supplementing domestic savings for capital formation in Korea, an unfavorable balance of payments was eased, and inflationary pressure was reduced. During the period 1953-61, the United States donated 95 percent of total foreign aid which amounted to some 8 per cent of Korea's GNP, 77 percent of capital formation and about 70 percent of total imports.[8] After 1957, however, foreign aid began to decline and this, in turn, brought an adverse impact on the Korean economy. Stated differently, Korea has been excessively dependent on the foreign aid. Subsequently, the Foreign Capital Inducement Law was promulgated in 1960.

2. The Bilateral Trade Period (1962 – Present)

Since the beginning of the 1960s, Korea has been experiencing re-markable changes: from a unilateral relationship to bilateral economic cooperation, from grant-in-aid to development loans and foreign direct investment, from a dependent to a self-sustaining economy, and from labor-intensive to capital-intensive industries. Someday Korea will become a "developed" nation.[9]

For the first time in her history, Korea had launched the Five-Year Economic Plan in 1962. Foreign aid was providing some $200 million worth of assistance a year, equivalent of about 10 percent of GNP, but the standard of living was still low. Economic stagnation, according to the planners, had its roots in inefficient management and defective institutions. The chief purpose of setting up the first development plan was to attain a self-sustaining economy with steady growth for a higher standard of livng.[10]

During the second half of the current century, the term "economic miracle" began to appear in economic literature, designating Germany and Japan. Now Korea has been added to the honor roll. In the past two decades, Korea has managed extraordinary and spectacular economic performance despite considerable odds.[11] Yet the actual economic growth surpassed the ambitious planners' expectations and surprised the rest of the world.[12] Many of the third world nations

---

[8] Edward S. Mason, et al., *op. cit.,* p. 185, Table 36.

[9] Hans W. Singer, for instance, is not so optimistic. Considering Korea's realistic economic situation, one of a few possibiolities would be assuming a leadership role within the third world like Brazil and Mexico. In other words, says he, Korea would remain a part of the third world and not just join the club of rich nations. See Hans W. Singer, "Has the Korean Model a Future in a Changing World?" (Seoul, Korea: Korea International Economic Institute, 1979), Seminar Series No. 30, p. 6.

[10] The Government of the Republic of Korea, *Summary of the First Five-Year Economic Plan, 1962-1966,* p. 9. Also the United States has taken a strong stand in advocating development planning in LDCs. See Albert Waterson, *Development Planning: Lessons of Experience* (Baltimore, Md.: Johns Hopkins University Press, 1969), p. 36.

[11] See Parvez Hasan and D.C. Rao, *Korea,* pp. 3-11.

Table 4.   *Summary of Exports and Imports, 1952-81*

(In million U.S. dollars)

Year	Exports				Imports				Annual Growth of GNP (%)
	Total	Growth Rate (%)	To the U.S.	% of Total	Total	Growth Rate (%)	From the U.S.	% of Total	
1952	27.7				214.2				
1953	39.6	43.0			345.4	61.3			
1954	24.2	-38.9			243.3	-29.6			5.1
1955	18.0	34.4	7.4	41.1	341.6	40.4	37.9	11.1	4.5
1956	24.6	36.7	10.9	44.3	386.1	13.1	87.0	22.5	-1.4
1957	22.2	-9.8	4.1	18.5	442.2	14.5	110.0	24.9	7.6
1958	16.5	-25.7	2.9	17.6	378.2	-14.5	209.0	55.3	5.5
1959	19.8	20.0	2.1	10.6	303.8	19.7	147.6	48.6	3.8
1960	32.8	65.7	3.6	11.0	343.5	13.1	133.7	38.9	1.1
1961	40.9	24.7	6.8	16.6	316.1	-8.0	143.4	45.4	5.6
1962[a]	54.8	34.0	12.0	21.9	421.8	33.4	220.3	52.2	2.2
1963	86.8	58.4	24.3	28.0	560.3	32.8	284.1	50.7	9.1
1964	119.1	37.2	35.6	29.9	404.4	-27.8	202.1	50.0	9.6
1965	175.1	47.0	61.7	35.2	463.4	14.6	182.2	39.3	5.8
1966	250.3	42.9	95.8	38.3	716.4	54.6	253.7	35.4	12.7
1967[b]	320.2	27.9	137.4	42.9	996.2	39.1	305.2	30.6	6.6
1968	455.4	42.2	237.0	52.0	1,462.9	46.8	449.0	30.7	11.3
1969	622.5	36.7	315.7	50.7	1,823.6	24.7	530.2	29.1	13.8
1970	835.2	34.2	395.2	47.3	1,984.0	8.8	584.8	29.5	7.6
1971	1,067.6	27.8	531.8	49.8	2,394.3	20.7	678.3	28.3	9.4
1972[c]	1,624.1	52.1	758.9	46.7	2,522.0	5.3	647.2	25.7	5.8
1973	3,225.0	98.6	1,021.2	31.7	4,240.3	68.1	1,201.9	28.3	14.9
1974	4,460.4	38.3	1,492.2	33.5	6,851.8	61.6	1,700.8	24.8	8.0
1975	5,081.0	13.9	1,536.3	30.2	7,274.4	6.2	1,881.1	25.9	7.1
1976	7,715.1	51.8	2,492.5	32.3	8,773.6	20.6	1,962.9	22.4	15.1
1977[d]	10,046.5	30.2	3,118.6	31.0	10,810.5	23.2	2,447.4	22.6	10.3
1978	12,710.6	26.5	4,058.3	31.9	14,971.9	38.5	3,042.9	20.3	11.6
1979	15,055.5	18.4	4,373.9	29.1	20,338.6	35.8	4,602.6	22.6	6.4
1980	17,504.9	16.3	4,606.6	26.3	22,291.7	9.6	4,890.2	21.9	-6.2
1981*	21,188.9	21.0	5,560.9	26.2	26,344.6	18.2	6,050.2	23.0	7.1

a, b, c, and d: The First, Second, Third, and Fourth Five-Year Plan periods.
* Provisional data. Exports are valued at f.o.b., imports at c.i.f.
Source: The Bank of Korea, *Economic Statics Yearbook,* various editions.
               Monthly Economic Statistics, various editions,
               Korea's National Income, 1953-1963,
               The 30-Year History of the Bank of Korea, 1980,
               pp. 430-431; *The 31st Annual Report,* 1980, p. 2,
               The Key Economic Index, February, 1982 (New York).
     The Korean Traders Association, New York Office, annual reports.

would like to "emulate South Korea's 20-year leap from poverty to relative prosperity."[13]

Throughout the 1960s and 1970s, as Table 4 shows, the average rate of growth was more than 10 percent a year, and per capita income was changing from $87 in 1962 to $1,636 in 1981. This has been projected to go up to $2,710 in 1986 when the Fifth Five-Year Plan ends.[14] Primary industry was shrinking from 40 percent to less than 25 percent. The most remarkable growth occurred in international trade: exports have been rising from a mere $41 million in 1961 to $21.2 billion in 1981. This is an average growth of 37.1 percent a year for the last two decades. In 1977 Korea celebrated the breaking of the $10 billion export target and within four years Korea has doubled the total.

During the First Five-Year Plan period (1962-66), exports were increasing at an annual rate of 43.9 percent with 7.8 percent growth in GNP per annum. During the second period (1967-71), the performance was reversed. Exports were increased at 33.7 percent per year while GNP was growing faster than the previous plan period at a rate of 9.7 percent 'per year. During the third period (1972-76), both exports and economic growth expanded: the former at the annual rate of 50.9 percent and the latter at 10.1 percent. This was accomplished in spite of the energy crisis. Again, as Table 4 shows, the fourth plan period (1977-81) registered a decline in the growth rate of both: exports were increasing only at 22.5 percent a year and the economy was growing only at 5.8 percent. In fact, the annual growth of GNP for 1980 was minus 6.2 percent, the first time since 1956. Imports, on the other hand, have been rising faster than exports. Korea has been suffering from a chronic deficit in her balance of payments.

Although the economic relationship between the two nations has changed from foreign aid to trade, the main force which made it possible for Korea to accomplish such a spectacular export performance is again the United States. In other words, as shown in Table 4, the United States absorbed the average of 35.7 percent of total Korean exports annually. To be specific, the gorwth rate for each of

---

[12] Norman Pearlstine, "How South Korea Surprised the World," *Forbes*, April 30, 1979, pp. 53-61.

[13] Urban C. Lehner, "What Put South Korea on the Fast Track?" *The Wall Street Journal*, May 3, 1982, p. 31.

[14] The Bank of Korea, *The Korean Economy: Performance and Prospects* (Mimeographed), January 27, 1982, p. 25.

the four five-year plan periods are 30.7 percent (1962-66), 48.5 percent (1967-71), 34.9 percent (1972-76), and 28.9 percent (1977-81), respectively. In the 1980s, however, Korea's exports to the U.S. decreased to slightly above 26 percent a year. At any rate, the United States was the leading importer of LDCs' manufactured goods in the 1960s and 1970s. Apparently, Korea's export strategy took advantage of her partner's global trade policy.[15]

The World Bank has observed Korea's trade from a different angle, i.e., efficient export growth can attain efficient import substitution. During the early stage of industrialization, Korea emphasized selective import substitution which brought favorable results. Her approach was to produce for both domestic and international markets which caused an increase in export-led growth and also an expansion of the domestic market. Clearly, the process illustrates complementarities between the two.[16] At the same time, Korean trade policy supports the connotation that there is a positive correlation between exports and GNP. Based on comparative advantage, better utilization of productive capacity, and improvements in technology which causes economies of scale, a nation reaps the gains from foreign trade.[17] Of course, the Korean experience presupposes a favorable international milieu and prosperous economic conditions in industrial market economies.

II. Analyses and Evaluation

1. Basic Data

As a reference, the following data are selected from various sources. Korea's GNP for 1981 was estimated at $63.4 billion, the average annual growth rate for gross domestic investment was 23.6 percent (1960-70) and 14.9 percent (1970-79), respectively. For 1981, the

---

[15] Jayati Datta-Mitra, "Structure of (Korea's) Exports and Imports," in *Korea*, Ed. by Parvez Hazan and D. C. Rao, p. 431. The United States and Japan absorbed more than 70 per cent of Korea's total exports until the early 1970s.

[16] *World Development Report, 1980*, The World Bank, pp. 23-24; Jayati Datta-Mitra, p. 439.

[17] Bela Balassa, "Korea's Place in the World Economy During the Fifteen-Year Plan Period (1976-91)," (Seoul, Korea: KIEI, 1977), Seminar Series, 77-09, p. 8.

figure corresponded to 27.3 percent of GNP. Per capita income (1981) was $1,636. Total exports and imports were 40.7 percent and 45.2 percent, respectively. The distribution of GDP (1978) was 24 percent in agriculture, 36 percent in industry, and service, 40 percent. The average annual growth rate in public consumption (1970-79) was 8.7 percent, private consumption, 8.0 percent.[18] Interest payments on foreign loans (1981) amounted to $3.6 billion, or 5.7 percent of GNP; Korea's foreign obligation at the end of 1981 was $32.5 billion. As of 1981, total gold and foreign exchange holdings were $6.9 billion.[19] The total population in 1981 was estimated at 38.7 million; the percentage of the labor force in agriculture, 41 percent, industry, 37 percent, and service, 22 percent; unemployment in 1981 was 4.5 percent. The adult literacy rate (1975) was 93 percent, life expectancy (1980), 65.9 years, and daily calory supply per capita as percentage of requirements (1977) was 119 percent.

2. Analyses

A. Foreign Aid

Foreign aid, like the movement of private capital, is a transfer of real resources from the donor to the recipient nations. The significant issues for our analytical purpose are (1) the degree of importance in the aid-receiving nation and timing, (2) the role of aid for a sustained devleopment process, (3) bilateral vs. multilateral aid programs,[20] and (4) the overall effectiveness of foreign aid.

First of all, the degree of importance of both economic and military aid in the case of Korea cannot be overstated. In fact, the development of contemporary economic relations between the two nations started with this kind of a "vertical" relationship, which is changing to a "horizontal" relationship.[21] The Marshall Plan was extended to former foes and friends alike. For Korea, it was fortunate to have this kind of friendly aid in order to be transformed from a "relief-oriented" to "development-oriented" country in the past three

---

[18] *World Development Report, 1981,* The World Bank, pp. 134-183.

[19] The Bank of Korea, *The Korean Economy, Performance and Prospects,* pp. 25, 33-35.

[20] See Delbert A. Snider, *Introduction to International Economics,* 7th ed. (Homewood, Ill.: Richard D. Irwin, Inc., 1979), p. 439.

[21] William Watts, "American Awareness of Korea Needs to be Enhanced," *The Korea Herald,* October 31, 1981, p. 5.

decades. Since 1972 aid has been reduced to almost nothing (see Table 2).

The positive aspect of American military aid was often overlooked. It not only could support the Republic of Korea armed forces but also helped the formation of human capital. The military personnel acquired technical skill, managerial knowledge and leadership experiences while they were in the service. They learned the importance of team work, strategy, and how to operate vehicles, airplanes, and electronic equipment. Moreover, the Korean armed forces have been managed by the latest techniques learned from the U.S. military system. Each year some 200,000 young men who were well trained and disciplined were joining the labor force in the private sector.[22] Even soldiers themselves helped to finish various civilian projects, such as the construction of roads and bridges, or giving a helping hand to the farmer. These experiences have proven to be the key factor in terms of "manpower export" to the Middle East in the 1970s.

Timing, however, presented a problem. Starting in 1956, Korea began to receive surplus farm products from the U.S. according to PL480. Due to a lack of consistent domestic farm policy and the mismanagement of the aid fund,[23] the inflow of surplus grains began to depress farm prices in Korea. Consequently, farmers and those who were directly engaged in primary industry suffered most.[24] In the past, both donor and recipient learned a good lesson because the difficulty was spilled over into the 1960s as we recognize a lover's quarrel:

> For the first three years (1954-1956) the Korean government had its way . . . Over the next four years (1957-1960) the American side was dominant . . . This was followed by two years of expansion (1961-1962) by the Park Government and two more years of American-imposed contraction (1963-1964). In general, the Koreans were overly ambitious and gave little consideration either to the inflationary consequences or to the need to mobilize domestic resources. Conversely, the Americans were overly restrictive, believing that greater stability would lead to more growth. . . .[25]

---

[22] Youngil Yim, "Sources of Economic Growth in Korea, With Emphasis on the Export Sector," (Seoul, Korea, KIEI), Seminar Series, 77-10 (November 1977), p. 26.

[23] For more critical and negative comments on the U.S. aid to Korea, see Hirokazu Matsumoto, *The South Korea in Convulsion* (in Japanese) (Tokyo, Japan: Iwanami Shoten, 1963), pp. 173-181.

[24] The same is true for the farmers in Burma, the Philippines, Thailand and Vietnam, who had been exporting their rice to India were unable to do so when India began to import surplus farm products from the U.S. under the PL480 program.

As for a sustained development process, United States aid has accomplished its goal in Korea, because foreign assistance was a catalyst for self-help development measures.[26] Aside from the relief-oriented aid program, economic assistance closed a foreign exchange gap when Korea was unable to increase her savings. Gradually, as the Korean economy began to grow, both savings and exports have been rising. For the period 1976-78, domestic savings accounted for more than 64 per cent of gross domestic capital formation.[27] Foreign trade reduced the need for more aid and this is cearly reflected in Table 2. Indeed, Korea has been transforming her economy from an *aid-sustained* growth to a *trade-sustained* growth process;[28] eventually she hopes to attain *self-sustained* development, although she has to meet heavy external debt obligations.

Ideally, multilateral aid programs are preferred to bilateral assistance. This is because the quality of aid may be improved and is less likely to be influenced by the donor's self-interest. Todaro explains:

> Donor countries give aid primarily because it is in their political, strategic, and/or economic self-interest to do so. While some development assistance may be motivated by moral and humanitarian reasons to assist the less fortunate (e.g., emergency relief programs), there is no historical evidence to suggest that over longer periods of time donor nations assist without expecting some corresponding benefits (political, economic, military, etc.) in return. . . .[29]

Moreover, multilateral program can avoid tying aid; it can meet both the short-run and long-run needs of the recipient because coordination of various sources of assistance may be facilitated.[30] Nevertheless, there has been a close economic tie between the U.S. and Korea which paved a way for the latter to attain a high rate of growth. Koreans themselves have become a development-minded people whose extraordinary efforts have paid off.

The overall effectiveness of foreign aid program brought the two nations closer. Any aid designating special projects has also proven to

---

[25] Edward S. Mason, et al., *op. cit.,* p. 305.

[26] Gerald M. Meier, *International Economics: The Theory of Policy* (New York: Oxford University Press, 1980), p. 337.

[27] The Bank of Korea, *Economic Statistics Yearbook, 1980,* p. 277 (Table 143).

[28] Gerald M. Meier, *op. cit.,* p. 337.

[29] Michael P. Todaro, *Economic Development in the Third World,* 2nd ed. (New York: Longman Inc., 1981), pp. 411-412.

[30] Gerald M. Meier, *op. cit.,* p. 338-339.

Table 5. Korean Students Studying in the United States

School Year	Total Foreign Students in the U.S.	Korean Students in the U.S.	Percentage of the total (%)
1954-55	34,232	1,197	3.5
1959-60	48,486	2,474	5.1
1964-65	82,045	2,604	3.2
1969-70	134,959	3,991	3.0
1974-75	154,580	3,390	2.2
1975-76	179,344	3,260	1.8
1976-77	203,509	3,630	1.8
1977-78	235,510	4,220	1.8
1978-79	263,940	4,980	1.9
1979-80	286,340	4,890	1.7
1980-81	311,880	6,150	2.0

Source: Institute of International Education, *Open Doors, Report on International Educational Exchange, 1980-81* (New York: Institution of International Education, 1981), pp. 1, 11.

be effective in Korea as it has been linked to the total investment programs. In addition, American aid also included a considerable amount of technical assistance. In the past three decades, numerous American technical advisers and professionals worked in Korea and they helped in every field. Many Koreans were sent to the United States for training and learning under the USAID programs.

Studying in the U.S. has been almost every young person's dream and many have realized their aspirations. This is partly because the Japanese disallowed Koreans from pursuing higher education until 1945 but the Koreans never gave up hope. Table 5 shows the number of Korean students in the U.S. Although the percentage has been declining, the absolute number has been increasing. It is true that many who had completed their studies in the U.S. did not go back to Korea. Consequently, the brain drain was a problem for the United States and Korea. This was a kind of foreign aid in reverse! Economic, political, sociological, and personal reasons are often cited as causes of the brain drain.[31]

---

[31] For more detailed causes, see Ki Hoon Kim, "The Economics of the Brain Drain: Pros, Cons, and Remedies," *Journal of Economic Development* 1 (July 1976), pp. 55-80; Walter Adams (Ed.), *The Brain Drain* (New York: Macmillan Co., 1968).

In retrospect, however, the brain drain was mutually beneficial for the two nations. During the 1950s and 1960s, the United States absorbed well-educated and productive Koreans who were "unemployed" or "underemployed." As the economy grew, the Korean government, along with the private sector, implemented the "brain gain" program. From cabinet members, professors, business managers and other professionals to artists and musicians, many have returned to Korea and have been contributing their talent and skills. The American-Korean Foundation provided an excellent service for Korean students who had completed their studies in the U.S. It issued newsletters which informed them of employment opportunities in Korea; it also arranged low-cost transportation.

Thus, the role of human capital in the development of Korea is by no means small. The existence of a highly productive and well-motivated human resources preceded the formation of physical capital in Korea. These two factors of production have been complementary to each other, and this is one of the key points in her economic miracle. In general, the third world tends to emphasize physical capital alone. If the Korean experience could be a guide, it would be a systematic and balanced supply of, and demand for both tangible and intangible capital.

B. The Economy as a Whole

As the deteriorating U.S. balance of payments and the third postwar recession persisted, American aid was reduced in 1957. This was the period when President Eisenhower changed the foreign aid program from a humanitarian and economic to a political purpose, and the grant-in-aid was replaced by a development loan fund. The overly dependent economy suffered at that time, but Korea undertook a series of new reforms, including anti-inflationary fiscal and monetary policy, better taxation methods, and improving the balance of payments. These were not easy.

In August 1953, a month after the war in Korea ended, the U.S. Office of Economic Coordinator for Korea was established. This is a concrete example of closer economic cooperation between the two nations. It coordinated U.S. economic and military aid so that the assistance program could be more efficient. Later, the ROK-U.S. Joint Economic Committee also contributed much to the stabilization of the Korean economy.

The Republic of Korea became a member of the IMF and IBRD on August 26, 1955. This in turn expanded economic activities abroad and facilitated the inflow of foreign capital to Korea. A series of Five-Year development plans may not be possible without having this kind of international experience.

An important issue for our analysis is planning and its consequences. As a result of the underdeveloped status of the economy, it was necessary to implement macroeconomic development planning. In the process, however, there was a concentration of economic power into the hands of the government. The banking system, including the Bank of Korea, became subordinate to the government.[32] This is nothing new. The law governing the Bank of Korea was amended so that the Ministry of Finance, not the central bank, has the final decision on monetary policy. This kind of vertical relationship eliminates the mutual checks-and-balances. The central bank should have an "independent" but healthy monetary policy for dynamic and innovative economic development.[33]

Fortunately, the Fifth Five-Year Plan (1982-86) includes an important change: Government intends to reduce its intervention in general private economic activities so as to "exploit the advantage of the free market mechanism." We welcome this kind of sensitivity and sincerely hope that this would be realized in the near future. The major priority tasks of the plan include: (1) consolidating the foundation for economic stability and enhancing efficiency, (2) improving the balance of payments, (3) promoting comparative advantage, (4) environmental protection, and (5) expanding social development. It seems that the Korean planners are moving in the right direction. The plan boils down to two major themes: economic stability and improvement in social welfare.

In the 1980s, Korea has to adopt more of a capital-intensive and technology-intensive export structure. The days of textiles, clothing, wigs, shoes, light electronics, and assembly-type manufactures are almost gone.[34] Korea must find new ways to increase domestic capital because the external debt service tends to add an accelerating burden on the balance of payments. Furthermore, an increase in R & D is

---

[32] The Bank of Korea, *The 30-Year History of the Bank of Korea* (Seoul, Korea, 1981), pp. 60-61.

[33] Ki Hoon Kim, "A Constitutional Amendment to Grant the Bank of Korea an Independent Status Proposed," *Dong-A Il Bo* (Daily News), May 7, 1980, p. 2.

[34] Hans W. Singer, *op. cit.*, p. 7.

highly desirable. At present, Korea is spending about 1 per cent of her GNP on her R & D programs. There are many specialized research and business organizations. They have excellent brains. Yet, technological transfer from the United States is vital to propelling Korea's development endeaver.

Among many organizations, one in particular stands out as it has been promoting better contemporary U.S.-ROK economic relations. Established on August 17, 1973, the KUSEC (Korea-U.S. Economic Council), and its counterpart in the United States, USKEC (U.S.-Korea Economic Council), a private, non-profit corporation, has been serving as an information center and clearing house for economic cooperation. The Council makes arrangements for consultations, conducting studies and providing information on trade, investment, and technical cooperation; sponsoring conferences; exchanging trade mission; and helping mutual visits and business ventures. This kind of partnership promotes better economic relations between the two nations. The centennial programs and celebration would enhance greater economic development and better understanding of the two nations.

C. Non-Economic Aspects

In addition, the defense program presents another close tie. The Korean War reinforced the strategic importance of Korea. This was already recognized by the U.S. when mainland China fell to Mao in 1949. Japan has been under U.S. pressure to increase her share of national defense. In fact, the future economic relationship between the U.S. and Korea will depend on the outcome of U.S.-China, U.S.-Japan, and U.S.-U.S.S.R. relationships. At present, South Korea is trying to open a dialogue between the South and North Korea. She is also trying to expand her economic relations with other communist nations. This series of international relations indicates that the Korean economy is still not free from her "dependency" even if she has transformed from aid to trade.

Cultural and religious aspects are noteworthy. In 1984, the Protestant churches in Korea will celebrate another centennial, commemorating the first arrival of the Protestant missionaries from the United States. These missionaries and their successors not only evangelized Koreans but also have been teaching democracy, social consciousness, and providing medical care. Korea is rapidly growing—

both in her economy and church members. In the United States, textbooks and cultural events should bring Korea and her culture up-to-date. The KACEC (Korean-American Cultural Exchange Committee) has initiated more specific programs. The Peace Corps, which had provided immeasurable contributions to Korea, has terminated its programs on August 7, 1981. Their 15-year services promoted better understanding between the two peoples.

Last year, Korea was able to manage a double coup—inducing the 1988 Olympics to come to Seoul, and the 1986 Asian Games as well. The 32-nation festival may open a dialogue between South Korea and her neighbors, North Korea and China.[35] Thus the decade of the 1980s provides an important challenge, and how the Republic of Korea will respond is yet to be seen.[36] Within the nation, it is highly desirable to restore more initiative in the private sector. The Japanese experience would be a good lesson: mutual cooperation between the government and free enterprise.

Koreans admire harmony as their national flag symbolizes. U.S.-Korea economic relations show a continuous harmony and reconciliation as the philosophy of "um" and "yang" indicates. Various centennial programs testify to this fact. The 5,000-year Korean history reflects hardships and oppression as well as invasion by strong neighbors. Somehow they have survived. Yet, the rich nations appear to show a sentiment toward protectionism[37] while the third world wants the "new international economic order." As one of the Korean proverbs says, "When the whales fight, it is the shrimp that suffers the most." When the rich nations adopt protectionism, it will hurt many innocent "Shrimps," including Korea.

Please save the shrimp!

---

[35] Robert Keatley, "South Korea's President Seeks Acceptance Abroad," *The Wall Street Journal,* January 18, 1982, p. 23.

[36] Robert Keatley, "Can South Korea Revive Its Economic Miracle?" *The Wall Street Journal,* December 21, 1981, p. 21.

[37] *The New York Times, International Economic Survey,* Section 12, February 14, 1982, p. 9. "Protectionism is no longer a risk," said Viscount Etienne Davignon, the EEC's Commissioner for Industry, "it is a probability."

CHAPTER 15

U.S.-ROK ECONOMIC INTERDEPENDENCE

Thomas A. D'Elia*

Economic ties between the U.S. and South Korea have grown rapidly over the past 30 years. During this time the relationship between the two countries has changed considerably. The partnership has moved steadily from the oneway, client-patron relationship that existed during the 1950s and 1960s toward a more mutually beneficial, two-way association.

Both countries derive substantial benefit from their close economic links. Although South Korea has broadened its economic horizons in recent years and has had great success at diversifying its economic ties, the U.S. still looms as Seoul's most important economic partner. The U.S. absorbs more of South Korea's exports and supplies more capital than any other country. The U.S. is also South Korea's second most important source of equity investment, foreign technology, and imports. Although the economic relationship is not nearly as important to the U.S., Washington, for its part, benefits from close ties with one of the most dynamic economies in the world. South Korea is the eleventh largest market for the U.S. and its largest non-OPEC LDC market.

The U.S. and South Korean economies are, to a considerable extent, complementary. With a substantially lower cost labor force, South Korea can produce labor intensive, low to medium technology manufactured goods at a comparative advantage relative to the U.S. The developed U.S. economy, in turn, has the advanced technology,

---

* The views expressed in this chapter are those of the author and do not represent the U.S. government.

the capital equipment, the agricultural supplies, and the raw materials that the developing, resource-poor South Korean economy needs.

Historical Perspective

The economic relationship between the two countries is vastly different today than it was 20 or so years ago. In the 1950s and early 1960s the relationship was largely one-way. In the early 1960s, South Korea's per capita income was below $100, imports were 10 times larger than its exports, the manufacturing base was minimal and the economy was overwhelmingly dependent on economic aid from the U.S. for its very survival. During these years, South Korean trade was minimal. Total two way trade between South Korea and the U.S. in 1962 was only $232 million, consisting of $220 million in South Korean imports and only $12 million in South Korean exports. Capital inflows from the U.S. largely took the form of grant aid. Between 1953 and 1961, the U.S. provided $2.6 billion in economic grant aid to South Korea in addition to $1.8 billion in military aid. Throughout the 1960s, economic grant aid to South Korea ranged from $100 million to $200 million per year. By 1970 grant aid was below $100 million and during the early 1970s had come to a virtual halt.[1]

Relationship in 1980

The economic relationship today is one of mutual benefit and is becoming increasingly interdependent. Two way trade has increased dramatically and reached $9.5 billion in 1980 of which $4.9 billion were South Korean imports from the U.S. and $4.6 billion were South Korean exports. Capital flows from the U.S. to South Korea are in the form of loans, rather than grants, and equity investment flows are in both directions.

---

[1] Agency for International Development, *U.S. Overseas Loans and Grants and Assistance from International Organizations.*

Trade Patterns

The U.S. is South Korea's most important market, taking 26% of Seoul's exports in 1980.[2] For several key products the U.S. share is even larger. The U.S. takes 35% or more of South Korean exports of electronics, footwear, leather products, toys and games, plywood, and machinery; all of which are among Seoul's top foreign exchange earners and sources of employment. These six commodities, together with textiles, metals, and transport equipment make up 85% of South Korean exports to the U.S. Cotton fabrics, outer garments, radios and TVs, iron and steel, and containers are among the largest commodities within these broad categories.

The importance of the U.S. market to the South Korean economy is underscored by Seoul's heavy dependence on exports for growth. Exports account for about 40% of South Korean GNP. Lacking in natural resources, export of manufactured goods is the only way for Seoul to provide jobs for a rapidly growing labor force—which is growing almost 3% per year; to raise still relatively low living standards—per capita income is below $1700; and to provide the large sums for defense against the North Korean threat—over 6% of GNP is allocated to defense. In short, South Korea must export to survive. As the world's largest market, the U.S. is crucial to South Korea's export-oriented economy. About 10% of South Korea's GNP is accounted for by exports to the U.S. The U.S. takes 20% of South Korea's textiles, which is by far Seoul's major industry and leading foreign exchange earner. The textile industry accounts for about one-fourth of industrial production, employment, and foreign exchange earnings in South Korea. In electronics, the U.S. takes almost 40% of total exports; since about 70% of electronics output is sold abroad, the U.S. market is vital to the success of the industry, absorbing more than one-fourth of its output. The electronics industry, in turn, accounts for more than 10% of manufacturing employment.

From the U.S. standpoint, imports from South Korea are a small share of total imports, accounting for less than 2% of the total in 1980.[3] In several specific areas, however, South Korean imports loom fairly large. This is primarily true in labor intensive, low to medium

---

[2] South Korea trade data are from Office of Customs Administration, Republic of Korea, *Statistical Yearbook of Foreign Trade*, 1980.

[3] U.S. trade data are from United Nations, *trade tapes*.

technology manufactured goods at the lower end of the price scale which account for the bulk of U.S. imports from South Korea. Higher value added, more capital intensive products, however, are assuming increased importance. Overall, 96% of U.S. purchases from Korea are manufactured goods. South Korea accounts for 16% of U.S. clothing imports, 17% of its footwear purchases from abroad, and 25% of its TV imports. The U.S. economy benefits from these purchases because of the lower labor costs in South Korea which contributes to less U.S. inflation. In steel, for example, labor costs per metric ton in 1980 were about $15 in South Korea compared with $172 in the U.S.

For South Korea, the U.S. is its second most important import source behind Japan. In 1980, the U.S. accounted for 22% of South Korean purchases from abroad. Agricultural commodities, specifically grains, are by far the largest purchase from the U.S. amounting to almost $1 billion in 1980 and making up about one-fifth of total purchases from the U.S. The U.S. has a near monopoly in the agricultural area, with a 90% share of the market. Good credit terms offered by the U.S. and a Korean desire to buy American and keep trade in balance are largely responsible for the dominant U.S. position in this area. Wheat, corn, and rice account for the the bulk of this trade. The U.S. also has a strong position in the textile area with a better than 50% share of the Korean market. Cotton accounts for the overwhelming percentage of this trade.

The U.S. is also a key supplier of industrial raw materials and capital equipment to South Korea including iron and steel, transport equipment, electrical machinery, industrial machinery, and chemicals. The U.S. share of the Korean market in the five areas ranges from 18% to 38%. These five commodities together with textiles and grains represent 73% of total Korean imports from the U.S. Other key commodities include pulp and hides and skins in each of which the U.S. has a better than 40% market share.

In recent years the U.S. share of the Korean market in several industrial areas has risen appreciably as Seoul has diversified away from Japan. In transport equipment, for example, the U.S. share rose from 16% in 1978 to 37% in 1980. The Korean government has attempted to reduce its large bilateral trade deficit with Japan by purchasing more of its industrial raw materials and capital equipment from the U.S. In 1978, Japan had a better than 40% market share of Korean imports in all major industrial areas.

For the U.S. the fast growing South Korean market is a major export growth area. South Korea's ranking as an export market has risen steadily in recent years. In 1980, South Korea was the eleventh largest export market for the U.S. and its largest non-OPEC LDC market. South Korea is also the U.S.'s largest market in Asia except for Japan. The U.S. sells more to Korea than it does to Brazil, China, or Australia and almost as much as it sells to Italy or Saudi Arabia. U.S. exports to South Korea have risen 25% annually between 1965 and 1980.

The complimentary and mutual benefit that derives from the trade links between the two countries is well demonstrated by looking at U.S. exports to South Korea. Excluding the grain sales, a great deal of the U.S. export growth to South Korea is generated as a result of Korea's own export drive. South Korea imports industrial raw materials from the U.S., adds value, then exports finished manu-factured goods abroad. Cotton is a good example; South Korea imports large amounts of raw cotton from the U.S.—$569 million in 1980 or 16% of total U.S. cotton exports, and exports cotton fabrics to the U.S. and other overseas markets. Similarly, Korea imports hides and skins from the U.S. and sells leather goods to the U.S. and other countries. In addition, South Korea imports much of the machinery and capital equipment needed to manufacture its textiles, electronics, etc. from the U.S. The high import context of South Korea's exports—about 32% in 1980—means that fast growing Korean exports leads to rapid U.S. export growth to Korea.

Investment Flows

The U.S. is the second largest source of equity investment in South Korea, behind Japan. U.S. equity investment in South Korea between 1962 and 1980 amounted to $252 million on an arrival basis. This represents 23% of South Korea's total investment from abroad. In 1980, the U.S. was the largest investor in Korea because of increased investment by U.S. firms already in Korea and a decline in Japanese inflows to Korea. In 1980, the U.S. invested $60 million in South Korea, accounting for 63% of total inflows.[4]

---

[4] Investment data are from Economic Planning Board, Republic of Korea.

U.S. investment in Korea has been largest in chemicals, electronics, petroleum refining, automobiles, and fertilizer industries. South Korea has benefited from the advanced technology induced through these ventures. U.S. firms, for their part, have benefited from lower production costs in South Korea. Profit remittances through the end of 1980 totaled $194 million.

A new development in the bilateral relationship in recent years and a further sign of the movement toward a more equal footing of the ties is the fact that South Korea has made several significant investments in the U.S.. As of the end of 1978, South Korea's equity investment in the U.S. was only $25 million in 34 projects. Since then, South Korea has invested in several large projects. In 1979, South Korea invested in a large coal project in Pa. as part of its resource development diplomacy. The venture is 100% Korean owned, involves $73 million and will produce 650,000 tons of coal per year.[5] South Korea also made its first investment in manufacturing in the U.S. in 1981 for an electronics plant in Alabama. The $5 million facility will produce 400,000 color TVs per year as well as refrigerators, microwave ovens, and audio equipment. Operations are expected to begin this year.[6]

Technology Flows

Closely tied to U.S. equity investment in South Korea has been the flow of U.S. technology. The U.S. is second to Japan as a source of foreign technology. Through 1980, South Korea signed 392 technology import contracts with the U.S., equal to 23% of the total. Although Japan accounted for 59% of the total, technology coming from the U.S. is more sophisticated than that coming from Japan.[7]

---

[5] *Korea Herald*, August 11, 1981.

[6] *New York Times*, May 12, 1981.

[7] Ungsuh K. Park, "U.S.-Korea Economic Relations in Trade and Technology Transfers," *Korea & World Affairs*, Vol. 5 (Winter 1981), p. 598.

Capital Flows

The U.S. is the largest source of foreign capital for South Korea, accounting for better than 25% of the total. U.S. capital inflows to South Korea (of one year or more) between 1959 and 1979 amounted to $4 billion.[8] South Korea is vitally dependent on U.S. capital flows to finance its economic development. At South Korea's early stage of development, capital from abroad is essential to finance industrialization. The domestic savings rate, although it has increased to 26%, is still too low to provide enough funds to finance development. Higher energy prices have helped to push South Korea's current account deficit to roughly $5 billion in each of the past two years. U.S. capital has been essential in financing these shortfalls.

For U.S. commercial banks, South Korea is a profitable market and they continue to take leading roles in South Korea's major eurocurrency loans. U.S. commercial bank exposure in South Korea is among the highest it is in any developing country. The U.S. Export-Import Bank has a larger exposure in South Korea than in any other country in the world. U.S. Ex-Im Bank loans have been instrumental in financing 6 nuclear power plants Seoul has purchased from the U.S.

Implications

South Korea's heavy dependence on exports and foreign capital for its economic survival, and the leading role the U.S. plays in these areas make Seoul very cognizant of the importance of close economic ties with the U.S.. Seoul attempts to keep trade roughly in balance; Seoul is well aware of the problems in the U.S.-Japanese economic relationship because of the trade imbalance and wants to avoid a similar situation in the future. At the same time, the importance of access to the U.S. market for its export goods makes Seoul very aggressive in seeking to minimize U.S. protectionist actions.

The close security ties between the two countries also have an impact on the economic relationship. South Korea does not want

---

[8] Economic Planning Board, *Handbook of Korean Economy*, 1980.

economic frictions to interfere with its security links with the U.S.. Washington, for its part, has a strong interest in seeing the South Korean economy do well because of its security commitments to that country.

U.S.-South Korea Trade

(Mil US$)

	South Korea Exports to U.S.	South Korea Imports from U.S.
1962	12.0	220.3
1963	24.3	284.1
1964	35.6	202.1
1965	61.7	182.3
1966	95.8	253.7
1967	137.4	305.2
1968	235.5	449.0
1969	312.2	530.2
1970	395.2	584.8
1971	531.8	670.3
1972	759.0	647.2
1973	1021.2	1201.9
1974	1492.2	1700.8
1975	1536.3	1881.1
1976	2492.5	1962.9
1977	3118.7	2447.4
1978	4058.3	3043.0
1979	4373.9	4602.6
1980	4606.8	4890.3

Source: Economic Planning Board, Seoul, Korea, *Major Statistics of Korean Economy*, 1981.

South Korea: Major Exports to U.S., 1980

	Mil US $	U.S. Share of SK Exports (%)
Textiles & Clothing	$1,011	21.5
Electronics & Electrical Machinery	708	37.9
Iron, Steel & Metals	641	25.6
Footwear	491	54.3
Transport Equipment	358	30.9
Leather Products	247	40.4
Toys & Games	165	50.4
Non-Electrical Machinery	141	36.7
Plywood	126	36.1

South Korea: Major Imports from U.S., 1980

	Mil US $	U.S. Share of SK Imports (%)
Grains	$974	89.5
Textiles	609	50.7
Iron, Steel & Metals	435	22.9
Non-Electrical Machinery	408	17.7
Electrical Machinery	396	26.8
Chemicals	355	21.7
Transport Equipment	397	37.4
Pulp & Paper	187	48.0
Hides & Skins	162	41.3

Source: Office of Customs Administration, *Statistical Yearbook of Foreign Trade,* 1980.

South Korea: Foreign Equity Investment Arrivals

(Mil US$)

	Total	from U.S.	U.S. Share of Total (%)
1962-66	16.7	16.0	95.9
1967-71	96.4	32.7	33.9
1972-76	557.0	87.5	15.7
1977	102.3	11.8	11.5
1978	110.5	14.8	13.4
1979	126.0	28.9	22.9
1980	96.2	60.4	62.8
Cumulative	1,100.6	252.0	22.9

Source: Economic Planning Board, *Handbook of Korean Economy*, 1980.

South Korea: Foreign Equity Investment Arrivals By Industry[1]
Cumulative 1962-1980

(Mil US$)

	Total	from U.S.	U.S. Share (%)
Chemicals	201.0	55.7	28
Electronics	143.3	34.9	24
Construction & Services	59.6	34.4	58
Petroleum	62.5	27.0	43
Transport Equipment	41.4	26.9	65
Fertilizers	43.3	23.5	54
Total	1,100.6	252.0	23

[1] Excludes foreign subsidiaries of U.S. multinationals.
Source: Economic Planning Board.

South Korea: Inflow of Foreign Loans – Arrival Basis

(Mil US $)

	Commercial		
	Total	from U.S.	U.S. Share (%)
1959-73	2314	756	33
1974-76	2260	784	35
1977	1242	259	21
1978	1929	303	16
1979	1622	180	11
Cumulative	9,367	2282	24

	Public		
	Total	from U.S.	U.S. Share (%)
1959-73	1752	966	55
1974-76	1568	186	12
1977	626	123	22
1978	818	176	22
1979	1085	236	22
Cumulative	5,849	1687	29

¹ Muturity of over one year
Source: Economic Planning Board, *Handbook of Korean Economy*, 1980.

SOURCES

Agency for International Development, *U.S. Overseas Loans and Grants and Assistance from International Organizations.*

Economic Planning Board, Seoul, Korea, *Handbook of Korean Economy*, 1980.

Economic Planning Board, Seoul, Korea, *Major Statistics of Korean Economy*, 1981.

Office of Customs Administration, Republic of Korea, *Statistical Yearbook of Foreign Trade*, 1980.

Park, Ungsuh K., "U.S.-Korea Economic Relations in Trade and Technology Transfers," *Korea & World Affairs,* Vol. 5 (Winter 1981).

United Nations, *trade tapes.*

CHAPTER 16

UNITED STATES DIRECT INVESTMENT AND ITS INTERNATIONAL PRODUCTION IN KOREAN MANUFACTURING INDUSTRIES

*Chung Hoon Lee**

Direct investment in Korea by the United States began in 1963 when the Gulf Oil Company was given permission to invest in petroleum refining. Since then there has been a continuous flow of US direct investment to Korea, its total cumulative value amounting to approximately $175 million by the end of 1978.

What are the salient characteristics of US direct investment in Korea? What are its effects on the economy of Korea? These are the questions which we attempt to answer in this paper. Where it is appropriate, we will also compare the characteristics of US direct investment in Korea with those of Japanese direct investment. Japan in fact has surpassed the United States in recent years in terms of both the number of investment projects and the total amount invested in Korea.

I

Korea's experience with direct foreign investment did not begin until 1960 when in January the Foreign Capital Inducement Law was promulgated. The intent of the Law, with its subsequent changes and revisions, was to encourage the inflow of foreign capital. This was done with an array of tax concessions and streamlined administrative

* The research reported here was partly supported by a grant from the East-West Center/University of Hawaii Collaborative Research Funds.

procedures dealing with foreign investment. What seems to be clear is that Korea has been by and large a highly hospitable place for direct foreign investment.

In order to provide an overall view of direct foreign investment in Korea we report in Table 1 the number of investment projects and the amount invested for various time-periods and for the United States, Japan and other countries. Up through 1976 the average annual number of US investment projects increased from about two a year during the 1962-66 period to about seven a year during the 1972-76 period. The number then increased to ten in 1977 and declined to eight in 1978. The basic trend seems to be an upward one although it is by no means a spectacular one. The average annual amount invested by US investors varied from period to period, ranging from a minimum of $4.5 million during the 1962-66 period to a maximum of $19.6 million during the 1972-76 period (in current dollars).

We find in Table 1 that through the end of the 1967-71 period the United States was the predominant source of direct investment in Korea. From then on, however, Japan surpassed it in terms of both the number of investment projects and the amount invested. In fact, by the end of 1978 there were altogether 578 investment projects in Korea with the total cumulative sum amounting to approximately $806 million. Of this sum Japan accounted for 57.9%, the United States 21.4% and Others 20.4%. Japan is now by far the most important source of direct foreign investment in Korea.

In order to measure the importance of US direct investment in Korea to its capital formation we compared the maximum average annual inflow of direct investment from the United States, $19.6 million during the 1972-76 period, with the gross capital formation in Korea in 1976. The latter is estimated at $6,244 million, which makes the contribution of US direct investment to the gross capital formation of that year a meager 0.3%. What we must conclude is that in terms of the contribution to capital formation US direct investment has been very much negligible. This point should not be taken to mean, however, that it has had only a negligible effect on the economy of Korea. Direct foreign investment has many varied effects on the economy of the host country than its contribution to capital formation. Its overall contribution to the host country cannot be appraised, therefore, without investigating its multifarious effects.

Table 2 reports a sectoral distribution of US direct investment in terms of the amount invested. It is most important in Chemicals &

Table 1. Direct Foreign Investment in Korea   (All Sectors)

(In thousand dollars)

		1962-66	1967-71	1972-76	1977	1978	Cumulative Total
UNITED STATES	Number of Projects	8	26	34	10	8	86
	Amount Invested	$22,614	$26,853	$98,040	$10,142	$17,157	$174,806 (21.7%)
JAPAN	Number of Projects	1	70	338	12	15	436
	Amount Invested	$186	$26,380	$296,064	$76,952	$67,238	$466,820 (57.9%)
OTHERS*	Number of Projects	2	16	26	7	5	56
	Amount Invested	$538	$20,357	$46,264	$41,604	$55,407	$164,170 (20.4%)
TOTAL	Number of Projects	11	112	398	29	28	578
	Amount Invested	$23,338	$73,590	$440,368	$128,698	$139,802	$805,796 (100%)

Source: Korea Industrial Bank, *Direct Foreign Investment and Its Economic Effects* (in Korean), 1979.
*Panama, Bermuda, Bahama, Hong Kong, West Germany, the Netherlands, the Great Britain, France, Iran and others.

Table 2. *Sectoral Distribution of US Direct Investment in Korea (End of 1978)*

	(in thousand dollars)	
Sectors	Amount Invested	
Food, Beverage & Tobacco	$4,682	(3.2%)
Textile, Wearing Apparel & Leather Goods	3,101	(2.1%)
Paper, Paper Products, Printing & Publication	390	(0.3%)
Chemicals & Petroleum Products	89,339	(61.3%)
Non-Metal Mineral Products	950	(0.7%)
Basic Metal	1,968	(1.4%)
Fabricated Metal Products, Machinery & Equipment	25,842	(17.7%)
Electric & Electronic	19,265	(13.2%)
Other Manufactures	172	(0.1%)
Manufacturing	$145,709	(100%)
Tertiary	$ 29,097	
All Sectors	$174,806	

Source: Korea Industrial Bank, *Direct Foreign Investment and Its Economic Effects* (in Korean), 1979.

Petroleum Products, amounting to 61.3% of the total amount invested in manufacturing industries. The second important group of industries are Fabricated Metal Products, Machinery & Equipment with 17.7%, and then follows Electric & Electronic with 13.2%. US direct investment in the rest of manufacturing industries is insignificant ranging from 0.1% in Other Manufactures to 3.2% in Food, Beverage & Tobacco. The top three groups, which together account for 92.2% of the total US direct investment in manufacturing industries, consist of industries which are relatively skilled labor-intensive. By and large it seems that US multinational firms in Korea are not there to take advantage of inexpensive unskilled labor. The technologies employed by these firms are of sophisticated type, requiring a relatively intense use of skilled labor.

Another characteristic of US direct investment in Korea is the fact that it tends to be a large-scale investment. As can be seen in Table 3, US investment is concentrated in the group of projects with a mini-

Table 3. Size-distribution of US Direct Investment in Korea
(End of 1978)

(in thousand dollars)

Sectors	Less than $200,000		$200,000 to $1 million		$1 million to $5 million		$5 million or more		Total	
	Number of Projects	Amount Invested	Number of Projects	Amount Invested	Number of Projects	Amount Invested	Number of Projects	Amount Invested	Number of Projects	Amount Invested
Manufacturing	22	$1,640 (1.1%)	29	$14,173 (9.8%)	10	$22,499 (15.4%)	6	$107,397 (73.7%)	67	$145,709 (100%)
Tertiary	7	$594 (1.9%)	4	$1,245 (4.3%)	5	$8,337 (28.7%)	3	$18,942 (65.1%)	19	$29,097 (100%)
All Sectors	29	$2,234 (1.3%)	33	$15,418 (8.8%)	15	$30,836 (17.6%)	9	$126,339 (72.3%)	86	$174,806 (100%)

Source: Korea Industrial Bank, *Direct Foreign Investment and Its Economic Effects* (in Korean), 1979.

mum of $5 million invested per project. In manufacturing alone 73.7% of the total US direct investment was accounted for by projects in this group. This contrasts with Japanese direct investment in Korea which has been carried out at a much smaller scale.

II

The preceding section discussed some of the characteristics of US direct investment in Korean manufacturing industries. It has informed us where it went in which amounts. What we would like to know now is what has resulted from the investment. Direct investment results in the establishment of foreign affiliates and what effects direct foreign investment has on the economy of the host country depend very much on the activities of the affiliates. In this section we will discuss some of these activities using data collected recently by the Economic Planning Board and the Korea Industrial Bank.

In 1979 the Economic Planning Board and the Korea Industrial Bank (EPB-KIB) jointly undertook a survey of foreign affiliates in Korea. A questionnaire was sent out to 785 affiliates, of which 593 responded. As of the end of 1978, 541 of those responded were in manufacturing industries. The number of US affiliates, for which we have usable responses, was 39 in 1974, 43 in 1975, 44 in 1976, 45 in 1977 and 53 in 1978. Since we wish to find out the activities of US affiliates for the 1974-78 period, we took the average of the figures for 1974 and 1978 as a representative figure for the period. For the values of sales and exports we used the average annual values for the 1974-78 period as their representative values.

For the purpose of analyzing the activities of US affiliates in Korean manufacturing industries, we grouped industries into four categories: 1) industries using labor-intensive, low-technologies; 2) industries using labor-intensive, high-technologies; 3) industries using capital-intensive, low-technologies; and 4) industries using capital-intensive, high-technologies. For classifying industries into these four categories we relied on Hufbauer's estimates (1970) of factor- and skill-intensities of US traded goods. Factor-intensity is thus measured as capital per man in US industries in 1963, and skill-intensity is measured as the percentage of professional, technical and scientific personnel employed in an industry in 1960. The respective median values of these estimates are then used as the criteria for classification. Thus, for example, an industry with an above-median value for capital-intensity and an above-median value for skill-intensity is classified as a capital-intensive, high-technology industry. Obviously, the use of Hufbauer's estimates requires the assumption that there is no factor- and skill-reversal over time and between countries.

Table 4 reports the average annual sales of US affiliates in the four industry groups. It is clear that in terms of the value of the average annual sales US international production in Korean manufacturing industries was highly concentrated in the capital-intensive, high-technology group (72%). What is striking is the fact that the combined share of the labor-intensive, high-technology group and the capital-intensive, high-technology group was 92% of the total average annual sales of all US affiliates, which amounted to approximately ₩748 billion. This figure is very close to the percentage of US direct investment that went into Chemicals & Petroleum Products; Fabricated Metal Products, Machinery & Equipment; and Electric & Electronic (92.2%). These are largely skill-intensive or high-technology industries. In the case of Korea we may therefore conclude that the industrial composition of US direct investment is a fairly accurate measure of the industrial composition of US international production.

We noted earlier that US direct investment in Korea was carried out at a relatively large scale amounting to $5 million or more. In order to see whether or not a similar pattern may be found in the size-distribution of affiliate operation, we calculated the average annual sales per establishment for the 1974-78 period. The figures reported in Table 5 show that the largest scale of operation was in the capital-

Table 4.   *Average Annual Sales of US Affiliates in Korean Manufacturing Industries (1974-1978)*

(in million ₩)

	Low-Technology	High-Technology	Sub-Total
Labor-Intensive	₩47,231 (6%)	₩152,469 (20%)	₩199,700 (27%)
Capital-Intensive	₩10,152 (1%)	₩538,008 (72%)	₩548,160 (73%)
Sub-Total	₩57,383 (8%)	₩690,477 (92%)	₩747,860 (100%)

Source: EPB-KIB Survey, 1979.

intensive, high-technology group. At the opposite end is the labor-intensive, low-technology group, which is about one-twentieth of the other group in terms of the average annual sales per establishment.

In Table 6 we show the share of annual sales exported. In the capital-intensive, high-technology group only 9% of the sales were exported. In the two labor-intensive groups the share of exports was at least 50% and the export-share for all manufacturing industries was 21%.

The preceding discussion leads us to conclude that US direct investment in Korean manufacturing industries was, at least up through 1978, largely in the capital-intensive, high-technology industries, carried out at a relatively large scale of $5 million or more. Its affiliates had a relatively large scale of operation and its output was primarily for the domestic market. We may thus characterize US direct investment in Korean manufacturing industries as an import-substituting type, as Kojima (1977 and 1978) has argued. As clearly demonstrated in this paper, some US direct investment were made in

Table 5. *Average Annual Sales Per Establishment for US Affiliates in Korean Manufacturing Industries (1974-1978)*

(in million ₩)

	Low-Technology	High-Technology	Sub-Total
Labor-Intensive	₩2,489	₩11,728	₩6,241
Capital-Intensive	₩3,384	₩53,801	₩42,166
Sub-Total	₩2,608	₩30,021	₩16,619

Source: EPB-KIB Survey, 1979.

Table 6. *Average Annual Exports/Average Annual Sales for US Affiliates in Korean Manufacturing Industries (1974-1978)*

	Low-Technology	High-Technology	Sub-Total
Labor-Intensive	61%	50%	53%
Capital-Intensive	31%	9%	9%
Sub-Total	56%	18%	21%

Source: EPB-KIB Survey, 1979.

the labor-intensive, low-technology industries. This is, however, relatively insignificant in terms of the amount invested and the value of sales. We may infer from this fact that US direct investment benefited skilled labor more than unskilled labor.

III

The host country benefits from direct foreign investment and subsequent international production within its boundary through an increase in allocative efficiency, an increase in technical efficiency and an improvement in technology. Allocative efficiency improves as the market becomes more competitive with the establishment of foreign affiliates; technical efficiency of indigenous firms improves due to competitive pressure from foreign affiliates and/or a demonstration effect; and the factor productivity of indigenous firms improves as superior technology of foreign affiliates is transferred to them. Some of these effects are, however, relevant only to host countries which are industrially developed already. For allocative efficiency and technical efficiency to improve with the establishment of foreign affiliates and industry consisting of indigenous firms must already be in existence.

For a developing host country probably the most important effect of direct foreign investment is that on indigenous industrialization. A salutary effect on indigenous industrialization is brought about through a demonstration effect, technology transfer and linkages.

First of all, the presence of foreign affiliates demonstrates profitable opportunities to indigenous entrepreneurs. The demonstration that certain activities can be profitably carried out in the country may induce indigenous entrepreneurs to start the same or similar economic activities. As the demonstration of a new product or more productive technology leads to its diffusion, so would the demonstration of a profitable economic activity lead to its diffusion.

The presence of foreign affiliates may bring about the transfer of technology to indigenous firms. The technology of foreign affiliates is transferred to the host country when some of the personnel trained by foreign partners move to indigenous firms or themselves establish new firms. How this transfer may take place is, perhaps, best described by Spencer (1965) in his description of the effect of an external military force present in a country lagging behind in technology. He found that the presence of US military force in Japan after World War II effected the transfer of technology and the establishment of indigenous firms, which became eventually equal or better in technological capability. According to Spencer, the transfer of technology occurred first in simple operation and maintenance of American equipment, in repair and overhaul capacity, then in manufacturing with imported parts and under the supervision of American technicians, and so on in an ascending order of technological complexity. He found the same process, albeit less strong, in the case of Korea. Since a foreign affiliate is present in the host country because of its technological advantage, what is true in the case of a foreign military force should also be true in the case of a foreign affiliate. We should also expect the transfer of technology from a foreign affiliate to occur in a similar manner with indigenous industrialization progressing gradually and in stages.

The linkage is another channel through which technology may be transferred and indigenous industrialization may be induced. The forward linkage of international production is probably minimal as the output of foreign affiliates is either for export or for import-substitution. The backward linkage could, however, play an important role in the transfer of technology as affiliates demand a higher level of specification for their materials than the specification demanded by indigenous firms. Even though initially there may be no linkage as there are no established local suppliers of the materials, the presence of affiliates could induce local production with their demonstrated need for them.

A question in which we are ultimately interested in this paper is what effect US direct investment has on indigenous industrialization of Korean manufacturing industries. In order to answer this question directly, we will need to specify a counterfactual model of industrialization and then compare the actual industrialization with a hypothetical one. This is an impossible task and we are forced to resort to an alternative, albeit less satisfactory, approach.

As discussed above, the presence of foreign affiliates may lead to indigenous industrialization through a demonstration effect and through linkages and technology transfer. These act as intermediates in the process of industrialization, and the presumption is that the larger their magnitude the greater their effect on industrialization is. What we propose to do here is to investigate the extent of linkages from US international production in Korean manufacturing industries and the transfer of technology as found in a sample of US affiliates in Korea.

In Table 7 we show the value of locally produced materials used by US affiliates as a percentage of the value of their total material usage for various years and for the four industry groups. For all manufacturing industries the backward linkage was only 5% for both 1974 and 1975 but it gradually increased to 16% in 1978. This increase could be interpreted as evidence of an increasing capability of the Korean economy to produce materials that met the specifications demanded by US affiliates. This is precisely what the linkage is supposed to bring about.

Although the linkage did increase over time between 1974 and 1978, it certainly cannot be said to be large as at most only 16% of the total materials used by US affiliates were supplied locally.

In order to find out whether or not the small linkage is due to a high concentration of US international production in petroleum refining, we grouped US affiliates into petroleum refining and the rest. It is clearly shown in Table 7 that the overall small linkage is due to the importance of US international production in Korea in petroleum refining. The linkage in that sector is close to zero where as the linkage in the rest of the manufacturing industries is substantially higher than the one for the manufacturing as a whole. In the rest of the industries excluding petroleum refining the linkage was 25% in 1974 rising to 47% in 1978.

One of the beneficial effects of direct foreign investment to the developing host country is supposed to be the transfer of superior foreign technology to indigenous firms. It has been questioned, however, whether or not the transfer would occur when direct foreign

Table 7. *The Percentage of Locally Supplied Materials to Total Material Usage of US Affiliates in Korean Manufacturing Industries*

	1974	1975	1976	1977	1978
All Manufacturing	5%	5%	8%	12%	16%
Petroleum Refining	0%	0%	0%	0%	0%
The Rest	25%	24%	30%	39%	47%

Source: EPB-KIB Survey, 1979.

investment is from a highly developed country such as the United States.

The question regarding the transfer of technology is whether or not there is the transfer from foreign partners of foreign affiliates to indigenous firms. But, before this transfer can occur, there must be the transfer of technology from foreign partners to indigenous personnel of the affiliates. If there is no such transfer, it is not likely that the transfer to indigenous firms would occur except, perhaps, through a demonstration effect. The first link in this chain of technology transfer is, therefore, the transfer of technology to indigenous personnel of foreign affiliates.

We took a sample of 21 US affiliates from those that had responded to the EPB-KIB questionnaire. There were four questions on the transfer of technology and management know-how. The first question inquires about the type of assistance provided by foreign partners to the operation of the affiliate. In the questionnaire there were seven types of assistance, and the figures in Table 8 show the proportion of the sample respondents that answered affirmatively to this question. The 95% confidence interval estimate of the universe proportion is also reported in the table.

According to the sample, 90% of US affiliates received technical assistance from their US partners and 48% received assistance in the

Table 8. *Affirmative Answers by US Affiliates in Korea to "What are the Types of Assistance Provided by your Foreign Partner?"*

(Sample = 21)

	Percentage of Affirmative Answers	95% Confidence Interval
(1) Management Know-How	33%	13% to 53%
(2) Patented Technology	43%	22% to 64%
(3) Technical Assistance	90%	77% to 100%
(4) Assistance in Marketing	48%	27% to 69%
(5) Assembly of Machinery and Maintenance	29%	10% to 48%
(6) Supply of Raw Materials and Intermediate Products	48%	27% to 69%
(7) Others	0%	

Source: EPB-KIB Survey, 1979.

supply of raw materials and intermediate products and in marketing. We may thus conclude that a majority of US affiliates received technical assistance, assistance in marketing and in supply of raw materials and intermediate products. What seems to be clear is that in general US partners provided assistance of various kinds to the operation of their affiliates.

The second question, somewhat related to the first, is that of whether or not there is the transfer of technology and management know-how to indigenous personnel. Although assistance of various kinds may be provided by foreign partners, they may not become part of the technological knowledge of indigenous personnel. To this question there are two possible answers, and the responses are distributed as shown in Table 9. Seventy-six percent of the respondents answered that technology was effectively transferred but only 33% answered that management know-how was effectively transferred. We do not know why there is such a difference. Our speculation is that management know-how is very much culture-bound whereas technology is not, and consequently, the latter would be more easily transferred than the former.

Foreign technology and management know-how, although effectively transferred to indigenous personnel, may not be regarded as having any beneficial effect on the economy of the host country. The responses to the third question thus reveal some interesting, albeit subjective, information on this issue. It asks about the extent of con-

Table 9.   *Answers by US Affiliates in Korea to "Has Technology or Management Know-How been transferred?"*

(Sample = 21)

Possible Answers to the Question	Technology		Management Know-How	
	Affirmative Answers	95% Confidence Interval	Affirmative Answers	95% Confidence Interval
(1) "Effectively Transferred"	76%	58% to 94%	33%	13% to 53%
(2) "Not Effectively Transferred"	14%	0% to 29%	24%	6% to 42%

Source: EPB-KIB Survey, 1979.

tribution made by foreign technology and management know-how. Three possible answers were provided in the questionnaire and the responses are distributed as shown in Table 10. Ninety-five percent of the respondents thought that the contribution of the technology transferred from US partners was large but only 8% thought the same for management know-how.

The fourth question inquires about the reasons for no transfer of technology and management know-how. The questionnaire provided four possible reasons, and the responses are as shown in Table 11. Six affiliates out of 21 in the sample responded to this question. This is as expected since those affiliates which received technology and management know-how would not have answered this question. Three out of the six found Korea's lack of absorptive capacity as the reason for non-transfer. Because of the very small sample size we must be, however, careful in interpreting this result.

A general conclusion that we may derive from the responses to these questions is that in the majority of US affiliates there was an effective transfer of technology to indigenous personnel which was re-

Table 10. Answers by US Affiliates to "What is the Extent of the Contribution made by Foreign Partners to Indigenous Technology and Management Know-How?"

(Sample = 21)

Possible Answers	Technology		Management Know-How	
	Affirmative Answers	95% Confidence Interval	Affirmative Answers	95% Confidence Interval
(1) Large Contribution	95%	86% to 100%	8%	0% to 20%
(2) No Large Contribution	5%	0% to 14%	19%	2% to 36%
(3) No Contribution As It Is Inferior to Indigenous Technology or Management Know-How.	0%		0%	

Source: EPB-KIB Survey, 1979.

*Table 11.   Reasons Given by US Affiliates for Non-transfer of Technology
and Management Know-How*

(Sample = 6)

Reasons	Affirmative Responses
(1) Lack of Absorptive Capacity	50%
(2) Restrictions Imposed in the Contract	17%
(3) Conscious Attempt to Prevent Transfer	0%
(4) Other Reasons	33%

Source: EPB-KIB Survey, 1979.

garded as being beneficial to the host country. The same cannot be said, however, regarding management know-how.

An important point to note here is that the fact that some respondents to the questionnaire thought the technology transferred by US direct investment was beneficial does not mean that it is necessarily so from the society's point of view. It is often argued that the technology transferred via multinational firms from an industrially developed country is "inappropriate" to the developing host country. According to this argument, the technology is too sophisticated, uses too much capital and requires too large a scale of operation. This is an issue, we must point out, that cannot be settled with a survey such as the one carried out by the EPB-KIB.

IV

What multinational firms do to the economy of a developing host country is a controversial issue. For some, they create employment, bring in scarce capital and entrepreneurial resources, create linkages, bring about the transfer of technology, and in general help in the process of industrialization. For others, multinational firms are an instrument of neocolonialism, exploiting the host country. Although they may not actually exploit the host country, technologies and products introduced by them are, some argue, "inappropriate" to the developing host country.

In this paper we tried to address ourselves to some of these issues, specifically in reference to US direct investment in Korea. It must be admitted, however, that we are still unable to render a verdict on the question of what US direct investment has done to the Korean economy. Has Korea gained from it or has there been a net loss? We do not have the answer yet.

What we have learned here is some specific characteristics of US direct investment and its international production in Korean manufacturing industries. If there is a clear message that we can find in this study, it is that direct foreign investment has not been a dominant link connecting the United States and the Republic of Korea.

REFERENCES

The Bank of Korea, *Economic Statistical Yearbook,* 1977.

Caves, R. E., "International Corporations: The Industrial Economics of Foreign Investment," *Economica,* February 1971, 1-27.

_____, "Multinational Firms, Competition, and Productivity in Host-Country Markets," *Economica,* May 1974, 176-193.

Economic Planning Board and Korea Industrial Bank, *Direct Foreign Investment and Its Economic Effects* (in Korean), Seoul, 1979.

Hufbauer, G. C., "The Impact of National Characteristics and Technology on the Commodity Composition of Trade in Manufactured Goods," in Vernon, R. (ed), *The Technology Factor in International Trade,* Columbia University Press, New York, 1970.

Kojima, K., *Japan and a New World Economic Order,* Westview Press, Boulder, 1977.

_____, *Direct Foreign Investment,* Praeger, New York, 1978.

Lee, C. H., "United States and Japanese Direct Investment in Korea: A Comparative Study," *Hitotsubashi Journal of* Economics, February 1980, 26-41.

_____, "Economic Activities of United States and Japanese Affiliates in Korean Manufacturing Industries: A Comparative Study," mimeographed, 1982.

Spencer, D., "An External Military Presence, Technology Transfer, and Structural Change," *Kyklos,* 1965, 451-474.

PART V

THE FUTURE OF U.S.-KOREAN RELATIONS
IN THE 1980s

CHAPTER 17

THE TRIANGLE: KOREA, THE UNITED STATES AND JAPAN

Ardath W. Burks

When the informed observer focuses on the far Pacific, a number of possible configurations come into view. Utilizing geometric figures, one can visualize a pentagon consisting of Korea, Japan, China, the USSR, and the United States. Americans most often see a quadrangle made up of Japan, China, the USSR, and the U.S. And then there are several triangles, for example (omitting Korea) Japan, China, and the USSR; (omitting Japan) Korea, China, and the USSR; and, of course (omitting China), Korea, Japan, and the U.S. All of these are useful figures, for they suggest subtle lines of cooperation and not so subtle lines of conflict. The lines become somewhat blurred when one includes other points, for example, the Republic of China (on Taiwan) and the Democratic People's Republic of (North) Korea. *Views of the Region*—There have been persistent attempts to widen the lines of sight, to include the entire Pacific region. The late Prime Minister Ōhira Masayoshi of Japan staked much of his career in a "Pacific Basin" concept. In May 1980, just before a massive heart attack felled him, Ōhira received a final report on the idea, a concept paper that occupied some 14 months' work. He promptly appointed Okita Saburō, who had headed the study group, to be foreign minister.[1]

To Prime Minister Ōhira, the Pacific Basin plan was one alternative to the historical ill-conceived Greater East Asia Co-Prosperity Sphere

---

[1] Mineo Nakajima, "Pacific Basin Cooperation Concept and Japan's Options," *Asia Pacific Community*, No. 9 (Summer 1980), 1-9. This journal (hereafter *APC*) has been in the forefront of a campaign to publicize a Pacific Community. For another view, see Lee Poh Ping, "Reflections on the Pacific Community Concept," *APC*, No. 8 (Spring 1980), 35-43.

(GEACPS). (He had detected in both Korea and in Southeast Asia nationalist sentiment which feared a revival of the GEACPS.) The "Pacific Basin" remained, however, a kind of slogan, designed to replace the even more vague "omnidirectional foreign policy" of the previous Fukuda government. Both contained some wishful thinking, a hope to avoid the "anti-hegemony" alliance among Japan, China, and the U.S. directed against the Soviet Union.

Moreover, such a sweeping plan had been enhanced by the short-lived "China boom," which stemmed from the long-term trade agreement (June 1978) and the treaty of peace and friendship (August 1978), both signed with China. On the other hand, even Ōhira's task force had recognized limits to the Pacific scenario:

> The Asia Pacific region has become so complicated and diversified an area that it can no longer permit pursuit of any kind of policy by only one's interpretation.[2]

Nonetheless, there has been discussion that eventually there *should* emerge a Pacific Treaty Organization (PTO)—embracing security pacts among and between the U.S., Japan, the Republic of Korea (ROK), the Philippines, and the ANZUS axis—parallel to the North Atlantic Treaty Organization (NATO). (Some comparisons of the NATO and U.S.-Japan pacts are outlined below.) Others were content to refer to a "Pacific Economic Community." Three experts have tended to use the OECD as a model, on which a future Pacific Community might be based.[3] The disadvantages in such parallels have been recognized: it remains doubtful whether the European Community—with its internal free trade, common external tariffs, and shared regulations—could be applied even to the U.S., much less to the entire Pacific.

Many nations, however, did express an interest in the Pacific Basin concept. Australia, for example, was anxious to expand economic relations with Japan and with the ROK. Seoul also expressed support, possibly because it was so dependent on Japan, but preferred inclusion of the Association of South East Asia Nations (ASEAN)

---

[2] Nakajima, "Pacific Basin," *loc. cit.*, 3.

[3] Peter Drysdale & Hugh Patrick, *An Asia-Pacific Economic Organization* (Washington: U.S. Government Printing Office, 1979); and Kiyoshi Kojima, *Economic Cooperation in a Pacific Community* (Tokyo: Institute of International Affairs, 1980). See also J.D.B. Miller, "A Pacific Economic Community: Problems and Possibilities," *APC*, No. 9 (Summer 1980), 10-20.

as well.[4]

In any case, it is doubtless more useful to concentrate on a narrower, a more manageable region. In this context, the policy planning framework of the U.S. Department of State seems more practicable. Country desks in the Department have been traditionally grouped along geo-political lines. Thus one is tempted to speak of relations in East Asia among the People's Republic of China, the Republic of Korea (ROK), Japan, and the U.S.. ROK-China relations are, however, so indirect and tentative; U.S.-China ties, still developing and being tested; and Japan-China links, still emergent, that the lines in the quadrangle are difficult to place in immediate policy perspective. Better still, one can concentrate on the ROK-Japan-U.S. triangle, in what the Department of State calls Northeast Asia.

The approach in this essay thus follows the somewhat more pragmatic guidelines adopted by Donald Hellmann, who argued for the existence of a specific regional subsystem. Such a unit embraces "'a pattern of relations among basic units in world politics which exhibits a particular degree of intensity,' plus an awareness of this pattern among the participating units."[5] Obviously geographic propinquity (to such an extent as to affect strategic planning) is a requirement, and this is fulfilled by the historic juxtaposition of interests, of the ROK, of Japan, and of the U.S.

There are certain other assumptions embedded in the analysis of this regional subsystem. First, despite the flurries of attention to intricate problems (as between the U.S. and Japan, and between Japan and the ROK) the economic take second place behind, indeed complement, the overriding strategic issues. This is true, second, because of the priority placed on defense from the very beginning by the incoming Reagan administration. It is also true, third, because the peninsula of Korea remains one of the most heavily armed and potentially explosive areas of the world. Strategic issues deserve priority attention, fourth and finally, because it is increasingly doubt-

---

[4] Han Sung-joo, "Thoughts on the Pacific Community Proposal: A Korean View," (unpubl. paper) Conference on the Pacific Community, Japan Center for International Exchange, Oiso, Japan, January 1980.

[5] This is a modification of a definition offered by Karl Kaiser, "The Interaction of Regional Subsystems," *World Politics,* XXI. 1 (October 1968), 86, cited by Donald C. Hellmann, *Japan and East Asia; the New International Order* (New York: Praeger, 1972), 19.

ful that a nation of the magnitude of Japan can long remain aloof from, while progressively more engaged in, the power politics of Northeast Asia.

One by-product of the analysis, perhaps only a hypothesis rather than an assumption, relates to Japan. Because of geographic location, historic circumstances, and strategic necessities, Japanese will not only step up the volume of debate on the defense issue (long taboo in Japan). Japan will also probably augment its capacity for conventional, if not nuclear, armament to reinforce the nation's interest in the region. In fact, the most likely issue to trigger an alteration in postwar Japanese attitudes and actions is precisely the strategic relationships in the tight triangle, the ROK, Japan, and the U.S.[6] For a slightly different focus on U.S.-Korean relations in the 1980s, we may now turn to the various views from corners of the Korean-Japanese-American triangle.

The View from America—It is apparent that since World War II Japanese foreign policy has rather faithfully accommodated to the American posture. Japanese themselves reflect on the fact that, in the 35-odd years since the end of the war, Japan has experienced no severe security crisis owing to U.S.-Japan defense arrangements.[7] It is equally apparent that the Republic of Korea (ROK) has had to adjust to the Northeast Asia policy of the U.S. The ROK has also been acutely aware of American influence filtered through Japan.

Since the majority treaty of peace (1952), Japan has been—for better or worse—a central component in "the San Francisco system." This system grew out of American post-surrender policy (especially after 1948), coupled with the U.S.-Japan security treaty (1953), which

---

[6] Robert A. Scalapino has also commented on strategic issues within the parameters of the "Northeast Asia area." Most likely, he assumes, is continuation of the U.S.-Japan security arrangement. Even so, as is indicated below, with relative decrease in American commitment and capability, Japan must decide how to fill the gap. A possibility would be to abandon the U.S.-Japan security treaty, in which case Japan would likely augment its military capabilities (while keeping them nonnuclear and for defense only); would seek a tripartite guarantee (the U.S., the USSR, and the PRC); and would request dissolution of all treaties directed against Japan. This option would, however, leave the status of Korea still unclear. See Robert A. Scalapino, "Perspectives on Modern Japanese Foreign Policy," in *The Foreign Policy of Modern Japan*, ed. by Robert A. Scalapino (Berkeley: University of California Press, 1977), 407-408.

[7] Ministry of Foreign Affairs, *Diplomatic Bluebook, 1980 Edition; Review of Recent Developments in Japan's Foreign Relations* (Tokyo: Foreign Press Center, n.d. [1980]), 25.

in turn profoundly affected by the conflict in Korea (in the 1950s).[8]

Beginning in 1951 when it was proposed, through 1960 when it was revised, the American-Japanese security pact had been accepted reluctantly by the Japanese as in a sense the price of a peace treaty. The core of the treaty was in Article 5, which provided for resistance to attack on either party *in Japan;* and in Article 6, which made arrangements for American use of "facilities and areas" in promoting *both* the interests of Japan's security *and* of "peace and security in the Far East." From the beginning, then, there was some ambiguity in the arrangement.

Although Japan was technically *not* bound to defend U.S. forces in *Korea,* it was recognized that the peninsula was clearly within the security ken of "the Far East." (Taiwan and, later, Vietnam were not.) Too much, it has been stated, has been made of the differences between the NATO and the U.S.-Japan security structures. True, the U.S. has undertaken to go to the defense of Japan, while Japan has not been committed to help except in case of an attack on American forces in Japan (thus has arisen in American circles the "free ride" argument). Nonetheless, as will be seen, repeatedly the Japanese prime minister has stated that the security of the ROK and stability in South Korea is "essential" to the security of Japan. If Japan has a priority regional interest, it is in the neighboring ROK.[9]

Because of continuing sensitivities in both Tokyo and Seoul, joint planning for security, however, had to be crude and conducted through the third party, the U.S. Nor at the time would it have been infallibly a net gain, in the American view, to have South Korea (or even Taiwan) under the cover of the American-Japanese security arrangement.

Meanwhile, toward the end of the Occupation Japan had become the "lynchpin" of American security machinery in East Asia. During the Korean conflict, Japan was the indispensable staging base and supply center. In American presidential campaigns, political parties competed to find suitable rhetoric. Some (Republicans) stated that Japan "would remain the main pillar of our Asian Policy." Others (Democrats) described Japanese friendship and cooperation as "the cornerstone of our Asian interests and policy."

---

[8] Richard B. Finn, "Continuity in Japan's Foreign and Defense Policies," *APC*, No. 10 (Fall 1980).

[9] Philip H. Trezise, "The Japan Relationship," *APC*, No. 8 (Spring 1980), 10.

So far as security policy was concerned, the year 1954 was crucial. In March Japan and the U.S. signed four Mutual Security Act (MSA) agreements which, in American legislative context, meant that the ally would be provided with weapons in exchange for an obligation on the part of the recipient to build up defenses. Japan promptly responded by presenting the Self-Defense Forces and Defense Agency Establishment bills to the so-called MSA Diet. To this point, Japan and the U.S. shared a "partnership" (which allowed both a senior and a junior partner). After 1954, in the American view the two powers moved toward "alliance" (which permitted greater equality).[10]

The steady movement toward an alliance was not, of course, without cost. A more equitable agreement was worked out by 1960, but so sensitive was the issue of rearmament in Japan that a prime minister (Kishi Nobusuke) was forced out upon the renewal of the security pact. Renewal for an indefinite term was made easier in 1970 by the American agreement on reversion of Okinawa to Japanese control, by the reduction of American forces in Japan's main islands, and by the reconciliation between Washington and Peking. Paradoxically, the American withdrawal from Vietnam caused concern in Japan because of the seeming retreat of U.S. Forces; on the other hand, it probably made the U.S.-Japan security arrangement more palatable.

In any case, it is significant to note that the United States profited from Japan's felt need for continued, if reduced, American forces—both in Okinawa and in Japan proper as well as in Korea—to protect Japanese interests in Korea.

The next major turning point in American security policy involving Japan came in 1973, when Secretary of State Henry Kissinger carried out a thorough review of American-Japanese relations. Three alternative courses, which could be adopted by Japan, were projected: (1) an independent foreign and security policy; (2) a closer orientation toward China, toward the USSR, or toward Southeast Asia; or (3) continued ties with the U.S. The study predicted continued but loosening links with the U.S. and over time greater freedom in foreign and security policies.[11]

Meanwhile, an early version of a "sharing-of-roles" doctrine had made its appearance. As early as 1969, in the Sato-Nixon communi-

---

[10] Murakami Kaoru, "Sengo bōei mondai ronsōshi," *Shokun* (October 1979), trans. and incorporated in "The Postwar Defense Debate in Review," in Foreign Press Center, Japan, *Japan's Defense Debate* (Tokyo: n.d. [1981]), 19.

[11] Finn, "Continuity," *loc. cit.*, 20.

que it was stated clearly that the security of the ROK was of vital importance to the security of Japan. Nevertheless, joint planning was approached with arm's-length reluctance by the Japanese out of political prudence. Not until 1975, in an agreement between Prime Minister Miki Takeo and President Gerald Ford, was a joint study designed. The report, "Guidelines for United States-Japan Defense Cooperation," appeared in 1978 and still limited planning to defense of the main islands (and Okinawa, after reversion). An addendum did provide for joint study of "facilitative assistance" that *might* be extended to U.S. forces outside Japan, in light of the fact that the U.S. was handling security problems that would affect Japan. It was *vis a vis* Korea that a division of labor first surfaced. When Sakata Michita, former director general of the Defense Agency, held talks with Secretary of Defense Harold Brown, late in 1980, it was agreed that the main axis of military cooperation would be between the U.S. and the ROK; of economic cooperation, between Japan and the ROK.[12]

Despite the reluctance of Japanese leaders to engage in joint planning with respect to areas outside Japan, however, American strategy clearly envisaged a direct connection between U.S. Forces Japan (USFJ) and the defense of the ROK. Moreover, the American Fifth Air Force (based at Yokota) continued to command units stationed in both Japan and in the ROK. U.S. Army supply units in Japan continued to regard support of U.S. Army units deployed in Korea as their main mission. Finally, the Fifth Air Force and marine units in Okinawa would be the first to be deployed, in case of an emergency on the Korean peninsula. By 1980, the next logical step was taken: the head of Japan's Defense Agency visited the ROK.[13]

Nonetheless, certain marked differences of opinion remained apparent. Leaders in the ROK joined the U.S. in criticism of Japan for its failure to increase defense expenditures. Tokyo in turn was thoroughly alarmed, as was the ROK, over the campaign promise made by President Carter (1976) to withdraw American forces from Korea. After the Soviet invasion of Afghanistan and President Carter's visits to Japan and to Korea, in 1979, both Tokyo and Seoul were relieved to learn that any withdrawal would be postponed through at least 1981. With the advent of a new, the Reagan,

---

[12] *Asahi shimbun,* April 11, 1981.
[13] Trezise, "The Japan Relationship," *loc. cit.*

administration, an entirely new environment was provided for U.S.-Japan-ROK relations.

Even before the inauguration of Ronald Reagan, Japanese were receiving new signals from Washington. In January, 1981, under a U.S.-Japan parliamentary exchange program, the chairman of the House Armed Services Subcommittee, Representative Samuel Stratton, made his eighth visit to Japan since 1971. He bluntly stated that the proposal, made by President Carter, to withdraw troops from the ROK, had been "completely crazy."[14]

Shortly after the Reagan inauguration, the Japanese press highlighted the views of Professor Robert Pfaltzgraf (Tufts University), who had been invited to Japan by the Defense Agency. (Pfatzgraf had not entered the new administration, but had advised the president during the campaign and in the transition.) In March 1981, he was widely quoted as proclaiming that it was good for the U.S. to have reconfirmed its commitment to the ROK, since such a step served to maintain the strategic balance in East Asia. He had added that, although obviously Beijing could not so proclaim, the Chinese interest in the stability of the Korean peninsula was the same as that of the U.S. and Japan.[15]

Incidentally, the lesson inherent in the visit by Chun Doo Hwan (before his inauguration) to President Reagan (just after his inauguration)—the very first official visit to the new administration—was not lost on any of the powers concerned. Obviously, the Japanese press noted, the diplomacy of a "strong America" was first spelled out in Northeast Asia.

On the other hand, the renewed American commitment to the ROK, which was welcome in Tokyo, was accompanied by certain implications with regard to Japan's defense effort, which were not entirely welcome in Tokyo. As early as January 1981, these implications had been spelled out by Representative Stratton.

Although Stratton greeted the renewed commitment to Korea with enthusiasm, he pointed out that this was only one among many American responsibilities spread throughout Asia. With Soviet deployment of forces in Cam Ranh Bay to the South, and in the Kuriles to the North, "the U.S. no longer has the capability to defend Japan, especially to take over on all-out basis, the security of

---

[14] *Sankei shimbun,* January 16, 1981.
[15] *Sankei shimbun,* March 20, 1981.

Japan."[16] The American Chief of Naval Operations had stated to Stratton's subcommittee that the U.S. now has responsibilities in three oceans (the Atlantic, the Pacific, and the Indian). It has ships, he had reported, to cover only 1.5 of these oceans.

In similar fashion, Japanese correspondents being briefed on Oahu in Hawaii were informed that U.S. Forces Pacific now total about 320,000 personnel. After the Soviet incursion into Afghanistan, two combat groups—about 25 ships and 20,000 personnel centered on two aircraft carriers of the Seventh Fleet—were deployed into the Indian Ocean. Diego Garcia, a British atoll in the Indian Ocean, became the advance base with B-52 strategic bombers flying in from Guam (often via Okinawa or Japan).[17] And thus a new "sharing-of-roles" doctrine appeared.

In January 1981, the U.S. Defense Department released its 1982 National Defense Report, which provided "a coalition strategy" based on "appropriate sharing of roles with our allies."[18] The Americans were thus assuming a wider area for strategic planning. "Team Spirit 81" exercises involved U.S. Forces Korea (USFK), the Twenty-Fifth Division (Oahu), and the Seventh Division (Fort Ord, California). "RIMPAC" (Rim-of-the Pacific exercise) embraced components in the U.S., in Canada, in Australia, as well as in Japan. Obviously, the U.S. was expecting Japan to increase its defense capability to cover not only Japan (especially Hokkaidō), but also the Western Pacific approaches with tactical air power (ASDF), maritime capability (MSDF), and anti-submarine operations.[19]

Therein lay a difference in interpretation, between American and Japanese planners, of closer joint planning. The Japanese government persisted in stressing the defense of only Japan within constitutional limitations. To understand fully this different emphasis, it is necessary to turn briefly to Japanese attitudes.

The View from Japan—Since the end of the Occupation (1945-52), Japan has been inextricably bound to the U.S. in what has been referred to above as "the San Francisco system." This system included the peace treaty and parallel U.S.-Japan security treaty. In 1954, as has been pointed out, Japan undertook to build up defense capability (but *only* for the defense of Japan) in return for Mutual

---

[16] *Sankei shimbun,* January 16, 1981.
[17] *Asahi shimbun,* March 31, 1981.
[18] *Asahi shimbun,* March 31, 1981.
[19] Interview with Robert Pfaltzgraf, *Sankei shimbun,* March 20, 1981.

Security (MSA) assistance from the U.S. It was perhaps the first step from a "partnership" toward an "alliance."[20]

Although the earliest pacts of 1953-54 were subject to constant criticism (especially during the dramatic renewal struggle of 1960); and although at first American bases in Japan did not enjoy the support of majority Japanese opinion,[21] nonetheless Japanese suffered the dependence inherent in the security arrangements. Through the 1960s, the majority Liberal-Democratic Party (LDP)-led government put up with the security tie as the lesser of two evils. The alternative would have been to face up to building Japan's own defense system, and the Establishment in Japan was far too busy doubling, tripling, even quadrupling national income.

By 1981, some 55 percent of Japanese polled held that the U.S.-Japan security arrangement was "serving the interests of Japan."[22] It was the very first time that more than half of those questioned so replied. Paradoxically, just as the U.S.-Japan security treaty had taken root, Japanese were finding the system inadequate. The steady shift in opinion may be explained in several, sometimes contradictory, ways.

In the first place, despite the 1960 *demo,* the renewal and revision of the security treaty of that year did produce a more equitable agreement. Second, the renewal in 1970 was made easier not only by the reversion of Okinawa—"the end of the war" against the U.S., in Prime Minister Sato's terms—but also by the reduction of American facilities on the main islands, as well as by application of the so-called *hondo-nami* ("same-as-mainland") formula. That is to say, the U.S. agreed to "prior consultation" on deployment of major components out of Japan (including Okinawa); and the U.S. presumably recognized Tokyo's three-non-nuclear policy, namely, Japan would not build, possess, or allow the introduction of, nuclear weapons.

It must be remembered that in the Sato-Nixon negotiations of 1969-70, what was involved was not only the reversion of Okinawa (without nuclear weapons), but also a hypothetical emergency on the

---

[20] See above in text; and above, note 10. Murakami, "Sengo bōei," *loc. cit.,* 19; and Finn, "Continuity," *loc. cit.,* 19.

[21] See Douglas H. Mendel, Jr., *The Japanese People and Foreign Policy* (Berkeley: University of California Press, 1961), esp. Table 15, 107.

[22] *Asahi shimbun,* March 25, 1981. On the other hand, also in 1981 when asked if the U.S., in case of an emergency, would certainly come to the aid of Japan, some 59 percent expressed skepticism. *Asahi shimbun,* April 4, 1981.

Korean peninsula. Thus on the one hand, the U.S. was restricted by the principle of prior consultation; on the other hand, Japan took the first step in expansion of its responsibility. Prime Minister Sato assumed (along with President Nixon) that the security of the ROK was essential to the security of Japan. At the time, the prime minister stated: "In the event of an armed attack on the Republic of Korea in which U.S. forces would be compelled to use their bases in Japan as advance bases for combat operations, the government of Japan would take a forward-looking attitude toward prior consultation and make a prompt decision."[23]

A third factor in the slow but steady shift in Japanese defense attitudes arose out of a decade of spectacular economic growth, itself partially a by-product of relatively low expenditures on security. Growth was accompanied by a heightened sense of nationalism. The Tokyo Olympics (1964) and Expo '70 (Osaka) were only symptoms of the stronger self-identity.[24]

A fourth factor illustrated the paradox: the American military presence in Asia, as had been predicted by the Nixon Doctrine (1969), steadily diminished. This made the American-Japanese security arrangement more palatable. In growing Japanese opinion, however, the American withdrawal left a vacuum. By the fall of Saigon in 1975, American conponents had been reduced in Thailand, in Taiwan, in the Philippines, and even in Japan. In 1976, enthusiasm began to turn to alarm as President Carter announced that U.S. forces might be withdrawn from South Korea.

Fifth, the two "Nixon shocks" of 1971 served to sever the umbilical cord between the U.S. and post-treaty Japan. They were closely followed by the "oil shock," the embargo of 1973, which further forced Japanese to reconsider security measures.

A sixth factor also contained contradictions. Normalization of relations as between Washington and Beijing and between Tokyo and Beijing, it is true, served to remove a bone of contention between Japanese and Americans. Moreover, the People's Republic of China displayed a complete change, a favorable attitude toward the U.S.-Japan security axis and even toward Japan's Self-Defense Forces. This too made the American agreement less subject to attack on the

---

[23] Murakami, "Sengo bōei," *loc. cit.*, 26.

[24] Hereinafter, the factors listed follow closely the analysis made by Takubo Tadae, "The Recent Debate Over Defense," *Japan's Defense Debate*, cited, 10-13.

domestic political front,[25] but it also carried worrisome implications. Tokyo squirmed to avoid the hostile reaction from Moscow.

Indeed, the sixth and final factor was what the press called "the Soviet threat." Americans stressed the invasion of Afghanistan in 1979, but even before that Tokyo had watched with concern the Soviet military buildup (to division strength) in what Japan called the "northern territories." These were, of course, the southern Kuriles, still claimed by Japan as original territory and still occupied by the USSR.

It is understandable, then, in light of these developments that Japan's security policy—specifically, Japan's posture toward Korea—contains ambivalence. At the very least, Japanese attitudes are in transition.

Japan has entered a "new age" according to the magazine of opinion, *Sekai* ("World"), marked above all by the nation's escape from the one-sided relationship of dependence upon the U.S. True, Tokyo has followed Washington's lead on the Afghanistan issue and, more recently, on Poland.[26] At the same time, Japanese have been impressed by what may be called the "Stratton thesis." It was Representative Stratton who, following the lead of the new administration, called for joint planning under, and strengthening of, the U.S.-Japan security arrangement. Stratton threw further doubt, however, on the ability of the U.S. to provide security to Japan with conventional weapons. The implication was clear: Japan would have to increase its defense efforts.[27]

The current Japanese position on defense reflects just such a dependence-independence transition. Technically, Japan remains bound by the Japanese-inspired, American-approved "peace" clause (Article 9) of the Constitution.[28] Although some die-hard opponents

---

[25] For example, the opposition Kōmeitō (Clean Government Party), known for its close relations with China, displayed a sharp swing toward a posture supportive of the security treaty. Takubo, *loc. cit.*, 12.

[26] *The New York Times*, February 24, 1982, reported that Japan had joined in selective diplomatic and economic sanctions against the USSR, for encouraging military rule in Poland. Tanaka Naoki prepared the article on the "new age," *Sekai*, February 1981.

[27] *Sankei shimbun*, January 16, 1981.

[28] Murakami, "Sengo bōei," the essay cited, refers to Article 9: "Aspiring sincerely to an international peace based on justice and order, the Japanese people forever renounce war as a sovereign right of the nation and the threat or use of force as a means of settling international disputes. In order to accomplish the aim of the preceding paragraph, land, sea, and air forces, as well as other war potential, will never be maintained. The right of belligerency of the state will not be recognized."

of rearmament still argue that the SDF, used even for the defense of Japan, is unconstitutional, a consensus in public opinion agrees with the government that Japan never relinquished its right of self-defense. And yet almost two-thirds of those polled remain opposed to constitutional revision to clarify the issue. Two out of three Japanese also remain opposed to using naval components (MSDF) to protect sea lanes, through which critical raw materials are transported to industrial Japan. In the face of recent increases in defense expenditures, some 57 per cent of those polled oppose the steady rise in the proportion of the budget devoted to security. As might be expected, almost three-fourths of all Japanese surveyed are against the arming of the SDF with nuclear weapons.[29]

In light of the results of such survey research, the official government stance on defense reflects caution. For example, to cite a government spokesman, "the Self-Defense Forces are prohibited to despatch units to foreign lands even for the purpose of self-defense." Tokyo continues to maintain the three-non-nuclear policy, even though the official position is that the Constitution does not, in fact, prohibit the use of tactical nuclear weapons for defense. Nonetheless, maintenance of *any* offensive weapons (for example, ICBMs or long-range bombers) is still prohibited.[30]

Even within the government, there have been two schools of thought on defense matters. The former Director-General of the Japan Defense Agency (JDA), Kanemaru Shin (supported by about 60 Diet members), advocated an increase in defense expenditures to about 2.5 percent of GNP and represented the "rapid-promotion" faction. Prime Minister Suzuki Zenko was the symbolic leader of the "gradual promotion" faction, which aims to maintain defense expenditures at or below 1 percent of GNP. Suzuki presided over a delicate equilibrium, which clearly demonstrates that constituencies for rapidly increased defense expenditures are weak. Moreover, the powerful Ministry of Finance provided yet another barrier to proportionate increase of expenditures.[31]

In fact Prime Minister Suzuki, at the beginning of his regime (July 1980), contributed to confusion abroad with regard to Japan's intentions. He adopted reports written by a research group from the previ-

---

[29] *Yomiuri,* February 9, 1981; *Asahi shimbun,* March 25, 1981.

[30] Ito Keiichi, "Japan's Defense Policy," *APC,* No. 10 (Fall 1980), 3-4 (Ito was secretary-general, National Defense Council).

[31] *Asahi shimbun,* April 14, 1981. With the election of Nakasone Yasuhino, in November 1982, the strengthening of the "rapid-promotion" faction was expected.

ous Ohira administration and established a national comprehensive security council. Suzuki's concept of "comprehensive security," like that of the late Prime Minister Ohira, included "security in the fields of resources and energy and foodstuffs, because security cannot be ensured by the use of defense power alone." Suzuki was quoted as saying: "Japan should become a porcupine, not a lion or a tiger."[32]

As among the three powers—Japan led by Suzuki, the U.S. led by Reagan, and the ROK led by Chun—herein lay a continuing point of friction. The U.S. and the ROK believed that "comprehensive security" was a euphemism screening a continuing reluctance to define security in military terms. Both Seoul and Washington were critical of Japan in its failure to define security in military terms.

The government in Tokyo, however, had to manage uneasiness over the hawk-like Reagan administration. Among opposition parties, even the Kōmeitō, which increasingly had displayed a more sympathetic attitude toward U.S.-Japan security arrangements, decried the danger of collapse of *détente.* The Democratic Socialist Party (DSP), which had also shown a pragmatic stance in defense matters, urged Japan to cooperate in non-military fields of economic aid and technological assistance. A spokesman for the Japan Socialist Party (JSP) argued that Japan should resist U.S. demands for increased defense expenditures, and make efforts toward building a peaceful international environment. The Japan Communist Party (JCP) announced that the Reagan administration intends to reconstruct the cold war strategy of putting the world under American control. Japan must aim at neutrality, the communists proclaimed.[33]

Nevertheless, despite the government's caution in face of shrill

---

[32] *Asahi shimbun,* April 30, 1981; see also issues of April 14 and April 28. Mrs. Thatcher of England had also expressed reservations on the American penchant for placing priority on military security alone. A Gallup poll conducted in the U.S. for Fuji TV-*Sankei shimbun* in December 1981 added to the zoological metaphors. In the American mind, the survey showed, Japan's image changed from that of a tiger to that of a peacock. The Japanese were viewed, *Sankei shimbun* concluded, as an arrogant people who tend to show off.

[33] An excellent summary of opposition party stands was contained in *Mainichi,* January 21, 1981. The Kōmeitō position was defined by International Bureau Chief Kuroyanagi; the DSP policy, by International Bureau Chief Watanabe. JSP spokesman Kawakami was quoted, saying, "A strong American cannot be realized, after all." On another occasion, he remarked, "We know that we are a country which cannot have war." (Editorial Committee panel, *Asahi shimbun,* February 1, 1981). The JCP position was outlined by International Department Chief Tachiki.

opposition, the Japanese—like a blind man tapping his way over a stone bridge—had crossed to a new frontier of opinion. Beginning about 1978, a vigorous defense debate broke out and had continued ever since. Historically the dialogue was significant, for thereafter Japanese, really for the first time, were arguing as to *what* to do rather than *whether* to do anything.

There were, of course, among the ubiquitous professor-critics, those who continued to maintain that the principle of unarmed neutrality springs from Japanese tradition. Thus, the existent Constitution, "far from embodying an idealism divorced from reality, is an extremely realistic document whose purpose is to guarantee the security of national life." In contrast, the president of Japan's Research Institute for Peace and Security denounced both the opposition and the government, as moving from "utopian pacifism to utopian militarism." In January 1978, Chairman Takeiri Yoshikatsu of Kōmeitō announced that his party was ready to acknowledge the utility of the SDF. In March 1979, in the shadow of the Soviet military buildup in the southern Kuriles, the chief of staff of Japan's ground forces (GSDF) stated flatly that the National Defense Program Outline (approved by the cabinet in 1976) needed revision.[34]

An issue of the prestigious monthly journal, *Bungei Shunjū* (July 1979), next published a full-scale debate on the defense issue. In capsule, Professor Morishima Michio (then teaching at the London School of Economics) argued that, in case of an expected emergency to the North Japan should, "in return for the political right of self-determination," promptly surrender to the Soviet Union. In rebuttal, Professor Seki Yoshihiko (Waseda University) urged Japan to rely on its own strength, pending the arrival of aid from the U.S. Significantly, the furor of debate was followed by the Soviet invasion of Afghanistan on December 27, 1979.[35]

---

[34] See Kamishima Jiro, "The Tradition and Realism of Demilitarization," 47-56; Inoki Masamichi, "From Utopian Pacifism to Utopian Militarism," 33-46—both in *Japan's Defense Debate*, cited. See also Takubo, "The Recent Debate," cited, 7-8. In the dialogue legal aspects were raised by Justice Minister Okuno Seisuke, in September 1980: since the Constitution was adopted under "instructions from the occupation forces," he welcomed a review and the drafting of a new constitution. Only a few years before, in January 1978, when Chairman Kurisu Yoshikatsu of the Joint Staff Council had raised the problem of defense command in an emergency, he was forced to resign. Despite a hail of criticism, Okuno kept his job.

[35] Since *Bungei Shunjū* enjoys the largest circulation of all monthly magazines in Japan, the Morishima-Seki debate caused a sensation throughout the country. Takubo,

The July 1980 issue of *Shokun* carried an important essay, which was representative of a new dimension of the defense debate. It was titled "The Nuclear Option" and was prepared by Shimizu Ikutaro, who had been the ideological leader of the struggle against the security treaty renewal in 1960. In a complete reversal of form, Shimizu argued that, since the American nuclear umbrella had sprung leaks, Japan should build up its defense capability. Its options were: (1) to possess nuclear arms; (2) to possess delivery vehicles (but leave nuclear weapons in American hands); (3) to permit the U.S. to station nuclear weapons in Japan; or (4) openly to allow U.S. forces to bring nuclear arms into or out of Japan. All of these probably, three certainly, would serve to amend the three-non-nuclear policy.[36]

In an uncanny coincidence, which served to tie Korea into this ongoing debate and to recognize a *fait accompli*, members of the Tokyo Peace Committee released a report of surveillance of the Yokota air base for 38 days ending in February 1981 (during U.S.-ROK joint maneuvers, "Team Spirit 81"). Observation yielded seven nuclear strategic attack planes (six A4M Skyhawks and one A6E Intruder, components in the Marine Wing Unit (MWU)), which were en route from the U.S. to Korea via Japan. The *Mainichi* concluded, "The suspicion has become still stronger that nuclear weapons themselves have been brought into Yokota Air Base." As the *Asahi Shimbun* pointed out, it was only one more step to the next frontier, the deployment of American theater nuclear weapons in East Asia, including Japan. Apparently the Japanese were being administered antihistamines to offset their nuclear allergy.[37]

"The Recent Debate," *loc. cit.*, 9-10.

[36] Takubo, "The Defense Debate," *loc. cit.*, 9-10. In many Japanese book stores there are now large, special sections devoted to publications on the defense issue. See *Look Japan*, XXVII. 310 (January 10, 1982).

[37] *Mainichi*, March 13, 1981; *Asahi shimbun*, April 6, 1981. During 1981 there were several illustrations of the continuing Japanese allergy to nuclear weapons. Under the U.S.-Japan security arrangement, the Americans publicly acknowledged Tokyo's three-non-nuclear policy; but they argued that "introduction" (Japanese, *mochikomi*) meant landing and installation of nuclear weapons, not transit through Japan's ports or territorial waters. Earlier, retired American military personnel had admitted that U.S. forces had brought in and out of Japan nuclear weapons. To clarify this situation, early in the year former Ambassador Edwin O. Reischauer stated publicly that there had been an "understanding" that U.S. forces might carry nuclear weapons in transit and, indeed, that they had brought in such weapons. The result was a typhoon of reaction in the press. The U.S. position was firm: there would be no discussion of the location of nuclear weapons. The Japanese government position was far less convincing: passage of

To conclude this treatment, perhaps it will be useful to sketch the present status of Japanese defense. As a matter of fact, the current development of security components rather accurately reflects the transition in Japanese attitudes. The government has gradually built up and improved capability "appropriate to an exclusively defensive posture," in line with four successive annual programs dating from the National Defense Program Outline implemented in fiscal year 1977.[38] The fiscal year 1981 budget showed an increase of defense expenditures of 7.6 percent over the preceding year. It was this increase that Secretary of Defense Casper Weinberger called "inadequate"; the defense plan on which it was based, "outdated," since it had been formulated five years before. With personnel costs and supplements (added in September 1981), the Japanese pointed out, the increased total reached expenditures of 2.4 trillion yen (or a 9.7 percent increase, roughly parallel with NATO members' efforts). In any case it was, as Foreign Minister Ito Masayoshi told Secretary Weinberger, Japan's best effort "within the framework of restrictions of the Constitution."[39]

The most striking feature of the draft budget for fiscal year 1982 is the appropriation of almost 2.6 trillion yen for defense. This represents only a 7.5 percent increase, but the aggregate makes up for the first time in 26 years a rate of growth which outpaces the increase in general accounts expenditure. The 1982 pattern constitutes not only an increased *share* within Japan's budget; it also marks an increase devoted to the improvement of the *quality*, rather than the quantity, of SDF components.[40]

---

such weapons, Tokyo stated, would require prior consultation; since the U.S. has not, even once, asked for prior consultation, therefore, there had been no introduction! Later, in June, when the U.S. carrier *Midway* called at its home base, Yokosuka, thousands of demonstrators protested the presence of the ship. A far more serious incident occurred in April, when the American nuclear-powered, missile-carrying (Polaris) submarine, *George Washington*, rammed and sank a Japanese vessel in waters near Japan. Both failure to engage in efficient and prompt rescue operations (one newspaper referred to the 'hit-and-run accident') and an inordinate delay in notifying Tokyo left many Japanese unconvinced of the sincerity of the U.S. Washington later acknowledged responsibility and paid compensation. See *Tokyo shimbun*, April 13, 1981; *Sankei shimbun*, April 12, 1981.

[38] Public Information Division, Defense Agency, "Defense of Japan; White Paper on Defense (Summary)," *Defense Bulletin*, IV. 2 (October 1980), 15.

[39] *Mainichi*, March 27, 1981. In 1980 the Stockholm International Peace Research Institute ranked Japan seventh in the world in level of defense expenditures. The International Strategic Research Institute, London, ranked Japan eighth.

In recent years, the personnel quota of land forces (GSDF) has been 180,000 men; effective personnel have been held at about 86 percent of quota strength (about 13 divisions). A maritime capability (MSDF) is projected to include something over 40,000 personnel with about 60 ships, 14 submarines, and 190 aircraft, all designed for patrol and anti-submarine activities. Air components (ASDF) are projected at about 45,000 personnel with something under 500 aircraft (F-104Js, F-86Fs, and F-4EJs). The Base Air Defense Ground Environment (BADGE) is in place (since 1967), but is subject to modernization. The major mission of all SDF is to have the ability to sustain a holding operation, particularly in the Hokkaidō region, until help arrives.[41]

The View of Korea—Other essays in this collection, prepared by observers far more skilled in Korean affairs, will comment on the view from Korea. Suffice it here to add some remarks on how the outsiders—Japanese and Americans—regard the public stance of the ROK and how they view the Korean problem.

As has been mentioned, on February 2, 1981 the new president in Washington received General Chun Doo Hwan. In leaving the Blue House in Seoul (only a few weeks before the South Korean election) and going to the White House in Washington, Chun thus improved his presidential chances, reinforced the aura of his legitimacy, and conveyed the image of a confident leader. Later, in April in an interview with the Japanese press, the minister of national unification, Lee Bum Suk reported a new mood of confidence and maturity among the middle class in the ROK, as compared with the turbulence of student rebellions of two decades before. "A large number of the people of the ROK hope for the maintenance of the *status quo,*" Lee claimed. A major boost to Seoul's morale came late in the year, when the International Olympic Committee named the capital as site for the 1988 games. On January 5, 1982, President Chun freed the popula-

---

[40] The defense share of the budget is projected to reach 10 percent in 1983; see *Japan Times Weekly*, XII.6 (February 6, 1982), 3; also XII.1 (January 2, 1982), 2, for the 1982 budget. *The Liberal Star* (published by the LDP), XI. 122 (February 10, 1982), 2, carried a major story on defense expenditures in the 1982 budget.

[41] JDA, "White Paper on Defense (Summary)," *loc. cit.*, especially the chart, "Current Strength of Self-Defense Forces," 16. See also Foreign Press Center, Japan, "Summary of 'Defense of Japan' by Defense Agency, August 14, 1981" (Doc. W-81-7); Japan Institute of International Affairs, ed. *White Papers of Japan, 1979-80*, 27-42; and *Bungei Shunjū*, November 1980, for a dialogue between the director-general of the JDA, Omura Joji, and Professor Eto Shinkichi of the University of Tokyo.

tion from a restriction which had lasted three decades, by lifting the curfew.[42]

Both Washington and Tokyo were impressed too by Chun's seeming initiatives toward the Democratic People's Republic of (North) Korea. In his administrative policy speech of January 12, 1981, the ROK president had invited Chairman Kim Il Sung of the DPRK to visit Seoul, without attaching any conditions. He had stated that it was a matter of "supreme importance" to make the fatherland a united, independent, and democratic nation-state. In the same speech, Chun promised to improve relations with "non-hostile" states (meaning China) as well as with "non-aligned" nations (meaning ASEAN, to which Chun paid a successful visit during the year).[43]

Although a Japanese newspaper called Chun's proposal for top-level visits between Seoul and Pyongyang "epochal," it also admitted that the plan would not be soon realized. Again in his New Year's policy statement delivered before the National Assembly January 22, 1982, President Chun proposed that the two Koreas appoint pleni-potentiaries (rank of cabinet minister) to staff liaison missions in Seoul and in Pyongyang. On January 26, DPRK Vice President Kim Il rejected the latest proposal, stating that withdrawal of U.S. troops from South Korea would clear the "main obstacle" to reunifi-cation. On February 10, the vice president issued a counter-proposal, calling for a "conference" of 100 political figures representing the two Koreas to discuss reunification.[44]

With regard to Seoul's attitude toward Tokyo, it is now apparent

---

[42] On Chun's visit to Reagan, see *Nihon Keizai*, January 24, 1981; also Editorial, "Reagan and Chun," *Monthly Review of Korean Affairs* (hereafter *MRKA*), III.1 (Jan./Feb. 1981), 3-4. For Lee's statement, see *Asahi shimbun*, April 4, 1981; also Editorial, "Japan-ROK Cooperation," *Japan Times Weekly*, XII.3 (January 16, 1982), 12.

[43] *Tokyo shimbun*, January 13, 1981; see also *Sankei shimbun*, January 13, 1981 and *Mainichi*, January 14, 1981.

[44] *Asahi shimbun*, January 14, 1981. A Foreign Ministry spokesman, commenting on the 1981 initiative, said, "That is an extremely bold proposal. I do not think that it will be realized immediately, but the holding of dialogues between the North and the South is necessary for peace in the Korean peninsula." See *Sankei shimbun*, January 13, 1981. For the 1982 initiative and reply, see Ogawa Masaru, "ROK Initiatives," *Japan Times Weekly*, XII. 7 (February 13, 1982); also dispatches by Richard Halloran (Washington) and Henry Scott Stokes (Seoul). *The New York Times*, January 22, 27 and the issue of February 11, 1982.

that South Korean leaders had underestimated the hostile Japanese reaction to the verdict in the case of dissident Kim Dae Jung.[45] Once President Chun decided in January 1981 to appease Washington (and at the same time Tokyo), by commuting Kim's death sentence, the way was open for more normal relations. Ambassador Choi Kyung Nok, who had been serving in Tokyo since September 1980 and who spoke in fluent Japanese, was quoted: "We are brother nations— closer than any other countries in the world in terms of racial blood, history, and geography."[46]

In Seoul on May 15, 1981, President Chun used less hyperbole and stressed the practical importance of summit talks with Tokyo: "I want them to be talks where we will reach the same view on the strategic importance of the Han peninsula." Repeatedly the president referred to the costly burden of defense shouldered by the people of the ROK, who were thus (Chun spoke frankly) also ensuring the security of Japan. In August 1981, the ROK presented its bill for this burden, asking for $10 billlon over five years (the economic assistance tied directly to security affairs). Tokyo balked, but it was apparent that Seoul wanted a Japanese defense buildup to aid U.S. and ROK forces in Korea and to protect the sea lanes leading to Northeast Asia.[47]

---

[45] Mr. Kim, it will be remembered, was a prominent opposition leader, who had been kidnapped from a Tokyo hotel (doubtless by personnel with ties to the ROK government). Seoul had made a "political settlement" with Tokyo to the effect that Mr. Kim would not be charged with any activity in Japan. On September 17, 1980, Foreign Minister Ito expressed gravest concern over the death sentence handed down by the ROK government. Obviously, Chun decided to commute the sentence before his visit to Washington in January 1981. The *Tokyo shimbun* called the Kim case a "thorn in the throat"; *Asahi shimbun* January 24, 1981 carried comments by the LDP and all opposition parties. In a press conference in Tokyo, ROK Ambassador Choi was bitter in his reference to the dissident leader: "He is not as big a figure as he is claimed to be in the international community.'" See *Japan Times Weekly*, XXI. 9 (February 28, 1981).

[46] Ambassador Choi was stressing the importance of a Chun-Suzuki summit meeting. See *Japan Times Weekly*, XXI. 9 (February 28, 1981).

[47] For Chun's statement, see *Asahi shimbun*, May 16, 1981. President Chun's remark, tying Japan to the defense of the ROK, was made on the occasion of his inauguration, to a Japan-ROK parliamentary league meeting in Seoul. For the financial negotiations, see *Japan Times Weekly*, XXI. 34 (August 22, 1981). Early in 1982, apparently the request was pared to $6 billion, subject to negotiation. See Ogawa, "ROK Initiatives," *loc. cit.*, XXII. 7 (February 13, 1982). In February, while looking forward to an official visit to Seoul, Premier Suzuki was quoted as predicting a satisfactory solution to the government loan problem. Details were being worked out prior

Meanwhile, the Japanese press was giving almost equal time to the views of the DPRK. Utilizing a visit to Pyongyang by a JSP mission led by Chairman Asukata Ichiō in March 1981, Chairman Kim Il Sung expressed concern about the strengthening of military power in Japan. The "unified military structure" constructed among Japan, the U.S., and the ROK, he added, implies a "conspiracy" to occupy South Korea forever. "We will not wage war first," the chairman proclaimed. A declaration establishing a non-nuclear peace zone in Northeast Asia would be "meaningful," Kim said. Finally, Pyongyang is ready to confer with Seoul "at any time," *on the condition* that a person other than Chun be in power. "We do plan to hold talks with various strata of people," the chairman concluded.[48]

Now turning briefly to Japanese views, although they may not embrace Ambassador Choi's concept of "brother nations," nonetheless the Korean peninsula always looms large in Tokyo's planning. Tokyo's official posture is to the effect that peace and stability in the Asia-Pacific region are indispensable to Japan's security and prosperity. More specifically, "The maintenance of peace and stability in the Korean peninsula is important for peace and security in East Asia, including Japan." In a slight contradiction, Japan's purposes are "to maintain and promote friendly relations with the Republic of Korea," and to create an environment so "as to ease tensions in the Korean peninsula." Borrowing the phrasing of its constitution, "in order to accomplish these aims" Japan will remain devoted to peace and will not become a military power.[49]

---

to a foreign ministers' meeting scheduled for May: see *The Korea Herald*, February 24, 1982. Tokyo sources, however, predicted that the Japanese government would offer only $4 billion in loans over five years. See *Japan Times Weekly*, XXII. 8 (February 20, 1982).

[48] *Yomiuri*, March 15, 1981.

[49] Ministry of Foreign Affairs, *Diplomatic Bluebook, 1980*, cited, 27, 28, 35-36. In an editorial Ogawa Masaru referred to the ROK as "Japan's closest, yet most distant neighbor." See "Mending Japan-ROK Ties," *Japan Times Weekly*, XXI. 32 (August 8, 1981). In an article by Okazaki Hisako (published under a pen name), the Counsellor to the Foreign Ministry complained of the general neglect of Korean studies in Japan. See Nagasaki Notoru, "Gaps in the General Knowledge of the Japanese People," *Shokun*, September 1976. In his conference with Prime Minister Suzuki in February 1981, Vice Foreign Minister Sunobe Ryōzo (formerly ambassador to the ROK for four years) may have been engaged in wishful thinking when he reported that a "younger generation" in the ROK is becoming increasingly interested in Japan. See *Mainichi*, February 6, 1981.

Consistently with such non-military views, Tokyo has concurred in the American view that the DPRK has the *potential* to win out over the ROK in a conventional war; but it has preferred to agree with Beijing that an attack is unlikely. Following along logically, it is the view of many Japanese that the political, economic, and foreign relations of the ROK are entirely too sophisticated to be managed by "military politics." Unlike the era of the 1961 coup, the problems are too complex to be controlled by the military establishment. Others have argued that Tokyo is in complicity with Seoul to destroy democracy.[50]

In any case, in the American view (shared by the leaders of the ROK), Japan's posture has been, beyond the "free ride" in security (and to shift the figure), something like wanting the rice cake and wanting to eat it too. Among numerous illustrations, one may cite the exchange in March 1981 among Foreign Minister Ito, President Reagan, Secretary of State Haig, and Secretary of Defense Weinberger. Ito stated that Tokyo appreciated the commitment made in the U.S.-ROK communique that American troops would remain in the peninsula "for the stability of Northeast Asia." Ito gratuitously repeated the thesis that an attack from the North was unlikely, however, whereupon both Haig and Weinberger pointed out the *reason,* namely, the stationing of American troops in South Korea. The implication was clear: Japan too should help out.[51]

---

[50] In the Fall of 1980 in testimony before the Diet, a JDA counsellor estimated that DPRK forces had increased from 24 divisions (430,000 men) to 40 divisions (600,000 men). In a puzzling commentary, Chief Cabinet Secretary Miyazawa Kiichi noted that the analysis expressed the judgment of only military experts. He added, "It will be inconsistent with our national interest to conclude that North Korea is a potential threat." See *Sankei shimbun* (Kyōdo), January 25, 1981; also issue of March 20, 1981. See also Kazunobu Hayashi, "Developments in South Korea," *APC,* No. 9 (Summer 1980). On "military politics" see Gregory Henderson, "The Fifth Republic's Military Politics," *MRKA,* III. 3 (May/June 1981), III. 4 (July/August 1981); and on Japanese-American responsibility, Donald L. Ranard, "The Ineptitude of American and Japanese Policy Toward Korea," *MRKA,* II. 8 (August 1980), II. 9 (September/October 1980). Henderson served in Seoul as political and cultural officer in the U.S. embassy for seven years; Ranard was political counsellor in the embassy (1959-62) and director of the Office of Korean Affairs, Department of State (1970-74).

[51] On the Ito visit and exchanges, see *Mainichi,* March 24, 25, 1981. Ito repeated this opinion prior to a visit by ROK Foreign Minister Lho Shin Yong; *Nihon Keizai,* April 29, 1981. Mass media in Seoul strongly criticized Ito for his statement; *Tokyo shimbun,* May 2, 1981. For a slightly different, more pessimistic view of China's capacity to restrain North Korea, see Kim Gabh-chol, "The Effect of Changes in China on North

There are those who have argued that there are only two serious alternatives in effectively maintaining stability and security in East Asia. One, a unilateral U.S. move to revive its powerful military presence in the region, is less likely in light of its worldwide responsibilities, domestic economic difficulties, and the continued reluctance of the American people. The other would be Japan's decision, granted within the context of an expanded Japanese-American treaty arrangement, to take the lead in building an effective regional security system in Northeast Asia.[52]

The latter is somewhat unlikely too. As has been pointed out, there remain sharp differences, not only between Seoul and Tokyo but also between Tokyo and Washington as to the nature of the danger. Despite the highly public "Soviet threat," paradoxically Japanese are not convinced that Soviet forces, spread thin along the China border, are prepared to take direct action against Japan. While Washington, as has been described, must indeed make strategic plans for the entire Asia-Pacific region, Japan continues to coordinate actions in constitutionally defined, limited terms of self-defense of Japan proper. Nor is Japan's inhibition simply because of an amendable legal obstacle. Even the question of an "alliance" with the U.S. is still a sensitive public issue. American leaders are going to have to accommodate to the fact, and there is ample evidence to show, that Japan is *not* quite prepared to become a military super power.[53]

Korean Politics" (abstract of the original in Korean), *Sino-Soviet Affairs,* V. 2 (April 1981), 139-142. (This journal is published by The Institute for Sino-Soviet Studies, Hanyang University, Seoul, Korea.)

[52] A recent, interesting analysis is Taketsugu Tsurutani, *Japanese Policy and East Asian Security* (New York: Praeger, 1981). This monograph is unusual because, although it displays a command of published, original-language materials and extensive contacts with human resources in the region—that is to say, it is a scholarly study—it also moves along to highly subjective judgments and even policy recommendations.

[53] As to the Japanese view that the "Soviet threat" is exaggerated, see the statements of Sakata Michita (LDP, chairman of the House of Representatives Special Security Committee), *Asahi shimbun,* February 1, 1981. Prime Minister Suzuki was cited as quoting an old Japanese proverb: "No wild boar bigger than the mountain will appear." *Asahi shimbun,* April 30, 1981. After the Suzuki-Reagan summit (May 1981), Foreign Minister Ito publicly resigned, taking responsibility for the confusion arising out of the use of the word, "alliance," in the communique. Despite the painstaking attempts of the prime minister to play down use of the term, there is no doubt that the government deliberately used the word and thus signalled a change in attitude. See *Nihon Keizai,* May 10, 1981. In reply to queries as to what should be Japan's future role, Japanese respondents were divided as follows: those who urged scientific, techno-

The clue to steadily increased effort on the part of Japan lies once again, às in history, in Korea. While Americans always keep a wary eye on the big-power rival, the Soviet Union, Japan keeps an eye on the Han peninsula. Former Premier Tanaka Kakuei, in talks with Premier Zhou En-lai at the time of normalization of relations between Tokyo and Beijing, stated categorically: "If war were to break out, once again, at the 38th parallel on the Korean peninsula, we will revise the Constitution."[54]

Most likely is a steady increase in American military presence, not only in Northeast and in East Asia, but also through Southeast Asia and into the Indian Ocean. More slowly but steadily, Japan will increase the quality (if not quantity) of strategic capacity, not only for what might be called the inevitable defense of Japan but also for wider coordinated functions. These functions will include protection of vital sea lanes approaching Northeast Asia and, even more likely, joint planning with the U.S. and ROK to maintain what Japan calls "essential" stability on the Korean peninsula.[55]

Japanese caution—and the notorious inertia in the Tokyo decision-making process—should never obscure the most salient fact, so far as either Korea, the U.S., and Japan are concerned. Japan has the potential for great-power status in the region. Cautiously, but with deliberate speed, Japan is moving toward fulfilling that potential. The implications of Japanese rearmament for Northeast Asia are beyond exaggeration.

---

logical, and cultural exchange—31%; economic cooperation—31%; participation in diplomacy—20%; service as a bridge between the U.S. and USSR—5%; role in military affairs—1%; see *Asahi shimbun*, March 25, 1981.

[54] *Yomiuri*, June 21, 1981; see also Ogawa Masaru, "Debate Over Defense," *Japan Times Weekly*, XXII. 4 (January 23, 1982).

[55] Japan is not likely to act unilaterally as mediator between South and North Korea because of the Kissinger formula, which prohibits Washington from bilateral contacts with Pyongyang. See Tsurutani, *op. cit.*, 159. The commitment was reinforced in the Chun-Reagan summit; see *Asahi shimbun*, February 5, 1981. Japan's Defense Plan General Outline was drawn up on the premise of maintaining the *status quo* in Korea; *Tokyo shimbun*, February 4, 1981.

CHAPTER 18

NORTH KOREAN POLICY TOWARD
THE UNITED STATES

Jae Kyu Park

This paper is composed of three sections. The first section deals with the history of North Korean policy toward the United States from the time of the Korean War to the present; the second section investigates the methods the North Korean government has employed to implement its policy toward the United States; and the third section attempts to assess the impact of North Korean policy toward the United States on the security of the Republic of Korea.

I. Changing Characteristics of North Korean Policies Toward the United States

Since the time of North Korea's military conflict with the United States in the Korean War, the North Korean government has usually considered the United States its arch-enemy with its unceasing anti-U.S. propaganda among both North Korean people and the third world countries. However, along with its persistent denunciations of the United States, it has also attempted to approach the U.S. Government since the *rapprochement* of U.S.-China relations in the early 1970's. This section of the paper will look at the changing themes of North Korean denunciations of the United States and, at the same time, the changing methods of North Korean approaches to the United States from the early 1950's to the present. In describing the changing characteristics of North Korean policy toward the United States, the contextual factors in which these changes have taken place will be given a special emphasis here because they are important in understanding the dynamics of North Korean policy changes. The period this paper covers can be divided into three parts according to the characteristics of North Korean policies toward the United States: (1) the period of North Korea's extreme hostility toward the United States (the time of the Korean War—the end of the 1960's); (2) the period of the so-called "people's diplomacy" (the early 1970's—1974); and (3) the period of governmental approaches to the United States (1974—the present).

1. The Period of North Korea's Extreme Hostility Toward the United States

Throughout the entire period from the outbreak of the Korean War to the end of the 1960's, North Korea had not kept any significant contact with American people or government officials except for the time of armistice negotiations between the two countries in the early 1950's. On the contrary, North Korea bombarded the United States with extremely hostile verbal attacks almost everyday.

Although the nastiness of North Korean propaganda against the United States during this period is a well-known fact particularly to the people of the Republic of China, it may be interesting to look at a few examples of North Korean denunciations of the United States to understand the style of the former's denunciations directed against the latter country. For one example, there is the term, "U.S. imperialism," in the North Korean "Dictionary of Political Terms," and it is defined as the "most barbarously piratical invader and head of all other imperialistic countries."[1] For another example, many poems and essays bitterly criticizing the United States are found in North Korean textbooks of Korean language, and the following example may be enough to illustrate the style of North Korean denunciations of the United States: "Let us destroy the most violent and imperialistic burglar, the United States. That barbarous beast is treading upon our villages, streets and harbors. Let us save our brothers from its barbarism."[2] For other examples, North Korea used to accuse the United States of having been responsible for the division of the country, and also used to stress that South Korean troops instigated by the

---

[1] Sahoekwahakwon (Institute of Social Science), ed., *Jungchi Yong O Sajun* (Dictionary of Political Terms), Pyongyang: Sahoekwahak Chulpansa, 1970, p. 246.

[2] *Kuk O* (The Korean Language), Tokyo: Hakwoo Sobang, 1965, p. 6.

U.S. invaded North Korea first at the time of the Korean War. North Korean hostility toward the United States may be said to have reached a peak when it captured the U.S. intelligence ship, Pueblo, in January 1968 and shot down a U.S. reconnaissance plane, EC-121, in April 1969. The North Korean government charged the U.S. with having infringed upon its territorial sea and air in both of these instances, contrary to the facts themselves. The North Korean government is still continuing its verbal attacks against the United States in similar styles as just noted here, but such attacks were most frequent and intense during the period from the Korean War to the end of the 1960's.

What are the factors which made North Korea consistently denounce the United States with such bitterness and intensity as seen in the styles of North Korean propaganda against the United States? First of all, it should be pointed out that the "cold war" between the United States and the Soviet Union was the most distinctive characteristic of this period. Although the polarized military confrontation between them was an important feature of the "cold war," more than the military confrontation was involved in it. This was none other than the ideological competition in which the United States advocated liberal democracy as an ideal political order of all nations while the Soviet Union called for the establishment of a communistic political system specially in the third world countries. Both sides displayed Messianic missions to propagate their respective ideologies among other countries during this period, and it was in this period of ideological contention between the two superpowers that North Korea had shown an extreme hostility and hatred toward the United States.

Second, the North Korean government could be active in launching its verbal attacks against the United States all the more because the split between China and the Soviet Union had not taken an explicit form until the mid-1960's. North Korea also used to have closer relations with the third world countries than the Republic of Korea during most of this period, and could maintain such friendly relations with them by having supported their anti-imperialism, anti-colonialism and anti-racism. In particular, since the time of the Bandung Conference among the third world countries in April 1955, North Korea has made it a basic goal of its foreign policy to isolate U.S. "imperialism" from other countries for the weakening of its international strength. In short, North Korea had little to lose by denouncing the United States in the international environment of the 1950's and 1960's.

Third, the description of the contextual factors which led the North Korean government to take an extremely hostile anti-U.S. stance cannot be complete without considering the domestic situation of North Korea during the same period of time. The period of the "cold war" between the two super-powers coincided with that of system consolidation in domestic politics of North Korea, and the leaders of the North Korean government needed an outside enemy upon which they could justify their exploitative policies vis-à-vis the people of North Korea. The United States served as such an object for North Korean domestic politics. It is clear that North Korean denunciations of the United States were intended for its domestic consumption as much as for its foreign propaganda.[3]

2. The Period of "People's Diplomacy" Toward the United States

The leaders of the North Korean government began to soften their aggressive attitude toward the United States from the early 1970's—the time in which they also agreed to talk with the government of the Republic of Korea. Why did they show such a policy change toward the United States as well as toward the Republic of Korea from this time? It can be understood easily if the international characteristics of this period are taken into account in brief. As is well known, it was in the early 1970's that U.S.-China and Japan-China *rapprochement* were made following the *détente* between the United States and Soviet Union, and the North Korean government had to make a policy change toward the United States lest it should be isolated from the international environment of *détente* and *rapprochement* starting from this time. In particular, the *rapprochement* between the United States and China was important for motivating North Korean leaders to soften their attitude toward the United States. It seems that they had a feeling of fear about the U.S.-China *approchement* at first, but they soon decided to take advantage of the U.S.-China *rapprochement* for the accomplishment of the following three goals. First, they had long been demanding the withdrawal of U.S. troops from the Republic of Korea, and aimed to accomplish this goal by

---

[3] Kim Yu Nam, "Linkage Framework as uihan Bukhan Jungchi Yonku Model" (Research Model of North Korean Polity in Linkage Framework), *Kukje Jungchi Nonchong* (The Korean Journal of the International Relations), Korean Association of International Relations, 1977, p. 47.

taking an reconciliatory gesture toward the people of the United States. It was also exactly for this goal that they agreed to talk with the leaders of the Republic of Korea. Second, they tried to join various international organizations and to improve the international images of North Korea for the strengthening of their diplomatic activities, and may have thought that they could accomplish this goal better by softening their barbarous accusations against the United States. Third, they wished to import western technology and even capital to accelerate the process of North Korean economic development, and the softening of their belligerent attitude not only toward the United States but also toward the Republic of Korea was again necessary for the accomplishment of this economic goal.

Besides the softening of North Korea's verbal attacks against the United States, the most conspicuous change of North Korean policy at this point of time can be found in the decision of the North Korean government to grant visas to U.S. journalists and scholars who wished to visit Pyongyang. Shortly after former U.S. President Nixon's visit to China, the North Korean government allowed H.E. Salisbury of *The New York Times,* S.S. Harrison of *The Washington Post* and Professor Jerome Cohen of Harvard University to enter their country for the first time in the history of North Korea. These visits to North Korea were soon followed by the visits of many Korean-Americans teaching in American universities and colleges such as Professor Yung-hwan Jo of Arizona State University, Professor Dae-sook Suh of the University of Hawaii and Professor Young-chin Kim of George Washington University. North Korean leaders who met with these visitors invariably emphasized that the United States should withdraw its troops from the Republic of Korea for a peaceful unification of the divided country, while stressing their wish to establish friendly relations with the people of the United States.

North Korean policy toward the United States at that time was well reflected in Kim Il-sung's conversation with Salisbury published in *The New York Times.*[4] Kim said at first that the United States had a bad reputation among the people of North Korea because U.S. "imperialism" invaded North Korea in 1950. Then, he went on to say that North Korea should prepare itself for another outbreak of war in the Korean peninsula in view of the U.S. threat to its security, and that the best preparation for such a contingency was to educate its people

---

[4] *The New York Times,* May 26, 1972.

to hate U.S. "imperialism." Nevertheless, he did not fail to point out a possibility of improving North Korea's relationship with the United States. For this improvement, he proposed two prerequisites: (1) the withdrawal of U.S. troops from the Republic of Korea and (2) the faithful attitude of the United States toward North Korea. There is nothing unusual about the former prerequisite since it has always been a North Korean demand. However, a change of North Korean policy toward the United States may be seen in the latter prerequisite, about which Kim said: "Our country's relationship with the United States is totally up to the attitude of the leaders of its government . . . If the U.S. government changes its policy toward us, we will also accordingly change our policy toward the United States." This statement may imply that Kim wished to improve North Korea's relationship with the United States even prior to its fulfilment of the first prerequisite North Korea demanded formally. Finally, Kim emphasized the importance of "people's diplomacy" for the improvement of the relations between the two countries, saying that he did not oppose the people of the United States but wished to establish friendship with them, despite his opposition to the "reactionary" policies of the government of the United States.

3. The Period of Governmental Approaches to the United States

It may be said that North Korea has been trying to establish governmental contacts with the United States from early 1974, when its Supreme People's Assembly adopted a resolution calling for a direct negotiation with the U.S. government for the replacement of an armistice agreement between the two countries with a peace treaty. For reasons proposing a direct negotiation between the two countries regarding the matter of the peace treaty without including the Republic of Korea, North Korean leaders alleged falsely that the government of the Republic of Korea was unwilling to talk with them on this matter and that the United States actually controlled the armed forces of the Republic of Korea. More specifically, they proposed: (1) the mutual guarantee not to attack each other and the elimination of any element of danger of a direct military conflict between the two countries; (2) the immediate halt of arms competition between South and North Korea along with a U.S. decision not to deliver any more military weapons and equipment to the Republic of Korea; (3) the earliest withdrawal of foreign troops from the Korean peninsula; and (4) the guarantee not to use the southern part of the Korean peninsula as a military base of a foreign country.[5]

Why did North Korea propose a peace treaty with the United States and seek to have governmental contacts with the United States at this point of time? First of all, with this proposal, North Korean leaders wished to justify their refusal to continue a dialogue with South Korean leaders as well as their failure to accept the late President Park's proposal of a non-aggression pact between South and North Korea. Second, they also wished with this proposal of the peace treaty to encourage the withdrawal of U.S. troops from the Korean peninsula and, at the same time, to discourage U.S. military assistance to the Republic of Korea. These are the main motivations behind North Korea's proposal of the peace treaty with the United States, but it is necessary to look at the objectives North Korea wished to accomplish with this proposal more closely in order to understand its implications in full. First, the proposal was to imply that propaganda was directed toward both the people of the Republic of Korea and the leaders of foreign countries. North Korea may have wished to create support for its proposal especially among those Koreans who were critical of the Park government, and thereby to weaken the security consciousness of the Korean people in general. North Korean leaders also wished to gather support for it among the leaders of foreign countries, which in turn may have helped to isolate the Republic of Korea internationally. Second, the proposal was an attempt to achieve an autonomous position from China and the Soviet Union quarrelling against each other. North Korea has been in the state of dilemma between these two communist neighbors because it needed the support of both of them for its security and development. North Korea may have wished to lessen its dependence upon them by proposing this proposal of the peace treaty.

Since its proposal of the peace treaty with the United States, North Korea has continued its efforts to make direct contact with the government of the United States. In July 1975, Kim Il-sung himself, in his meeting with a pro-North Korea Japanese Diet member, Utsunomiya Tokuma, expressed his wish to negotiate with the government of the United States under the condition of equality between the two countries.[6] In September 1976 and January 1977, Kim Il-sung made official overtures for a direct negotiation again by sending former President

[5] *Nodong Shinmun* (Workers' Daily), March 26, 1974.
[6] *Yomiuri Shimbun*, August 17, 1975.

Carter messages calling for the improvement of mutual relations through then President of Pakistan, Ali Bhutto.[7] It shou'd be noted at this point that Kim's overtures toward the United States were brought about by President Carter's policy change. During his campaign period, he promised to withdraw U.S. troops from the Republic of Korea gradually, and after his election pursued to implement his campaign promise of troop withdrawal. In January 1977, President Carter sent Kim Il-sung a reply to his message through President Bhutto. In March of the same year, President Carter repealed a regulation which had so far prohibited U.S. citizens' from traveling to North Korea, and expressed his hope to improve relations with former adversaries in Asia including North Korea in his speech to the General Assembly of the United Nations.

However, President Carter soon came to change his policy on the troop withdrawl from the Korean peninsula, and President Reagan confirmed the military commitment of the United States for the security of the Republic of Korea. Official contacts between the two countries were made more difficult by these developments in U.S. policy toward the Republic of Korea. Nevertheless, the North Korean government has not stopped its efforts to establish governmental relations with the United States. In July 1980, a member of the House of Representatives in the U.S., Stephen Solarz, paid a visit to Pyongyang, and in September of the same year former State Department spokesman, Tom Reston, went to North Korea. In June 1981, Professor Donald Zagoria of City University of New York also visited North Korea, and there are many other U.S. journalists, scholars, and Korean-Americans who have already been to Pyongyang or who wish to visit there in the future. According to Professor Zagoria, North Koreans are expecting visits of a Harvard group, some other American academicians, and a dozen Korean-American scholars in the near future.[8] The North Korean government has been using these visitors to convey its wish to talk directly with the United States, and will mount its efforts to woo American intellectuals and Korean-Americans for this purpose. Needless to say, the final objective North Korea wishes accomplish in wooing American intellectuals and government officials is to drive a wedge between the Republic of Korea and the United States, however difficult it may be to accomplish such a goal.

---

[7] *Chung-Ang Ilbo*, March 19, 1977.

[8] Donald S. Zagoria, *Report on My Trip to North Korea, June 23-26, 1981.* monographed paper.

II. Organizations, Contents and Methods of North Korean Propaganda Toward the United States

The North Korean government has so far failed to keep any official contact with the government of the United States except in Panmunjom where North Korean and U.S. delegates get together from time to time to discuss matters regarding armistice. Short of any official contact between these two countries, propaganda has been a major means of the North Korean government not only to express its policy toward the United States but also to implement it. This section of the paper will examine organizational framework, contents and methods of its propaganda very briefly.

1. Organizations

North Korea can use three organizational frameworks for the implementation of its propaganda toward the United States: (1) North Korean observation team in the United Nations; (2) pro-North Korean friendship associations and research teams of Kim Il-sung's thought in the United States; and (3) the U.S. Communist Party and other radical underground organizations in the United States. North Korean observers can have access to the diplomats of all the member countries of the United Nations in New York, and their propaganda activities toward U.N. delegates can also have an indirect effect upon the people and officials of the United States. As prominent pro-North Korean friendship associations, here are the American-Korean Friendship Information Center which was founded by pro-North Korean radical Americans in New York in August 1970, and the Committee for Solidarity with Korean People which was established by Americans of a similar ideological bent in Berkeley in June 1971. In 1975, small research teams for the study of Kim Il-sung's thought were organized by pro-North Korean Americans especially on university campuses. The number of members of these organizations is not large and their activities have only marginal influence even on progressive American intellectuals. Nevertheless, they serve as an access point through which the North Korean government can reach the people of the United States.

The North Korean government has kept its relations with the Communist Party of the United States since the end of the 1960's, and it also serves as a channel of North Korean propaganda toward the people of the United States, although its effectiveness is very dubious. North Koreans invited leaders of the U.S. Communist Party including its head and executive committee chairman to Pyongyang at the end of the 1960's and in the early 1970's, but there is no evidence that North Koreans extended more invitations to the members of the U.S. Communist Party after this time. Among radical underground organizations with which North Korea has once kept friendly relations, the Black Panthers may be said to have been most important for North Koreans. Its leader, Eldridge Clever, has been to Pyongyang many times, and it was rumored that he received funds for the operation of his Black Panther Party.

Finally, it should be noted that pro-North Korean associations of Korean-Americans began to be organized in the United States and Canada. For instance, in 1977, there were 9 such organizations in the United States, and the North Korean government has been mounting its efforts to penetrate the Korean-American community more deeply for many years.

2. Contents

Contents of North Korean propaganda toward the people and government of the United States consist of the following three components. First, as noted earlier, the North Korean government blames the division of the country and the subsequent outbreak of the Korean War exclusively on South Korea and the United States. Second, North Koreans used to portray South Korean reality only in dark color, but from the mid-1970's their denunciations of South Korean reality have been usually coupled with their recognition of economic development in South Korea. North Korean leaders may have wished to enhance persuasiveness of their denunciations against South Korea by accepting its economic success partially. In denouncing the Republic of Korea, North Koreans have usually pointed out a widening gap between the rich and poor, poverty of South Korean farmers and workers, and foreign capitalists' exploitation of Korean workers. It may be interesting to note here that North Korean propaganda attributed the increase of the unemployed in the United States to the increasng investment of American capitalists in the Republic of Korea. North Koreans may have wished to turn the unemployed Americans against the Republic of Korea with such propaganda.[9] Recently, North Koreans have been

---

[9] *Operation War Shift: Position Paper* (New York: F.A.I.C., 1971).

denouncing the present government of the Republic of Korea more nastily than ever before, and they will continue to do so in the foreseeable future. Third, the North Korean government carried out massive propaganda activities to propagate the thought of Kim Il-sung and his efforts to unify the divided country under a confederal system among the people of the United States. It is not necessary to elaborate on this point as it is a well-known fact among us.

3. Methods

There are three methods by which North Korean propaganda can reach the people and government officials of the United States. First, North Koreans use mail service for their propaganda activities. They send out numerous kinds of their publications to Korean-Americans, American intellectuals, research institutes, libraries and embassies of communist and third world countries in the United States. These publications include *Pyongyang Times, Eastern Horizon, Current Scene,* and *Korea,* and also such Korean publications as *Nodong Shinmun* (Workers' Daily), *Keunloja* (Workers), *Deungdae* (Light Tower) and *Kim Il-sung Sonjip* (Selected Works of Kim Il-sung). It should also be noted here that pro-North Korean American intellectuals publish a journal, *Korea Focus,* in the United States and write books on Korean problems from the standpoint of the North Korean government. Second, North Koreans use U.S. the mass media for their propaganda activities. They have frequently advertized Kim Il-sung's thought, his unification efforts, and North Korean development in prominent U.S. newspapers. Third, as noted earlier, they invite American intellectuals to Pyongyang or grant visas to those Americans who wish to visit North Korea, and use them as a channel through which they try to get close to the American public and government.

III. North Korean Policy Toward the United States and the Security of the Republic of Korea

It is now necessary to reconsider the objective of North Korea's reconciliatory gesture toward the United States in order to see its possible impact upon the security of the Republic of Korea and the Pacific region in general. Professor Holsti's three objectives of foreign policy[10] is useful in reconsidering the objectives North Korean government tries to accomplish with its reconciliatory overtures toward the United States. First of all, what is the core value or interest the North Korean government attempts to promote with this policy toward the United States? The core interest involved in this policy is to communize the whole Korean peninsula by force in the near future. To accomplish this goal, it is very necessary for North Koreans to induce the Americans to withdraw their troops from the Republic of Korea, because it is the presence of U.S. troops in the Korean peninsula that has restrained North Korean armed forces from invading the Republic of Korea for a long time since the end of the Korean War in 1953. This intention of North Korea behind its proposal of the peace treaty with the United States is clear if we take account of the following facts. First, North Korea has been building up its military strength massively for many years, while proposing peace treaties with the United States and its troop withdrawal. According to a Pentagon intelligence estimate of North Korea's military strength in January 1979, North Korea had over 40 combat divisions with 600,000 or 700,000 men, while it had 29 combat divisions with 44,000 soldiers according to prior estimates. It also had twice as many aircraft, four times as many ships, and three times as many tanks as South Korea at that time. It was actually due to such a military build-up on the part of North Korea that President Carter stopped the full implementation of his plan to withdraw U.S. troops from the Korean peninsula. Second, North Korea stopped the South-North dialogue unilaterally several years ago, and is still refusing to talk with the government of the Republic of Korea about peaceful unification of the divided country. Although Kim Il-sung proposed the unification of the country under a confederal system, it is nothing more than a pretext with which to refuse South Korea's call for a dialogue with North Korea. In particular, President Chun Doo Hwan invited Kim Il-sung to the Republic of Korea, and exprssed his willingness to visit North Korea in January 1981, but Kim Il-sung has flatly refused to accept this proposal up to now. If the leaders of the North Korean government really wish to accomplish a peaceful unification of Korea, how can they achieve it without talking with the leaders of the South Korean government?

---

[10] K.J. Holsti, *International Politics: A Framework for Analysis* (New Jersey: Prentice-Hall, 1972), p. 131.

The North Korean government has so far failed to enter into direct negotiation with the United States government concerning the peace treaty and its troop withdrawal, but succeeded in attracting American intellectuals to North Korea. As Professor Zagoria reported after his recent visit to North Korea. North Koreans are expecting more Americans to come to their country, and are actually encouraging them to do so by extending invitations to influential Americans who are sympathetic with them or even by trying to bribe some of the American visitors to their country as one Korean-American professor who refused to accept money from Kim Il-sung revealed. As noted earlier, it seems that North Korean leaders are using these visitors as a channel through which they can convey their policy to the leaders of the U.S. government. However, the core interest of North Korea's policy to accept American visitors is to drive a wedge between the Republic of Korea and the United States by trying to persuade them to become the supporters of North Korea instead of the Republic of Korea. North Korean leaders may also understand the role of public opinion in the American political process, and wish to contribute to the making of U.S. public opinion favorable to their cause.

What are the middle-range objectives North Korea aims to accomplish with its policy of reconciliatory overtures toward the United States? They are to improve its international image and to enhance its international status on the one hand, and to isolate the Republic of Korea on the other hand. If North Korea succeeds in establishing its official relationship with the United States in the near future, it would certainly contribute to enhancing the international status of North Korea, while weakening that of the Republic of Korea. Even if North Korea does not succeed in its efforts to strengthen its relations with the United States, such efforts themselves may help to improve its image among many other countries of the world.

Finally, what is the long-range goal of North Korean policy toward the United States? It is to deprive the United States of her influence and role in the international politics of the Far East, but it is not necessary to discuss this at this point since the realization of such a goal cannot be imagined at the present time.

The government of the United States should understand the real objectives of North Korea's policy change, and has so far adopted appropriate policy of refusing any governmental contact with North Korea. The United States government should not open diplomatic relations with North Korea so long as North Korea refuses to have a dialogue with the Republic of Korea to ease a tension in the Korean peninsula and the two North Korean allies, the Soviet Union and China, refuse to open their respective doors to the Republic of Korea. If the United States enters into negotiations unilaterally with the North Korean government without securing these two prior conditions, it would isolate the Republic of Korea internationally, and eventually undermine the security of South Korea and the security system of the Pacific region in general.

The government of the United States has been allowing its citizens to visit North Korean communists since the early 1970's, and now does not have any regulatory power to restrain or to stop American citizens' visit to North Korea since it repealed such a regulation in 1977. The number of American visitors to North Korea may increase for some time to come simply because there are still many Americans curious about this small communist country. Furthermore, China has been attacting many American visitors since the establishment of diplomatic relations with the United States, and some of these visitors may also wish to visit its neighboring country, North Korea. The Republic of Korea is concerned about such increasing tendency of American visitors to travel to North Korea because it gives an opportunity for North Koreans to develop its support base among the American citizens. If the American visitors have courage to tell North Koreans what they do not want to hear about the Republic of Korea and international reality, it may help North Korean leaders to rectify their beliefs and policy goals, but it cannot be expected that most of the visitors have such courage. The government of the United States should keep a close eye on the American visitors to North Korea lest they should form a separate group who supports the policy goals of North Korea in opposition to those of the United States. In particular, the U.S. government should be aware of North Korean intention to organize the pro-Pyongyang Federation of Korean residents in the United States. The pro-Pyongyang Federation of Korean residents in Japan, as is well-known, has long been serving as a base upon which North Koreans attempt to manipulate international opinion as well as to penetrate Korean society by sending their spies. North Koreans will exert their utmost efforts to create a similar organization among Koreans in the United States. It is not unthinkable that the American visitors to North Korea can foster a climate of opinion infavorable to the Republic of Korea,[11] although it is not likely to happen at the present time. It is not unthinkable, either, that some Korean-

American visitors to North Korea may try to found the pro-Pyong-yang Federation of Korean residents in the United States, although it is not now likely that they will succeed in receiving support from a significant number of Korean residents in the United States. If such an unlikely phenomenon appears in the near future, it will also undermine the security of not only the Republic of Korea but also the Pacific region.

IV. A Concluding Remark

In sum, the North Korean government has usually shown extreme hostility throughout the entire period of the post-Korean war era, but has somewhat softened its hostile attitude by advocating "people's diplomacy" with the United States from the early 1970's. It has been trying to establish governmental contacts with the United States since 1974, when its Surpeme People's Assembly proposed direct negotiations with the United States to discuss the matter of a peace treaty between the two countries. Recently, its leaders invited a number of Americans especially Korean Americans to their country in the apparent hope that they could foster a climate of opinion favorable to direct talks between the United States and North Korea.

A major means through which North Korea can implement its policy toward the United States has been that of propaganda, a North Korean observation team in the United Nations, pro-North Korean friendship associations and research teams and U.S. Communist Party. These have thus far served as the organizational basis for North Korean propoganda. The contents of the propoganda have re-

---

[11] Some American visitors to North Korea have already advocated a direct negotiation between the United States and North Korea. At a Hawaii conference in commemoration of the centennial Korean-American relations Professor Byung C. Koh has strongly insisted on the necessity of such a talk. Shortly before this conference, Professor Manwoo Lee wrote a paper specifically on this subject. Major points of his arguments in it are as follows: "The United States foreign policy should not be dictated by South Korea. The United States should take its own initiative toward North Korea"; "The United States should unilaterally enter into bilateral talks with North Korea on a peace treaty" and "The American interest in Korea is no longer strategic." Manwoo Lee, "U.S.-North Korean Relations: Problems and Prospects," paper presented at the 23rd Annual Convention of the International Studies Association, Cincinnati, Ohio, March 24-27, 1982.

flected North Korea's changing policies toward the United States.

The core interest behind North Korea's reconciliatory overtures toward the United States is to induce the Americans to withdraw their troops from the Republic of Korea, and thereby to communize the whole Korean Peninsula. Its middle-range objective is to improve its international image on the one hand and to isolate the Republic of Korea on the other. However, North Korea has not succeeded in accomplishing any of its policy goals so far, mainly because the United States did not accept its reconciliatory overtures.

The Republic of Korea and the United States have just celebrated the centennial year of their mutual relations. The relationship between the two countries has been changing from an asymmetric one to a more mature partnership for the last 34 years, and it is on this ground that the United States has not taken any unilateral decision regarding her North Korean policy. With the advent of the Reagan administration the United States is showing even more respect toward South Korean wishes in this matter. It is imperative for both countries to contrive to take a common posture toward North Korea in the second century of their relations as in the previous few decades.

CHAPTER 19

NORTHEAST ASIAN SECURITY: SHARING RESPONSIBILITIES

Edward A. Olsen

The Korean War supposedly taught American policy makers two primary lessons: no more land wars in Asia and stand by an ally. The advent of tensions in Vietnam put those two lessons in conflict with each other. The reasons for the United States' entry into and expanded involvement in the Vietnam quagmire were many and complex. However, in the recesses of Washington's composite mind was one nagging fear that facilitated the process of the United States' entanglement in Southeast Asia. Great apprehension was widespread among American decision makers in the 1960s and early 1970s that one of the key lessons from our Korean War experiences not be forgotten. The need to stand by an ally at all costs was embedded in the American psyche by events in Korea. If allies are to stand a chance of persevering in their confrontation with common implacable foes, they must be backed to the hilt.

Since the United States' steadfastness in Korea clearly played a major role in maintaining Northeast Asian peace and stability during the Korean War and after, the lesson seemed certain. Washington had to remain steadfast beside its faithful South Vietnamese allies so they too could do what the South Koreans did. As we know all too well things did not go as hoped. The debacle in Vietnam cast considerable doubt upon the sagacity of the lesson Americans attempted to transfer from Korea to Vietnam. In the wake of the United States' defeat in Vietnam the conventional wisdom started to shift. Post Vietnam War revisionism flourished, finding new "lessons" from American foreign and defense policies in Asia. One continuing problem with popular American evaluations of history is that we as a mass society are poor historians. We tend to be too selective in choosing useful facts, too simplistic in assessing those "facts" in another setting where they may not be applicable, and —as a result—we regularly produce faulty analyses. So it was after Vietnam.

In the mid- and late-1970s a new conventional wisdom prevailed: no more Vietnams. Never again would the United States be lured into supporting an unsupportable regime or fighting its battles for it. In that mind-set Americans sought to apply the "lessons" of Vietnam. The United States in the 1970s gradually evolved into an overcautious superpower. Several problems arose. The American will to resist aggressive behavior softened. They physical capabilities of the United States to resist armed aggression weakened. Washington's commitment to its commitments wavered. The degree to which the United States' will, capabilities, and commitment actually deteriorated is debatable, but there clearly was some decline in these facets of Washington's foreign policy. More importantly, there were widespread perceptions in the United States and abroad that Washington was retrenching. Rightly or wrongly, the Carter administration bore most of the responsibility for that state of affairs.

Several policies of the Carter administration contributed to the institutionalization of the "no more Vietnams" syndrome in American foreign policy. Foremost on the list was Carter's flexibility toward foreign demands, particularly his willingness to accomodate Third World pressures on economic, political, and security issues. United States foreign policy became guilt-laden and its policy makers appeared anxious to atone for past wrongs. Around the world the United States demonstrated a readiness to prevent another Vietnam by pressing human rights reforms on our client states and allies, by urging greater self-reliance by our allies, and by reassessing Washington's commitments. Though other examples abound, in few of them did these three characteristics stand out as clearly as they did in U.S.-Korea relations during the 1970s.

Washington pressed Seoul to upgrade its own security both because South Korea's economic status could support such expenditures and because the Carter administration wanted to reduce its ground force presence in Korea. The reasons for Carter's troop cutback proposals is obscure, but seem to stem largely from a Carter campaign idea that developed its own momentum. The memory of "Koreagate" also rankled popular and official perceptions of South Korea, greatly complicating bilateral ties. Though linkage between these events and Carter's human rights policies was denied, many South Korean leaders saw linkage as Washington pressed Seoul to clean up its act on the human rights front. Clear signals were sent that South Korean repression was dangerous to the prospects for Seoul's political stability and, in turn, to the stability of the American commitment to South Korea. Washington had its setbacks in Vietnam (and Nicaragua and Iran) in mind as it sought to apply the latest variety of foreign policy "lesson" to Korea. Officials in Washington did not want Park Chung Hee to become another Thieu, Somoza, or Shah. They feared that prospect was on the horizon and up until Park's assassination were doing their best to prevent its occurence.

The election of President Reagan brought into power a new group of lesson learners. The Reaganite conservatives never were dissuaded from their long cherished convictions by the post-Vietnam revisionists. To the new team the choices seemed simple. Either Washington reasserted the prerogatives of a superpower to project activist foreign and defense policies in pursuit of American national interests or the United States would face the inevitable supremacy of its mortal enemies. Obviously, given those options, there was—and is—no alternative to the first choice. The main problem with this accurate if simplistic worldview is devising the means to implement it. In the case of Korea, there seemed to be a clear cut process of implementation. The Reagan administration consciously chose to back away from the Carter era policies of caution, criticism, and cutbacks.

From the outset of the Reagan term in office these three C's were out of fashion. Washington threw caution and criticism to the wind in its wholehearted support for Seoul. The wisdom of that decision is yet to be determined. If it, in fact, buys South Korea time to reinvigorate its political and economic well being after the trauma initiated by the Park assassination, Washington's unqualified support for Chun Doo Hwan will be proven a correct policy. However, if Chun et al fail to lead South Korea effectively and that country's domestic troubles mount, Reagan's support for Chun will almost certainly bear bitter fruit.

Though the overall impact of the Reagan administration's less cautious and less critical attitudes toward South Korea may in time prove more important, over the short term and in the realm of regional security, the administration's jettisoning of Korean troop cutbacks is likely to have the greatest impact.

As part of this administration's program of strengthening existing commitments to allies, there was little reason to expect Korean troop cutbacks to be held in high esteem. The reversal of that ill-conceived Carter policy was a logical result of the Reagan neo-revisionists' desire not to learn the wrong lessons from Vietnam. From their perspective the error in Vietnam was more a matter of what the United States did not do and less what it did do. American mistakes supposedly revolved around failing to keep our commitment to help an ally *win*. So that Washington does not repeat its Vietnam mistakes in Korea the Reagan administration has recommitted the United States to its treaty relationship with South Korea, pledging Washington not to be a fickle ally and putting North Korea on notice that it will not be able to pull off a victory like Hanoi's.

Such pronouncements have been well received on both sides of the Pacific. To many Americans such sentiments are the stuff of which American foreign policy should be made. Though candidate Reagan contributed to the rising sense of pugnacious nationalism in the United States by his campaign attacks on Carter era vacillation and ineptitude in international affairs, President Reagan now is more a beneficiary of that nationalism than he was as a candidate. As long as there are no major foreign policy disasters, President Reagan can count on rapid popular support for assertive foreign and defense policies. The American public is tired of seeing the United States manhandled and berated. They want strong leadership. Consequently, Reagan's recommitment to South Korea is well received among many in the American public who are familiar with it.

Naturally it was, and is, well received by the South Koreans. Seoul had argued consistently that pre-Reagan Washington did not put proper value on its relations with South Korea. It lobbied ardently for a reassessment of U.S. policy toward Korea, urging pragmatism about dissent and realism regarding the threat posed by North Korea. Seoul was supported in this stance by Tokyo. The Japanese used their considerable influence to encourage continued close U.S.-ROK ties in all areas, particularly on the security front. Together these two key allies had little difficulty in "converting" the already persuaded Reaganites.

If all the assumptions presented by the South Koreans, the Japanese, and the mainstream Reaganite conservatives were accurate, there would not be any reason to find fault with the latest interpretations of history's "lessons." However, there are flaws in the assumptions that obfuscate the situation.

Current United States policy in Korea is misapplying the real lesson of Vietnam. Where we went wrong in Southeast Asia was not a matter of our policy consistency or inconsistency. Instead, we failed by not adjusting our policies in a timely manner to our evolving interests. As our interests changed in Southeast Asia according to circumstances, so should our policies been altered. The same is true in South Korea (or anywhere else for that matter.) It is foolish to be consistent solely for the sake of consistency and its value in reassuring an ally. If that ally can be reassured and strengthened by other means —i.e., by changing American policy—then there is nothing inherently wrong or damaging about following such a course of action.

In Korea the United States has misapplied the lessons of Vietnam by viewing any cutbacks in the U.S. troop presence as almost a sellout, and—most dangerous—as an invitation to North Korean aggression. In place of reneging, Washington has opted for a strengthened commitment so that the conservatives' version of "no more Vietnams" will be the lasting version.

In place of that option there needs to be more thought given to the reality of contemporary American interests in Korea and its environs. The nature of existing American commitments to South Korea are reasonably well known. The United States maintains large numbers of uniformed personnel—primarily Army and Air Force—committed to South Korea's defense. Though the United States is not legally locked into the automatic defense of South Korea and—via the standard requirement that American constitutional processes will be adhered to —has a way out of fulfilling its existing commitments even during a crisis, for all practical purposes the United States is pledged to the automatic defense of South Korea. The troop presence dictates this. The frequent reassurances given to Seoul and Tokyo by Washington strongly suggest this. And the Reagan administration's predisposition to put alliances on a pedestal make unlikely any move away from this view of the United States' commitment to South Korea.

Despite all these existing factors, it is time to reassess the relationship. A *more* conservative perception than the Reagan administration's view of American interests in Northeast Asia should be brought to bear. The Reagan administration is allowing its status quo-ism in Korea to supercede a truly conservative assessment of the United States' interests in the region of which Korea is only part.

As I have suggested elsewhere,[1] it is time for a fundamental reassessment of American interests in the Northeast Asian region. Contemporary American national interests must be given first priority, not Washington's commitments based on a set of interests that were applicable to the 1950s. Essentially the United States has three long-standing interests in the Japan-Korea area: maintaining strategic stability, maintaining smooth political relations, and furthering the United States' economic interests in the area. To date Washington has put far more emphasis on the first two interests and much less on the economic side. That was proper in the 1950s and 1960s when Japan and South Korea were neither capable of facing nor prepared to adjust to the geopolitical threats outside powers posed. The United States met that task willingly. In exchange for the stability and political equanimity gained, the United States endured some economic costs in terms of aid expenditures and competition. Conditions started to change in the 1970s as both Northeast Asian allies became more capable of doing for their own security what the United States was doing on their behalf. Moreover, the economic costs to the United States mounted steadily during this period.

From an American perspective the relationship between the United States and its Northeast Asian allies increasingly took on the overtones of an "unequal treaty" similar to those denounced by Asians in the 19th century. This observation may surprise Asians, but if they look objectively at the situation they should see some similarities. What does the United States do for its Northeast Asian allies? First, it provides the security essential for their existence, without demanding any reciprocity by the Japanese or South Koreans. Despite the benefits they receive, neither is obligated to come to the defense of the United States or to each other's aid in the event of an attack. It is a one-way affair for each. Second, the United States is a key supplier of raw materials for the Japanese and South Korean economies. Third, the United States is a key consumer market for the products of the Japanese and South Korean economies. These American supplier and consumer roles are vital to both Northeast Asian allies. Of course, Americans too profit from these relationships. However, in a sense the United States' relationship with Japan and South Korea does have certain semi-colonial aspects.[2] The United States provides

---

[1] "Changing U.S. Interests in Northeast Asia," *World Affairs,* Spring 1981, pp. 346-365.

and pays for the basic security of both allies, supplies large portions of each's imported raw materials, and purchases a major share of each's manufactured products. Is it, therefore, surprising that this relationship might be labeled an "unequal" one?

In the present analysis no attempt has been made to separate Korea from Japan as elements of the United States' Northeast Asian policies. This undoubtedly will upset many Koreans and Japanese who frequently want to keep their respective bilateral relations with the United States discrete entities. Koreans, in particular, are adamant on this issue. They do not want to be treated as an adjunct to Japan. Japanese tend not to think seriously enough about the trilateral linkage to worry about it. That too is a problem.

Frankly there never has been, is not now, and probably never will be any valid reason for the United States to keep its bilateral security relations with its Northeast Asian allies separate. For appearance's sake—to mollify Korean and Japanese emotionalism—Washington has not been crudely heavy handed in making this point, but let there be no doubt in anyone's mind that in United States policy for the region Japan is, to quote Ezra Vogel, "Number One." This is true not only in comparison to Korea, but in reference to any other Asian state.

Japan's present capabilities and its potentials necessitate such an American perception. The implications of this for South Korea are serious. Most of what the United States has done in, to, and for South Korea has been done because of Washington's interests in Japan. Washington did what it thought Japan should have done if it had been, at first, capable of doing and, subsequently, willing to do in light of domestic political constraints in both South Korea and Japan. The United States' policies in Korea today reflect those perceptions of what Japan's "natural" geopolitical responsibilities are.

The fundamental problem the United States faces today in Northeast Asia is that the Japanese have been overprotected by Washington's regional security policies. Because American officials have been very sensitive to Japanese domestic opposition to an expansion of Tokyo's security role and to South Korean domestic suspicions of

---

² For insights into this seldom considered aspect of the United States' global role, see Eugene J. McCarthy, "Is America the World's Colony?," *Policy Review*, Summer 1981, pp. 120-124.

Japanese motives, Washington has not chosen to press its interests
forcefully. By its inaction Washington has permitted an atmosphere
of ignorance, complacency, and distrust to permeate the United
States' relationships in Northeast Asia. It is incredible that the
Japanese still do not recognize widely the benefits Japan derives from
its U.S. security treaty. The treaty is criticized frequently in Japan as
largely in the United States' interests and dangerous to Japan because
it acts like a magnet for Soviet attack. That is a nonsensical view and
Washington should not hesitate in saying so. Tokyo gains at least as
much from its U.S. treaty as does Washington. A strong case can be
made that Japan gains more than the United States. Furthermore,
Tokyo gains a great deal from the presence of American forces in
Korea and from the contributions made to regional security by South
Korea's large forces and defense expenditures. Neither the Japanese
government nor the Japanese public are willing to admit candidly
how much they benefit. Seoul already is telling Tokyo to accept these
facts, but to little avail. That view of US-ROK-Japan interdependency
failed to persuade Tokyo to be forthcoming with the economic aid
Seoul requested in 1981 as a form of *quid pro quo* arrangement to
compensate South Korea for the regional security responsibilities it
bears. Clearly Seoul's argument is sound and Washington should lend
its weight forcefully behind South Korea's position.

Washington also has a job awaiting it on the other side of the
Tsushima straits. Seoul's encouragement of popular South Korean
suspicions of Japanese motives may be understandable, but it should
not be tolerated. Koreans do harbor bitter memories of Japanese
colonial rule. That period and its legacy cannot be erased. Neither can
contemporary Japanese arrogance be readily ignored. Furthermore, it
is easy to sympathize with Seoul's periodic interest in taking a club to
Korea's everpresent Japanese bogeyman. South Korea's leaders sometimes need a whipping boy to vent domestic and international tensions. Washington's not very prudent attitude toward that South
Korean need has been one of relief that the scapegoat is Japan and
not the United States. None of this should be sanctioned any longer
by American policy makers. The Japan of the 1980s is not the Japan
of yesteryear. Washington knows it, Tokyo knows it, and Seoul
knows it. It is foolish for the United States to try to shield its two
Northeast Asian allies from the inevitability of more intimate and
more pragmatic relations of all sorts. Interjecting an American buffer
only delays the day of reckoning when Japan must face up to its

range of options vis-a-vis South Korea and when Seoul must decide how to respond to Tokyo's options.

From the standpoint of American interests in Northeast Asia several objectives are evident. The United States must stop being ambiguous about its desires for a greater Japanese role in regional security. Today's Japan is worthy of trust. Its interests generally mesh very well with those of the United States and are even closer to those of South Korea. There is no valid reason why the United States should not seek—and make clear to South Korea that it is seeking—a much larger regional security role from Japan. Tokyo has the most to gain and lose in the region and it ought to take primary responsibility for regional security. Certainly Japan is capable of undertaking such a task. Tokyo has the luxury of dragging its feet and rejecting past American pressures to do more only because the United States bends over backwards to do Japan's duty.

To rectify this situation the United States should shed its remaining inhibitions about Japan. Washington should be unequivocal in its pressures on Tokyo to supplant Japan's American-supplied "proxy" forces in Japan and in the area. It is vital to the United States' global interests that Japan's regional role resume a more appropriate stature. Washington, Tokyo, and Seoul need to put Japan's geopolitical role in a new perspective. In terms of bilateral US-Japan security relations this "new perspective" should mandate a revised treaty relationship, calling for true reciprocity on Japan's part and recognition of Japan's substantial gains from the treaty. Such a treaty would not permit the Japanese to keep their heads in the sand. They would be compelled to face the realities of a changing international milieu and to make some perhaps difficult decisions.

Probably the most difficult decisions would focus on Korea. If Tokyo is to assume its proper regional role, it is inevitable that the United States stop fulfilling Japan's duty in Korea. If what Washington and Seoul have done and are doing in Korea militarily is of value to Japan's interests, and there is abundant evidence that it is, then Tokyo should be willing to do something to alleviate the existing demands on the resources of its two allies. To start, Tokyo must accept the United States' and South Korea's forces in Korea as Japan's "allies." This will not be easy, witness the somewhat contrived uproar that grew out of Tokyo's acceptance of the United States as an "ally" during Prime Minister Suzuki's visit to Washington in 1981. That ridiculous flap underscores the ostrich-like attitudes of most Japanese when it comes to security issues. The Japanese need to be forced to recognize their interests in Northeast Asian security; they will not do it voluntarily. To reach that goal one excellent means exists: a diminution of the United States' armed presence in Korea. This is not meant as a suggestion that the United States return to Carter era cutback policies. Instead, the United States should maintain its commitments, but in an altered way. American ground forces can be reduced a bit—not incidentally freeing them for more pressing demands elsewhere—but keeping a small body of ground forces in South Korea to act as both a "trip wire" for Northern aggression and as reassurance for the South Koreans that American pressures on Japan to do more militarily will not go beyond some well defined bounds. Specifically those bounds must certainly preclude any possibility of Japanese ground forces ever again entering Korea. No one in Japan, Korea, or the United States wants that to occur. The memories it would stir would be counterproductive to any possible security gains. Moreover, South Korea's ground forces alone are capable defensively of meeting any challenges North Korea could pose. All the ROK forces require from abroad is some material aid. Only in those terms might Japan—like the United States—become involved with South Korea's ground forces.

However, there is every reason why Japan and South Korea can and should cooperate much more closely than they do today in their mutual security.[3] This cooperation should be carried out via each country's naval and air forces and—as Seoul has suggested—via Japanese economic aid to alleviate the large costs South Korea bears for Northeast Asian security. The exact nature of naval and air cooperation should be worked out by both countries in consultation with the United States. Mutual visits, exchange of forces, joint exercises, joint commands, interchangeable equipment, and sharing of intelligence all stand out as likely possibilities. To spur such cooperation the United States should first seek to integrate both allies' forces into trilateral exercises and planning. Second, and sooner rather than in the distant future, the United States should phase out gradually some of its non-nuclear naval and air force activities in both Japan and South Korea with an eye on providing incentives for both allies to

---

[3] The writer addressed the existing low level of bilateral Japan-South Korea defense relations in "Japan-South Korea Security Ties," *Air University Review*, May-June 1981, pp. 60-73.

supplant the United States' role, preferably via cooperative Japan-ROK defensive measures.

In short, the United States' changing interests in Northeast Asia mandate a somewhat reduced American armed presence in order to facilitate the assumption of certain tasks by the Japanese. The United States needs to edge slowly away from its unilateral commitment to South Korea. This transition should not be seen as an attempt by Washington to dump its burden on Tokyo at the expense of Seoul. Instead, and accurately, it should be seen as an effort to get Japan to assume its rightful share of regional burdens in cooperation with the United States and South Korea. There should be emphasis on the development of a multilateral commitment to regional Northeast Asian stability, working toward the eventual peaceful reunification of the Korean peninsula. None of these moves would require any changes in the existing set of American commitments commonly described as the United States' "nuclear umbrella." On the contrary, the assumption by Japan of a stronger sub-nuclear regional security role should enhance the United States' sense of commitment to its Northeast Asian allies' nuclear security precisely because of those allies' willingness to shoulder their fair share of the burden.

Clearly the most difficult aspect of implementing such a transfer of responsibilities will be surmounting the endemic hostility between the two potential strong allies. The mutual enmity characterizing Japan-Korea relations is well known. This should not, however, continue to preclude the United States from forcing the issue. For too long the United States has acted as a barrier shielding its two Northeast Asian allies from each other's barbs. Frequently this American role has been the cause of needless damage to the United States' position. This policy was wise in its time. When Korea was utterly weak and Japan was incapable of expanding its defense capabilities, any American effort at that time to push the two allies closer together would have been both fruitless and damaging to long term American interests. That is no longer true. It is time for Washington to encourage Tokyo and Seoul to confront each other frankly. The long delayed experience should be cathartic and almost certainly will produce a healthier relationship in the end. If Washington stops shielding them from each other, in time Tokyo and Seoul should be able to come to a pragmatic working arrangement for closer security relations. Despite the rhetoric which beclouds Japan-South Korea ties today the two countries have more interests in common with each other than either has with the

United States. If they can agree to put the past in the past, they should be able to come to terms and not blows. They share an essentially common cultural-ethnic outlook. Their traditional and modern societal values overlap in broad areas. Their contemporary economic interests are very similar and grow ever more alike as South Korea emulates with increasing success the development path pioneered by Japan. Though the Japanese still deny it, their strategic interests overlap in significant ways. With the proper prodding by the United States there is every reason why Japan and South Korea in conjunction with their mutual ally across the Pacific should be able to cooperate in many endeavors, particularly in security matters.

If the United States fails to learn the real "lesson" from its past experiences in Korea and Vietnam—the need to adapt its policies to altered circumstances—and keeps intact outdated commitments to both Japan and South Korea, there is a strong likelihood that Washington will not best serve American interests over the long run. The United States has too many new and pressing obligations worldwide to be hamstrung by outdated commitments in Northeast Asia that can better be served by other means. If Japan and South Korea are capable of cooperatively bearing the brunt in Northeast Asia with strong but relatively reduced support from the United States—and they are—then they should do so. It is vital that Washington urge now, and ultimately insist, that Tokyo and Seoul move rapidly toward that goal.

In urging this course of action Washington must be prepared for some side effects. Admittedly there could be negative side effects. Some colleagues in all three countries have responded to my suggestions that the United States force the issue by contending it would inevitably destabilize trilateral ties. There are several reasons why this apprehension seems unwarranted. First and foremost, if Tokyo and Seoul know Washington is utterly serious about compelling closer trilateral security ties, each ally will do its utmost to deal pragmatically with the other. Irrational emotions cannot and will not be permitted to get in the way.

Domestically, in all three countries, the impact of closer ties should be salutary; not destabilizing. The American public should gain greater respect for Tokyo and Seoul's readiness to meet common problems. The Japanese public ought to appreciate more empathetically South Korea's long standing sense of strategic responsibility. Some of that responsibility probably will rub off on the Japanese.

Inside South Korea the perception of Japan as a valuable ally should prove doubly salutary. First, it will reduce Seoul's tendency to make Tokyo a scapegoat for bilateral tensions. Secondly, Japan is likely to prove a more effective influence for domestic political reform in South Korea, both as a viable object lesson in Asian democracy and as a less easily manipulated ally. In other words, as a real ally for South Korea, Tokyo is less likely than Washington to tolerate indefinitely Seoul's repression of democratic rights.

On the international front some fears have been expressed to the writer that the present proposal for a tougher American attitude toward Northeast Asia might well encourage another round of cold—or hot—war in the region. Such fears would be justified if one assumed that the Japanese are likely to be led like sheep into assuming a large share of exactly the same burdens now borne by the United States in precisely the same way. Under those circumstances, one can visualize clearly the Soviet Union and North Korea becoming very edgy. Their dire predictions of an American inspired plot to create a trilateral super pact in the region would be verified. However, none of this is likely to happen because the Japanese are not "sheep."

One of the most positive results of enmeshing the Japanese more thoroughly in an expanded Northeast Asian security system is likely to be Tokyo's enhanced ability to influence the directions of regional strategy. Many Americans are prone to ridicule Japanese concepts of "comprehensive security" as too idealistic. Such ridicule is unwarranted. There is ample reason to praise Japanese desires to infuse more respect for the political and economic aspects of regional stability. The Japanese viewpoint is only faulty when it comes to Tokyo's notion of the proper division of labor among allies. The Japanese want to bear substantial political and economic burdens but leave the military burden to the United States. In light of the changes which have occurred in Japanese and Korean potentials for military cooperation, the United States can no longer tolerate unequal burdens. That is precisely the issue we are addressing here. Clearly the United States has every right to expect Japan to do something more militarily for the common good. However, there is no sound reason why Japan should not seek to do more militarily within the provisions of its comprehensive security doctrine.

If there is going to be a trilateral partnership in Northeast Asia, it is only logical to expect the Japanese strategic worldview to be given equal credibility. Washington and Seoul must adjust to Japan's hopes

and aspirations for the region's peace and stability. To the extent that
Japan can influence its two allies over the coming years all three must
anticipate greater openness toward eventual regional disarmament,
proposals for creating a nuclear-free zone in Asia, pragmatism vis-a-
vis North Korea, flexibility when responding to the Soviet Union, and
a generally less ideological predisposition.

As a result of these potential Japanese moderating influences, it is
difficult to see now movement toward Northeast Asian trilateral
security cooperation can be seriously considered a destabilizing
factor. On the other hand, treating Japan and its policies as equals
will take some getting used to by Seoul and Washington, However,
there is no real choice. If the United States and South Korea truly
want Japan to act like a responsible partner, Tokyo, Seoul, and
Washington will have to pay careful attention to each other's concerns. Frequently observers of Asian affairs express fear that it will be
difficult for the Japanese to adjust to new responsibilities. There is
some reason for such worry, witness pre-war Japanese behavior.
However, as long as Japan is not forced into an American-made
strategic mold, there is little reason to really worry about adverse
Japanese reactions. Surprisingly, it may be far more difficult for
Washington and Seoul to adapt to Japan's more prudent strategic
outlook. While the process of allied adaptation will be difficult at
times as each side adjusts to altered roles and perceptions, it will not
be destabilizing in any important sense. In fact, there is every reason
to hope that regional stability will be enhanced as burdens are shared
on an increasingly equitable basis.

The United States had better do something quickly to adjust its
commitments in South Korea and Japan for one simple reason.
Despite the seeming assertiveness of the American public and of
Washington after President Reagan's election, a Vietnam hangover still
permeates American thinking about Asia. Americans today may
permit Washington great latitude in foreign entanglements, but any
sign that one of the two erstwhile lessons—i.e., "another land war in
Asia"—might be relearned the tough way would send shock waves
throughout the United States' electorate. Asia remains a special case.
Any calls upon the United States to meet its existing commitments in
Asia had better be for unquestionably worthwhile causes. None of
the United States' Asian allies' existing "causes" are likely to stand
up to severe Vietnam style scrutiny. In Northeast Asia Japan's reluctance to carry its own defense burden and South Korea's damaging

image problems make their claims to rapid American support more problematical than they should be. Both countries would be far better served by their alliance with the United States—as would American national interests—if their claims on an American commitment are brought into accord with the contemporary burdens, capabilities, and potentials of all three states.

INDEX